Fundamentals
of
Real Estate
Appraisal

5th Edition

William L. Ventolo, Jr. • Martha R. Williams

Terry V. Grissom, Ph.D., MAI, SREA Consulting Editor

REAL ESTATE EDUCATION COMPANY
a division of Dearborn Financial Publishing, Inc.

©1975, 1977, 1980, 1983, 1987, 1990 by
Dearborn Financial Publishing, Inc.

Published by Real Estate Education Company
A division of Dearborn Publishing, Inc.

Printed in the United States of America.

92   10   9   8   7   6

Sponsoring Editor: Margaret M. Maloney
Project Editor: Ronald J. Liszkowski
Cover Design: Vito DePinto
Interior Design: Edwin Harris

Library of Congress Cataloging-in-Publication Data

Ventolo, William L.
    Fundamentals of real estate appraisal / William L. Ventolo, Jr.,
Martha R. Williams : Terry V. Grissom, consulting editor.—5th ed.
        p.   cm.
    ISBN 0-7931-0012-7
    1. Real property—Valuation.   I. Williams, Martha R.
II. Grissom, Terry V. (Terry Vaughn)   III. Title.
HD1387.V45   1990
    333.33′2—dc20   8977064
                                                              CIP

Contents

About the Authors

William L. Ventolo, Jr., a former vice president of Development Systems Corporation and its subsidiary, Real Estate Education Company, received his M.S. in psychology from the University of Pittsburgh. Mr. Ventolo has developed and authored numerous industrial training programs and manuals, including a comprehensive dealership accounting correspondence course used by the Ford Motor Company. In addition to *Fundamentals of Real Estate Appraisal*, he has authored or co-authored many textbooks for the national marketplace, including *Mastering Real Estate Mathematics, Residential Construction, The Complete Home Inspection Kit* and *Principles of Accounting*, all **currently published by Dearborn Financial Publishing, Inc. Mr. Ventolo resides in Sarasota, Florida.**

Martha R. Williams, who received her J.D. from the University of Texas, was a writer and editor for ten years before becoming an attorney, and has worked on materials ranging from primary-level English books to medical monographs. She has found the appropriate forum for combining both her legal and writing interests as author of *California Real Estate Appraisal* and co-author of *Fundamentals of Real Estate Appraisal, California Real Estate Principles* and *Agency Relationships in California Real Estate*. She acted as Consulting Editor on the eleventh edition of *Modern Real Estate Practice* and was revision author of the latest edition of the *Real Estate Principles Course Study Guide* published by the Real Estate Education Center of the California Community Colleges. She also serves as Editor of the *Real Estate Educators Association Journal*. Ms. Williams resides in Marin County, California.

Preface

In recent years, no area of real estate practice has been under as intense scrutiny as that of appraising. The federal call for strict education and licensing criteria is being heeded by the states. Current efforts are intended to make education and other prelicensing requirements for appraisers comparable to those of other areas of professional practice.

The present interest in appraiser qualifications is partly the result of recent, volatile market conditions that have proved there can be no easy assumptions, even when dealing with such an historically appreciating asset as real estate. There is no substitute for the well-reasoned opinion of a competent appraiser. Of course, the skill and judgment required to make a reliable appraisal must begin with a thorough knowledge of appraisal fundamentals. Ideally, that knowledge relates appraisal theory to practice, so that the student knows how to apply what is learned.

Fundamentals of Real Estate Appraisal is designed to help both the student and the established professional relate appraisal theory and technique to practice. Explanations of the basic approaches to appraising are thorough yet concise. The many questions, exercises and forms throughout the text increase its day-to-day usefulness as a practical, hands-on tool.

Acknowledgments

The authors wish to thank those who participated in the preparation of the fifth edition of *Fundamentals of Real Estate Appraisal.*

Terry V. Grissom, M.B.A., Ph.D., MAI, SREA, served as consulting editor, offering the insight of his years of appraisal practice and skill as an educator. Dr. Grissom is an Associate Research Economist for the Real Estate Research Center at Texas A & M University where his topics of investigation include real estate appraisal, real estate development, portfolio management and urban land economics. Prior to his involvement with the Research Center, Dr. Grissom was the director of the real estate program at the University of Texas at Austin. He has also had extensive experience as a real estate practitioner, serving as a salesman and staff appraiser for a private real estate firm. His papers and articles have appeared in *Appraisal Review Journal, Appraisal Journal, The Real Estate Securities Journal* and *The Real Estate Market Advisor.*

John E. Spurgeon of The Princeton Group, San Francisco, helped update the cost figures. Other useful reviews were provided by:

> Robert W. Chaapel
> National College of Appraisal and Property Management
> Atlanta, GA
>
> George R. Harrison, MSA, AAR
> Lincoln Graduate Center
> San Antonio, TX
>
> Robert S. Martin, MAI, CRE, SREA
> Martin & Associates
> Winston-Salem, NC
>
> Michael Milgrim
> American Institute of Real Estate Appraisers
> Chicago, IL
>
> Lawrence Sager
> Madison Area Technical College
> Madison, WI

Milton J. Tharp
Tennessee Real Estate Education System, Inc.
Nashville, TN

Henry E. Ormonde, CREA
Ormonde & Associates—Realty Division
Natick, MA

Terrence M. Zajac, DREI
Terry Zajac Seminars
Scottsdale, AZ

James H. Boykin, Ph.D., MAI, SREA, served as consulting editor on earlier editions of this book, and his assistance was always appreciated. Reviewers of earlier editions included Linda W. Chandler, Clay Estes, Donald A. Gabriel, Robert C. Gorman, Gary Hoagland, Robert Houseman, Joseph H. Martin, John F. Mikusas, Robert L. Montney, Kenneth E. Ritter, Margaret E. Sprencz, Paul C. Sprencz and Bryan K. Swartwood, Jr.

In addition to those mentioned, numerous instructors, students and real estate professionals have offered many useful comments and suggestions over the years. We thank all who have contacted us and welcome additional comments on this edition.

Finally, the authors thank the staff of Real Estate Education Company for their fine efforts. Margaret M. Maloney, sponsoring editor, coordinated the manuscript revision and review with admirable patience and persistence. Ronald J. Liszkowski helped shepherd the manuscript through the production process. Loretta Faber's efforts in copyediting the manuscript are appreciated.

William L. Ventolo, Jr.
Martha R. Williams

Introduction

Appraising has always been a unique part of the real estate industry. The appraiser's estimate of property value has a significant effect on many aspects of a real estate transaction, whether the transaction involves a sale, transfer, insurance policy, mortgage loan, real estate tax levy or some other purpose. Unlike most of the other people involved in the transaction, the appraiser's compensation is not based on the value of the subject property. As a result, the appraiser has no vested interest in the estimation of value and can objectively evaluate the relative merits, appeal and value of a property.

Impartiality, objectivity, knowledge of appraising fundamentals and the quality of judgment that comes only with experience are the professional appraiser's chief credentials. The real estate appraiser's impartiality and objectivity make it unlikely that his or her prerogatives will be abused. The appraiser's knowledge and experience provide the basis for an accurate appraisal.

The value of real estate has risen dramatically during the past twenty years and consumes an ever greater portion of individual and business income. Yet the marketplace still fluctuates and not every property will increase in value over time. Many may lose value. Under such market conditions the appraisal is even more important; shortcut assumptions that work in a time of rising prices will produce devastating results. In recent times, stagnating or decreasing real estate prices have resulted in many appraisals being questioned. Appraiser qualifications have inevitably become part of the discussion on how to avoid the "overappraisal" of property. Those qualifications are discussed in this Introduction.

Appraiser Licensing

Historically, only a few states required the licensing of real estate appraisers, although every state had strict licensing requirements for both real estate brokers and salespeople. In 1986, California became the first state to adopt standards for a certified appraisal and a certified appraisal report. The California law did not specify qualifications for appraisers but mandated the minimum requirements that an appraisal must meet before it can be labeled *certified*.

In 1987, Louisiana became the first state to provide for the voluntary certification of real estate appraisers. Florida, which already required real estate appraisers to have a real estate license, soon initiated a similar program. Iowa, Minnesota, Texas, Washington and Wyoming joined the ranks by mid-1989, and the remaining states should not be far behind.

Major impetus to appraiser licensing and certification has come from the federal government. Circular A-129 of the Office of Management and Budget (OMB), signed by OMB Director Joseph Wright on November 25, 1988, applies to all federal agencies under OMB's jurisdiction. Circular A-129 requires that the agencies determine by July 1, 1991, which transactions, because of their size or complexity, need a state-certified appraisal prepared by a state-certified appraiser. All other appraisals must be performed by appraisers licensed or registered as required by the state involved. Appraisal standards must meet or exceed those developed by the Appraisal Standards Board of the Appraisal Foundation. Qualifications for a state-certified appraiser and a state certifying examination must meet or exceed those produced by the Appraisal Foundation's Appraiser Qualification Board.

The OMB action may not provide a satisfactory alternative to federal appraiser licensing, particularly as proposed in House of Representatives Bill 3675 (the Real Estate Appraisal Reform Act), originally introduced before Congress by Rep. Doug Barnard on November 20, 1987.

The Appraiser's Work

The professional real estate appraiser estimates the value of real property (land and/or buildings). The value sought may be for any number of reasons, such as setting a sales price or determining insurance coverage. The appraiser's client can be a buyer, a seller, a corporation, a public agency or a real estate broker. Although real estate brokers still make many routine appraisals themselves, it is now common practice to rely on the practiced judgment of a professional whose sole interest is in estimating the value of real property.

An appraiser's estimate of a property's value usually is in writing and may be a letter simply stating the appraiser's estimated value. Most often, however, it is a longer document called an *appraisal report*. To make such a report, the appraiser must conduct a thorough study of the appraised property, its geographical area and economic trends. The appraiser must be able to read a legal description and recognize the exact boundaries of the subject property. The appraiser also must have some knowledge of building construction to recognize the quality and condition of the subject property.

The appraiser must know market conditions—why some properties are more desirable than others—as well as how to analyze income and expense statements so that an evaluation of a property's potential earnings can be made.

In short, the appraiser needs some of the expertise of the surveyor, the builder, the broker, the accountant, the economist and the mortgage lender. An appraisal takes into account the many factors that influence a property's value; therefore, an experienced appraiser can make an important contribution to any real estate transaction.

Educational Background and Training

Colleges and private schools, as well as professional associations, offer courses in real estate appraising, but there are many other courses at both high school and college levels that give the appraiser some of the necessary educational background. The appraiser must be able to work easily with mathematical computations. He or she will be computing land and building areas and construction costs and performing all of the steps necessary to determine investment income. For this last area, a knowledge of accounting techniques would be invaluable. A course in statistics would also help in studying trend indicators such as those found in census and economic reports.

Geography and urban sociology are also important. Because the appraiser must be able to recognize and describe the driving forces behind population movements and economic trends, economics and city planning courses would be useful. A knowledge of building construction or engineering will help the appraiser in recognizing building components and their value contribution to the property.

General real estate courses of interest to appraisers and available through colleges and private schools are geared primarily to prospective real estate salespeople and brokers, who must be licensed by their state real estate offices. Most real estate appraisers enter the field in this way—gaining the experience of handling real estate transactions and learning the market through firsthand experience. In some states, you must be a licensed real estate broker to accept an appraisal assignment.

The beginning appraiser will usually spend years in some area of real estate, possibly as a researcher for an experienced appraiser, before developing the competence to warrant being hired for his or her appraisal skill. Government agencies and some financial institutions often have their own appraiser training programs.

Of course, with the increasing availability of small, easily programmed office computers, the appraiser's qualifications would be incomplete without the ability to use appraisal-based computer applications. Even the small real estate or appraisal office can now take advantage of the computer's storage and problem-solving capabilities. Programs designed to help organize and speed data retrieval in making appraisals are already on the market, and more are being developed. Although there never will be a substitute for the skilled, informed judgment of the professional appraiser, use of appropriate resources, including computers, can help the appraiser function more efficiently and more accurately.

An appraiser's main credential ultimately will be the expertise that comes only after performing many appraisals. The most competent appraiser will also maintain a high level of professional practice by keeping up to date on developments within the field, reading appraisal and other publications and attending seminars and courses.

Assignments Available

The service of a qualified appraiser is a recognized essential in many situations. In a real estate transaction involving either the sale or lease of real property, an appraisal may be desired to:

- help set the seller's asking price;
- help a buyer determine the fairness of the asking price;
- set a value for real property when it is part of an estate;
- estimate the relative values of properties being traded;
- set value on property involved in corporate mergers, acquisitions, liquidations or bankruptcies;
- determine the amount of a mortgage loan; or
- set rental rates.

In addition, other uses of real estate requiring appraisals include:

- determining building insurance value;
- assessing property for taxes;
- setting gift or inheritance taxes;
- estimating remodeling costs;
- determining development costs;
- discovering a vacant property's most profitable use;
- ascertaining whether the present use of a property is its most profitable use; and
- estimating the value of property in a condemnation proceeding.

Employment Opportunities

The types of appraisals noted above give some indication of employment opportunities available to professional real estate appraisers.

The appraiser may be self-employed, working as a sole practitioner or perhaps using the services of a staff of other appraisers. A few appraisal companies have offices in major cities coast to coast, employing the services of hundreds of appraisers.

Aside from appraisal companies, many other sources of employment are open to appraisers. Government agencies hire the greatest number of appraisers. Appraisers' reports are used as a basis for establishing a variety of tax and condemnation values. Federal agencies, such as the Federal Housing Administration (FHA) and Veterans Administration (VA), appraise properties before insuring or guaranteeing mortgage loans. Both the FHA and VA use independent fee appraisers almost exclusively. Agencies involved in such matters as road construction, urban renewal, conservation and parkland all employ appraisers.

Institutions such as banks, savings and loan associations, mortgage banking firms and insurance companies may have staff appraisers. Other companies, such as large industrial organizations and chain stores, hire appraisers to serve their real estate departments by inspecting and judging the condition of land and buildings before entering into a purchase or lease agreement.

Individuals considering the purchase or lease of real estate may hire an appraiser, although most appraisals involving sale or trade transactions between individuals will be under the control of a real estate broker. The broker will either make an appraisal or rely on an independent appraiser he or she has worked with and trusts.

The importance of objective, accurate appraisals cannot be overstated. The wide range of activities for which the appraiser's services are required eventually touches the lives of every citizen.

Professional Societies

As a way of establishing professional credentials and keeping up to date in the appraisal field, the appraiser may seek membership in an appraisal society. Such groups usually have regular meetings, publish professional journals, hold seminars and conduct appraisal courses. Usually they have education, experience and examination requirements for membership.

The major appraisal and related societies are listed below. Member designations are listed in the order of their requirements—the most easily acquired first.

Accredited Review Appraisers Council, San Antonio, TX
   Publishers of *The Review Appraiser*
   Member designation: AAR (Accredited in Appraisal Review)

American Association of Certified Appraisers, Inc., Cincinnati, OH
  Member designations, noncertified: Affiliate and R-1 (Residential—
  First Level); certified: CA-R (Certified Appraiser—Residential),
  CA-S (Certified Appraiser—Senior) and CA-C (Certified Appraiser
  —Consultant)

American Institute of Real Estate Appraisers, Chicago, IL
  Publishers of *Appraisal Journal* and *Appraiser,* as well as a number of special reports and books
  Member designations: RM (Residential Member) and MAI (Member of the Appraisal Institute)

American Society of Appraisers, Herndon, VA
  Publishers of *Technical Valuation,* a professional journal, and the
  Appraisal and Valuation Manual
  Member designations: ASA (Senior Member), ASR (Senior Resi-
  dential Member) and FASA (Fellow)

American Society of Farm Managers and Rural Appraisers, Inc.,
  Denver, CO
  Member designations: AFM (Accredited Farm Manager) and ARA
  (Accredited Rural Appraiser)

American Society of Professional Appraisers, Atlanta, GA
  Member designations: CRRA (Certified Residential Real Estate
  Appraiser) and CCRA (Certified Commercial Real Estate Appraiser)

American Society of Real Estate Appraisers, Atlanta, GA
  Member designations: RSA (Residential Senior Appraiser), and
  CSA (Commercial Senior Appraiser)

Appraisal Institute of Canada, Winnipeg, Manitoba, Canada
  Publishers of *The Canadian Appraiser,* a technical journal, and
  Appraisal Institute DIGEST, a newsletter
  Member designations: CRA (Canadian Residential Appraiser) and
  AACI (Accredited Appraiser Canadian Institute)

International Association of Assessing Officers, Chicago, IL
  Publishers of *The International Assessor* and the *Assessors Jour-
  nal*, as well as many specialized booklets and manuals
  Member designations: CPE (Certified Personalty Evaluator), AAE
  (Accredited Assessment Evaluator), CAE (Certified Assessment
  Evaluator) and RES (Residential Evaluation Specialist)

International Right of Way Association, Inglewood, CA
  Publishers of *Right of Way* magazine
  Member designation: SR/WA (Senior—Right of Way Association)

National Association of Independent Fee Appraisers, Inc., St. Louis,
  MO
  Publishers of *The Appraisal Review*
  Member designations: IFA (Member), IFAS (Senior Member) and
  IFAC (Appraiser-Counselor)

National Association of Master Appraisers, San Antonio, TX
Publishers of *The Master Appraiser*
Member designations: MRA (Master Residential Appraiser), MFLA (Master Farm and Land Appraiser), MSA (Master Senior Appraiser) and CAO (Certified Appraisal Organization)

National Association of Real Estate Appraisers, Scottsdale, AZ
Publishers of *Appraisal Report*
Member designation: CREA (Certified Real Estate Appraiser)

National Association of Review Appraisers and Mortgage Underwriters, Scottsdale, AZ
Publishers of *Appraisal Review Journal*
Member designations: CRA (Certified Review Appraiser) and, in Canada, RRA (Registered Review Appraiser)

National Residential Appraisers Institute, Amherst, OH
Publishers of *Appraisers News Network*
Member designations: CMDA (Certified Market Data Analyst), GSA (Graduate Senior Appraiser) and SCA (Senior Certified Appraiser)

National Society of Real Estate Appraisers, Inc., Cleveland, OH
Publishers of *National Report*
Member designations: RA (Residential Appraiser), CRA (Certified Real Estate Appraiser) and MREA (Master Real Estate Appraiser)

Society of Real Estate Appraisers, Chicago, IL
Publishers of *Appraisal Briefs* and *The Real Estate Appraiser and Analyst*
Member designations: SRA (Senior Residential Appraiser), SRPA (Senior Real Property Appraiser) and SREA (Senior Real Estate Analyst)

Professional Ethics and Standards of Practice

Appraisal Societies

The major appraisal societies, including many of those listed above, have been leaders in establishing standards of appraisal practice as well as in defining ethical conduct by members of the profession. In 1985, representatives from nine appraisal groups formed an Ad Hoc Committee on Uniform Standards of Professional Appraisal Practice. The organizations included:

- American Institute of Real Estate Appraisers;
- American Society of Appraisers;
- American Society of Farm Managers and Rural Appraisers;
- Appraisal Institute of Canada;

- International Association of Assessing Officers;
- International Right of Way Association;
- National Association of Independent Fee Appraisers;
- National Society of Real Estate Appraisers; and
- Society of Real Estate Appraisers.

The standards that were published in 1986, and amended in 1987, cover real estate, personal property and business appraisals as well as other topics. They are now the Uniform Standards of Professional Appraisal Practice of the Appraisal Standard Board of the Appraisal Foundation, discussed below.

As an example of the high level of professional practice espoused by the professional appraisal organizations, the Code of Professional Ethics of the American Institute of Real Estate Appraisers is reproduced here. It is a useful summary of the responsibilities of a conscientious, professional appraiser.

Code of Professional Ethics*

Canon 1.   A Member or Candidate of the Appraisal Institute must refrain from conduct that is detrimental to the Appraisal Institute, the real estate appraisal profession and the public.

Canon 2.   A Member or Candidate must assist the Appraisal Institute in carrying out its responsibilities to the users of appraisal services and the public.

Canon 3.   In the performance of an appraisal assignment, each analysis and opinion of a Member or Candidate must be developed and communicated without bias and without the accommodation of the Member's or Candidate's personal interests.

Canon 4.   A Member or Candidate must not violate the confidential nature of the appraiser-client relationship.

Canon 5.   In promoting an appraisal practice and soliciting appraisal assignments, a Member or Candidate must use care to avoid advertising or solicitation that is misleading or otherwise contrary to the public interest.

Canon 6.   A Member or Candidate must comply with the requirements of the Appraisal Institute's Standards of Professional Practice.

---

*Reprinted by permission of the American Institute of Real Estate Appraisers.

Appraisal Foundation

The Appraisal Foundation, headquartered in Washington, D.C., is a nonprofit corporation that was established in 1987 to create and finance the Appraisal Standards Board and the Appraiser Qualification Board. Members of the Appraisal Foundation include the American Institute of Real Estate Appraisers, American Society of Appraisers, American Society of Farm Managers and Rural Appraisers, International Association of Assessing Officers, International Right of Way Association, National Association of Independent Fee Appraisers, National Society of Real Estate Appraisers and Society of Real Estate Appraisers, as well as the American Bankers Association, American Real Estate and Urban Economics Association, Mortgage Bankers Association, Real Estate Educators Association, Urban Land Institute and U.S. League of Savings Institutions.

The Appraisal Standards Board and the Appraiser Qualification Board will establish the minimum appraisal and appraiser qualifications recently mandated by the Office of Management and Budget.

Federal Regulation

The important role of all real estate professionals in providing access to housing for every resident of the United States has been recognized by Congress. The Fair Housing Amendments Act of 1988, effective March 12, 1989, prohibits discrimination in the selling, brokering or appraising of residential real property because of race, color, religion, sex, handicap, familial status or national origin.

CHAPTER 1

Principles of Appraising

What is a real estate appraisal? An *appraisal* is an unbiased estimate of property value. An appraisal includes a description of the property under consideration, the appraiser's opinion of the property's condition, its utility for a given purpose and/or its probable monetary value on the open market. The term *appraisal* is used to refer to both the process by which the appraiser reaches certain conclusions and the written report in which those conclusions are explained and justified. With an objective, well-researched and carefully documented appraisal, all parties involved, whether in a sale, lease or other transaction, are aided in the decision-making process.

A reliable estimate of value is sought by many parties for many different reasons. The seller wants to know the value of the real estate to determine an appropriate selling price, the buyer wants to pay no more than necessary and the broker wants to realize the maximum commission. Financial institutions insist on an appraisal to determine the amount of money they should lend to a credit applicant. Appraisals are also used to estimate value for taxation and insurance purposes and in condemnation proceedings. In addition, owners of nearby properties will take a proprietary interest in the selling price because it will probably directly affect the value of their properties.

The value of real estate is estimated primarily by comparing vacant and improved properties similar to the appraised property. The similar property may be one that has sold recently (as in the *sales comparison approach*) or, if there is a building, the similar property may be a newly constructed building on a comparable site (as in the *cost approach*). The buyer of an income-producing property will be interested both in recent rentals and sales prices of other similar rental properties (as in the *income capitalization approach*).

All three approaches to value make use of basic concepts of real estate ownership and take into account certain economic principles that influence property value.

Basic Concepts

Land Versus Site

The earth's surface, and everything under or on it, is considered *land*. The substances *under* the earth's surface may be more valuable than the surface itself. *Mineral rights* to solid substances (such as coal and iron ore), as well as those that must be removed from beneath the surface to be reduced to possession (such as oil and gas), may be transferred independently of the rest of the land. *Water rights* provide access to our increasingly important surface and underground water supplies.

Within limitations, the air rights *above* the earth's surface are also considered the landowner's property. Transferable air rights have facilitated construction of high-rise buildings.

When land is *improved* by the addition of utilities (water, gas, electricity) or other services (such as sewers), it becomes a *site* and may be considered suitable for building purposes.

Real Estate and Real Property

Real estate is the land itself and all things permanently attached to it. The rights of ownership of real estate are referred to as *real property*. These rights of ownership, often called the *bundle of rights,* include the rights to use, rent, sell or give away the real estate as well as to choose *not* to exercise any of these rights. The bundle of rights inherent in the ownership of real estate may be bought and sold in a real estate transaction. The terms *real estate* and *real property* are frequently used interchangeably.

Taxation, Eminent Domain, Escheat and Police Power

Other rights, however, are reserved by law for public (government) exercise and limit an owner's full enjoyment of ownership rights. The right of *taxation* enables the government to collect taxes and to sell the property if the taxes are not paid. Private property may be taken for public use, upon payment of just compensation, by the right of *eminent domain*. If the owner of real property dies leaving no qualified heirs, ownership of the property may revert to the state by the right of *escheat*. The *police power* of government enables it to establish zoning ordinances, building codes and other measures that restrict the use of real estate to protect the health, safety, morals and general welfare of the public.

Personal Property

The real estate appraiser must be aware of nonrealty items to be included in the appraisal, such as personal property, business value, contractual arrangements, lease premiums, finance premiums, and so forth, and should value those items separately.

Any tangible items not permanently attached to real estate are classified as *personal property*. Items of personal property are usually not included in an appraisal of the real property. A permanent attachment would be an item that could be removed only by causing serious injury either to the real estate or the item itself. A window air conditioner would ordinarily be considered personal property, but if a hole were cut in a wall expressly for the installation of that air conditioner it would probably be considered part of the real estate.

The parties involved in a transaction should agree on what items to consider part of the real estate. In the absence of such an agreement, however, legal action might ultimately decide the issue. In that event, the intent of the installer (whether to make a permanent or temporary installation), the method of installation (whether permanent or temporary) and other actions of the parties would be considered.

Appraising

A given parcel of real estate may have many different values at the same time, depending on the objective or purpose of the appraisal. Some of these are:

assessed value	cash value	salvage value
inheritance tax value	market value	depreciated value
mortgage loan value	insurance value	replacement value
capitalized value	appraised value	lease value
book value	rental value	

To *appraise* something means to estimate the dollar amount of one of its values. Appraisers for banks, savings and loan associations or other lenders will probably be seeking the market value of the properties they inspect for mortgage loan purposes. Depreciated value is used in one appraising approach to estimate market value; rental value may be used in another. City and county real estate taxes are based on assessed value.

Market Value

The definition of *market value* has undergone considerable scrutiny in recent years, as the automatic assumption of consistently rising values has proved unreliable. The following definition came out of a California court decision and has been widely used by appraisers:

Market value is the highest price estimated in terms of money which the property would bring if exposed for sale in the open market, with reasonable time allowed in which to find a purchaser, buying with knowledge of all of the uses and purposes to which it is adapted and for which it was capable of being used.

In 1986, the Federal Home Loan Mortgage Corporation (FHLMC) and Federal National Mortgage Association (FNMA) revised the definition of the market value of real estate, which had formerly used the "highest price" standard. Market value is now considered the *most probable price* real estate should bring in a sale occurring under normal market conditions. The appraiser's estimate typically will be chosen from a range of values; the highest value in that range is not necessarily an accurate reflection of expected market value.

The definition of market value approved by those agencies will be used in this book.

The appraiser's estimate of market value will assume an *arm's-length transaction* in which four conditions must be present:

1. Neither the buyer nor the seller is acting under duress.
2. The real estate has been offered on the open market for a reasonable length of time (some properties would be expected to take longer to sell than others).
3. Both buyer and seller are aware of the property's potential, including its assets and defects.
4. No unusual circumstances are present, such as favorable seller financing or the seller's need for cash in a hurry.

Sales Price

Sales price is what a property actually sells for—its transaction price. This price may differ from market value because many factors can prevent a sale from being an arm's-length transaction. The need of either principal (buyer or seller) to close the transaction within a short period of time will limit that party's bargaining power. On the other hand, if a seller receives an offer for less than the asking price, which was the market value of the property, but the offer is made only one week after the property is put on the market, the seller may decide that a quick sale is worth losing the higher price that might have been received if the property were left on the market longer. The buyer and seller may be relatives, friends or related companies, and one or both could voluntarily limit their bargaining power. Also, the buyer may have a pressing need to acquire the property, such as to add to an adjoining site.

Exercise 1.1

Indicate whether each of the following items is real estate, real property or personal property.

1. window screens

2. draperies

3. a furnace

4. venetian blinds

5. central air-conditioning

6. kitchen cabinets

7. a child's playhouse

8. a portable room heater

9. rose bushes

10. the right to sell land and any building attached to the land

Which of the following factors would be likely to prevent an arm's-length transaction?

11. seller's immediate job transfer to another city

12. new highway construction

13. delinquent tax sale

14. location across the street from a grade school

15. flooding in basement not revealed by seller

Answer the following question.

16. Why is the distinction between real estate and personal property important to the appraiser?

Check your answers against those given in the Answer Key at the back of the book.

Basic Value Principles

While many property owners could probably make a fairly accurate guess as to the current value of their property, they would still be unable to identify all or most of the factors that contribute to that value. The knowledge of precisely what those factors are, and how they influence and can be expected to influence property value, is part of what lends credence to the appraiser's estimate of market value.

The basic value principles are interrelated, and their relative importance will vary depending on particular local conditions. Supply and demand may be the paramount factor in a burgeoning oil boomtown, while in a period of economic recession competition among existing retail stores may foreclose development of new stores. Even climatic or geological conditions are important, such as when unexpected heavy rainfall creates the threat of destructive mudslides.

It is the appraiser's task, then, to consider the subject property in light of all the following principles.

Substitution

The upper limit of value of a given real property is basically determined by using the principle of *substitution*. The worth of the real estate is influenced by the cost of acquiring an equally desirable substitute or comparable property. The value of an appraised property may be found by applying this principle to the three basic approaches to value, which are discussed later in this chapter under "Methods of Appraisal."

Highest and Best Use

Of all the factors that influence market value, the primary consideration is the *highest and best use* of the real estate. The highest and best use of a property is its most profitable legally and physically permitted use, that is, the use that will provide the highest present value. This applies to both the land itself, considered vacant (whether or not a building is on it at present) and the improved property (whether improvements are existing or proposed). The highest and best use evolves from an analysis of the community, neighborhood, site and improvements. This analysis should reveal the intensity and length of the stated use or uses. A highest and best use study may be made to find the most profitable use of a vacant site or to determine the validity of a proposed site utilization. The local planning department would be consulted to learn of any potential change in the permitted uses. If there already is a structure on the property, the highest and best use study may make one of several assumptions: the site could be considered vacant, with the cost of demolishing the existing structure taken into account when estimating profits from any other use of the site; the cost of refurbishing the existing structure could be considered in light of any increased income that might result; the structure could be considered as is, that is, with no further improvements; and the structure might be considered adaptable to new uses.

Every case must be studied on its own merits, considering zoning or other restrictive ordinances as well as current trends. For example, many gas stations have closed since the early 1970s. Before that time, most such facilities would probably have been used again only as gas stations. However, with the current trend toward drive-in facilities, from restaurants and dry-cleaning shops to almost every other type of retail outlet, some former gas stations have been converted to other types of drive-in businesses. In effect, the highest and best use for such properties in some instances has been redefined.

Although appraisers make highest and best use studies, most appraisers ordinarily do not include detailed narration for every highest and best use option in an appraisal report. They should nevertheless consider each option in arriving at a highest and best use conclusion. A property's highest and best use may be redefined at a later date, just as its appraised value may fluctuate downward or upward.

Externalities

The principle of *externalities* states that influences outside a property may have a positive or negative effect on its value. For example, the federal government's direct participation in interest rate controls, in mortgage loan guarantees, in slum clearance and rehabilitation, and so forth, has had a powerful impact in stimulating or retarding the housing supply and increasing or decreasing the level of home ownership. Values of homes and all other types of real property are directly affected by governmental action or inaction. External influences affecting value can be found at the regional, city and neighborhood levels as well. At the neighborhood level, for instance, property values can be enhanced even by decorative features such as fresh paint, flowers and plush lawns.

Supply and Demand

As with any marketable commodity, the law of *supply and demand* affects real estate. Property values will rise as demand increases and/or supply decreases. The last building lot in a desirable residential development will probably be worth much more than the first lot that was sold in the development, assuming a consistent demand.

The effect of supply and demand is most obvious on the value of older buildings in very desirable areas, usually in cities, where demographic trends (population size and distribution) may bring heavy demand for housing to neighborhoods that have already seriously deteriorated. A building in such an area, even if it required extensive remodeling to meet current building codes, might have increased in value several times because of the increased demand. Thus it should be remembered that demand relates to the supply of a particular type of property *in a given location*—and not to property in general.

Conformity, Progression and Regression

In general, particularly in residential areas of single-family houses, buildings should follow the principle of *conformity;* that is, they should be similar in design, construction, age, condition and market appeal to other buildings in the neighborhood. Nonconformity may work to the advantage or disadvantage of the owner of the nonconforming property. A house that has not been well maintained but is in a neighborhood of well-kept homes will benefit from the overall good impression created by the neighborhood and its probable desirability. This is an example of the principle of *progression*. In an example of the principle of *regression,* a house that has been meticulously maintained but is in a neighborhood of homes that have not received regular repair will suffer from the generally unfavorable impression created. In the same way, an elaborate mansion on a large lot with a spacious lawn will be worth more in a neighborhood of similar homes than it would in a neighborhood of more modest homes on smaller lots. From the appraiser's viewpoint, the major concern is whether the improvements, or components, are typical.

Contribution

In an appraisal for market value any improvement to a property, whether to vacant land or a building, is worth only what it adds to a property's market value, regardless of the improvement's cost. In other words, an improvement's *contribution* to the value of the entire property is counted, not its intrinsic cost. The principle of contribution is easily applied to certain housing improvements. A remodeled basement usually will not contribute its total cost to the value of a house. A second bathroom, however, may well increase a house's value by more than its installation cost.

The principle of conformity may overlap with the principle of contribution. For example, if a house's exterior is its major flaw and other houses nearby are well kept, the addition of new siding may be worth several times its cost because the house will then blend in with those nearby. The appraiser's opinion, therefore, should be governed by a feature's contribution to market value—not by its reported cost.

Law of Increasing Returns and Law of Decreasing Returns

Improvements to land and structures eventually will reach a point at which they will have no positive effect on property values. When money spent on such improvements produces a proportionate or greater increase in income or value, the *law of increasing returns* is in effect. At the point when additional improvements bring no corresponding increase in income or value, the *law of decreasing returns* is operating.

Competition

Retail properties are always susceptible to *competition*. For example, as the profits of a store increase, similar stores are attracted to the area. This competition tends to mean less profit for the first business because the profits are now going to more than one store. Unless total sales increase, there probably will not be enough sales to support very many stores, and one or more will be forced out of business. Occasionally the opposite is true, and more competitors serve as a stimulus to the area, making a center of trade for the products being sold (such as in a shopping center).

Change

All property is influenced by the principle of *change*. No physical or economic condition remains constant. Just as real estate is subject to natural phenomena—earthquakes, tornadoes, fires, violent storms and routine wear and tear of the elements—the real estate business (as is any business) is subject to the demands of its market. It is the appraiser's job to keep aware of past and perhaps predictable effects of natural phenomena as well as the changes in the marketplace. Remember that persons buy property for its future benefits. Also, mortgage lenders may hold a mortgage for 25 to 30 years on the appraised property.

Growth, Equilibrium and Decline

In terms of the effects of change on real property, ordinary physical deterioration and market demand have indicated three stages through which an improved property will pass: (1) *growth,* when improvements are made, and property demand expands; (2) *equilibrium* or *stability,* when the property undergoes little change; and (3) *decline,* when the property requires an increasing amount of upkeep to retain its original utility while demand slackens. This principle also applies to an entire neighborhood. Demand may increase of course, as has occurred in many urban areas, providing the needed impetus for major property renovation. In essence, this can be thought of as a fourth stage of a property's life cycle—*revitalization.*

Anticipation

Real estate has historically proved to be a generally appreciating asset. As such it is usually bought with the expectation of its future higher value. This *anticipation* of higher value is usually fulfilled because land offers a fixed supply to what has proved to be a continually growing demand. However, anticipation may also lower value if property rights are expected to be restricted or if the property somehow becomes less appealing to prospective buyers.

For example, a residential area scheduled to undergo condemnation for highway construction might represent anticipation in either of its forms. Owners of residential property immediately adjacent to the highway may expect property values to decline as traffic noise and pollution increase. Owners of residential property far enough away from the highway to avoid those problems may expect property values to rise as their property is made more accessible to surrounding business and shopping areas.

Land-use requirements are often anticipated by developers who wish to be ready with the necessary residential, commercial or industrial facilities to meet the demand they expect. The predicted need might or might not materialize, however, which is why real estate as an investment still contains an element of risk. In short, real property is very often purchased for its anticipated future benefits, whether for production of income, a tax shelter or future appreciation.

Conclusion

The principles discussed are not just pure theory but the keys to understanding *why, when* and *how* certain factors act to influence the value of real property. If the appraiser understands these principles, he or she can form opinions based on knowledge and understanding, not guesswork.

Exercise 1.2

Which basic value principle(s) does each of the following case problems illustrate?

1. Carl Snyder owns a vacation home near a small town almost 300 miles from the city in which he lives and works. He doesn't use his vacation house more than three weeks every year. The last time he stayed there, he noticed that a gas station had been built a few hundred yards down the road. After talking to the owner, he discovered that a zoning change had been put into effect to allow construction of a new shopping center on land adjacent to the gas station. Mr. Snyder realizes that his property won't be suitable as a vacation retreat once the shopping center is built.

2. Marian Nelson customized the family room of her new home by having a special wall niche built for her harpsichord, a mural painted on one wall, intricately carved wainscotting installed on every wall and small ledges chiseled in the stone of the fireplace so that she could display her glass miniatures. Mrs. Nelson decided that the improvements were justified because, even though she knew she would not be living in the home for many years, she could always realize the worth of the improvements whenever she sold her home.

3. A structurally sound office building rents for $15.00 per square foot but lacks air-conditioning. A similar, air-conditioned building rents for $18.50 per square foot.

4. Two grocery stores are located on the same city block, and both have had good business for ten years. One store is modernized—new cash registers and lighting fixtures are installed, and more efficient stock control is put into effect. Because the store is part of a chain, remodeling costs are absorbed without general increase in prices. The other grocery store begins losing customers.

5. A 100-unit apartment building designed for middle-income persons over 55 years of age is in very good condition. The owners plan extensive remodeling and redecorating to be financed by raising rents as needed. The plans will probably take four years to complete. None of the apartments will be altered, but the building's exterior will be completely redone, and the lobby will be furnished with expensive carpeting, chairs and a chandelier. The lobby remodeling is done first; the tenants seem pleased, and no major objection is made to the resultant rent increases. After the second year, however, many tenants object to the continued increases and choose not to renew their leases. The owners have difficulty finding new tenants.

6. A single-family neighborhood is located adjacent to an airport. Excessive noise caused by airplanes flying overhead and the potential danger they create have adversely affected the value of homes in the immediate area.

Check your answers against those given in the Answer Key at the back of the book.

Methods of Appraisal

Each appraisal approach uses some of the principles defined earlier. In addition, each approach has its own terms, some of which will be mentioned briefly in the following summaries of the three methods. All of them will be explained more fully in later chapters.

Sales Comparison Approach

The *sales comparison* approach to appraising makes the most direct use of the principle of substitution. The appraiser finds three to five (or more) properties that have sold recently and are similar to the subject property under appraisal. The appraiser notes any dissimilar features and makes an adjustment for each by using the following formula:

$$\frac{\text{Sales Price of}}{\text{Comparable Property}} \pm \text{Adjustments} = \frac{\text{Indicated Value of}}{\text{Subject Property}}$$

The appraiser adds the value of the feature present in the subject property but not in the comparable and subtracts the value of a feature present in the comparable but not in the subject property. Major adjustments include those made for physical (on-site) features, locational (off-site) influences, conditions of sale (buyer-seller motivation and financing terms) and time from date of sale. After going through this process for each of the comparable properties, the appraiser selects a market value for the subject property that is the adjusted value of the comparable(s) most like the subject.

EXAMPLE: House A, which sold for $55,000, is comparable to house B, the subject property, but has a garage valued at $5,000. House B has no garage. In this case, using the formula for the sales comparison approach, the market value of the subject property would be reached as shown below.

$$\$55,000 - \$5,000 = \$50,000$$

House B is valued at $50,000.

EXAMPLE: House X, the subject property, is 15 years old. A comparable property, house Y, is 15 years old and sold for $70,000 one year before the time of this appraisal. Because of the length of time since the sale of house Y, the appraiser has determined that 10 percent added to the sales price is an accurate reflection of the increase in property values over the year. In this case, using the formula for the sales comparison approach:

$$\$70,000 + (10\% \times \$70,000) = \text{Value of Subject Property}$$
$$\$70,000 + \$7,000 = \$77,000$$

House X is valued at $77,000.

Vacant land is valued in the same way, by finding other comparable properties and adding or subtracting, as necessary, the worth of any improvements present in either the subject or comparable property and not in the other. Features of vacant land might include installation of utilities, composition of soil, terrain, shape, zoning and favorable location.

Cost Approach

In the *cost* approach, the appraiser estimates the value of any improvements to the land (such as structures) in terms of their cost *new*. The appraiser then subtracts any loss in value owing to the *depreciation* of the improvements. Finally, the appraiser adds an estimate of value of the site itself, usually found by sales comparison analysis. The formula for the cost approach is:

$$\frac{\text{Cost of}}{\text{Improvements New}} - \frac{\text{Depreciation on}}{\text{Improvements}} + \text{Site Value} = \text{Property Value}$$

Depreciation may occur through either *deterioration* (effects of wear and tear or the elements) or *obsolescence.* Obsolescence can be *functional,* such as outmoded room layout or design, or *external,* caused by changes in factors outside the property, such as zoning, the property's highest and best use or supply and demand.

EXAMPLE: A house being appraised is similar in size, design and quality of construction to a new house that has a construction cost of $125,000. The house being appraised has depreciated by 20 percent due to lack of maintenance and is on a lot valued separately at $35,000. Using the cost approach formula:

$125,000 – (20% × $125,000) + $35,000 = Property Value
$125,000 – $25,000 + $35,000 = $135,000

The estimated value of the property is $135,000.

EXAMPLE: A warehouse that would cost $350,000 to construct today has depreciated 25 percent in its lifetime and is on land valued at $110,000. What is the property's total estimated value by the cost approach?

$350,000 – (25% × $350,000) + $110,000 = Property Value
$350,000 – $87,500 + $110,000 = $372,500

The estimated value of the property is $372,500.

Income Capitalization Approach

The *income capitalization* approach is based on the net annual income, or investment return, that a buyer expects from the property. The price that the buyer will pay will be determined by the probable return the property will yield from the investment.

Remember that the income capitalization approach is based on *net operating income.* Rents are *not* net operating income. All the expenses of maintaining the building, such as upkeep and management, must be subtracted from *potential gross income* (scheduled rents plus any other income) to realize net operating income.

If a property's net operating income is known, as well as the buyer's required rate of investment return, value can be computed by using the formula:

$$\frac{\text{Net Operating Income}}{\text{Rate of Return}} = \text{Property Value}$$

Or:

$$\frac{I}{R} = V$$

EXAMPLE: A buyer wants a 10 percent investment return. He is interested in a medical office building that produces a net operating income of $22,500 per year. What would the buyer be willing to pay for the building?

$$\frac{\$22,500}{10\%} = \$225,000$$

The property value necessary to produce the expected net operating income is $225,000.

If a buyer has only a certain amount to invest and wants a specific rate of return from his investment, he would use a variation of the formula given above.

Property Value × Rate of Return = Net Operating Income

Or:

$$V \times R = I$$

EXAMPLE: To receive a 12 percent return from an investment of $100,000, what would be the required net operating income of the purchased property?

$$\$100,000 \times 12\% = \$12,000$$

The net operating income would have to be $12,000.

Exercise 1.3

Using the formula for the approach specified, solve each of the following appraisal problems.

Sales Comparison Approach:

House X is being appraised. It is very similar to house Y, but house Y has an in-the-ground swimming pool valued at $7,000. House Y sold two months ago for $78,000. What is the market value of house X using the formula for the sales comparison approach?

Cost Approach:

A retail store, built 15 years ago, has depreciated about 30 percent overall. It would cost $130,000 to build today, and similar sites are now worth $52,000. What is the market value of this store using the formula for the cost approach?

Income Capitalization Approach:

An apartment building provides a net annual rental income of $14,500. The current owner wants to offer a prospective purchaser a 15 percent investment return. What will the asking price be if it is the same as the market value found by the formula for the income capitalization approach?

Check your answers against those given in the Answer Key at the back of the book.

Relationship of Approaches

The three approaches to appraising obviously have distinct requirements: comparable property sales (sales comparison approach), cost and depreciation estimates (cost approach) and investment return (income capitalization approach). These requirements determine which appraisal method will be given the most weight in the appraiser's final estimate of the market value of the subject property.

As a general rule, the sales comparison approach is most useful with single-family residences, the cost approach is most useful with non–income-producing property and the income capitalization approach is most useful with investment property.

Most appraisals will require the use of more than one approach, especially when land value must be distinguished from building value. This is true in using the cost approach to find building value. There are other instances when land value must be separated from building value, such as for tax valuation purposes. These will be discussed later in this book.

EXAMPLE: If a 25-year-old school building is to be sold, what approach would be given the most weight in estimating its market value?

School buildings are not usually on the market, so there probably would be no recent, nearby, comparable sales. If the building could be used as office or other rental space as it stood, or with a little remodeling, the income capitalization approach might be feasible. The approach given the most weight, however, would probably be the cost approach, because the high cost of constructing a similar new building would probably be the most significant selling factor.

Exercise 1.4

Decide which appraisal approach(es) would normally carry the most weight in valuing each of the following properties.

1. a factory

2. an automobile showroom and garage

3. a public building formerly used as a town hall

4. farmland surrounded by commercial and industrial developments

5. a one-story retail store in a busy downtown business district

6. an older, single-family residence in a neighborhood changing to high-rise apartments

7. a medical office building in a suburban shopping center

8. a single-family, owner-occupied residence

9. a church

10. a small, outdated roadside restaurant adjacent to a new apartment complex

Check your answers against those given in the Answer Key at the back of the book.

Data Collection

Finding the information necessary to utilize any of the appraising approaches, whether comparable properties, cost figures or investment return, involves collecting the appropriate *data*. Specific data about the property itself, general data about the surrounding area and data applicable to the appraisal approach being used must be found.

Figure 1.1 on page 17 is a flowchart that outlines the steps to be followed in carrying out an appraisal assignment. The steps are:

1. *State the problem.* The property to be appraised must be identified by legal or other description, and the purpose of the appraisal must be considered. The appraiser and client must agree on what the appraisal is to accomplish. The property interest may be less than full ownership, such as a tenant's interest in a lease or the right to use an easement or right-of-way; or title may be held in partnership, by a corporation or jointly with other individuals. Once the appraiser knows the property interest to be appraised and why the appraisal is necessary—whether for insurance purposes, to find

FIGURE 1.1   The Appraisal Process

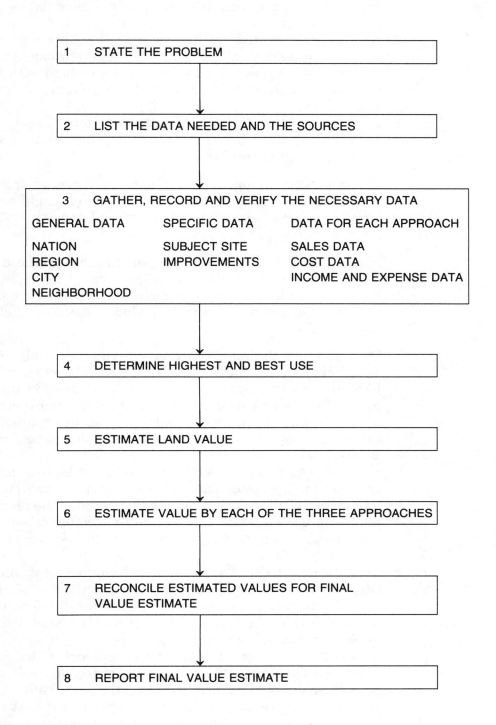

market value or simply to determine rental value—the approach(es) best suited to the property can be chosen. Occasionally only one approach will be appropriate, since only limited data will be available for some properties.

2. *List the data needed and the sources.* Once the appraiser knows which approach(es) will be used, the information needed can be itemized. The appraiser must be familiar enough with the sources of information to state exactly what the sources for the particular case will be.

3. *Gather, record and verify the necessary data.* The types of data needed must be collected and recorded for future use, and the accuracy must be verified.

   The appraiser compiles general data on the geographic and economic features of the nation, region, city and neighborhood. Property location, as influenced by both natural and economic factors, is often of critical importance.

   Regardless of the interest being appraised, specific data on the subject property (including a detailed physical description) must be obtained. Particularly when comparable properties are to be found, the physical description should include all items likely to affect market value.

   Depending on the approach used, the appraiser also will gather sales data on comparable properties, cost data on construction of a like property or income and expense data based on the property's history. All sources should be double-checked against other sources, especially when obtaining the sales price of a comparable property. In such a case, at least one of the sources should be a party to the transaction.

4. *Determine highest and best use.* Through a highest and best use analysis the appraiser analyzes and interprets the market forces that influence the subject property to determine the property's most profitable use on which to base the final value estimate. The appraiser may conclude that the highest and best use of the land is *not* its present use.

5. *Estimate land value.* The location and improvements of the subject site (except for buildings) are compared to those of similar nearby sites. Adjustments are made for any significant differences, and the adjusted prices of the properties most like the subject site are used to estimate the value of the subject site.

6. *Estimate value by each of the three approaches.* Using the *sales comparison* approach, the sales prices of recently sold comparable properties are adjusted to derive an estimate of value for the property under appraisal. In the *cost* approach, the cost of property improvements, less depreciation on improvements, is added to site value. In the *income capitalization* approach, value is based on the rental income the property is capable of earning.

7. *Reconcile estimated values for final value estimate.* The appraiser must correlate the information and decide what conclusions can be drawn from the volume of collected facts. The appraiser never

simply averages differing value estimates. The most relevant approach, based on analysis and judgment, receives the greatest weight in determining the estimate that most accurately reflects the value sought.

8. *Report final value estimate.* Finally, the appraiser presents his or her conclusion of value in the form requested by the client.

Conclusion

Real estate includes the land at and beneath the surface of the earth, the airspace above it and improvements (both buildings and fixtures) to the land. Real property is the ownership of certain rights in land and its improvements.

One of the many values of real property is market value—the most probable price property can be expected to bring in a sale occurring under normal market conditions—an arm's-length transaction. To estimate property value accurately, the appraiser must be familiar with the economic principles that affect value.

In making an appraisal, the appraiser first defines the value sought. After a thorough study of the subject property and its geographic area, the appraiser uses the different appraisal approaches to make an estimate of the property's value.

Throughout the rest of this book, we will discuss how each step in the appraisal process is accomplished.

You have now completed Chapter 1. If you feel you understand the material in this chapter, take the Achievement Examination. If you would like to review the material in the chapter first, do so. The Achievement Examination will serve both to test your comprehension and to review the chapter highlights. If after taking the examination you find you are unsure about certain points, review those points before continuing with the next chapter.

Achievement Examination 1

1. The property of a person who dies leaving no heirs passes to the state by the right of:

   a. acquisition. b. escheat. c. condemnation. d. eminent domain.

2. Condemnation of private property for public use is called the right of:

   a. seizure. b. escheat. c. eminent domain. d. acquisition.

3. Name the approach that normally would be the most useful in valuing each of the property types listed below.

   a. residential properties
   b. investment properties
   c. public and religious-use properties

4. Distinguish between real property and real estate.

5. Explain the difference between market value and sales price.

6. Property A in a neighborhood sold for $80,000. It is very similar to property B, which you are appraising, except that property A has a two-car garage worth $6,000. Using the formula for the sales comparison approach, calculate the market value of property B.

7. An office building has depreciated 40 percent since it was built 25 years ago. If it would cost $425,000 to build today, and if similar sites are selling for $175,000, what is the market value of the property using the formula for the cost approach?

8. You are appraising a single-story building, which rents for $24,000 per year. If you determine that a 13% return was justified on this investment, what would be your value estimate of the property using the income capitalization approach formula?

Identify the major value principle described in each case below.

9. A less expensive house tends to gain in value because of more expensive neighborhood houses.

10. The value of a property tends to be limited by what it costs to buy another property similar in physical characteristics, function or income.

11. Plans have been announced for a multi-million-dollar shopping center to be built next door to a vacant lot you own. Property values in the area of the proposed site will tend to increase as a result of this announcement.

12. The rental value of vacant land can sometimes be greater than it would be if the land were improved with a building.

13. In many downtown areas, parking lots make more profit than older office buildings.

14. An investor will probably pay more for the last 20 lots in an area where the demand for houses is great than for the first 20 lots in the same area.

15.   The cost of installing an air-conditioning system in an apartment building is justified only if the rental increase that can be expected as a result of the installation exceeds the amount spent.

Check your answers against those given in the Answer Key at the back of the book.

CHAPTER 2

The Data Collection Process

The Appraisal Process

The appraisal process, discussed in Chapter 1, is shown in the flow-chart (Figure 2.1) on page 24. Almost every step in the appraisal process involves determining, gathering, recording or verifying the many kinds of data the appraiser needs to make an estimate of value.

In step 3 of the appraisal process, the appraiser will need to know:

- general data on the nation, region, city and neighborhood;
- specific data on the subject site and improvements;
- sales data for the sales comparison approach;
- cost and accrued depreciation data for the cost approach; and
- income and expense data for the income capitalization approach.

Without knowledge of the sources and reliability of available data, the appraiser would be unable to perform the job properly. The type of property being appraised will dictate the emphasis to be placed on the types of data collected. A factory in an industrial area, for instance, will require more services than a home in a residential area. Thus the appraiser makes an integrated analysis, moving from general data to that required for the specific appraisal approach, always keeping the subject property in mind.

The Data Bank

Appendix A is the Data Bank, which lists the sources of information the appraiser may use. It also presents different kinds of data needed in each step of the appraisal process.

FIGURE 2.1   The Appraisal Process

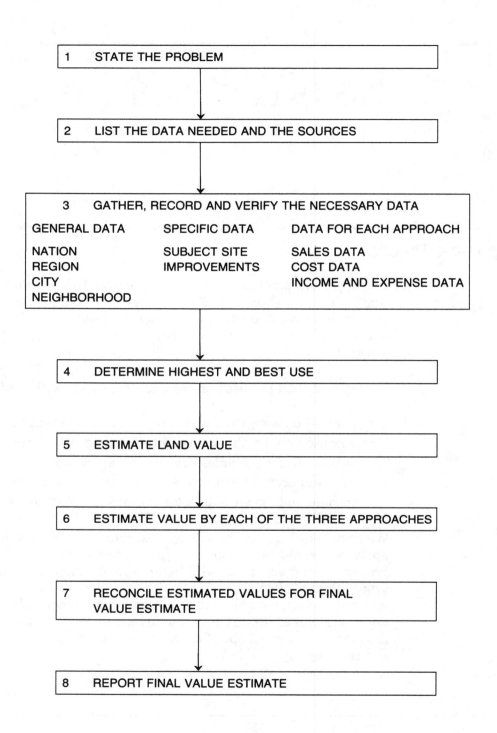

The Source List

Forty-five sources to which an appraiser should have access are listed on the first page of the Data Bank. Some already may be familiar to you; if you have ever owned real estate you will recognize even more. You will be referring to the source list throughout the rest of this book. Blanks are provided at the end of the list so you can enter any additional sources of information available to you that have not been included.

Kinds of Data needed

Following the source list in the Data Bank are eight charts detailing the types of specific information needed in each category. Each type of information called for in the chart is keyed to one or more of the 45 sources of information itemized in the source list. (If you add any sources to the list, key them to the appropriate types of information.)

Each chart tells what kinds of information you need for that category as well as the sources to be used to obtain that information.

EXAMPLE: In inspecting a site in a new subdivision, you notice that construction work is going on along the sides of the roadway. There are no workers present, however. How can you find out what kind of work is under way?

In the chart for specific data about the subject site, you would look up "Improvements" and find that there are four possible sources of information—numbers 1, 12, 20 and 28 in the source list. The sources are (1) personal inspection; (12) city hall or county courthouse; (20) county or city engineering commission; and (28) public utility companies. Because you have already inspected the property personally, you would contact the other sources, the most pertinent one first. In this case, the county or city engineering commission could probably tell you the reason for the construction activity. The department that issues building permits should have the information you need.

Exercise 2.1

Refer to the Data Bank and list the source(s) for the following information.

1. lot size

2. new construction in the area

3. proposed zoning changes

4. population size

5. nearest schools and churches

6. municipal services

7. recent zoning changes

8. utility easements

9. property tax assessment

Check your answers against those given in the Answer Key at the back of the book.

Data Forms

The best way to make sure that no details of the property, its area or the approaches to value are overlooked is to use a form for recording the necessary information. Such a form specifies the types of information needed and provides a place to record it.

The rest of this chapter includes forms for neighborhood data, site data and building data. Forms for regional and city data are not given here. By using the sources listed in the Data Bank, the appraiser should be able to build an accurate profile of the region and city. Once compiled and analyzed, this information will change infrequently, but inevitably change will occur. It is the appraiser's job to keep up to date on economic indicators such as employment level, business starts (and failures) and political trends that could signal governmental policy changes affecting property values.

Neighborhood Data Form

A Neighborhood Data Form, such as the one shown in Figure 2.2, will help the appraiser gather some of the basic information needed for every appraisal report. The appraiser will probably not have to complete a new Neighborhood Data Form for each appraisal, since many of the appraisals to be made will be within the same neighborhood. Some categories of neighborhood data will have to be updated every year or two.

Although the Data Bank in Appendix A will supply sources for much of the neighborhood information, a considerable amount of fieldwork will still be necessary. For example, when checking a neighborhood the appraiser should note the general condition of all houses in the area. Are the homes large or small? How well are the properties landscaped? Are the lawns well kept? Do the surrounding houses conform architecturally? Answers to these questions tell much about the quality of life in the neighborhood. In most cases, visual inspec-

FIGURE 2.2   Neighborhood Data Form

NEIGHBORHOOD DATA FORM

BOUNDARIES: ADJACENT TO:

    NORTH _____   _____

    SOUTH _____   _____

    EAST _____   _____

    WEST _____   _____

TOPOGRAPHY: _____ ☐ URBAN ☐ SUBURBAN ☐ RURAL

STAGE OF LIFE CYCLE OF NEIGHBORHOOD: ☐ GROWTH   ☐ EQUILIBRIUM   ☐ DECLINE

% BUILT UP: _____ GROWTH RATE: ☐ RAPID ☐ SLOW ☐ STEADY

AVERAGE MARKETING TIME: _____ PROPERTY VALUES: ☐ INCREASING ☐ DECREASING ☐ STABLE

SUPPLY/DEMAND: ☐ OVERSUPPLY ☐ UNDERSUPPLY ☐ BALANCED

CHANGE IN PRESENT LAND USE: _____

POPULATION: ☐ INCREASING ☐ DECREASING ☐ STABLE   AVERAGE FAMILY SIZE: _____

AVERAGE FAMILY INCOME: _____ INCOME LEVEL: ☐ INCREASING ☐ DECREASING

PREDOMINANT OCCUPATIONS: _____

TYPICAL PROPERTIES:	% OF	AGE	PRICE RANGE	% OWNER OCCUPIED	% RENTALS
VACANT LOTS					
SINGLE-FAMILY RESIDENCES					
2–6-UNIT APARTMENTS					
OVER 6-UNIT APARTMENTS					
NONRESIDENTIAL PROPERTIES					

TAX RATE: _____ ☐ HIGHER ☐ LOWER ☐ SAME AS COMPETING AREAS

SPECIAL ASSESSMENTS OUTSTANDING: _____ EXPECTED: _____

SERVICES: ☐ POLICE ☐ FIRE ☐ GARBAGE COLLECTION   OTHER: _____

DISTANCE AND DIRECTION FROM

    BUSINESS AREA: _____

    COMMERCIAL AREA: _____

    PUBLIC ELEMENTARY AND HIGH SCHOOLS: _____

    PRIVATE ELEMENTARY AND HIGH SCHOOLS: _____

    RECREATIONAL AND CULTURAL AREAS: _____

    CHURCHES AND SYNAGOGUES: _____

    EXPRESSWAY INTERCHANGE: _____

    PUBLIC TRANSPORTATION: _____

        TIME TO REACH BUSINESS AREA: _____ COMMERCIAL AREA: _____

    EMERGENCY MEDICAL SERVICE: _____

GENERAL TRAFFIC CONDITIONS: _____

PROXIMITY TO HAZARDS (AIRPORT, CHEMICAL STORAGE, ETC.): _____

PROXIMITY TO NUISANCES (SMOKE, NOISE, ETC.): _____

tion should disclose whether the neighborhood will likely retain its character and value or decline gradually. There is no way the appraiser can avoid such work, and there is no reason to do so. Not only is a thorough, firsthand knowledge of the area of tremendous value to an appraiser, it is essential for an accurate estimate of the property's value.

Although most of the categories of neighborhood data are self-explanatory, some require background knowledge if the appraiser is to record them accurately. *Neighborhood boundaries,* for instance, are determined by considering:

1. natural boundaries (actual physical barriers—ravines, lakes, rivers and highways or other major traffic arteries);
2. differences in land use (changes in zoning from residential to commercial or parkland);
3. average value or age of homes; and
4. income level of residents.

When filling out the Neighborhood Data Form, record the street name or other identifiable dividing line and note the type of area adjacent to the subject neighborhood at that boundary. A residential property adjacent to a park will usually have a higher value than a similar property adjacent to a gravel pit, for instance.

Stage of life cycle.   A typical neighborhood usually goes through three distinct periods in its life: *growth, equilibrium* and *decline.*

When an area is first developed, property values will usually increase until few vacant building sites remain. At that point, the houses in the neighborhood will tend to be in equilibrium at their highest monetary value and prices will rarely fluctuate downward. With increasing property deterioration, the area will usually decline both in value and desirability. The process is enhanced by the availability of new housing nearby, successive ownership by lower-income residents who may not be able to afford the increasing maintenance costs of older homes, and conversion of some properties to rental units, which may not be properly maintained. As properties decrease in value, some may even be put to a different use, such as light industry, which in turn further decreases the attractiveness of the surrounding neighborhood for residential use. The neighborhood's life cycle may start over again due to *revitalization*—a period when demand increases, providing the stimulus needed for neighborhood renovation.

The classic pattern described above is the result of general economic growth coupled with increasing consumer demand and the availability of land for housing and commercial development. In recent years, this pattern has been subjected to volatile market conditions.

In the 1970s, rapid inflation, high interest rates and a prolonged period of economic recession combined with limited land availability to make property ownership increasingly expensive and beyond the means of many more people than formerly. Existing housing became much more desirable, and, for many, making repairs and improvements to an older building became a viable alternative to buying a new home. In response to this slowing of residential life cycles and the demand for tax-sheltered investments, developers concentrated on commercial structures, such as office buildings, overbuilding (at least temporarily) many desirable urban and suburban areas.

By the mid-1980s, a much lower rate of inflation, declining interest rates and indicators of a general economic recovery helped revive the sluggish real estate housing market. The number of new building starts rose as demand increased, and the pace of development helped compensate for the slower preceding years. The Tax Reform Act of 1986 greatly limited the use of real estate as a tax shelter, but that limitation has placed new emphasis on the necessity for prudent investment. A competent appraisal is an important means of helping to determine the soundness of an investment.

In some areas, housing growth is now deliberately limited for environmental or other reasons. In those areas, the state of equilibrium may be much longer than would otherwise be the case.

The appraiser must be sensitive to all of the factors that determine value, including economic, social and governmental influences, to gauge accurately their effect on neighborhood development.

Proximity to hazards and nuisances.   The proximity of the neighborhood, or any part of it, to hazards or nuisances has become very important. The current awareness of environmental factors and the discovery of more factors that are injurious to health or safety have made some properties undesirable. The mere potential for danger (such as chemical storage facilities) may have the effect of lowering property values in nearby areas. The appraiser should be aware of these factors, as well as ones that have been alleviated (such as factory smoke pollution that may have been drastically reduced).

Site Data Form

The Site Data Form shown in Figure 2.3 can be used to record the information needed to describe the subject site.

First, a complete and legally accurate description of the property's location must be obtained and a sketch made to show the property's approximate shape and street location. A public building or other landmark could also be shown on the sketch to help locate the site. The topography (surface features) of the site should be noted as well as the existence of any natural hazards, such as location in or near a floodplain, earthquake fault zone or other potentially dangerous condition.

FIGURE 2.3   Site Data Form

SITE DATA FORM

ADDRESS: _____

LEGAL DESCRIPTION: _____

_____

_____

_____

_____

_____

DIMENSIONS: _____

SHAPE: _____ SQUARE FEET: _____

TOPOGRAPHY: _____ VIEW: _____

NATURAL HAZARDS: _____

☐ INSIDE LOT   ☐ CORNER LOT   FRONTAGE: _____

ZONING: _____ ADJACENT AREAS: _____

UTILITIES: ☐ ELECTRICITY   ☐ GAS   ☐ WATER   ☐ TELEPHONE

☐ SANITARY SEWER   ☐ STORM SEWER

IMPROVEMENTS: DRIVEWAY: _____   STREET: _____

SIDEWALK: _____   CURB/GUTTER: _____   ALLEY: _____

STREETLIGHTS: _____

LANDSCAPING: _____

TOPSOIL: _____ DRAINAGE: _____

EASEMENTS: _____

DEED RESTRICTIONS: _____

SITE PLAT:

Other important features of the site are its size in square feet, location in terms of position in the block, utilities, improvements, soil composition and view. The historically higher value of a corner lot location may not hold true in residential areas having lots 50 feet or more in width. The comparative privacy of a house on a corner lot is offset if other lots offer distances of 20 feet or more between houses. Then, too, a particular corner may front on busy streets, a detriment to residential property. The opposite would be true for a commercial site, however, where a high traffic count would be desirable.

Soil composition is important because if the soil is unable to support a building, piles will have to be driven to carry the weight. A rock bed within a few feet of the surface may require blasting before a suitable foundation can be established. In either case, the cost of preconstruction site preparation would decrease the site's value.

Knowledge of the subject site's zoning, which will affect its future use, is necessary, as is knowledge of current zoning of surrounding areas. A site zoned for a single-family residence may be poorly used for that purpose if the neighborhood is declining and multiunit buildings are being built nearby. In such a case, the feasibility of changing the zoning to multiunit residential construction might be analyzed by making a highest and best use study.

Finally, any easements or deed restrictions should be noted. Any part of the site that cannot be used for building purposes should be clearly designated, as should any other limitation on site use. Such limitations could raise or lower site value. An easement, for example, allows airspace or below-ground space for present or future utility installations or a right-of-way for others to travel over the property. A deed restriction, usually set up by the property's subdivider, may specify the size of lots used for building, the type or style of building constructed, setbacks from property lines or other factors designed to increase the subdivision's homogeneity and make property values more stable.

Building Data Form

The Building Data Form (Figure 2.4) is applicable to residential housing. Some of the information, such as room designations, would not be used for industrial or commercial properties. Any category that does not apply to a particular property can simply have a line drawn through it. Because residential properties are the kind most frequently appraised (they outnumber other types of property and also have a higher ownership turnover), separate industrial and commercial building forms will not be included here.

Even before entering a single-family house, the appraiser is called on to make certain value judgments. Approaching the house from the street, the appraiser mentally records a first impression of the house,

FIGURE 2.4 Building Data Form

BUILDING DATA FORM

ADDRESS: _____

NO. OF UNITS: _____ NO. OF STORIES: _____ ORIENTATION: N S E W

TYPE: _____ DESIGN: _____ AGE: _____ SQUARE FEET: _____

	GOOD	AVERAGE	FAIR	POOR
GENERAL CONDITION OF EXTERIOR				
FOUNDATION TYPE _____ BSMT./CRAWL SP./SLAB				
EXTERIOR WALLS: BRICK/BLOCK/VENEER/STUCCO/				
WOOD/ALUMINUM/VINYL				
WINDOW FRAMES: METAL/WOOD				
STORM WINDOWS: ____ SCREENS: ____				
GARAGE: _____ ATTACHED/DETACHED				
NUMBER OF CARS: ____				
☐ PORCH ☐ DECK ☐ PATIO ☐ SHED				
OTHER _____				
GENERAL CONDITION OF INTERIOR				
INTERIOR WALLS: DRY WALL/PLASTER/WOOD				
CEILINGS: _____				
FLOORS: WOOD/CONCRETE/TILE/CARPET				
ELECTRICAL WIRING AND SERVICE: _____				
HEATING PLANT: _____ AGE: _____				
GAS/OIL/WOOD/ELECTRIC				
CENTRAL AIR-CONDITIONING: _____ AIR FILTRATION: ___				
NUMBER OF FIREPLACES: _____ TYPE: _____				
OTHER _____				
BATHROOM: FLOOR___WALLS___FIXTURES _____				
BATHROOM: FLOOR___WALLS___FIXTURES _____				
BATHROOM: FLOOR___WALLS___FIXTURES _____				
KITCHEN: FLOOR___WALLS___CABINETS _____				
FIXTURES _____				

ROOM SIZES	LIVING ROOM	DINING ROOM	KITCHEN	BEDROOM	BATH	CLOSETS	FAMILY ROOM
BASEMENT							
1ST FLOOR							
2ND FLOOR							
ATTIC							

DEPRECIATION (DESCRIBE):

    PHYSICAL DETERIORATION _____

    FUNCTIONAL OBSOLESCENCE _____

    EXTERNAL OBSOLESCENCE _____

its orientation and how it fits in with the surrounding area. At the same time, the appraiser notes and records information about the landscaping. Next, the external construction materials (for the foundation, outside walls, roof, driveway, etc.) and the condition of each are listed and the general external condition of the building is rated. Finally, the appraiser measures each structure on the site, sketches its dimensions and computes its area in square feet.

Once in the house, the appraiser notes and evaluates major construction details and fixtures, particularly the interior finish, the kind of floors, walls and doors, the condition and adequacy of kitchen cabinets, the type and condition of heating and air-conditioning systems, paneled rooms, fireplaces, and all other features that indicate quality of construction. The appraiser also observes the general condition of the house—for evidence of recent remodeling, the presence of cracked plaster, sagging floors or any other signs of deterioration—and records room dimensions and total square footage.

The appraiser then notes the general condition of the building, giving consideration to three kinds of depreciation:

1. *Physical deterioration.* The effects of ordinary wear-and-tear and the action of the elements.
2. *Functional obsolescence.* The inadequacy of features in the design, layout or construction of the building that are currently desired by purchasers, or the presence of features that have become unfashionable or unnecessary. Fixtures such as bathtubs or vanities also fall into this category. A kitchen without modern, built-in cabinets and sink would be undesirable in most areas.
3. *External obsolescence.* A feature made undesirable or unnecessary because of conditions outside the property. A change of zoning from residential to commercial might make a single-family house obsolete if such usage does not fully utilize (take full monetary advantage of) the site.

The kinds of depreciation and how each affects the value of the property are explained in greater detail in the chapters on the specific appraisal approaches. When the appraiser first records the building data, it is enough to make a general estimate of the degree of physical deterioration, functional obsolescence or external obsolescence present in the property.

In appraising a multiunit residential building the appraiser will record the building data in the same way as for a single-family house except a multiunit building will have more information to evaluate, possibly in many categories. If apartment and room sizes are standard, this work will be greatly simplified. If there are units of many different sizes, however, each apartment must be recorded. In such a case, a floor-by-floor room breakdown would not be as useful as an apartment-by-apartment breakdown. Since most multiunit apartments are standardized, a typical floor plan indicating the size, placement and layout of the apartments would be the easiest and best way to show them.

There are some physical features that an appraiser may not be able to learn about a house or apartment building without actually tearing it apart. But if a checklist of items to be inspected, such as those on the Building Data Form, is prepared in advance, most of the building's deficiencies as well as its special features, can be identified. If the appraiser can supply all of the information required on this form and know enough about construction to recognize and record any features not itemized on the list, he or she will have as thorough an analysis of the building as required for any appraisal method.

As you go through the rest of this book you will be filling out all of the forms presented in this chapter. You may review this chapter whenever necessary. If you have difficulty computing building or lot areas, refer to Appendix B, which has been included to lead you through the mathematics involved in area and volume problems.

Exercise 2.2

Describe the house shown below, in as much detail as possible, on the basis of what you can determine from the photograph alone.

Achievement Examination 2

In the space below, lay out a form that could be used to collect sales data on properties comparable to a single-family residence being appraised. Itemize specific property characteristics, such as building size and number of rooms, that should be similar or identical in comparable properties.

Compare your form to the one given in the Answer Key at the back of the book.

CHAPTER 3

Residential Construction*

Real estate appraisers must know their product. In terms of residential real estate, this means knowing the construction features that determine quality, show good craftsmanship and indicate good upkeep or neglect, especially through visible flaws that could indicate significant structural damage. By being aware of current architectural trends and construction standards, the appraiser can gauge a property's desirability, marketability and value. The purpose of this chapter is to explain the basic construction features of wood-frame residential houses so you can better judge and evaluate them.

Wood-frame construction, whether covered by weatherboarding or veneered with brick or stone, is the type most frequently used in single-family houses. Wood-frame houses are preferred because:

- they are less expensive than other types;
- they can be built rapidly;
- they are easy to insulate against heat or cold; and
- greater flexibility of design is possible, thereby enabling architects and builders to produce a variety of architectural styles.

Building fundamentals that will be considered in this chapter include:

- municipal regulations, such as building codes;
- plans and specifications;
- architectural styles and designs;
- terms and trade vernacular used in residential construction; and
- the practical approach to recognizing, judging and comparing the quality of the various house components.

---

*The material in this chapter is adapted from *Residential Construction,* 2nd, by William L. Ventolo Jr. (Chicago: Real Estate Education Company, 1990).

PART I: PLANNING AND DESIGN

Regulation of Residential Construction

Building codes for the construction industry were established when the Building Officials Conference of America (BOCA) combined with the National Board of Fire Insurance Underwriters to set forth rules to ensure both comfort and safety for homeowners. These standards became the forerunners of present municipal building codes. Today FHA and VA standards serve as models for municipal building codes, which place primary importance on materials, structural strength and safe, sanitary conditions. Such building codes set the *minimum construction standards* that must be met by builders.

Plans and Specifications

Careful plans and specifications are required to comply with building codes. These must be in sufficient detail to direct the builder in assembling the construction materials. Working drawings, called *plans* or *blueprints,* show the construction details of the building, while *specifications* are written statements that establish the quality of the materials and workmanship required.

An owner may engage an architect to design a house and prepare plans and specifications for its construction. Professional architects are recognized as members of the American Institute of Architects (AIA). The architect's services may include negotiating with the builder and inspecting the progress of the construction, as well as preparing plans and specifications. Architects' fees, usually based on the hours spent on a given project, may vary from 6 percent to 15 percent of the total cost of the finished house, depending on the services rendered.

Other specialists may be involved in residential construction, including the *mechanical engineer,* who provides the heating, air-conditioning and plumbing plans and specifications; the *structural engineer,* who ensures that the foundation will support the structure and specifies the amount of steel required for reinforcing the foundation and the type and mix of concrete to be used; and the *soil engineer,* who may assist in determining the stability of the land on which the foundation is to be built. The soil engineer's investigation, coupled with the structural engineer's knowledge, will determine the details of the foundation.

House Styles

Although details of construction are rigidly specified by building codes, house styles may vary greatly. There are no absolute standards, and real estate values rest on what potential buyers, users and investors think is desirable as well as on what they consider to be attractive.

House styles can be grouped under two broad categories: *traditional* and *contemporary*.

Traditional Styles

Past architectural styles appeal to many prospective homeowners. Within this nostalgic design category, traditionalists have a wide range

---

FIGURE 3.1   Traditional House Styles

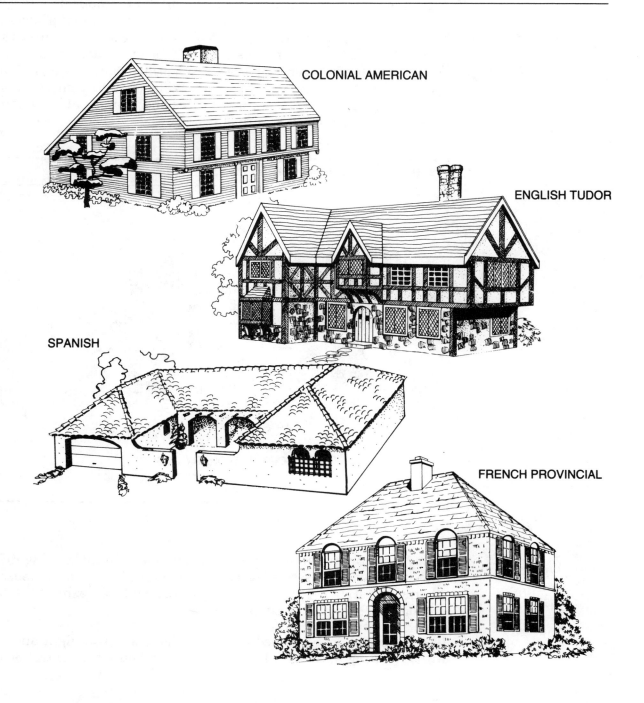

COLONIAL AMERICAN

ENGLISH TUDOR

SPANISH

FRENCH PROVINCIAL

of individual styles to choose from: *Colonial American, English Tudor, Spanish* and *French Provincial*—to name a few (see Figure 3.1). The handling of architectural details gives the traditional house its unique flavor. Fortunately, the detailing for many traditional houses no longer need be handcrafted because good reproductions are now mass produced. Ready-made entrance doors, mantels, moldings and parquet floors bear a close resemblance to their handcrafted prototypes.

Contemporary Styles

Although many contemporary houses appear uncomplicated, they are often clever examples of how to make the best use of materials and space. A distinctive contemporary look relies on the straightforward expression of the structural system itself for major design impact. One great benefit of contemporary residential architecture is its responsiveness to indoor–outdoor living. Walls of sliding glass doors, large windows, skylights, decks, terraces and atriums all contribute to this relationship (see Figure 3.2).

FIGURE 3.2   Contemporary House Styles

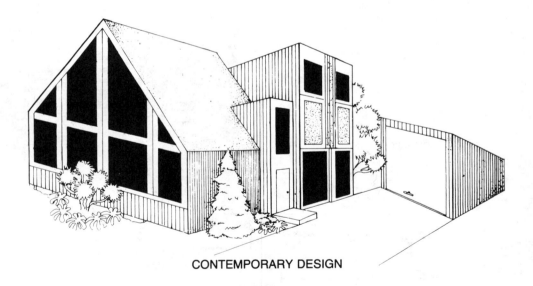

CONTEMPORARY DESIGN

House Types

Today's new materials and modern techniques can make a big difference in the way houses are designed and built. The modern house, whether its style is contemporary or traditional, can exhibit the latest conveniences and building innovations.

Large areas of double-paned glass open houses to sun, light and view without letting in cold drafts. A good modern house has central heating, which enables homeowners to enjoy big rooms and large windows without discomfort. Air-conditioning has eliminated the need for cross-ventilation from two exposures in every room, although a house providing cross-ventilation will be attractive to the energy-conscious consumer.

The one-story house.   The one-story house, often referred to as a *ranch,* has all the habitable rooms on one level. Its great advantage is the absence of steps to climb or descend, except to a basement. Because no headroom is required above the ceiling, the roof of a one-story house is usually pitched low. The low height simplifies construction, too, but this does not necessarily mean a lower cost, since foundation and roof areas generally are larger than in other types of housing. The ranch is one of the easiest houses to maintain.

The one-and-a-half-story house.   The one-and-a-half-story, or *Cape Cod,* house is actually a two-story house in which the second-floor attic space has sufficient headroom to permit up to half the area being used as livable floor area. It has two distinct advantages: economy in cost per cubic foot of habitable space and built-in expandability (see Figure 3.3).

The two-story house.   The two-story house offers the most living space within an established perimeter; the living area is doubled on the same foundation. Certain economies are inherent in the two-story plan: plumbing can be *lined up;* winter heating is utilized to the best advantage—heat rises to the second floor after warming the ground floor. More house can be built on a smaller lot with a two-story plan. The roof is smaller, relative to the overall floor area, as is the foundation required.

The split-level house.   The split-level has four separate levels of space. The lowest level is what would ordinarily be called the basement. Situated below the outside finished grade, it usually contains the heating and air-conditioning system. The next area—the one raised a half-flight from the basement level—is extra space common only to a split-level house. The floor here is even with, or close to, the outside grade; it usually includes the garage and recreation room. Living and sleeping levels are above, taking up the total room area in a typical one-story ranch house of equivalent size.

The split-entry house.   The split-entry design, sometimes called a *raised ranch,* is a fairly recent architectural approach to residential housing. Basically it is a one-story house *raised* out of the ground about half way. The resulting greater window depth gives better light to the basement area, making it a more usable space for recreation rooms, baths, bedrooms or other uses. In effect, the square footage of the house is doubled at a modest cost increase—merely that of finishing the rooms on the lower level (see Figure 3.4).

FIGURE 3.3 Types of Houses: One-Story, One-and-a-Half-Story

ONE-STORY HOUSE

ONE-AND-A-HALF-STORY HOUSE

Manufactured houses. Mention manufactured housing and most people visualize "prefab" buildings and flimsy trailers of the 1960s. That image nags at the manufactured housing industry, which accounts for nearly 10 percent of the nation's entire housing stock. In recent years, builders have been working hard to overcome those long-held biases against factory-built housing by turning out sturdier, better-looking products.

There are four basic types of manufactured houses, each characterized by the extent of assemblage completed in the factory:

1. *Mobile home.* This is the most complete and least expensive of the manufactured houses, needing only to be anchored to a foundation and connected to utilities.

FIGURE 3.4   Types of Houses: Two-Story, Split Styles

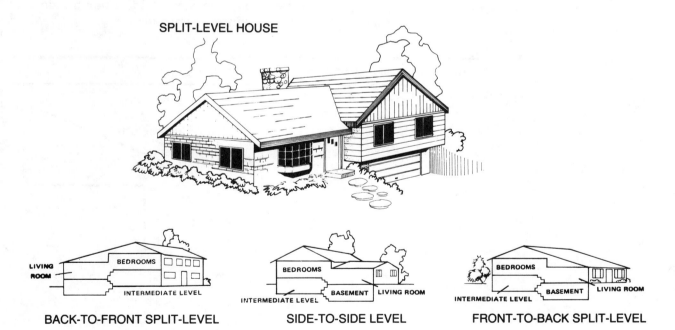

2. *Modular house.* This comes from the factory in single or multiple room sections, which are then fitted together at the construction site.
3. *Panelized house.* At the factory, entire wall units, complete with electrical and plumbing installations, are constructed and transported to the site where final assembly begins. With the foundation laid, the house can be enclosed within a week.

4. *Precut house.* As the name implies, materials are delivered to the construction site already cut and ready to assemble. Each piece should fit perfectly in its place, eliminating costly time for measuring and cutting materials on site.

Orientation: Locating the House on the Site

A house correctly oriented and intelligently landscaped, with windows and glass doors in the right places and adequate roof overhang, can save thousands of dollars in heating and air-conditioning bills over the years. A house well located on its lot also contributes to full-time enjoyment and use of house and grounds. Improper positioning is probably the most common and costly mistake made in house planning today.

Facing to the South

Ideally, a house should be positioned on the lot so that the main living areas have the best view and also face *south*. It has been scientifically established that the south side of a house receives five times as much sun heat in the winter as in summer, and the north side receives no sun heat at all during winter months.

FIGURE 3.5   Sunlight Exposure

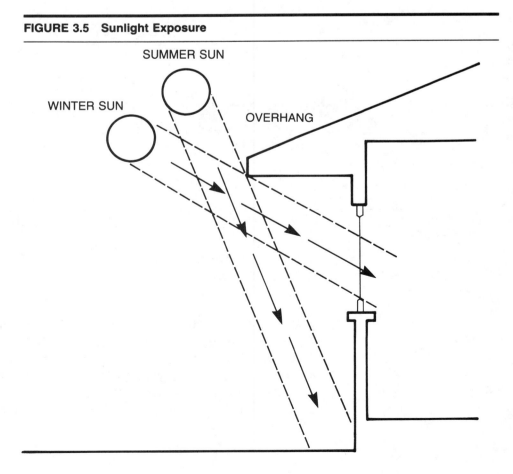

Unless some measures of control are used, the same sunshine that helps to heat a house during the winter will make it uncomfortable during the summer. Figure 3.5 shows how this can be corrected very easily. Because the summer sun rides high in the sky, a wide roof overhang will shade the windows by deflecting the direct heat rays. A roof overhang will not interfere with the sunshine in winter months because the winter sun travels a much lower arc and shines in at a much lower angle than the summer sun.

View

The location of a house can also depend on the view. If the site has an interesting long view to the east or west, it might be well to take advantage of it, in spite of the sun factor. Even if a site does not have a good long view, a short view of a garden or patio can be just as interesting if carefully planned.

Outdoor Space

Another important step in good site planning is to divide the lot into three different zones: *public, service* and *private*. The *public zone* is the area visible from the street—usually the land in front of the house. Zoning regulations specify how far back a house must be placed on a lot. The *service zone* consists of the driveway, the walks and the area for garbage cans and storage of outdoor equipment. It should be designed so that deliveries can be made to the service door without intrusion into the private area. The *private zone* is the outdoor living space for the family. An expanse of lawn, a patio, a garden, barbeque pit and play area are included in this zone.

It is obvious that the minimum amount of valuable land be allocated for public and service use and the maximum amount for private enjoyment.

Interior Design

The interior design of a house is essential to a convenient and comfortable living arrangement. Within each house are zones that correspond to the daily functions of the occupants. These areas should be easily accessible while offering privacy to family members.

Circulation Areas

Circulation areas, consisting of halls, stairways and entries, often make the difference between a good floor plan and a poor one. A study of a floor plan will reveal traffic patterns. Can people get directly from one room to another without crossing other rooms? Is there direct access to a bathroom from any room? Is the stairway between levels located off a hallway or foyer rather than a room?

Zones Within a House

Interior zoning refers to the logical arrangement of the rooms inside a house. Ideally, every house should have three clear-cut zones to accommodate the three main activities: *living, sleeping* and *working* (see Figure 3.6). The *living zone* contains the living, dining and family rooms. The *sleeping zone* contains the bedrooms. The *work zone* includes the kitchen, laundry area and perhaps a workshop. Each zone should be separate from the others so that activities in one do not interfere with those in another.

FIGURE 3.6   Zones in a House

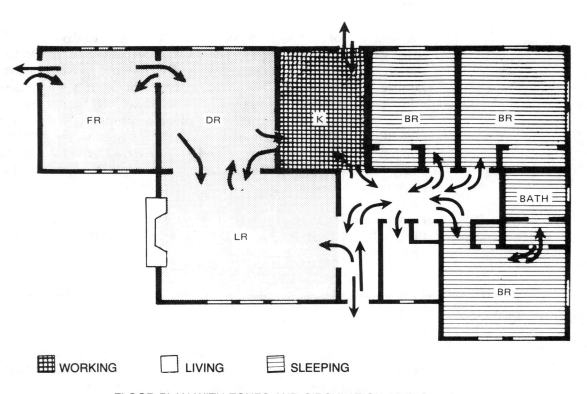

■ WORKING   □ LIVING   ▤ SLEEPING

FLOOR PLAN WITH ZONES AND CIRCULATION AREAS.

The living zone.   In small houses, the *living room* is the center of family life and entertainment. In houses large enough to have both a living room and a family room (sometimes called a recreation or "rec," room), the living room is a quiet room for reading and conversation. It should be close to the front door, next to dining space and away from sleeping areas. If there is a view, it should best be from the living room. The room should have a south orientation to obtain maximum daylight in summer and maximum sunlight in winter.

The *family room,* the center of noisiest activity, should be as far from bedrooms and the living room as possible. However, it should be close to the kitchen so that food is only a few steps away and near an outside entrance to allow people to come and go without having to walk through other rooms in the house. Because the family room is the indoor "action center," view is not too important; nor does it matter much which side of the house the room is on.

People spend only a few hours a day eating, so a separate room for that purpose alone is expensive space. Even so, a separate *dining room* is useful, especially for social or business entertaining. If a separate dining room is too expensive, people will compromise and use a dining space that is part of the living room, so long as there is some visual separation between the two. Also, dining space in the kitchen, either in an alcove or a large bright corner, is a feature of many homes.

The sleeping zone.   Bedrooms don't need a view or a lot of sunlight, but they should be on the cool side of the house—north or east—and on the quiet side, away from noisy rooms such as the family room and kitchen. They should be out of sight from the entrance door and living area so that they don't have to be kept meticulously clean.

How many bedrooms should a house have? From 1945 to 1970, the number of bedrooms in most new homes grew to three and then to four. Families today are smaller, so the trend is swinging back to the three-bedroom house. The market for two-bedroom houses is generally limited to empty nesters and young couples without children.

The work zone.   As the control center of the house, the *kitchen* should be conveniently located and should afford direct access to the dining area and the front entrance. It should be close to the garage so that groceries don't have to be carried far.

The nerve center of the kitchen, shown in Figure 3.7, is its *work triangle,* the arrangement of the refrigerator, sink and range in relation to each other. The location of these and other appliances is dependent on the plumbing and electrical connections. For maximum efficiency, the triangle should have a total perimeter of at least 12 feet but no more than 22 feet, with plenty of countertop space and cabinets. The room must be well ventilated to keep it free of cooking odors.

The *laundry* area is also found in the work zone. The best location for laundry equipment is a utility room or a ventilated closet off the bedroom hall. As a compromise, it may be placed off the family room, in the basement or in the garage.

FIGURE 3.7   Kitchen Work Triangle

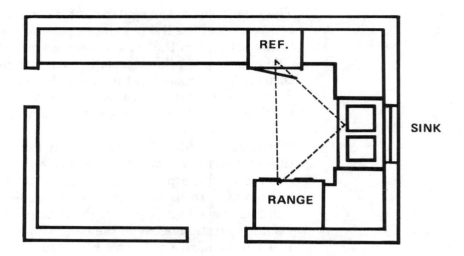

Bathrooms

As a general rule, allow one bathroom for every two adults and one for every three children. For convenience there should be a toilet and lavatory on every level. A complete bathroom can be put in a five-foot-by-seven-foot space, but the trend is toward bathrooms about twice that size.

A good floor plan locates bathrooms close to bedrooms, in an area where children can reach them easily from outdoors, and in a private, convenient spot for guest use. Developers usually prefer to build from plans that have bathrooms back to back or, in multistory houses, one above the other. This saves plumbing costs, but it usually limits the variability of the floor plan.

Storage Space

A sound floor plan will include a closet at least four feet wide by two feet deep for every person in the family, a linen closet big enough to hold blankets, a guest closet near the front door and, in colder climates, a closet near the rear door. Other storage areas to look for are places for books, toys and games, tools and out-of-season clothing. Larger areas for building or repairing things, storing garden tools, bicycles and other outdoor equipment, as well as bulk storage for "junk," are invaluable. Kitchens should have lots of storage space, all of it within reach of a shorter-than-average person.

Garage

A garage can have any orientation, but the best place for it is on the west or north, where it can protect living space from the hot afternoon sun in summer and from howling winds in winter. More important than orientation is convenience. A garage should be close to the kitchen; it should not block light out of other rooms. The garage should always be big enough for two cars. Even with small cars, it should have inside dimensions of at least 23 feet by 23 feet.

Basement

A basement provides low-cost space for heating and cooling equipment, bulk storage and so forth. Because the builder has to go below frost line with the foundation anyway, a basement adds little to the building cost in cold climates (but more as you go south).

If the building site slopes so that a ground-level entrance can be provided, a basement is good for workshops and family rooms. It stays cool in summer and warm in winter.

Exercise 3.1

List some economic advantages basic to the following house types.

One-and-a-half-story house

Two-story house

Split-entry house

How can the orientation of a house on its lot contribute to monetary savings and the enjoyment of a house and its grounds?

A study of a floor plan can show whether or not a house is well planned and logically arranged. In relation to the following areas, what important factors would make for a well-planned house?

circulation areas

the kitchen

the living room

the sleeping zone

storage space

Check your answers against those given in the Answer Key at the back of the book.

PART II: CONSTRUCTION DETAILS

Throughout this section, certain terms will be followed by a bracketed number. The number refers to the corresponding term in Figure 3.18, the house diagram at the end of this chapter, which provides an overall picture of how housing components fit together into the end product. For example, *footing* [1] means the component labeled 1 in the house diagram.

Foundations

The foundation of the house is the substructure on which the superstructure rests. The term *foundation* includes the footings, foundation walls, columns, pilasters, slab and all other parts that provide support for the house and transmit the load of the superstructure to the underlying earth. Foundations are constructed of cut stone, stone and brick, concrete block or poured concrete. Poured concrete is the most common foundation material because of its strength and resistance to moisture. The two major types of foundations are *concrete slab* and *pier and beam*, shown respectively in Figures 3.8 and 3.9.

FIGURE 3.8   Concrete Slab Foundations

MONOLITHIC SLAB

FLOATING SLAB

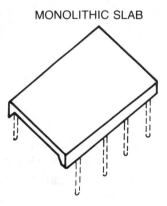
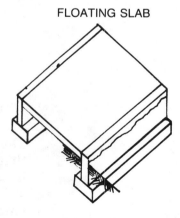

Concrete slab.   A *concrete slab foundation* is composed of a concrete slab supported around the perimeter and in the center by concrete beams sunk into the earth. It is made of poured concrete reinforced with steel rods. The foundation slab rests directly on the earth, with only a waterproofing membrane between the concrete and the ground. Foundations formed by a single pouring of concrete are called *monolithic,* while those in which the footings and the slab are poured separately are referred to as *floating.*

Pier and beam.   In a *pier and beam foundation,* the foundation slab rests on a series of isolated columns, called *piers,* that extend above ground level. The space between the ground and the foundation is called the *crawl space*. Each support of a pier and beam foundation consists of a *pier* [55], or column, resting on a *footing* [57], or base. The pier, in turn, supports the *sill* [8], which is attached to the pier by an *anchor bolt* [7]. The *floor joists* [10] that provide the major support for the flooring are placed perpendicular to and on top of the sills.

FIGURE 3.9:   Foundation, Pier and Beam

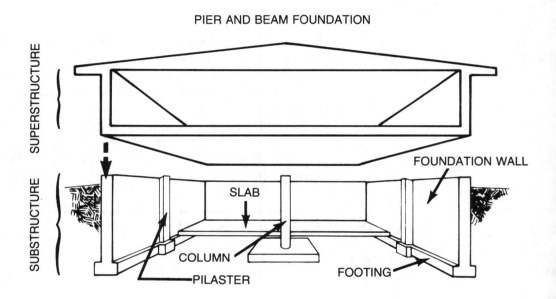

Termite Protection

The earth is infested with termites, extremely active antlike insects that are very destructive to wood. Before the slab for the foundation is poured, the ground should be chemically treated to poison termites and thus prevent them from coming up through or around the foundation and into the wooden structure. The chemical treatment of the lumber used for sills and beams and the installation of metal *termite shields* [9] will also provide protection.

Radon Gas

Radon is a colorless, odorless, tasteless radioactive gas that comes from the natural breakdown of uranium. It can be found in most rocks and soils. Outdoors, it mixes with the air and is found in low concentrations that are harmless to people. Indoors, however, it can accumulate and build up to dangerous levels. High radon levels in the home can increase risk of lung cancer (currently the only known health effect). The surgeon general recently drew attention to the danger of radon by announcing that it is second only to smoking as a cause of lung cancer.

How does radon get into a house? The amount of radon in a home depends on the home's construction and the concentration of radon in the soil underneath it. Figure 3.10 shows how radon can enter a home through dirt floors, cracks in concrete foundations, floors and walls, floor drains, tiny cracks or pores in hollow block walls, loose-fitting pipes, exhaust fans, sump pumps and many other unsuspected places, including even the water supply.

A lot of the variation in radon levels has to do with the "airtightness" of a house: The more energy efficient a home is, the more likely it will have higher radon levels. The average house has one complete

FIGURE 3.10   Common Radon Entry Routes

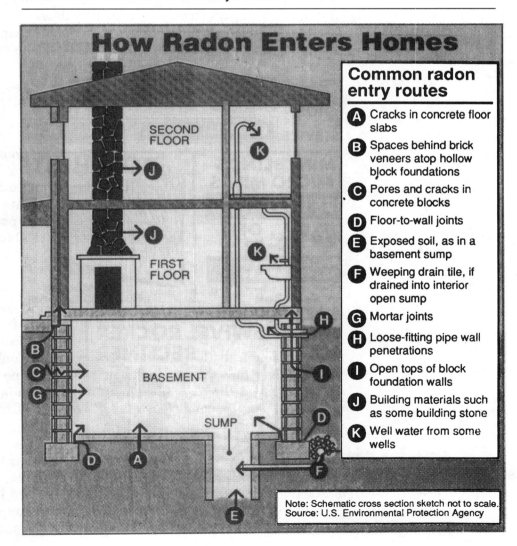

How Radon Enters Homes

Common radon entry routes

A Cracks in concrete floor slabs
B Spaces behind brick veneers atop hollow block foundations
C Pores and cracks in concrete blocks
D Floor-to-wall joints
E Exposed soil, as in a basement sump
F Weeping drain tile, if drained into interior open sump
G Mortar joints
H Loose-fitting pipe wall penetrations
I Open tops of block foundation walls
J Building materials such as some building stone
K Well water from some wells

Note: Schematic cross section sketch not to scale.
Source: U.S. Environmental Protection Agency

air exchange every six to seven hours; that is, about four times a day all the air from inside the house is exchanged with outside air. The tighter the house, the more likely it is that the air exchange will come from beneath the house from the air over the soil, which may contain high levels of radon gas.

Exterior Structural Walls and Framing

After the foundation is in place, the exterior walls are erected. The first step in erecting exterior walls is the *framing*. The skeleton members of a building to which the interior and exterior walls are attached are called its *frame*. The walls of a frame are formed by vertical members called *studs* [15], which are spaced at even intervals and are attached to the sill. Building codes typically require that, for a one-story house the stud spacing not exceed 24 inches on center. For a two-story house the spacing may not exceed 16 inches. Studs rest on *plates* [12] that are secured to and rest on the *foundation wall* [4]. In constructing walls and floors, the builder will install *firestops* [43] as needed or required. These are boards or blocks nailed horizontally between studs or joists to stop drafts and retard the spread of fire.

Figure 3.11 shows three basic types of wood frame construction: *platform, balloon* and *post and beam*.

Platform frame construction.   Today, the most common type of frame construction for both one- and two-story residential structures is *platform* frame construction. In platform construction only one floor is built at a time, and each floor serves as a platform for the next story. The wall studs are first attached to the upper and lower plates, and the entire assemblage is then raised into place and anchored to the sill.

Balloon frame construction.   The second type of framing is *balloon* construction, which differs from the platform method in that the studs extend continuously to the ceiling of the second floor. The second floor joists rest on *ledger boards* or *ribbon boards* set into the interior edge of the studs. The balloon method gives a smooth, unbroken wall surface on each floor level, thus alleviating the unevenness that sometimes results from settling when the platform method is used. The balloon method is usually employed when the exterior finish will be brick, stone veneer or stucco.

Post and beam frame construction.   The third type of frame construction is *post and beam frame*. The ceiling planks are supported on beams that rest on posts placed at intervals inside the house. Because the posts provide some of the ceiling support, rooms can be built with larger spans of space between the supporting side walls. In

FIGURE 3.11   Frame Construction Types

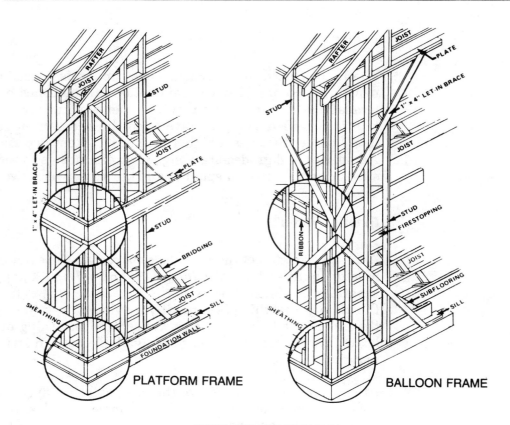

PLATFORM FRAME

BALLOON FRAME

POST AND BEAM FRAME

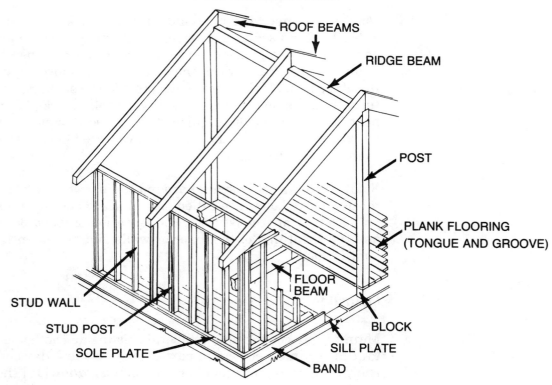

some houses the beams are left exposed and the posts and beams are stained to serve as part of the decor.

Lumber

The lumber used in residential construction is graded according to moisture content and structural quality as established by the National Grade Rule. Grading rules require dimension lumber (2″ × 4″, 2″ × 6″) that is classified as *dry* to have a moisture content of 19 percent or less. Lumber that has a higher moisture content is classified as *green*. All species and grades are assigned stress ratings to indicate their strength when used in spanning distances between two supports.

Exterior Walls

After the skeleton of the house is constructed, the exterior wall surface must be built and the *sheathing* [19] and *siding* [20] applied. The sheathing is nailed directly to the *wall studs* [15] to form the base for the siding. Sheathing is generally insulated drywall or plywood. If the house is to have a masonry veneer, the sheathing may be gypsum board. Fabricated sheathings are available both in strip and sheet material.

After the sheathing is added, the final exterior layer, called *siding,* is applied. This siding may be asphalt, shingles, wood, aluminum, stone, brick or other material.

Masonry veneer versus solid brick.   Brick *veneer* is a thin layer of brick often used as a covering on a frame house to give the appearance of a solid brick house. If the masonry is merely decorative and the walls are of wood, then the house is masonry veneer. On the other hand, if the brick walls provide the support for the roof structure, then the house is all masonry, or solid brick. A masonry veneer house may be distinguished from a solid masonry house by the thickness of the walls; the walls of a veneered house are seldom more than eight inches thick.

Small outlets evenly spaced around the base of the masonry perimeter of a brick house are called *weep holes.* These openings provide an outlet for any moisture or condensation trapped between the brick and the sheathing of the exterior walls and are essential for proper ventilation.

Insulation

Maintaining comfortable temperatures inside the home is an important factor in construction, particularly in these days of high-cost energy. To ensure adequate protection, *insulation* [17] should be placed in the exterior walls and upper floor ceilings. *Rock wool* and *fiberglass* are commonly used insulation materials. Combinations of materials, such as fiberglass wrapped in aluminum foil or rock wool formed into batt sections that can be placed between the studs, are also available.

The effectiveness of insulation depends on its resistance to heat flow—its R-value—rather than just on its thickness. Different insulating materials have different R-values; therefore, different thicknesses are required to do the same job. The larger the R-value, the more resistance to heat flow and the better the insulation.

How much R-value is needed? The minimum property standards for federally financed construction call for R-11 or R-13 insulation within the walls and R-19 or R-22 in the attic. R-values are additive. For example, if you already have an R-13 value of insulation in a particular location and you want it to be R-35, you can use a layer of R-22 to achieve an R-35 value.

Upgraded insulation guidelines.   The U.S. Department of Energy (DOE) has recently upgraded its insulation recommendations to homeowners, increasing its suggested minimum R-value to accommodate the country's various climates. The new R-values are now specific to zip code areas and take into account climate, heating and cooling needs, types of heating used and energy prices. The DOE estimates that 50 to 70 percent of the energy used in the average American home is for heating and cooling. Yet most of the houses in the United States are not insulated to recommended levels. In an attic insulation study, for example, it was found that the average insulation level in attics is about R-20, but the DOE now recommends an average of R-40. The new guidelines cover other areas of the home as well, including ceilings, floors, exterior walls and crawl spaces. Because insulation is relatively inexpensive, the cost/benefit ratio makes increased insulation levels worthwhile.

Asbestos and urea formaldehyde.   Two kinds of home insulation to be avoided are asbestos and urea formaldehyde. Asbestos insulation, embedded in ceilings and walls by builders of another era, is no longer used because it is believed to cause cancer if its fibers get into the lungs. Urea formaldehyde also may be a potential health hazard, and its use is banned in most parts of the United States. It often emits noxious odors and toxic fumes, causing nausea and other irritations if inhaled. If you suspect a house has either asbestos or urea formaldehyde insulation, bring in a qualified inspector to examine all questionable areas.

Roof Framing and Coverings

Residential roofs are made in several styles including gable, saltbox, hip and flat, as shown in Figure 3.12.

FIGURE 3.12   Roof Designs

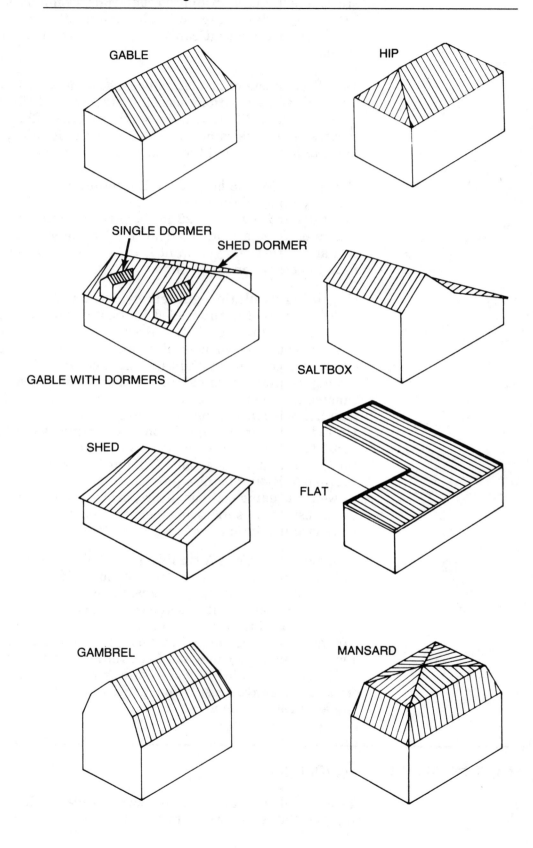

Roof construction includes the *rafters* [30], *sheathing* [40] and *exterior trim* or *frieze board* [42]. The skeletal framings are classified as either conventional or truss (see Figure 3.13).

Joist and rafter roof framing.   A *joist and rafter* roof consists of *rafters* [30], *collar beams* [31], *ceiling joists* [27] and *ridge board* [33]. Rafters are the sloping timbers that support the weight of the roof and establish the roof's pitch, or slant. The collar beams give rigidity to the rafters; the ridge board aligns and receives the rafters.

Truss roof framing.   A *truss* roof has four parts: *lower chords, upper chords, W diagonals* and *gusset plates*. The lower chords are similar to the ceiling joists, whereas the upper chords are the equivalent of the rafters in a joist and rafter roof. The *W* diagonals are the equivalent of the collar beams and are called *W* because they support the rafter chords in the form of the letter *W*. The gusset plates are solid pieces of metal or wood that add rigidity to the roof. All integral parts are assembled and held in place by gusset plates, bolt connections or nails. A truss roof is generally prefabricated at a mill and set in place in sections by cranes, whereas a joist and rafter roof is assembled piece by piece on the site.

Exposed rafter roof framing.   *Exposed,* or *sloping, rafter* roofs are often used with post and beam frame construction. The rafters are supported by central support posts and by the exterior walls. However, there are no ceiling joists or lower chords to provide additional support. The rafters in this type of roof are often left exposed for decorative purposes.

Exterior Trim

The overhang of a pitched roof that extends beyond the exterior walls of the house is called an *eave* [24], or *cornice,* shown in Figure 3.14. The cornice is composed of the soffit, the frieze board, the facia board and the extended rafters. The *frieze board* [42] is the exterior wood-trim board used to finish the exterior wall between the top of the siding or masonry and eave, or overhang, of the roof framing. The *facia board* is an exterior wood trim used along the line of the butt end of the rafters where the roof overhangs the structural walls. The overhang of the cornice provides a decorative touch to the exterior of a house as well as some protection from sun and rain.

Roof Sheathing and Roofing

With the skeleton roof in place, the rafters are covered with sheathing. The type of sheathing to be used depends on the choice of outside roofing material. Most shingles are composed of asphalt and are laid over plywood covered with felt building paper. If wood shingles are used, spaced sheathing of one-inch-by-four-inch boards may be used for providing airspace that allows the shingles to dry after rain.

FIGURE 3.13:   Roof Framing Systems

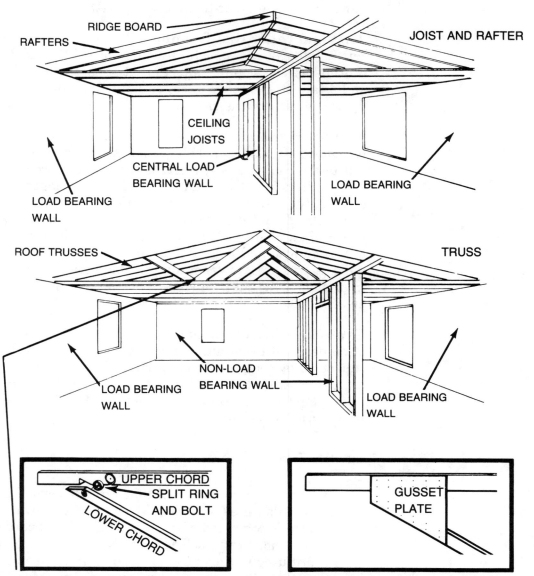

In a truss roof the upper and lower chords are joined together by either a gusset plate or a split ring and bolt.

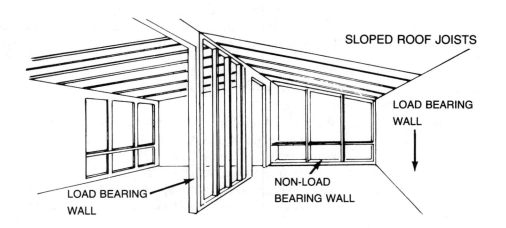

FIGURE 3.14   Eave or Cornice

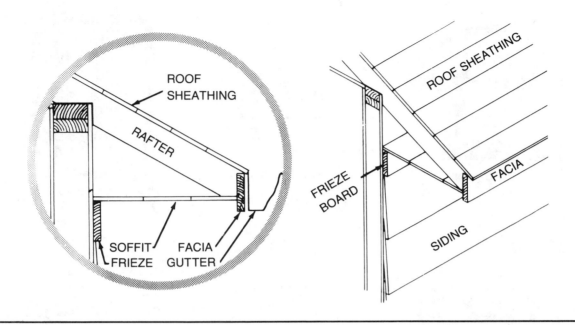

Exterior Windows and Doors

Windows and doors contribute to the overall tone of a house as well as provide a specific function. Skillfully placed doors regulate traffic patterns through the house and provide protection from intruders. Windows, in turn, admit light and a view of the exterior.

Types of Windows

Windows, as shown in Figure 3.15, come in a wide variety of types and sizes, in both wood and metal (usually aluminum). Wood is preferred where temperatures fall below freezing. Although metal windows require less maintenance than wood, the frames get colder in winter and panes frost up and drip from moisture condensation. Windows may be *sliding, swinging* or *fixed.* A window might span more than one category if part of it is fixed and another part slides.

Sliding windows.   The most commonly used window today is still the sliding window. Of the two typical types of sliding windows, the double-hung window is still most popular among builders, particularly in traditional houses. The *double-hung window* has an upper and lower sash both of which slide vertically along separate tracks. This arrangement allows cool air to come in at the bottom and warm air to go out through the top. Unfortunately, only half the window can be opened at any one time for ventilation, and it cannot be left open during a hard rain. The *horizontal sliding window* moves back and forth on tracks. As with the double-hung type, only 50 percent

FIGURE 3.15   Types of Windows

DOUBLE-HUNG

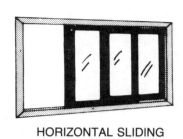

HORIZONTAL SLIDING

CASEMENT

JALOUSIE

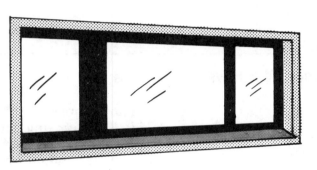

FIXED

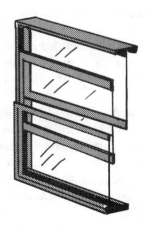

STORM

SKYLIGHT

of this window may be opened for fresh air. However, sliding windows usually provide more light and a better view.

Swinging windows. Casements and jalousies are two common types of swinging windows. *Casement windows* are hinged at the side and open outward. One advantage of the casement window is that the entire window can be opened for ventilation. *Jalousie,* or *louver,* windows consist of a series of overlapping horizontal glass louvers that pivot together in a common frame and are opened and closed with a lever or crank. In a sunroom or sunporch, the jalousie combines protection from the weather with maximum ventilation.

Fixed windows. A *fixed window* usually consists of a wood sash with a large single pane of insulated glass that cannot be opened for ventilation. It provides natural light and at the same time gives a clear view of the outside. Fixed windows are often used in combination with other windows.

Storm windows. A winter necessity in most parts of the country, *storm windows* fit either on the inside or the outside of the prime windows. Storm windows are usually made of aluminum, although older houses sometimes have wooden ones and newer houses may have the plastic type.

Storm windows can reduce summer air-conditioning bills as well as winter heating costs. Many homeowners who have air-conditioning now leave on their storm windows year-round.

The triple-track, self-storing unit that has built-in screens and storm windows is the most convenient type because it is permanently installed. A glass panel can be easily switched to a screen panel by moving the panels up or down in their tracks. Also, they do not require storage during off-seasons.

Skylights. *Skylights* can bring both natural illumination and the heat of the sun into rooms. A skylight lets about five times as much daylight into an area as a window of the same size. As a result, a skylight can make a small space appear brighter and larger than it actually is. A skylight is also an excellent way to bring light into a room with an obstructed or unsightly view.

Because older skylights tended to be poorly insulated and badly placed, they were labeled energy wasters. But with a little guidance on purchasing and placement, they can actually save energy in winter and in summer.

The local climate is the single most important factor in determining the right skylight. In cold climates, heat loss through the skylight can be a problem; in warm climates, heat gain through the unit can translate into higher cooling costs. Therefore, skylights, like windows, should generally be installed on the south side of a house in a colder climate or on the north side of a house in a warmer climate.

In a predominantly cold climate, a clear domed skylight combined with an insulating shade or storm window is the best choice. Conversely, in a warm climate, frosted or tinted skylights that open to vent excess heat and feature a shading device work best. Although the tint will reduce illumination slightly, it can also help to cut down on glare and heat gain.

Location of Exterior Doors

Exterior doors control passage in and out of the house. They are usually found in three locations around the house. The *main entrance door,* usually the most attractive and most prominent door, serves as both a passage and a barrier. It should be located on the street side of the house. The *service door* leads outside from rooms such as the kitchen, utility room, basement or garage and is important for good traffic flow in the house. The *patio door* is like the picture window in tying together indoors and outdoors. This door usually opens from a family room, living room or dining area onto a patio, porch or terrace.

Types of Doors

Exterior doors are made from wood or metal and are usually 1¾ inches thick. Interior doors usually have a thickness of 1⅜ inches.

Doors are most often classified by construction and appearance—the four most common types being *flush, panel, siding glass* and *storm and screen* (see Figure 3.16).

Flush doors.   *Flush doors* are most often constructed of hardwood face panels bonded to *solid* cores or *hollow* cores of light framework. Solid cores are generally preferred for exterior doors because they provide better heat and sound insulation and are more resistant to warping. Hollow-core doors are about a third as heavy as the solid-core type and are commonly used for interior locations, where heat and sound insulation are not critical.

Panel doors.   Available in a variety of designs, *panel doors* may be used for either interior or exterior application. They consist of *stiles* (solid *vertical* members of wood or metal) and *rails* (solid *horizontal* members of wood or metal) enclosing flat plywood or raised wood panel fillers or, in some types, a combination of wood and glass panels.

Sliding glass doors.   *Sliding glass doors* have at least one fixed panel and one or more panels that slide in a frame of wood or metal.

FIGURE 3.16   Types of Doors

PANEL

FLUSH

SCREEN DOOR

SLIDING GLASS

Like a window sash, the door panels are composed of stiles and rails and may hold either single or insulating glass.

Storm and screen doors.   *Storm doors* are made either with fixed glass panels, to improve weather resistance, or with both screen and glass inserts, to permit ventilation and insect control. In areas with moderate year-round temperatures, *screen doors* (without glass inserts) are frequently used. Combination doors combine the functions of both storm and screen doors with interchangeable glass and screen panels. Self-storing storm doors contain the equivalent of a two-track window, accommodating two inserts in one track and another in the adjacent track. The glass and screen inserts slide up and down just as they do in a vertical storm window.

Storm doors will have some impact on fuel bills, but not as much as most other energy improvements that can be made. Like storm windows, they can reduce summer air-conditioning bills as well as winter heating costs.

Interior Walls and Finishing

Interior walls are the partitioning dividers for individual rooms and are usually covered with *plasterboard* [46], although *lath* [45] and *plaster* [47] may be used. The terms *drywall* and *wallboard* are synonymous with plasterboard. Plasterboard is finished by a process known as *taping and floating.* Taping covers the joints between the sheets of plasterboard. Floating is the smoothing out of the walls by the application of a plaster texture over the joints and rough edges where nails attach the plasterboard to the wall studs. Texturing may be used in some areas as a final coating applied with a roller onto the plasterboard prior to painting.

The final features added to a home include (1) *floor covering,* (2) *trim,* (3) *cabinet work* and (4) *wall finishings* of paint, wallpaper or paneling.

Floor coverings of vinyl, asphalt tile, wood (either in strips or blocks), carpet, brick, stone or terrazzo tile are applied over the wood or concrete subflooring.

Trim masks the joints between the walls and ceiling and gives a finished decorator touch to the room. Trim, which is usually wood, should be selected in a style that is complementary to the overall decor of the house.

Cabinet work may be either built in on the job or prefabricated in the mill. Cabinets should be well constructed to open and close properly and should correspond with the style of the house.

Wall coverings are one of the most important decorator items in the home. Paint and wallpaper should be selected for both beauty and utility. Prefinished wood fiber and plastic panels such as polyethylene-covered plywood paneling are now widely used in less formal rooms. Either ceramic or plastic tiles are still used extensively as bathroom wall coverings.

Plumbing

The plumbing system in a house is actually a number of separate systems, each designed to serve a special function. The *water supply system* brings water to the house from the city main or from a well and distributes hot and cold water through two sets of pipes. The *drainage system* collects waste and used water from fixtures and carries it away to a central point for disposal outside the house. The *vent piping system* carries out of the house all sewer gases that develop in drainage lines. It also equalizes air pressure within the waste system so that waste will flow away and not back up into fixtures. The *waste collecting system* is needed only when the main waste drain in the house is lower than sewer level under the street or when the house has more than one drainage system. The *house connection pipe system,* a single pipe, is the waste connection from the house to the city sewer line, to a septic tank or to some other waste disposal facility.

Plumbing must be installed subject to strict inspections and in accordance with local building codes, which dictate the materials to be used and the method of installation. Sewer pipes are of cast iron, concrete or plastic, while water pipes are of copper, plastic or galvanized iron. Recently, wrought-drawn copper and plastic have been used more frequently because they eliminate piping joints in the foundation slab.

Plumbing Fixtures

Bathtubs, toilets and sinks are made of cast iron or pressed steel coated with enamel. Fiberglass is a new material for these fixtures and is gaining in popularity. Plumbing fixtures have relatively long lives and often are replaced because of their obsolete style long before they have worn out.

Water Heater

Water is almost always heated by gas or electricity. Water heaters come in several capacities, ranging from 17 gallons up to 80 gallons for residential use. A 30-gallon water heater is usually the minimum size installed. After water is heated to a predetermined temperature the heater automatically shuts off. When hot water is drained off, cold water replaces it, and the heating unit turns on automatically.

Water Softener

Much of the United States has *hard water,* so characterized when water contains more than five grains of salt per gallon. These salts tend to clog pipes, leave a scum on plumbing fixtures when mixed with soap and make washing of clothing and glassware difficult. The most common method of removing these salts is with a water softener. All water entering the house passes through the softener, which contains a bed of resin that absorbs the salts. The resin needs to be regenerated periodically with common salt.

Heating and Air-Conditioning

Warm-air heating systems are most prevalent in today's houses. A forced warm-air system consists of a furnace, warm-air distributing ducts and ducts for the return of cool air. Each furnace has a capacity rated in British Thermal Units (BTUs). The number of BTUs given represents the furnace's heat output from either gas, oil or electric firing. A heating and cooling engineer can determine the cubic area of the building as well as its construction, insulation and window and door sizes and from this data compute the furnace capacity required to provide heat for the building in the coldest possible weather.

All gas pipes for heating and cooking are made of black iron. Gas pipes are installed in the walls or run overhead in the attic, where adequate ventilation is possible. They are never placed in the slab.

Almost all new homes today are centrally air-conditioned. Air-conditioning units are rated either in BTUs or in tons. Twelve thousand BTUs are the equivalent of a one-ton capacity. An engineer can determine the measurements and problems inherent in the construction and layout of the space and from this information can specify the cooling capacity required to service the space or building adequately.

Combination heating and cooling systems are common in new homes. The most prevalent is the conventional warm-air heating system with a cooling unit attached. The same ducts and blower that force warm air are used to force cool air. The cooling unit is similar to a large air conditioner.

Many heating experts believe the heat pump will eventually replace today's conventional combination heating and cooling systems. The small heat pump is a single piece of equipment that uses the same components for heating or cooling. The most commonly used system for small heat pumps takes heat out of the ground or air in winter to warm the air in the house and takes warm air out of the house in summer, replacing it with cooler air. The main drawback to the heat pump has been its initial cost. Once installed, however, it operates very economically and requires little maintenance. It works most efficiently in climates where winter weather is not severe, but new improvements make it adequate even in northern states.

Technical aspects of heating and air-conditioning should be handled by an experienced and qualified authority, although the homeowner should give due consideration to the operation and maintenance of the unit. Filters should be cleaned regularly and return-air grilles and registers should be clear and clean for passage of the circulating air. The thermostat controls should be well understood and properly set. The compressor and fan motors should receive regular maintenance.

Solar heating.   The increased demand for fossil fuels in recent years has forced builders to look for new sources of energy. One of the most promising sources of heat for residential buildings is *solar energy*. There are two methods for gathering solar energy: *passive* and *active*. Figure 3.5 shows the simplest form of solar heating—a *passive* system in which windows on the south side of a building take advantage of winter sunlight. A passive system can be improved inside the house by having water-filled containers, which are warmed by the sun dur-

FIGURE 3.17   Active Solar Hot Water Heating System

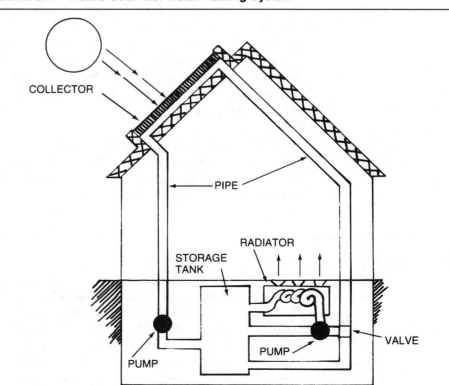

ing the day and reradiate warmth into the room during the night. Such a system takes up space inside the home, however, and is not compatible with most decorating schemes. If those considerations are unimportant, and if there is adequate available sunlight, a passive solar heating system can be installed easily and at low cost.

Most solar heating units suitable for residential use are *active* systems that operate by gathering the heat from the sun's rays with one or more *solar collectors*. Water or air is forced through a series of pipes in the solar collector to be heated by the sun's rays. The hot air or water is then stored in a heavily insulated storage tank until it is needed to heat the house.

Active solar heating systems have some drawbacks. They are more expensive than conventional heating systems, and if local utility costs are low enough the addition of a solar system to an existing house may be impractical. The heat production of a solar system is limited by both storage capacity and the need for good (sunny) weather, which means that most such systems must have an independent heating unit for backup. There is general agreement that most forms of whole-house solar heating systems cost more than the value received. There is also as yet no economical system that uses solar power to air-condition a home, although a great many people, including scientists working for the government, are exploring paths to solar cooling.

On a related note, solar heaters for swimming pools continue to provide a low-cost way of heating pool water. Solar pool heaters, in fact, constitute the largest single use for solar equipment.
Construction of solar heating systems recently has been boosted by the availability of tax credits and, in some areas, low- or no-interest loans from utility companies for energy-saving home improvements. Such incentives, in addition to the satisfaction that comes from being more energy self-sufficient, have helped increase the desirability of solar heating systems.

The U.S. government is one of the best sources on solar topics—whether for general information, the names of companies or organizations in the business, the names of architects familiar with solar design or suggested references for further study.

Electrical System

A good residential electrical system has three important characteristics. First, it must meet all National Electrical Code (NEC) safety requirements: each major appliance should have its own circuit, and lighting circuits should be isolated from electrical equipment that causes fluctuations in voltage. Second, the system must meet the home's existing needs and have the capacity to accommodate room additions and new appliances. Finally, it should be convenient; there should be enough switches, lights and outlets located so that occupants will not have to walk in the dark or use extension cords. Electrical service from the power company is brought into the home through the transformer and the meter into a *circuit breaker box* (or a *fused panel* in older homes). The circuit breaker box is the distribution panel for the many electrical circuits in the house. In case of a power overload, the heat generated by the additional flow of electrical power will cause the circuit breaker to open at the breaker box, thus reducing the possibility of electrical fires. It is the responsibility of the architect or the builder to adhere to local building codes, which regulate electrical wiring. All electrical installations are inspected by the local building authorities, which assures the homeowner of the system's compliance with the building code.

Residential wiring circuits are rated by the voltage they are designed to carry. In the past, most residences were wired for only 110-volt capacity. Today, because of the many built-in appliances in use, 220-volt to 240-volt service is generally necessary. *Amperage,* the strength of a current expressed in amperes, is shown on the circuit breaker panel. The circuit breaker panel (or fuse panel) should have a capacity of at least 100 amperes. A larger service (150 to 200 or more amperes) may be needed if there is electric heat, an electric range, or if the house has more than 3,000 square feet. New wiring will be required if the existing board is only 30 to 60 amperes in capacity. If there are fewer than eight or ten circuits, it will probably be necessary to add more. Each circuit is represented by a separate circuit breaker or fuse. A house with a lot of electrical equipment may require 15 to 20 or more circuits.

Exercise 3.2

Where are solid- and hollow-core doors used generally? Why?

Two of the separate plumbing systems in a house are the vent piping system and the water supply system. What is the purpose of each?

What is the major advantage of the heat pump?

List three important characteristics of a residential electrical system.

What is the basic difference between balloon and platform construction? Which is preferred?

Define the following features of residential construction and give the purpose of each:

firestopping

circuit breaker box

ridge

monolithic slab

sill

Check your answers against those given in the Answer Key at the back of the book.

Basic Terms

The following terms and concepts were introduced or discussed in this chapter. If you are not sure of the meaning or application of any of these terms, restudy the chapter.

amperage
anchor bolt
architectural style
BTUs
balloon frame
building code
building plan
  (blueprint)
building
  specifications
casement window
ceiling joist
chords
circuit breaker box
collar beam
concrete slab
  foundation
cornice
crawl space
double-hung window
drainage system
eave
exposed rafter roof
  framing

facia board
firestops
floating
floating slab
floor joist
flush doors
footing
foundation wall
frame
framing
frieze board
gusset plate
insulation
jalousie window
joist and rafter roof
monolithic slab
110-volt wiring
panel doors
pedestal
pier and beam
  foundation
pier
piling
plate

platform frame
plasterboard
post and beam frame
rafter
rails
ribbon board
ridge
R-value
sheathing
siding
sill (beam)
sliding window
solar heating
solar collector
stiles
stud
taping
truss roof framing
220-volt wiring
veneer
vent piping system
weephole

FIGURE 3.18 Construction of a House

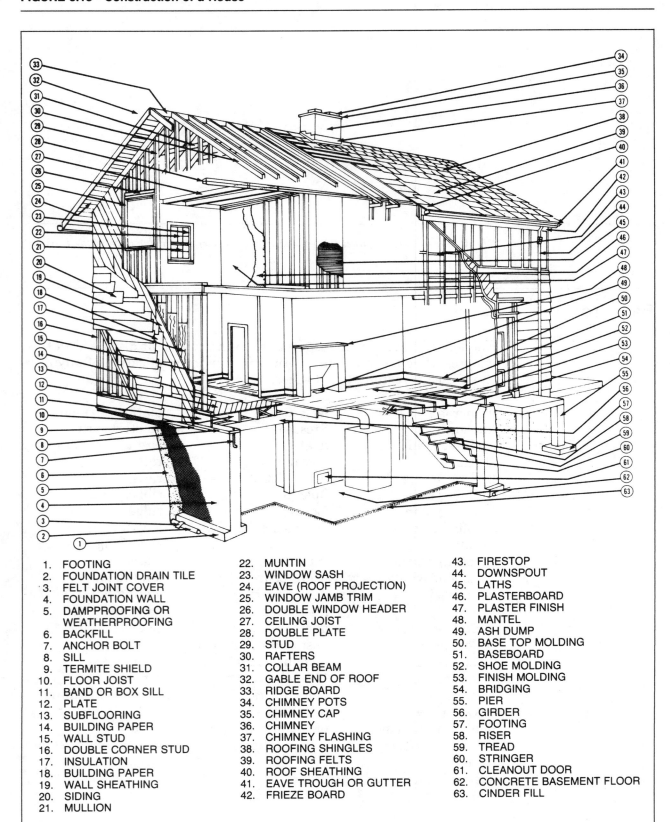

1. FOOTING	22. MUNTIN	43. FIRESTOP
2. FOUNDATION DRAIN TILE	23. WINDOW SASH	44. DOWNSPOUT
3. FELT JOINT COVER	24. EAVE (ROOF PROJECTION)	45. LATHS
4. FOUNDATION WALL	25. WINDOW JAMB TRIM	46. PLASTERBOARD
5. DAMPPROOFING OR WEATHERPROOFING	26. DOUBLE WINDOW HEADER	47. PLASTER FINISH
6. BACKFILL	27. CEILING JOIST	48. MANTEL
7. ANCHOR BOLT	28. DOUBLE PLATE	49. ASH DUMP
8. SILL	29. STUD	50. BASE TOP MOLDING
9. TERMITE SHIELD	30. RAFTERS	51. BASEBOARD
10. FLOOR JOIST	31. COLLAR BEAM	52. SHOE MOLDING
11. BAND OR BOX SILL	32. GABLE END OF ROOF	53. FINISH MOLDING
12. PLATE	33. RIDGE BOARD	54. BRIDGING
13. SUBFLOORING	34. CHIMNEY POTS	55. PIER
14. BUILDING PAPER	35. CHIMNEY CAP	56. GIRDER
15. WALL STUD	36. CHIMNEY	57. FOOTING
16. DOUBLE CORNER STUD	37. CHIMNEY FLASHING	58. RISER
17. INSULATION	38. ROOFING SHINGLES	59. TREAD
18. BUILDING PAPER	39. ROOFING FELTS	60. STRINGER
19. WALL SHEATHING	40. ROOF SHEATHING	61. CLEANOUT DOOR
20. SIDING	41. EAVE TROUGH OR GUTTER	62. CONCRETE BASEMENT FLOOR
21. MULLION	42. FRIEZE BOARD	63. CINDER FILL

Achievement Examination 3

For each of the following, describe the construction technique illustrated on the previous page.

1. foundation

2. wall framing

3. exterior walls

4. interior walls

5. windows

6. roof framing

7. roof coverings

8. floor coverings

Check your answers against those given in the Answer Key at the back of the book.

CHAPTER 4

The Sales Comparison Approach

The most widely used appraisal method for valuing residential property and vacant land is the sales comparison approach, using the principle of substitution. The sales comparison approach requires that the appraiser collect sales data on comparable nearby properties that have sold recently, then make adjustments to allow for individual differences between the subject property and comparable properties. When these differences have been allowed for, the appraiser will be able to select the resultant value indication that best reflects the market value of the subject property. Expressed as a formula, the sales comparison approach is:

$$\frac{\text{Sales Price of}}{\text{Comparable Property}} \pm \text{Adjustments} = \frac{\text{Indicated Value of}}{\text{Subject Property}}$$

In this chapter, you will trace the progress of a typical appraisal using the sales comparison approach by following the applicable steps outlined in the appraisal flowchart shown in Chapter 1. A single-family residence and lot will be appraised as the sales comparison method is discussed. At the end of the chapter, you will be given the information needed to complete your own appraisal analysis of a single-family residence using the sales comparison approach.

Review of Basic Terms

Market Value

Market value is the most probable price property should bring in a sale occurring under normal market conditions—an arm's-length transaction. Market conditions also include the economic, political and social forces that influence value. Examples include antigrowth initiatives that limit the supply of housing as well as rising interest rates that make homes less affordable and thus decrease demand.

Every sale is unique, of course, and the appraiser making an estimate of market value is making an estimate only. There is no guarantee that the estimated market value will be realized in a future sale of the appraised property. Because the sales comparison approach makes use of market data, it is also called the *market data* or *direct market comparison* approach.

Sales Price

Sales price is the closing sales price of a property—its transaction price. If a real estate transaction met all the requirements specified in the definition of market value perfectly, then the sales price generally would equal market value. Because there are so many market variables at work in the typical transaction, the contract sales price negotiated by the parties very often will not be the same as the property's estimated market value. Market value is the most probable price the property normally should bring, while sales price is the price it did or will command.

Step 1   State the Problem

The property must be identified along with the property rights to be valued. The value sought must be defined and the date of valuation specified. Any limiting conditions on the scope or use of the appraisal also must be determined. Throughout this book, we will assume that the appraiser is trying to find the market value of the subject property.

Exercise 4.1

The exercises throughout the text of this chapter will give you information on the sample appraisal you will be carrying out as you study the sales comparison approach. You are to complete each exercise, referring to the explanation just covered, if necessary; then check your results against those given in the Answer Key at the back of this book. If necessary, correct your responses before proceeding to the next text discussion.

The single-family residence located at 2130 West Franklin Street, Lakeside, Illinois, is to be appraised. State the problem, telling which value is being sought and the appraisal method that will be used to achieve it.

Check your answer against the one given in the Answer Key at the back of the book.

Step 2   List the Data Needed and the Sources

The appraiser must determine the types of data needed and where they can be located. Certain data must always be obtained—information about the region, city and neighborhood as well as facts about the property being appraised. When the sales comparison approach is used, sales data on comparable properties must be obtained.

Chapter 2, "The Data Collection Process," shows forms used to record the data needed. These data collection forms have already itemized the types of information that may be required for the neighborhood, site and building analyses.

No forms are given for regional and city data because a single, updated file in the appraiser's office would normally contain all regional data, and much of the city data already would be included in the neighborhood data form. Geographical boundaries of a city would generally encompass more than a single neighborhood, however; there usually would be a correspondingly greater variety of economic factors. Again, all of this information would be best collected in a single, comprehensive, updated file, so that data needed for individual appraisals could be compiled easily.

The special form to be used for the sales comparison approach is the Comparable Sales Chart, Figure 4.1 on page 93. The chart will be filled out at several stages during the sales comparison analysis. The various categories will be explained as they are used in this chapter.

Step 3   Gather, Record and Verify the Necessary Data

Data needed by the appraiser must be collected and recorded for future use.

General Data

The appraiser begins step 3 of the appraisal process by gathering, recording and verifying general data on the region, city and neighborhood. As described in Chapter 2, these are the easiest kinds of data to compile, and their sources require the least authentication. The neighborhood data is the only information that will necessitate significant fieldwork. Of course, all data collected will need to be reverified for each subsequent appraisal. The appraiser would have to update the data as special assessments were made, tax rates changed or other categories varied.

A temptation to insert "canned" regional and city data should be avoided. The appraiser should continually ask, "Does this informa-

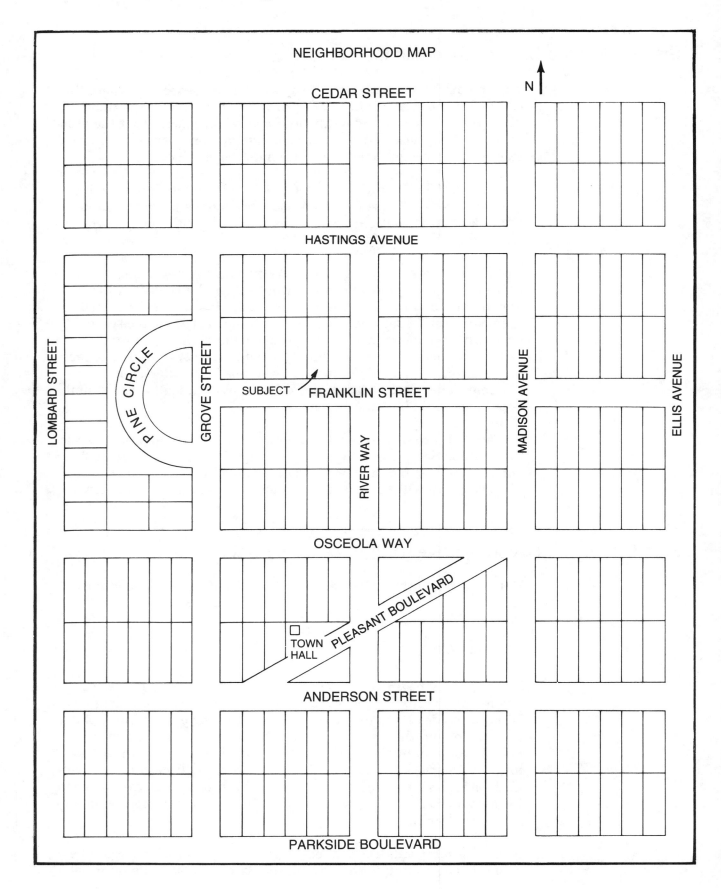

NEIGHBORHOOD MAP

tion assist me in reaching an estimate of the property's highest and best use and its market value?" If not, it should be excluded from the report.

The appraiser should also always ask, "What special factors should be considered in this particular appraisal?" An imminent zoning change, a proposed development or some other factor with the potential to affect property values may be discovered by the diligent appraiser.

Exercise 4.2

If you have not already done so, read the explanation of the Neighborhood Data Form in Chapter 2. Then, fill out the blank form on page 83 with the information supplied here. All of the information pertains to this chapter's sample appraisal. Since regional and city data would probably already have been gathered for the appraiser's file, they will not be used for the sample appraisal.

When you have finished, check your completed form against the one given in the Answer Key at the back of the book. Correct all errors and fill in all missing pieces of information on your form.

The neighborhood map on page 80 shows the location of 2130 West Franklin Street, Lakeside, Illinois, the subject of the sample appraisal. For this appraisal, you can assume that the subdivision is the neighborhood under analysis.

Lakeside is a city of just over 300,000 people. The boundaries of the subdivision are Lombard Street, Cedar Street, Ellis Avenue and Parkside Boulevard. Parkside forms a natural boundary to the south, since it separates the subdivision from parkland. Lombard divides the subdivision from expensive high-rise apartments to the west, forming another boundary. Ellis to the east separates the subdivision from an area of retail stores, and Cedar Street to the north provides a boundary between the single-family residences of the subdivision and a business district and area of moderately priced apartments. Parkland is gently rolling; built-up areas are level.

In the subdivision map, fewer than 1 percent of the lots are shown as vacant, and sales of those are infrequent. This neighborhood, then, has probably reached what stage of its life cycle? (Answer by checking the appropriate box on the Neighborhood Data Form.)

This subdivision is still known locally as the "Gunderson" area, which was its name at its founding, but it has since been incorporated as a part of the neighboring larger city. The area has a few two- and three-apartment buildings on Lombard Street that are about 20 years old, but 90 percent of the housing has been built within the past eight years. The apartment buildings average $185,000 to $275,000 in value, make up no more than 1 percent of the entire neighborhood, and usually have one apartment that is owner occupied.

The area is considered very desirable for middle-income families (yearly income $25,000 to $35,000 and rising steadily). Almost all homes are owner occupied.

About 2 percent are rented. Average home values are in the $110,000 to $140,000 range. Sales prices have kept up with inflation, and demand has stayed in balance with the number of homes put on the market although average marketing time is now four months. The property at 2130 West Franklin is typical of at least several dozen other properties in the area, all brick ranch houses with full basements and attached garages, on lots 50 feet by 200 feet. Other houses in the area are either split-level or two-story, the latter usually having aluminum or wood siding.

All utilities have been installed throughout the subdivision, and assessments for water and sewer lines, sidewalk installation and asphalt street surfacing were made and paid for eight years ago when the improvements were made. Since the area has been incorporated, it has city fire and police services as well as garbage collection. The property tax rate is $5 per $100 of assessed valuation, comparable to rates charged in similar nearby neighborhoods.

There is a community hospital two miles south at Parkside and Saginaw, and public grade schools and high schools are no more than ¾ of a mile from any home. Parochial grade schools are available within a mile, and a parochial high school is within two miles. Presbyterian, Episcopal and Roman Catholic churches are located in the area, as is a synagogue.

The average size of families in this neighborhood is 4.2, and most working people are in white-collar occupations. Some residents are self-employed, and some are in skilled trades.

Many area residents work in the nearby business district or in the commercial area, where a concentration of 80 retail stores as well as theaters and other recreational facilities offers a wide range of goods and services. Business and commercial areas are within two miles.

There are smaller groups of stores, primarily supermarkets, on Madison and Cedar streets and a public library branch at Cedar and Grove.

A superhighway two miles away that bisects the business district connects the area to major interstate routes. Bus service is available on Lombard and Cedar streets and Ellis Avenue, with excellent service during rush hours. The highest concentration of office buildings in the business district is no more than 15 minutes by bus from any house in the area, and the commercial area takes about the same time to reach. Emergency medical facilities are within a 15-minute drive of any home.

There are no health hazards within the neighborhood, either from industry or natural impediments. The busiest street through the neighborhood, Madison, is still mainly residential and generally quiet, except for rush hours. No change from current land use is predicted, and there are no nuisances, such as noise-producing factories or construction yards.

The above information should be filled in on the Neighborhood Data Form on page 83. When you have finished, check your form against the completed one in the Answer Key at the back of the book. Correct all errors and fill in all missing pieces of information on your form.

NEIGHBORHOOD DATA FORM

BOUNDARIES: ADJACENT TO:

    NORTH _____   _____

    SOUTH _____   _____

    EAST _____   _____

    WEST _____   _____

TOPOGRAPHY: _____ ☐ URBAN ☐ SUBURBAN ☐ RURAL

STAGE OF LIFE CYCLE OF NEIGHBORHOOD: ☐ GROWTH   ☐ EQUILIBRIUM   ☐ DECLINE

% BUILT UP: _____ GROWTH RATE: ☐ RAPID ☐ SLOW ☐ STEADY

AVERAGE MARKETING TIME: _____ PROPERTY VALUES: ☐ INCREASING ☐ DECREASING ☐ STABLE

SUPPLY/DEMAND: ☐ OVERSUPPLY ☐ UNDERSUPPLY ☐ BALANCED

CHANGE IN PRESENT LAND USE: _____

POPULATION: ☐ INCREASING ☐ DECREASING ☐ STABLE   AVERAGE FAMILY SIZE: _____

AVERAGE FAMILY INCOME: _____ INCOME LEVEL: ☐ INCREASING ☐ DECREASING

PREDOMINANT OCCUPATIONS: _____

TYPICAL PROPERTIES:	% OF	AGE	PRICE RANGE	% OWNER OCCUPIED	% RENTALS
VACANT LOTS	____				____
SINGLE-FAMILY RESIDENCES	____				____
2–6-UNIT APARTMENTS	____				____
OVER 6-UNIT APARTMENTS	____				____
NONRESIDENTIAL PROPERTIES	____				____

TAX RATE: _____ ☐ HIGHER ☐ LOWER ☐ SAME AS COMPETING AREAS

SPECIAL ASSESSMENTS OUTSTANDING: _____ EXPECTED: _____

SERVICES: ☐ POLICE ☐ FIRE ☐ GARBAGE COLLECTION   OTHER: _____

DISTANCE AND DIRECTION FROM

    BUSINESS AREA: _____

    COMMERCIAL AREA: _____

    PUBLIC ELEMENTARY AND HIGH SCHOOLS: _____

    PRIVATE ELEMENTARY AND HIGH SCHOOLS: _____

    RECREATIONAL AND CULTURAL AREAS: _____

    CHURCHES AND SYNAGOGUES: _____

    EXPRESSWAY INTERCHANGE: _____

    PUBLIC TRANSPORTATION: _____

       TIME TO REACH BUSINESS AREA: _____ COMMERCIAL AREA: _____

    EMERGENCY MEDICAL SERVICE: _____

GENERAL TRAFFIC CONDITIONS: _____

PROXIMITY TO HAZARDS (AIRPORT, CHEMICAL STORAGE, ETC.): _____

PROXIMITY TO NUISANCES (SMOKE, NOISE, ETC.): _____

Specific Data

Using the separate forms detailed in Chapter 2, information will be recorded for both site and building.

Land versus site. Land, as defined earlier in this book, is the earth's surface, including the ground below it and the airspace above it. To be considered a building site, land must have some utilities present or available. Sewers, especially, may not be constructed until there are enough houses in the immediate vicinity to warrant the required assessment. Electricity is usually required, as are water, telephone and gas lines.

Exercise 4.3

The following information is applicable to the sample site at 2130 West Franklin Street. Use it to fill in the Site Data Form on page 85.

The legal description of the lot is:

Lot 114 in Block 2 of Gunderson Subdivision, being part of the Northwest ¼ of the Southeast ¼ of Section 4, Township 37 North, Range 18, East of the Third Principal Meridian as recorded in the Office of the Registrar of Titles of Grove County, Illinois, on April 27, 1970.

The lot is 50 feet by 200 feet, rectangular, with 50 feet of street frontage. (The first lot dimension given is usually street frontage.) There are streetlights but no alley. The street is paved with asphalt, as is the driveway, which is 24 feet wide and 30 feet long. Sidewalk and curb are concrete. The land is level, with good soil and a good view.

Neither storm nor sanitary sewers have ever overflowed. There is an easement line running across the rear 10 feet of the property. Deed restrictions stipulate that the house must be no closer than 10 feet to side property lines, 30 feet to the street and 50 feet from the rear property line. The current structure does not violate these restrictions. Water, gas, electric and telephone lines have been installed. The lot is nicely landscaped, with low evergreen shrubbery across the front of the house and a view of the tree-lined parkway (the space between the sidewalk and curb). The backyard has several fruit trees.

When you have completed your Site Data Form, check it against the one given in the Answer Key at the back of the book. Correct any errors and fill in any omissions on your form.

Structures. A Building Data Form, such as the one shown on page 87 and explained in Chapter 2, details the many physical variances that may be present in residential structures. Where more than one item appears on a line, the condition of each can be noted separately, if necessary. The form in this book may be used for single-family

SITE DATA FORM

ADDRESS: _____

LEGAL DESCRIPTION: _____

_____

_____

_____

_____

_____

DIMENSIONS: _____

SHAPE: _____ SQUARE FEET: _____

TOPOGRAPHY: _____ VIEW: _____

NATURAL HAZARDS: _____

☐ INSIDE LOT   ☐ CORNER LOT   ☐ FRONTAGE: _____

ZONING: _____ ADJACENT AREAS: _____

UTILITIES: ☐ ELECTRICITY   ☐ GAS   ☐ WATER   ☐ TELEPHONE

☐ SANITARY SEWER   ☐ STORM SEWER

IMPROVEMENTS: DRIVEWAY: _____   STREET: _____

SIDEWALK: _____   CURB/GUTTER: _____   ALLEY: _____

STREETLIGHTS: _____

LANDSCAPING: _____

TOPSOIL: _____ DRAINAGE: _____

EASEMENTS: _____

DEED RESTRICTIONS: _____

SITE PLAT:

residential buildings. Specialized forms would be used for commercial or industrial buildings or multifamily structures, reflecting the required changes in construction and room designations.

Exercise 4.4

The following information is applicable to the sample single-family residence at 2130 West Franklin Street. Use it to complete the Building Data Form on page 87.

The subject building is six years old, a seven-room brick ranch house with a concrete foundation. It has wood window frames and doors and aluminum combination storm and screen windows and doors (all only two years old). The general outside appearance and appeal of the house are good. The wood trim was recently painted, and the house probably will not be in need of tuckpointing for at least five years. The attached two-car garage is also brick, and the wood overhead door was painted at the same time as the house trim. The house has a full basement with a 100,000 BTU gas forced-air furnace, which is in good condition, and a central air-conditioning unit. There are no special energy-efficiency items. The basement has concrete floor and walls, and there is no evidence of flooding. The wiring is 220-volt.

The general condition of the interior is good. The walls and ceilings are ½-inch drywall, with ceramic tile on the lower five feet of the walls in both full bathrooms. Family room walls are wood paneled. Except for tile and wood surfaces, all of the walls are painted. Floors are hardwood, with wall-to-wall carpeting in living and dining rooms, and vinyl tile in kitchen, family room and both bathrooms. Each full bathroom has a built-in tub and shower, lavatory with vanity, mirrored cabinet and toilet with wall-hung tank. The half-bath has a vanity lavatory and toilet. All bathroom fixtures are white.

The kitchen has 12 feet of colonial-style wood cabinets, with built-in double-basin stainless steel sink, dishwasher, coppertone range with oven and hood with exhaust fan and coppertone refrigerator. All appliances will be sold with the house.

The living room is 16 feet by 18 feet with a closet 2 feet by 4 feet. The dining room is 9 feet by 14 feet. The kitchen is 12 feet by 13 feet. The family room is 10½ feet by 17 feet. The bedrooms are 12 feet by 16 feet with a closet 2 feet by 8 feet; 10 feet by 10 feet with a closet 2 feet by 4 feet; and 9½ feet by 12 feet with a closet 2 feet by 5 feet. The full bathrooms are both 6 feet by 8 feet, and one has a closet 1½ feet by 2 feet. The half-bath is 4 feet by 7 feet. The house has a total of 1,300 square feet of living space, calculated from its exterior dimensions, and is functionally adequate.

Check your completed Building Data Form against the one given in the Answer Key at the back of the book. Correct any errors and fill in any omissions.

BUILDING DATA FORM

ADDRESS: _____

NO. OF UNITS: _____ NO. OF STORIES: _____ ORIENTATION: N S E W

TYPE: _____ DESIGN: _____ AGE: _____ SQUARE FEET: _____

	GOOD	AVERAGE	FAIR	POOR
GENERAL CONDITION OF EXTERIOR				
FOUNDATION TYPE _____ BSMT./CRAWL SP./SLAB				
EXTERIOR WALLS: BRICK/BLOCK/VENEER/STUCCO/				
WOOD/ALUMINUM/VINYL				
WINDOW FRAMES: METAL/WOOD				
STORM WINDOWS: ___ SCREENS: ___				
GARAGE: _____ ATTACHED/DETACHED				
NUMBER OF CARS: ___				
☐ PORCH ☐ DECK ☐ PATIO ☐ SHED				
OTHER _____				
GENERAL CONDITION OF INTERIOR				
INTERIOR WALLS: DRY WALL/PLASTER/WOOD				
CEILINGS: _____				
FLOORS: WOOD/CONCRETE/TILE/CARPET				
ELECTRICAL WIRING AND SERVICE: _____				
HEATING PLANT: _____ AGE: _____				
GAS/OIL/WOOD/ELECTRIC				
CENTRAL AIR-CONDITIONING: _____ AIR FILTRATION: ___				
NUMBER OF FIREPLACES: _____ TYPE: _____				
OTHER _____				
BATHROOM: FLOOR___WALLS____FIXTURES _____				
BATHROOM: FLOOR___WALLS____FIXTURES _____				
BATHROOM: FLOOR___WALLS____FIXTURES _____				
KITCHEN: FLOOR___WALLS____CABINETS _____				
FIXTURES _____				

ROOM SIZES	LIVING ROOM	DINING ROOM	KITCHEN	BEDROOM	BATH	CLOSETS	FAMILY ROOM
BASEMENT							
1ST FLOOR							
2ND FLOOR							
ATTIC							

DEPRECIATION (DESCRIBE):

  PHYSICAL DETERIORATION _____

  FUNCTIONAL OBSOLESCENCE _____

  EXTERNAL OBSOLESCENCE _____

Data for Sales Comparison Approach

In using the sales comparison approach, data is collected on sales of comparable properties. Only recent sales should be considered; they must have been arm's-length transactions and the properties sold must be substantially similar to the subject property.

Recent sales.   In an area with many property sales, comparable properties that have sold within the past four to six months should be available. The appraiser should be prepared to explain the use of any comparable sale that occurred more than six months before the date of appraisal. In an area of slow property turnover, the appraiser may have to refer to comparable sales from as long as a year ago. In that event, the appraiser probably will need to make an adjustment to allow for the time factor. If other types of properties have increased in value over the same period, a general rise in prices may be indicated. The appraiser must determine whether the property in question is part of the general trend and, if it is, adjust the sales price of the comparable accordingly. This adjustment answers the question, "How much would this comparable property probably sell for in to-day's market?"

Similar features.   Though adjustments may be made for some differences between the subject property and the comparables, most of the following factors should be similar:

style of house	size of lot
age	size of building
number of rooms	terms of sale
number of bedrooms	type of construction
number of bathrooms	general condition

Ideally, the comparable properties should be from the same neighborhood as the subject property. Specific data, similar to that collected for the subject property, should be collected for completed sales of at least three comparable properties. Sales data on more than those three will have to be studied in some cases, since the first three properties the appraiser analyzes may not fit the general requirements listed above well enough to be used in the appraisal. An analysis of the sales properties not used directly in the report may be helpful in establishing neighborhood values, price trends and time adjustments.

The terms of sale are of great importance, particularly if the buyer has assumed an existing loan or if the seller has helped finance the purchase. The seller may take back a note on part of the purchase price (secured by a mortgage on the property) at an interest rate lower than the prevailing market rate. The seller may also "buy down" the buyer's high interest rate on a new loan by paying the lender part of the interest on the amount borrowed in a lump sum at the time of the sale. The argument has been made that, in a buydown, the sales price has been effectively reduced by the amount the seller has paid to the lender. In any event, the sales price should be considered in light of the cost to the buyer reflected in the method used to finance the purchase.

One way to appreciate the effect of financing terms on property affordability is to adjust selling prices to reflect financing variances by using the *cash equivalency* technique. With this technique, the monthly payment to be made by the buyer is compared to the required monthly payment on a new loan in the same principal amount, at the prevailing interest rate as of the sale date. The resulting percentage is applied to the amount of the purchase price represented by the principal of the low-interest loan. When this reduced amount is added to the amount paid in cash by the buyer to the seller, the result is an adjusted sales price that compensates for the effects of below-market-rate financing.

EXAMPLE: The total purchase price of a property was $200,000. The buyer made total cash payments of $50,000 and also assumed the seller's mortgage, which had a remaining principal balance of $150,000, bearing an interest rate of 10 percent, with monthly payments of $1,447.50. As of the date of sale, the mortgage had a remaining term of 20 years. Prevailing mortgages on a loan of equal amount and for a like term, as of the sale date, required a 12 percent interest rate with monthly payments of $1,651.65.

The percentage to be applied to the principal amount of the assumed loan is computed by dividing the actual required monthly payment by the payment required for a loan at the prevailing rate.

$$\frac{\$1,447.50}{\$1,651.65} = .8764 \text{ or } 87.64\%$$

The remaining principal amount of the loan is then multiplied by that percentage to find its adjusted value.

$$\$150,000 \times 87.64\% = \$131,460$$

The cash equivalency of the sale can be reached by adding the down payment to the adjusted value of the assumed loan.

$$\$50,000 + \$131,460 = \$181,460$$

The cash equivalency of this sale is $181,460

Note that use of the cash equivalency technique as the sole method of determining value is not permitted by such agencies as the Federal National Mortgage Association (Fannie Mae).

Ideally, since comparable properties should have comparable terms of sale, no adjustment for that factor will be necessary. However, if the appraiser has no choice but to use properties with varying financing terms, the selling prices should be adjusted to reflect realistically the effect of the financing in the marketplace, rather than simply be the result of a mechanical formula.

Arm's-length transactions.   Every comparable property must have been sold in an *arm's-length transaction,* in which neither buyer nor seller is acting under duress, the property is offered on the open market for a reasonable length of time and both buyer and seller have a reasonable knowledge of the property, its assets and defects.

In most cases, the slightest indication of duress on the part of either of the principals automatically excludes a transaction from consideration. If the sale has been forced for any reason (a foreclosure, tax sale, an estate liquidation, the need to purchase adjoining property or to sell before the owner is transferred), it is not an arm's-length transaction. If the principals are related individuals or corporations, this must be assumed to have affected the terms of the sale. Again, financing should be considered. If the down payment was extremely small, or none was required, such an exceptional situation might disqualify the sold property from consideration as a comparable, or at least require an adjustment.

Sources of Data

The preliminary search for data on sales of comparable properties will be made from one or more of the sources listed here. All sales data, however, must be verified by one of the principals to the transaction. The sources are:

1. The appraiser's own records. These offer the best sources of data. If four comparable properties are available from the appraiser's own records, only the sales prices will remain to be independently verified. (Even though the appraiser has researched the market value as thoroughly as possible, the actual selling price may not have been the same figure.)
2. Official records of deeds. The appraiser may keep a file of transactions held within the area, but all records will be available in the county or city clerk's office. Much of the specific information needed can also be culled from these records. In localities where transfer tax stamps must be recorded on deeds, such stamps may give an indication of selling price; they are not generally reliable sources of exact selling price, however. The tax rate may be based only on the actual cash amount paid at the closing of the sale, thereby excluding assumed mortgages, for instance. Tax stamps are also usually based on rounded amounts, such as $0.50 per each $500 of financial consideration, or a fraction thereof. Merely multiplying the number of stamps by $500 in such a case could result in a final estimate that is as much as $499 more than the actual cash amount. Too many or too few stamps may also be put on the deed deliberately to mislead anyone trying to discover the property's selling price.
3. The broker or salespeople involved in the sale.
4. The lawyers for the principals in the sale.
5. The principals themselves.

6. Records of sales published by some local real estate boards.
7. Newspapers. In particular, local newspapers may publish monthly or seasonal listings of sales in different neighborhoods. Any sale information taken from a newspaper should definitely be verified elsewhere, as this source is not generally reliable.
8. The real estate assessor's office. If property cards can be examined, these will ordinarily reveal sales price, deed book and page, zoning, age of dwelling, lot and dwelling dimensions and dates of additions to the house.

Exercise 4.5

1. You need some comparables for the sample appraisal being carried out in this chapter for a house that is six years old and has three bedrooms. Name four places you would look for sales data.

2. You are appraising a subject property fitting the following description:

   Built 10 years ago, has five rooms, 1½ baths, of average-quality construction, in a neighborhood where average annual family income is $20,000.

   There are five properties that have sold recently. These five properties are similar to the subject property except for these differences:

   Sale 1 has only one bath.
   Sale 2 is about 25 years old.
   Sale 3 needs paint.
   Sale 4 is in a slightly better neighborhood.
   Sale 5 has eight rooms and one bath.

   Which sales should be dropped from consideration as comparables, and why?

Check your answers against those given in the Answer Key at the back of the book.

Comparison Chart

The Comparable Sales Chart, Figure 4.1, lists the common significant property variables that warrant price adjustments. The categories of information are almost the same as those required in the

Uniform Residential Appraisal Report used by many government agencies, lenders and others. The chart has space for the subject property and comparables to be described and for the sales price of each comparable to be adjusted to account for significant property differences. In any given appraisal analysis, it may be necessary to include other categories of adjustment. (For the sample appraisal in this chapter, no additional categories of information will be needed.)

The subject property and each comparable should be identified by street address. The proximity of each comparable to the subject also should be noted, for this will be important in determining whether a value adjustment will be made for location. The sales price of each comparable, as well as the source of the market data used, should be recorded. The easiest way to complete the chart is to describe all the details of the subject property, then do the same for each comparable in turn.

Although years of experience may give an appraiser some intuitive knowledge of the value of property, the figure presented in the appraisal report must be as factual as possible. It is important to remember that the adjustment value of a property feature is not simply the cost to construct or add that feature, but what a buyer is willing to pay for it, typically a lesser amount. An estimate of market value must always consider the demands of the marketplace.

The appraiser must also avoid the temptation to make adjustments match a value he or she has already decided "feels" right for the subject property. The value the appraiser initially felt was the right one for the subject property may in fact be reached by further analysis. Even if this were true for every appraisal, though, it would not mean that the appraiser would have no further need to itemize specific price adjustments. The appraiser's report to the client must present the facts on which the value estimate was reached rather than a preconception of value. The appraiser's intuition is useful, however, if the final adjusted property value is far removed from what it should be. If the value estimate seems too high or too low, there may be adjustment factors that the appraiser has failed to consider, and more information must be gathered.

Usually there will be some dissimilarity between the subject property and a comparable. The accuracy of the market comparison approach, therefore, relies on the categories selected for adjustments and the amount of any adjustments made. The appraiser should avoid making unnecessary adjustments; that is, the appraiser should make only those adjustments considered by buyers, sellers and tenants involved with this class of property. The categories listed on the Comparable Sales Chart are the most significant factors, as they have the greatest effect on value in standard residential appraisals.

Sales or financing concessions. As noted earlier, this is important if a sale involved nonstandard financing terms, whether in down payment, type of loan or terms of loan.

FIGURE 4.1   Comparable Sales Chart

COMPARABLE SALES CHART

	SUBJECT	COMPARABLE NO. 1	COMPARABLE NO. 2	COMPARABLE NO. 3	COMPARABLE NO. 4	COMPARABLE NO. 5
Address						
Proximity to Subject						
Sales Price		$	$	$	$	$
Data Source						
VALUE ADJUSTMENTS	DESCRIPTION	DESCRIPTION | +(–)$ Adjustment	DESCRIPTION | +(–)$ Adjustment	DESCRIPTION | +(–)$ Adjustment	DESCRIPTION | +(–)$ Adjustment	DESCRIPTION | +(–)$ Adjustment
Sales or Financing Concessions						
Adjusted Value		$	$	$	$	$
Date of Sale/Time						
Adjusted Value		$	$	$	$	$
Location						
Site/View						
Design and Appeal						
Quality of Construction						
Age						
Condition						
Above Grade Room Count	Total | Bdrms | Baths	Total | Bdrms | Baths	Total | Bdrms | Baths	Total | Bdrms | Baths	Total | Bdrms | Baths	Total | Bdrms | Baths
Gross Living Area	Sq. Ft.	Sq. Ft.	Sq. Ft.	Sq. Ft.	Sq. Ft.	Sq. Ft.
Basement & Finished Rooms Below Grade						
Functional Utility						
Heating/Cooling						
Garage/Carport						
Other Ext. Improvements						
Special Energy Efficient Items						
Fireplace(s)						
Other Int. Improvements						
Add'l Adj.		☐+ ☐– | $	☐+ ☐– | $	☐+ ☐– | $	☐+ ☐– | $	☐+ ☐– | $
Adjusted Value		$	$	$	$	$

Date of sale. Adjustment will probably be necessary for a sale made six months or more before the date of appraisal.

Location. The comparable property should be in the same neighborhood as the subject property. (There may be no recourse except properties outside the immediate area if there have been few sales, if the subject property is in a rural area or if the subject is atypical—such as the only three-apartment building in an area of single-family houses. In such a case, the buildings chosen as comparables should at least come from comparable neighborhoods.) Within the same neighborhood, locations can offer significant variances, such as proximity to different land uses or frontage on a heavily traveled street. A property across the street from a park would tend to be more valuable than one across the street from a railroad switchyard. As mentioned earlier, corner lots no longer automatically command higher prices for single-family residences.

Site/view. Parcel size should be given and the site rated as good, average, fair or poor on the basis of physical features as well as view.

Design and appeal. The style of a house probably should follow the rule of conformity; that is, the design should be compatible with that of others in the neighborhood.

Quality of construction. If not the same as or equivalent to the subject property, quality of construction will be a major adjustment. Available comparables within a particular builder's subdivision typically will be of the same construction quality. Building cost estimating guides, published to assist builders (and appraisers, as you will learn in Chapter 6, "The Cost Approach"), can be used to rate construction quality as low, average, good or very good to excellent.

Age. Because most subdivisions are completed within a relatively short period of time, there will probably be no significant differences among comparables. A brand-new home would likely be valued by the builder, according to actual costs, overhead and profit. In older homes of good general condition, an age difference of five years in either direction usually is not significant. Overall upkeep is of greater importance, although the age of the house may alert the appraiser to look for outmoded design or fixtures or any needed repairs.

Condition. The overall condition of each property will be noted as good, average, fair or poor. An adjustment would be indicated if the comparable is in better or worse condition than the subject.

Above-grade room count. Total number of rooms in the house, excluding bathrooms and any basement (below-grade) rooms, is listed here. The number of bedrooms and baths and the total above-grade square footage are also noted. A major adjustment would be needed if the subject property had fewer than three bedrooms and the comparables had at least three, or vice versa. Total number of full baths (lavatory, toilet and tub or shower) and half-baths (lavatory and toilet) are tallied in this category. Modern plumbing is assumed, with an adjustment made for out-of-date fixtures.

Basement and below-grade finished rooms.   The appraiser should note any below-grade improvements, such as a finished basement.

Size of lot.   Except for irregularities that would make parts of a lot unusable, impair privacy or restrict on-site parking, differences in street frontage and total square footage are the most important considerations.

Landscaping.   Trees and other plantings should be of the same maturity as those of the subject property and of approximately the same quantity and quality.

Functional utility.   The building's overall compatibility with its intended use, as defined in the marketplace, should be noted. This category includes design features, such as layout and room size, that are currently desirable.

Heating/cooling.   The appraiser notes the type of heating unit and air-conditioning system, if any, of the subject and comparables.

Garage/carport.   If the subject property does not have one, any garage on a comparable property would require an adjustment. A garage on the subject property would be compared for type of construction and size.

Other exterior improvements.   Porch, Florida room, patio, pool or any other living or recreation area not part of the primary house area is included here.

Special energy-efficient items.   High R-factor insulation, solar heating units or other energy conservation features should be noted.

Fireplace(s).   The number and type of fireplaces should be recorded.

Other interior improvements.   An adjustment factor is indicated if either the subject property or one of the comparables has any other interior property improvement that adds to or subtracts from value. Luxurious finishing, such as real wood paneling, could add to a home's value.

Step 4   Determine Highest and Best Use

The highest and best use of real estate, whether vacant or with improvements, is its most profitable legally permitted, physically possible and financially feasible use. The highest and best use of real estate that has been improved by the erection of a structure or structures on it may take into account the existing improvements, or the land may be treated as if vacant.

Because of the wide use of zoning throughout the United States, consideration of highest and best use is generally limited to the property's present legally permitted uses. In the case of areas zoned for single-family residences, this use usually is accepted as the highest and best use. A change of zoning is occasionally possible, particularly when a subsequent nearby land use creates adverse conditions for enjoyment of residential property. As an example, property along a roadway that has become very heavily traveled by commercial vehicles as a result of nearby development may be rezoned for commercial use. Rezoning can never be assumed, however, and it usually entails a lengthy application and approval process. For the appraiser's purpose, only existing permitted land uses are considered unless otherwise specified by the client.

For purposes of this chapter, the present use of all properties used in the case study and exercises will be considered their highest and best use.

Step 5 Estimate Land Value

Because house (improvements) and lot are being valued together in the sales comparison approach, we will not make a separate estimate of land value. Land valuation techniques are discussed in the next chapter.

Step 6 Estimate Value by Sales Comparison Approach

Data Analysis

The most difficult step in using the sales comparison approach is determining the amount of each adjustment. The accuracy of an appraisal using this approach depends on the appraiser's use of reliable adjustment values. Unfortunately, the value of the same feature may vary for different types, sizes and overall values of property. Until an appraiser has the background of many appraisals in a given area, more comparable properties will have to be studied than just the three to six presented in the typical appraisal report. If the appraiser completes an adjustment chart for as many as 10 to 20 or more properties, a market pattern may be more evident and, with better documentation, the value of individual differences may be estimated fairly accurately.

Ideally, if properties could be found that were exactly alike except for one category, the adjustment value of that category would be the difference in selling prices of the two properties. Noting the individual differences of many properties at once should provide at least two such properties for every adjustment category.

The Sales Price Adjustment Chart is a source of information for adjustment values that can be used in a sales comparison approach. The appraiser can develop such a chart and use it to substantiate dollar amounts for adjusted values.

EXAMPLE: House A is very similar to house B, except that it has a two-car attached garage, and house B does not. House A sold for $134,000; house B sold for $125,500. Because the garage is the only significant difference between the two properties, its value is the difference between the selling price of $134,000 and the selling price of $125,500. So the value of the garage is $134,000 − $125,500, or $8,500.

For the background of adjustment values, the appraiser analyzes as many properties as needed to be able to isolate each significant variable. Most neighborhoods have very similar types of properties, so this is not as difficult a task as it may first appear.

Figure 4.2 is a Sales Price Adjustment Chart that has been completed for ten properties, all comparable to each other. Each relevant adjustment variable has been highlighted by a screen. *Although an appraiser ordinarily will need two or more instances of each variable as a check on the accuracy of an adjustment value, for the sake of brevity only one comparable with each variable is presented here.*

Because properties A, E and J exhibit no variables, they will be used to define the standard against which the worth of each variable will be measured. Property A sold for $121,000, property E for $120,500 and property J for $121,000. Because property E shows only a slight price decrease, $121,000 will be used as the base house value for a typical property in the neighborhood; that is, one having the most typical property features. Each variable can now be noted and valued.

Time adjustment.   Property H is identical in features to properties A, E and J, except for length of time since the date of sale. Market conditions over the past year indicate a period of general inflation. Property H was sold one year ago; properties A, E and J were all sold within the past six to eleven weeks. The adjustment value to be made in the case of a year-old sale is, therefore:

$$\$121,000 - \$111,000 = \$10,000$$

The $10,000 adjustment value can be expressed as a percentage of the total cost of the property.

$$\frac{\$10,000}{\$111,000} = .09009 = 9.009\% \text{ or simply } 9\%$$

FIGURE 4.2   Sales Price Adjustment Chart

SALES PRICE ADJUSTMENT CHART
COMPARABLES

	A	B	C	D	E	F	G	H	I	J
SALES PRICE	$121,000	$115,000	$122,000	$124,000	$120,500	$112,000	$136,000	$111,000	$126,000	$121,000
FINANCING	75% assump.	70% assump.	75% assump.	75% assump.	70% assump.	75% assump.	70% assump.	70 or 75% assump.	70% assump.	70% assump.
DATE OF SALE	6 wks.	2 mos.	3 wks.	5 wks.	6 wks.	5 wks.	3 wks.	1 yr.	5 wks.	11 wks.
LOCATION	resid.	resid.	resid.	resid.	resid.	highway	commercial	resid.	resid.	resid.
SITE/VIEW	good	good	good	good	good	good	good	good	good	good
SIZE OF LOT	50' × 200'	50' × 200'	50' × 200'	50' × 200'	50' × 200'	50' × 200'	50' × 200'	50' × 200'	50' × 200'	50' × 200'
DESIGN AND APPEAL	good	good	good	good	good	good	good	good	good	good
CONSTRUCTION	brick	aluminum siding	brick	brick	brick	brick	brick	brick	brick	brick
AGE	8 yrs.	7 yrs.	8 yrs.	6 yrs.	6 yrs.	7 yrs.	6 yrs.	7 yrs.	6 yrs.	7 yrs.
CONDITION	good	good	good	good	good	good	good	good	good	good
NO. OF RMS./BEDRMS./BATHS	7/3/2	7/3/2	7/3/2	7/3/2½	7/3/2	7/3/2	7/3/2	7/3/2	8/4/2	7/3/2
SQ. FT. OF LIVING SPACE	1,275	1,300	1,290	1,300	1,300	1,325	1,300	1,350	1,400	1,300
OTHER SPACE (BASEMENT)	full basement	full basement	full basement	full basement	full basement	full basement	full basement	full basement	full basement	full basement
FUNCTIONAL UTILITY	adequate	adequate	adequate	adequate	adequate	adequate	adequate	adequate	adequate	adequate
HEATING/COOLING	central heat/air	central heat/air	central heat/air	central heat/air	central heat/air	central heat/air	central heat/air	central heat/air	central heat/air	central heat/air
GARAGE/CARPORT	2-car att.	2-car att.	2-car att.	2-car att.	2-car att.	2-car att.	2-car att.	2-car att.	2-car att.	2-car att.
OTHER EXT. IMPROVEMENTS	patio	patio	patio	patio	patio	patio	patio	patio	patio	patio
SPECIAL ENERGY EFFICIENT ITEMS	none	none	none	none	none	none	none	none	none	none
FIREPLACE(S)	one	one	one	one	one	one	one	one	one	one
OTHER INT. IMPROVEMENTS	none	none	none	none	none	none	none	none	none	none
TYPICAL HOUSE VALUE	$121,000	$121,000	$121,000	$121,000	$121,000	$121,000	$121,000	$121,000	$121,000	$121,000
VARIABLE FEATURE		aluminum siding		extra half bath		poor location	commercial area	year-old sale	4th bedroom	
ADJUSTMENT VALUE OF VARIABLE										

In this case, the adjustment value of the variable is $10,000. If a one-year time adjustment was required for another property, the dollar value of the adjustment would be the amount derived by applying the percentage of value to that property's sales price.

Highway location.   Property F, on a less desirable site facing a busy highway, sold for $9,000 less than the standard; therefore, this poor location indicates an adjustment of $9,000.

Commercial area.   In this example, the $136,000 selling price of property G is considerably higher than that of properties in the residential area. Upon closer analysis, the appraiser discovered that property G was adjacent to the site of a new shopping mall and had been purchased by the mall developers for use as a parking area. Since property G represents an extraordinary situation, it should not be considered representative of the adjustment value warranted by location.

In the next exercise, you will find the remaining adjustment values used in the sample appraisal being carried out in this chapter.

Exercise 4.6

Complete the adjustment valuations for construction, number of bedrooms and number of bathrooms as indicated by the data on the previous page. Record all of the adjustments computed thus far, and those you will compute yourself, in the appropriate boxes in the Sales Price Adjustment Chart on page 98.

Date of Sale:

9%

Location: Highway

$121,000 − $112,000 = $9,000

Construction:

No. of Bedrooms:

No. of Baths:

_____

Check your completed chart adjustments against the ones given in the Answer Key at the back of the book.

_____

Exercise 4.7

In the sample appraisal, five properties, all within one-half mile of the subject, have been selected as comparables. A description of each property and its sale is given below. In each case, property information was supplied by the sales agent. Complete the Comparable Sales Chart on page 101. Needed information on the subject property and comparable 1 has already been recorded. In the same way, you are to insert the necessary information for comparables 2 through 5. A map of the neighborhood is shown on page 80. Current market rate financing available for the purchase of homes in this price range is 10¼ to 10½ percent, with a minimum down payment of 20 percent. All of the homes are of contemporary style, with no functional obsolescence.

1. 2017 Parkside Boulevard—an eight-year-old, seven-room brick ranch, in good general condition, with full basement, living room, kitchen, family room, three bedrooms and two full baths. The house, which has forced-air heating and air-conditioning, has a total of 1,275 square feet of living space. Landscaping is very attractive, with several large trees, shrubs and flower beds. The property has a view of the surrounding hills. There is a two-car attached garage. The lot is 50 feet by 200 feet. The buyer obtained a 10½ percent mortgage loan, making a down payment of 25 percent on the $113,000 sales price. The sale took place six weeks prior to the date of appraisal of the subject property.

2. 2135 Hastings Avenue—a seven-year-old, seven-room ranch, with 1,350 square feet of space, a full basement and forced-air heating and cooling. The house is in good condition; it is brick, with an attached two-car garage. There are three bedrooms, two full baths, living room, dining room, kitchen and family room. The lot is 50 feet by 200 feet, with good landscaping and a view of the hills filtered through shade trees in front and back yards. The buyer obtained a 10½ percent mortgage; the exact amount of the down payment is not known, but it was probably at least 25 or 30 percent. The purchase price was $119,000; the sale took place one year before the date of appraisal of the subject property.

3. 2209 Madison Avenue—a seven-room, 1,300-square-foot aluminum-sided ranch on a corner lot 50 feet by 200 feet, with attached two-car garage. The house has forced-air heating and air-conditioning. Landscaping is good and the house has a lovely view of the area. The house is eight years old and in good condition, with a living room, dining room, kitchen, family room, three bedrooms and two full baths. There is a full basement. The sales price was $117,500, and the purchase, two months before the date of this appraisal, was financed by the buyer's obtaining a 10¼ percent loan with a 25 percent cash down payment.

COMPARABLE SALES CHART

	SUBJECT	COMPARABLE NO. 1	COMPARABLE NO. 2	COMPARABLE NO. 3	COMPARABLE NO. 4	COMPARABLE NO. 5
Address	2130 W. Franklin	2017 Parkside Blvd.				
Proximity to Subject		within half-mile				
Sales Price		$113,000	$	$	$	$
Data Source	owner	sales agent				
VALUE ADJUSTMENTS	DESCRIPTION	DESCRIPTION | +(-)$ Adjustment	DESCRIPTION | +(-)$ Adjustment	DESCRIPTION | +(-)$ Adjustment	DESCRIPTION | +(-)$ Adjustment	DESCRIPTION | +(-)$ Adjustment
Sales or Financing Concessions	n/a	none				
Adjusted Value		$	$	$	$	$
Date of Sale/Time	n/a	6 wks. ago				
Adjusted Value		$	$	$	$	$
Location	quiet st.	heavy traf.				
Site/View	50 × 200 gd.	50 × 200 gd.				
Design and Appeal	ranch/good	ranch/good				
Quality of Construction	good	good				
Age	8 yrs.	8 yrs.				
Condition	good	good				
Above Grade Room Count	Total 7 | Bdrms 3 | Baths 2½	Total 7 | Bdrms 3 | Baths 2	Total | Bdrms | Baths	Total | Bdrms | Baths	Total | Bdrms | Baths	Total | Bdrms | Baths
Gross Living Area	1,300 Sq. Ft.	1,275 Sq. Ft.	Sq. Ft.	Sq. Ft.	Sq. Ft.	Sq. Ft.
Basement & Finished Rooms Below Grade	full basement	full basement				
Functional Utility	adequate	adequate				
Heating/Cooling	central h/a	central h/a				
Garage/Carport	2-car att.	2-car att.				
Other Ext. Improvements	none	none				
Special Energy Efficient Items	none	none				
Fireplace(s)	none	none				
Other Int. Improvements	none	none				
Add'l Adj.		□+ □- $	□+ □- $	□+ □- $	□+ □- $	□+ □- $
Adjusted Value		$	$	$	$	$

4. 2320 Pleasant Boulevard—an eight-room, 1,400-square-foot brick ranch on a 50-foot-by-200-foot lot, with attached two-car garage. Landscaping is good and well kept, and the six-year-old house is also in good condition. The view is of the surrounding hills. There is a living room, dining room, kitchen, family room, four bedrooms and two full baths. There is a full basement and forced-air heating and air-conditioning. The purchase price of $127,500 was financed by the buyer's paying 20 percent down and obtaining a 10¼ percent mortgage. The sale took place five weeks before the date of the subject appraisal.

5. 2003 Franklin Street—a seven-room, 1,300-square-foot brick ranch, on a 50-foot-by-200-foot lot, with good landscaping, pretty views and attached two-car garage. The house is seven years old, in good condition and has a living room, dining room, kitchen, family room, three bedrooms, two full baths and one half-bath, as well as a full basement. The house has forced-air heating and air-conditioning. The sale, which took place five weeks ago, was financed by the buyer's down payment of 25 percent on a 10½ percent mortgage loan. The purchase price was $125,000.

Record all of the data given above on the Comparable Sales Chart on page 101.

At this point in many appraisals, properties considered comparables are found to be unacceptable for one or more reasons. In this group of comparables for the sample appraisal, do any of the properties seem unacceptable? If so, why?

Check your answers and your completed chart with those given in the Answer Key at the back of the book.

Using the adjustment values you recorded on page 98, you are ready to complete a Comparable Sales Chart for the sample appraisal being carried out in this lesson.

First, the details of the subject property are recorded as well as the selling prices of the comparables. Then, all boxes representing features of comparables are lined through, except for the features that differ significantly from the subject property. Those features are to be assigned adjustment values. The chart on page 103 shows the box for all the adjustment computations lined through, except for those that actually require an adjustment.

Next, the adjustment values must be recorded. For example, comparable 1 is located on a major thoroughfare, while the subject property is on a quiet residential street. So the adjustment value computed earlier for location can be assigned to comparable 1 and entered in the location box for that comparable. Keep in mind that selling prices of comparable properties are adjusted to reflect the probable market value of the subject property. Because the subject property's location

COMPARABLE SALES CHART

	SUBJECT	COMPARABLE NO. 1	COMPARABLE NO. 2	COMPARABLE NO. 3	COMPARABLE NO. 4	COMPARABLE NO. 5
Address	2130 W.Franklin	2017 Parkside Blvd.	2136 Hastings Ave.	2209 Madison Ave.	2320 Pleasant Blvd.	2003 Franklin St
Proximity to Subject		within half-mile	within half-mile	within half-mile	within half-mile	within half-mile
Sales Price		$113,000	$119,000	$117,500	$127,500	$125,000
Data Source	owner	sales agent	sales agent	sales agent	sales agent	sales agent
VALUE ADJUSTMENTS	DESCRIPTION	DESCRIPTION / +(−)$ Adjustment	DESCRIPTION / +(−)$ Adjustment	DESCRIPTION / +(−)$ Adjustment	DESCRIPTION / +(−)$ Adjustment	DESCRIPTION / +(−)$ Adjustment
Sales or Financing Concessions	n/a	none / $	none / $	none / $	none / $	none / $
Adjusted Value						
Date of Sale/Time	n/a	6 wks. ago / $	1 yr. ago / $	2 mos. ago / $	5 wks. ago / $	5 wks. ago / $
Adjusted Value						
Location	quiet st.	heavy traf. / +9,000	quiet st.	quiet st.	quiet st.	quiet st.
Site/View	50×200 gd.	50×200 gd.	50×200 gd.	50×200 gd.	50×200 gd.	50×200 gd.
Design and Appeal	ranch/good	ranch/good	ranch/good	ranch/good	ranch/good	ranch/good
Quality of Construction	good	good	good	gd./alum sd.	good	good
Age	6 yrs.	8 yrs.	7 yrs.	8 yrs.	6 yrs.	7 yrs.
Condition	good	good	good	good	good	good
Above Grade Room Count	Total 7 / Bdrms 3 / Baths 2½	Total 7 / Bdrms 3 / Baths 2	Total 7 / Bdrms 3 / Baths 2	Total 7 / Bdrms 3 / Baths 2	Total 8 / Bdrms 4 / Baths 2	Total 7 / Bdrms 3 / Baths 2½
Gross Living Area	1,300 Sq. Ft.	1,275 Sq. Ft.	1,350 Sq. Ft.	1,300 Sq. Ft.	1,400 Sq. Ft.	1,300 Sq. Ft.
Basement & Finished Rooms Below Grade	full basement	full basement	full basement	full basement	full basement	full basement
Functional Utility	adequate	adequate	adequate	adequate	adequate	adequate
Heating/Cooling	central h/a	central h/a	central h/a	central h/a	central h/a	central h/a
Garage/Carport	2-car att.	2-car att.	2-car att.	2-car att.	2-car att.	2-car att.
Other Ext. Improvements	none	none	none	none	none	none
Special Energy Efficient Items	none	none	none	none	none	none
Fireplace(s)	none	none	none	none	none	none
Other Int. Improvements	none	none	none	none	none	none
Add'l Adj.		□+ □− $	□+ □− $	□+ □− $	□+ □− $	□+ □− $
Adjusted Value		$	$	$	$	$

is generally considered a more desirable one than that of comparable 1, the adjustment value of $9,000 computed earlier must be added to the sales price of the comparable to find what the subject property would be worth. So, "+$9,000" is recorded.

An adjustment will be a plus (+) if that feature is found in the subject but not the comparable or otherwise represents a higher value for the subject property. An adjustment will be a minus (–) if that feature is present in the comparable but not the subject or otherwise represents a lower value for the subject property.

Exercise 4.8

Record the remaining adjustments on the Comparable Sales Chart on page 103. You will be recording the following adjustments, using the adjustment values you computed in the last exercise:

Comparable 1—No. of Baths

Comparable 2—No. of Baths

Date of Sale

Comparable 3—Construction

No. of Baths

Comparable 4—No. of Bedrooms

No. of Baths

When you finish, check your figures against those given in the Answer Key at the back of the book.

Net Adjustments

Once the necessary adjustment values are recorded, they can be totaled for each comparable property. The chart on page 106 shows the net adjustment for comparable 1. The location adjustment factor of +$9,000 is added to the adjustment factor of +$3,000 for an extra bath, for a total adjustment of +$12,000.

To find the final adjusted value of comparable 1, its sales price and net adjustments are totaled. In this case $113,000 + $12,000 gives an adjusted value of $125,000.

Exercise 4.9

Complete the net adjustment and adjusted value computations for comparables 2, 3, 4 and 5 and record them on the chart on page 106.

Check your results against those given in the Answer Key at the back of the book.

Value Estimate

Using the adjusted values thus compiled, the appraiser can determine the appropriate estimate of market value to assign to the subject property using the sales comparison approach.

Even when the appraiser is dealing with comparable properties that are virtually identical, the adjusted values will rarely be identical. There will usually be at least some differences in real estate transactions, however minor, that will cause selling prices to vary. A seller in one transaction may be less inclined to make a counteroffer than a seller in another transaction. Or a buyer may think that he or she has to offer a certain amount less than the asking price.

Whatever the reasons, the adjusted values of the comparable properties probably will not be identical. It is the appraiser's task to choose the adjusted value that seems to best reflect the characteristics of the subject property. In other words, which comparable is most like the subject property? The adjusted value of that property will most likely represent the market value of the subject property.

Exercise 4.10

You have already completed the Comparable Sales Chart for this chapter's sample appraisal. Based upon what you have just read, which adjusted value indicates the estimate of market value of the subject property? Why?

Check your answers against those given in the Answer Key at the back of the book.

COMPARABLE SALES CHART

	SUBJECT	COMPARABLE NO. 1	+(-)$ Adjustment	COMPARABLE NO. 2	+(-)$ Adjustment	COMPARABLE NO. 3	+(-)$ Adjustment	COMPARABLE NO. 4	+(-)$ Adjustment	COMPARABLE NO. 5	+(-)$ Adjustment
Address	2130 W. Franklin	2017 Parkside Blvd.		2135 Hastings Ave.		2209 Madison Ave.		2320 Pleasant Blvd.		2003 Franklin St.	
Proximity to Subject		within half-mile		within half-mile		within half-mile		within half-mile		within half-mile	
Sales Price		$113,000		$119,000		$117,500		$127,500		$125,000	
Data Source	owner	sales agent		sales agent		sales agent		sales agent		sales agent	
VALUE ADJUSTMENTS	DESCRIPTION	DESCRIPTION		DESCRIPTION		DESCRIPTION		DESCRIPTION		DESCRIPTION	
Sales or Financing Concessions	n/a	none		none		none		none		none	
Adjusted Value			$		$		$		$		$
Date of Sale/Time	n/a	6 wks. ago		1 yr. ago	+10,700	2 mos. ago		5 wks. ago		5 wks. ago	
Adjusted Value			$		$		$		$		$
Location	quiet st.	heavy traf.	+9,000	quiet st.		quiet st.		quiet st.		quiet st.	
Site/View	50×200 gd.	50×200 gd.		50×200 gd.		50×200 gd.		50×200 gd.		50×200 gd.	
Design and Appeal	ranch/good	ranch/good		ranch/good		ranch/good		ranch/good		ranch/good	
Quality of Construction	good	good		good		gd./alum sd.	+6,000	good		good	
Age	6 yrs.	8 yrs.		7 yrs.		8 yrs.		6 yrs.		7 yrs.	
Condition	good	good		good		good		good		good	
Above Grade Room Count	Total 7 | Bdrms 3 | Baths 2½	Total 7 | Bdrms 3 | (Baths) 2	+3,000	Total 7 | Bdrms 3 | (Baths) 2	+3,000	Total 7 | Bdrms 3 | (Baths) 2	+3,000	Total 8 | Bdrms 4 | (Baths) 2	−5,000 / +3,000	Total 7 | (Bdrms) 3 | (Baths) 2½	
Gross Living Area	1,300 Sq. Ft.	1,275 Sq. Ft.		1,350 Sq. Ft.		1,300 Sq. Ft.		1,400 Sq. Ft.		1,300 Sq. Ft.	
Basement & Finished Rooms Below Grade	full basement	full basement		full basement		full basement		full basement		full basement	
Functional Utility	adequate	adequate		adequate		adequate		adequate		adequate	
Heating/Cooling	central h/a	central h/a		central h/a		central h/a		central h/a		central h/a	
Garage/Carport	2-car att.	2-car att.		2-car att.		2-car att.		2-car att.		2-car att.	
Other Ext. Improvements	none	none		none		none		none		none	
Special Energy Efficient Items	none	none		none		none		none		none	
Fireplace(s)	none	none		none		none		none		none	
Other Int. Improvements	none	none		none		none		none		none	
Add'l Adj.		□+ □− $	12,000	□+ □− $		□+ □− $		□+ □− $		□+ □− $	
Adjusted Value		$	125,000	$		$		$		$	

Conclusion

The most obvious advantage of the sales comparison approach is its simplicity. It is easily understood by nonappraisers and preferred by the courts. Relying on past sales information, it gives the appearance of being the most logical and the most objective of the three approaches to estimating value. If reliable market data can be found and such information can be related to the subject property, the approach has considerable validity.

The principal limitation of the sales comparison approach is the problem of insufficient comparable sales or, even worse, a situation in which no comparable sales exist. If the subject is unique, or if there are no comparable sales available, then the approach cannot be used.

Another difficulty is the need for making accurate adjustments, since two properties are seldom identical. Adjustments cannot be based on subjective (what the appraiser "feels" is right) evaluations of the differences between properties or locations. Even under the best of circumstances, differences in value due to variations among properties may be difficult to measure. Beyond this, it also may be difficult to determine whether a particular transaction was a genuine arm's-length transaction or whether peculiar circumstances affected the transaction.

Above all, the appraiser must be keenly attuned to market conditions and trends. The sales comparison approach should not become a mechanical exercise. The appraiser must always question the reliability of sales data in light of economic, political and social market pressures.

Achievement Examination 4

At the conclusion of this three-part problem you will estimate the market value of a single-family residence.

1. First, determine the adjustment value for each of the significant variables by completing the Sales Price Adjustment Chart on the next page.

2. The subject property is a seven-room house with two baths and is situated on land 65 feet by 145 feet. The property is located in the central part of the neighborhood. The house is seven years old and is in good condition. Additional details on the subject property are listed on page 110. Using the adjustment values you computed above, complete the Comparable Sales Charts on pages 110 and 111.

3. In your opinion, what is the market value of the subject property? $_____

SALES PRICE ADJUSTMENT CHART

COMPARABLES

	1	2	3	4	5	6	7
SALES PRICE	$119,500	$123,000	$116,600	$122,500	$112,800	$116,300	$123,000
FINANCING	80% S/L	75% S/L	70% S/L	75% S/L	75% S/L	70% S/L	80% S/L
DATE OF SALE	2 mos. ago	3 wks. ago	1 yr. ago	2 wks. ago	1 mo. ago	5 wks. ago	3 wks. ago
LOCATION	quiet resid.	quiet resid.	quiet resid.	quiet resid.	quiet resid.	quiet resid.	quiet resid.
SITE/VIEW	good	good	good	good	good	good	good
SIZE OF LOT	65' × 145'	65' × 145'	65' × 145'	65' × 145'	65' × 145'	65' × 145'	65' × 145'
DESIGN AND APPEAL	split lvl/ good	split lvl/ good	split lvl/ good	split lvl/ good	split lvl/ good	split lvl/ good	split lvl/ good
CONSTRUCTION	brick	brick	brick	brick	brick	brick	brick
AGE	7 yrs.	6½ yrs.	6 yrs.	7½ yrs.	7 yrs.	7 yrs.	7 yrs.
CONDITION	good	good	good	fair to good	good	good	good
NO. OF RMS./BEDRMS./BATHS	7/3/2	7/3/2	7/3/2	7/3/2	7/3/2	7/3/2	7/3/2
SQ. FT. OF LIVING SPACE	1,600	1,600	1,600	1,575	1,575	1,575	1,590
OTHER SPACE (BASEMENT)	finished half-bsmt.	finished half-bsmt.	finished half-bsmt.	finished half-bsmt.	finished half-bsmt.	finished half-bsmt.	finished half-bsmt.
FUNCTIONAL UTILITY	adequate	adequate	adequate	adequate	adequate	adequate	adequate
HEATING/COOLING	central heat	central heat/air	central heat/air	central heat/air	central heat	central heat/air	central heat/air
GARAGE/CARPORT	2-car att.	2-car att.	2-car att.	2-car att.	none	none	2-car att.
OTHER EXT. IMPROVEMENTS	porch	porch	porch	porch	porch	porch	porch
SPECIAL ENERGY EFFICIENT ITEMS	none	none	none	none	none	none	none
FIREPLACE(S)	one/brick	one/brick	one/brick	one/brick	one/brick	one/brick	one/brick
OTHER INT. IMPROVEMENTS	none	none	none	none	none	none	none
TYPICAL HOUSE VALUE							
VARIABLE FEATURE							
ADJUSTMENT VALUE OF VARIABLE							

COMPARABLE SALES CHART

	SUBJECT	COMPARABLE NO. 1		COMPARABLE NO. 2		COMPARABLE NO. 3		COMPARABLE NO. 4		COMPARABLE NO. 5	
Address											
Proximity to Subject											
Sales Price		$		$		$		$		$	
Data Source											
VALUE ADJUSTMENTS	DESCRIPTION	DESCRIPTION	+(-)$ Adjustment	DESCRIPTION	+(-)$ Adjustment	DESCRIPTION	+(-)$ Adjustment	DESCRIPTION	+(-)$ Adjustment	DESCRIPTION	+(-)$ Adjustment
Sales or Financing Concessions	n/a										
Adjusted Value		$		$		$		$		$	
Date of Sale/Time											
Adjusted Value		$		$		$		$		$	
Location	quiet res.										
Site/View	good										
Design and Appeal	good										
Quality of Construction	gd./brick										
Age	7 yrs.										
Condition	good										
Above Grade Room Count	Total 7 | Bdrms 3 | Baths 2	Total | Bdrms | Baths		Total | Bdrms | Baths		Total | Bdrms | Baths		Total | Bdrms | Baths		Total | Bdrms | Baths	
Gross Living Area	1,600 Sq. Ft.	Sq. Ft.		Sq. Ft.		Sq. Ft.		Sq. Ft.		Sq. Ft.	
Basement & Finished Rooms Below Grade	finished half-bsmt.										
Functional Utility	adequate										
Heating/Cooling	central h/a										
Garage/Carport	none										
Other Ext. Improvements	porch										
Special Energy Efficient Items	none										
Fireplace(s)	one/brick										
Other Int. Improvements	none										
Add'l Adj.		□+ □- $		□+ □- $		□+ □- $		□+ □- $		□+ □- $	
Adjusted Value		$		$		$		$		$	

COMPARABLE SALES CHART

	SUBJECT	COMPARABLE NO. 6		COMPARABLE NO. 7					
Address									
Proximity to Subject									
Sales Price		$		$		$		$	
Data Source									
VALUE ADJUSTMENTS	DESCRIPTION	DESCRIPTION	+(-)$ Adjustment	DESCRIPTION	+(-)$ Adjustment	DESCRIPTION	+(-)$ Adjustment	DESCRIPTION	+(-)$ Adjustment
Sales or Financing Concessions									
Adjusted Value		$		$		$		$	
Date of Sale/Time									
Adjusted Value		$		$		$		$	
Location									
Site/View									
Design and Appeal									
Quality of Construction									
Age									
Condition									
Above Grade Room Count	Total | Bdrms | Baths	Total | Bdrms | Baths		Total | Bdrms | Baths		Total | Bdrms | Baths		Total | Bdrms | Baths	
Gross Living Area	Sq. Ft.	Sq. Ft.		Sq. Ft.		Sq. Ft.		Sq. Ft.	
Basement & Finished Rooms Below Grade									
Functional Utility									
Heating/Cooling									
Garage/Carport									
Other Ext. Improvements									
Special Energy Efficient Items									
Fireplace(s)									
Other Int. Improvements									
Add'l Adj.		□+ □- $		□+ □- $,		□+ □- $		□+ □- $	
Adjusted Value		$		$		$		$	

CHAPTER 5

Site Valuation

In most residential appraising, *site,* rather than *land,* is valued. As noted in Chapter 1, a site is land that is ready for its intended use and includes such improvements as grading, utilities and access.

The basic principles and techniques for site inspection, analysis and valuation are the same whether the site is vacant or improved with a house and/or other structures. Site valuation encompasses aspects of the sales comparison and income capitalization approaches to value and is an integral part of the cost approach to value.

Separate Site Valuations

As indicated above, an appraiser can estimate the value of a vacant site or of vacant land suitable for development into sites. The appraiser can also value a site separately from the improvements (structures) on it. The major reasons for separate valuations are reviewed below.

Cost approach. Use of the cost approach to value is a primary reason for a separate site valuation, since site value must be distinguished from the cost of improvements.

$$\frac{\text{Cost of}}{\text{Improvements New}} - \frac{\text{Depreciation on}}{\text{Improvements}} + \text{Site Value} = \text{Property Value}$$

It is necessary to realize that although utilities can be termed *improvements* in defining a site, in the cost approach improvements usually refer to structures.

Assessments and taxation. Assessments may require separate site valuations because they are usually based on improvements to the land itself (such as utilities) rather than on any structural changes. In the same way, most states require separate valuations of site and structures for ad valorem taxation purposes.

Because land is not considered a wasting asset, it does not depreciate. For income tax purposes, the property owner figures depreciation on structures only and thus needs to subtract the site value from the total property value.

Income capitalization.   In the income capitalization approach to finding property value, one method, called the *building residual technique* (covered in detail in Chapter 7), requires the appraiser to find land value separately. The appraiser then subtracts an appropriate return on this value from the net income earned by the property to produce an indication of the income available to the building.

Highest and best use.   The determination of the highest and best use of a property can be a very complex process. An appraiser may be asked to make a highest and best use report, which is a thorough analysis of this factor alone. In that case, the appraiser would be required to make a detailed projection of the feasibility and profitability of the entire range of uses to which the property could be put, with or without structures.

Of course, most urban and suburban land is zoned for a particular purpose. The few highly developed areas that do not have zoning (such as Houston, Texas) usually rely heavily on deed restrictions to limit density and kinds of development. Site approval and building permits may also be required. The appraiser must consider not only the most valuable present and/or prospective use of a site but also whether a zoning change or other approval necessary for a particular use is likely. Although many appraisals will be limited to present permitted land uses, occasionally the appraiser will be asked to make a broader recommendation. In that case, the appraisal should be qualified by noting those factors that might or might not preclude such a case.

Condemnation appraisals.   Courts and condemnors often require that the appraiser separate site and building values in eminent domain cases.

Exercise 5.1

The major reasons for valuing sites separately from buildings have been discussed. List as many of these reasons as you can.

Check your answers against those given in the Answer Key at the back of the book.

Site Data

Identification.   The first step in site analysis is to identify the property. A complete and legally accurate description of the site's location must be obtained. The plot plan should include the site's property line dimensions and show its location within a given block.

Analysis. Once the subject has been properly identified and described, it must be analyzed in detail. A report on the site's highest and best use should be an integral part of the analysis and should include the study of trends and factors influencing value, the data collection program and the physical measurement of the site. Important features of the site are its size, location in terms of position on the block, utilities, improvements and soil composition, especially as related to grading, septic system or bearing capacity for foundations.

Knowledge of the subject site's zoning, which will affect its future use, is necessary, as is knowledge of the current zoning of surrounding properties in the area.

Finally, easements, deed restrictions or publicly held rights-of-way should be noted. Any part of the site that cannot be used for building purposes should be clearly designated, along with other limitations on the use of the site.

Methods of Site Valuation

Five methods are commmonly used in appraising sites:

1. *Sales comparison method.* Sales of similar vacant sites are analyzed and compared. After adjustments are made, the appraiser arrives at an estimate of value for the subject site.
2. *Allocation method.* This method is used when the land value of an improved property must be found. The ratio of land value to building value typical of similar improved properties in the area is applied to the total value of the subject property to arrive at the land value of the subject.

3. *Subdivision development method.* The costs of developing and subdividing a parcel of land are subtracted from the total expected sales prices of the separate sites, adjusting for the time required to sell all of the individual sites, to determine the value of the undivided raw land.

4. *Land residual method.** The net income earned by the building is deducted from the total net income of the property; the balance is earned by the land. The residual or leftover income is then capitalized to indicate the land value. The formula used for this method is:

Property Net Income − Building Net Income = Land Net Income

Land Net Income ÷ Land Capitalization Rate = Land Value

5. *Ground rent capitalization.** When a landowner leases land to a tenant who agrees to erect a building on it, the lease is usually referred to as a *ground* lease. Ground rents can be capitalized at an appropriate rate to indicate the market value of the site. For example, assume that a site is on a long-term lease with a ground rent of $100,000 per year. If the appropriate rate for capitalization of ground rent is 10 percent, the estimated value by direct capitalization is:

$$\$100,000 \div .10 = \$1,000,000$$

Sales comparison method.   There are no basic differences between the data valuation of improved properties and unimproved sites in the sales comparison method. Since sales comparison analysis and valuation have been discussed and illustrated in detail in Chapter 4, the basic points are simply reviewed here.

The sales comparison approach is the most reliable method of site valuation. Just as the value of a used house is estimated by the most recent sales prices of comparable houses in the neighborhood, the value of a site is judged largely by the same *comparison* method.

The appraiser's objective is to find the probable market value of the property being appraised by interpreting the data from sales of similar properties. Since no two parcels of land are identical, there will be differences to compensate for when the appraiser compares sales properties to the subject property. Typical differences include *date of sale, location, physical characteristics, zoning and land-use restrictions, terms of financing* and *conditions of sale.*

The adjustment process is an analysis designed to eliminate the effect on value of these differences. Each comparable property is likened as much as possible to the subject property. In adjusting the sales

---

*Since a comprehensive treatment of the residual techniques and the capitalization process is contained in Chapter 7, "The Income Capitalization Approach," these methods of site valuation will not be covered here.

price of a comparable property, lump-sum dollar amounts or percentages customarily are used. Adjustments are always applied to the sales price of the comparable property, *not* the value of the subject property. If the comparable property is inferior in some respect to the subject property, its sales price is increased by an appropriate dollar amount or percentage. If the comparable property is superior in some category, its sales price is decreased. The adjustment process, then, uses the modified sales prices of comparable properties in estimating the value of the subject property.

Exercise 5.2

Assume that a residential lot, 75 feet by 150 feet, sold one year ago for $20,000. In analyzing the market, you arrive at the following conclusions:

1. The subject is 12 percent or $2,400 more valuable as a result of price increases over the year since the comparable site was sold.
2. The subject site is 10 percent or $2,000 more valuable than the comparable site with respect to location.
3. The subject site is 15 percent or $3,000 less valuable with respect to physical features.

Complete the adjustment table below:

	Sales Price	Date	Location	Physical Features	Net Adj. + Or −	Adjusted Price
Dollar basis						
Percentage basis						

Check your answers against those given in the Answer Key at the back of the book.

Allocation method.   Land value may be treated as a percentage or proportion of the total value of an improved property. In many areas, land and building values have historically held a certain relationship to each other. If the approximate ratio of land value to building value is typically one to four, for instance, and a property improved with a structure is valued at $100,000, the land value is 1/5 of that amount, or $20,000. Part of the total property value is thus *allocated* to the site and part to the improvements.

Obviously, the allocation method is weak because it fails to take individual property differences into account. This method should be used only in situations where there is a lack of current sales data for vacant sites that are similar to and competitive with the subject site. It may also be useful as a gross check of an appraisal by another method.

Exercise 5.3

In a high-income suburban residential area, the ratio of building value to land value approximates three to one. What is the land value of a typical property valued at $147,000, using the allocation method?

Check your answer against the one given in the Answer Key at the back of the book.

Subdivision development method.   The *subdivision development method* is used to value a large tract when limited large land sales exist, but sales data on finished lots are available. The value of land with a highest and best use as a multiunit development may be found using this method by computing all probable costs of development, including the developer's profit and cost of financing, and subtracting those costs from the total projected sales prices of the individual units.

EXAMPLE: A 40-acre subdivision is expected to yield 160 single-family homesites after allowances for streets, common areas and so on. Each site should have an ultimate market value of $30,000 so that the projected sales figure for all the lots is $4,800,000 (160 × $30,000).

Based on an analysis of comparable land sales, it is concluded that lots can be sold at the rate of 60 in year 1, 70 in year 2, and 30 in year 3.

Engineers advise that the cost of installing streets, sewers, water and other improvements will be $10,000 per lot. Other costs (sales expenses, administration, accounting, legal, taxes, overhead, etc.) are estimated at 20 percent and developer's profit at 10 percent of gross lot sales.

Problem: Assume that the highest and best use of the land is for subdivision development and that there is an active demand for homesites. What price should a developer pay for this acreage based on a sales program taking three years to complete?

Solution:

Total projected sales:		
160 lots at $30,000 per lot		$4,800,000
Total projected development costs:		
Street grading and paving, sidewalks, curbs, gutters, sanitary and storm sewers for 160 lots at $10,000 per lot	$1,600,000	
Other costs, 20 percent of $4,800,000 (total projected sales)	960,000	
Developer's profit, 10 percent of $4,800,000 (total projected sales)	480,000	
Total development costs		3,040,000
Estimated value of raw land		$1,760,000
Raw land value per lot, $1,760,000 ÷ 160		$ 11,000

The amount that a developer should pay now in anticipation of the land's future value is computed by applying a reversion factor to its present estimated value undeveloped. The table on page 273 lists the computed factors at specified interest rates for an investment term of one to forty years. This table allows you to compute the time value of money—from some point in the future backward to the present time. In essence you are taking a sum of money to be paid later and *discounting* it, or subtracting from it, the compound interest it would earn from the present time until the time when it is to be paid. By this process of discounting, you can find out what its value is today.

In the example problem, the developer's expected yield of 10 percent discounted to present worth for one year gives a reversion factor of .909; two years, a reversion factor of .826; and three years, a reversion factor of .751.

The present worth of lot sales is thus computed:

First year:	60 lots at $11,000 per lot = $660,000	
	$660,000 discounted to present worth at 10% for one year (.909)	$599,940
Second year:	70 lots at $11,000 per lot = $770,000	
	$770,000 discounted to present worth for two years (.826)	636,020
Third year:	30 lots at $11,000 per lot = $330,000	
	$330,000 discounted to present worth for three years (.751)	247,830
	Present value of $1,760,000 discounted partially 1, 2 and 3 years	$1,483,790

In this oversimplified example, a developer would be justified in paying $1,483,790 for the raw land for subdivision purposes.

Exercise 5.4

The following building costs have been predicted for a 72-unit residential subdivision planned to utilize a 30-acre tract:

Engineering and surveying	$ 23,000
Roads	117,000
Grading and leveling all sites	46,000
Utilities	129,000
Marketing	72,000
Financing	182,000
Taxes	47,000
Administration, accounting and other professional services	118,000
Developer's profit	200,000

Projected sales figures for the lots are:

48 lots at $27,000 each, discounted to present worth at 12 percent for one year (factor: .893)

16 lots at $32,000 each, discounted to present worth at 12 percent for two years (factor: .797)

8 lots at $36,000 each, discounted to present worth at 12 percent for three years (factor: .712)

(The higher lot prices reflect expected price increases over time.)

Estimate the market value of the raw acreage using the subdivision development method.

Determine how much a subdivider would be justified in paying for the raw land for development.

Conclusion

Appraisers are frequently called on to value sites, whether improved or unimproved. In determining the highest and best use of a property, for instance, the site itself is the prime consideration; its most profitable use, which may not be its present use, is found.

The appraiser can choose among a variety of site valuation methods, making use of sales of comparable sites (sales comparison method), income streams (land residual method), costs of development compared to projected sales income (subdivision development method), site-to-building value ratios (allocation method) or conversion of ground rents into a present worth estimate through the capitalization process (ground rent capitalization method).

Achievement Examination 5

1. Explain how the terms *land* and *site* differ.

2. Why would an appraiser need to know site valuation:

    a. in the cost approach?

    b. for assessments?

3. Name five site valuation techniques.

    Which method is preferred, and why?

Check your answers against those given in the Answer Key at the back of the book.

CHAPTER 6

The Cost Approach

In the cost approach to appraising, the present cost of constructing all of the improvements on a site, less their loss in value due to depreciation, is added to the value of the site as if vacant, to determine property value. The basic principle involved is that of *substitution*. The cost of a new building is substituted for that of the existing one, with some adjustment to compensate for depreciation of the existing building due to general deterioration and other factors. The appraiser will find the cost to build either a structure that is identical in design and material to the subject (reproduction cost), or a structure that has the same utility as the subject (replacement cost). The formula for the cost approach is:

$$\text{Reproduction or Replacement Cost of Improvement(s)} - \text{Accrued Depreciation} + \text{Site Value} = \text{Property Value}$$

One drawback to the cost approach is that the value of a new structure is presumed to be equal to its cost. This may not be true if the structure does not represent the highest and best use of the site. In other words, the value of an inappropriate structure, such as a large hotel on a little-traveled backroad, may not equal the cost to build it.

Another drawback to the cost approach, particularly with regard to appraising single-family residences, is that builders' costs may vary greatly depending on the number of units produced and the individual builder's profit margin. Ultimately, the appraiser may have to make market comparisons of builders' costs in the same way that selling prices are compared.

Because land alone is rarely considered a *wasting* (depreciating) asset, the cost approach is not generally used in estimating site value. Site value, as the last part of the cost approach equation, is computed by the sales comparison approach, as explained in the previous chapter. The location and improvements of the subject site (except for buildings) are compared to those of similar nearby sites. Adjustments are made for any significant differences, and the adjusted prices of the properties most like the subject site are used to estimate the value of the subject site.

The cost approach involves the addition of building and site values, each computed separately; thus it is also called the *summation* method of appraising.

In this chapter, the distinction between replacement cost and reproduction cost will be explained, and the methods of computing building cost and the different types of depreciation will be analyzed. Refer to the Construction Glossary as needed.

Reproduction Cost Versus Replacement Cost

Reproduction cost is the dollar amount required to construct an exact duplicate of the subject building, at current prices. The *replacement cost* of the subject building is the current construction cost of a building having the same utility; that is, one that can be used in the same way.

In most cases, the reproduction cost of the subject building is used to find the estimate of value by the cost approach. Determining the price of constructing an identical new property is not always feasible, however. The exacting details of workmanship present in an older home may make it impossible to duplicate today at a reasonable price. So a home with the same number, type and size of rooms would be used to find the replacement cost, rather than the reproduction cost, of the subject property.

The building cost, whether reproduction or replacement, will be for a *new* building, at current prices. The condition of the building at the time of the appraisal is not a factor at this point. Building cost is a measure of the quality of the building in terms of how expensive it would be to rebuild or replace and is not a measure of the building's condition. An allowance for the condition of the subject building, as well as any other adverse influences, is made when accrued depreciation is subtracted in the second part of the cost approach equation.

Exercise 6.1

Replacement costing (rather than reproduction costing) would likely be used in valuing which house shown on page 125? Why?

Check your answers against those given in the Answer Key at the back of the book.

Finding Reproduction Cost

The appraiser using the cost approach will compute the cost to construct a building, whether it is the subject building or its functionally identical replacement. There are four methods for finding the reproduction cost of a building:

1. *Index method.* A factor representing the percentage increase to the present time of construction costs is applied to the original cost of the subject property.
2. *Square foot method.* The cost per square foot of a recently built comparable structure is multiplied by the number of square feet in the subject property.
3. *Unit-in-place method.* The construction cost per unit of measure of each component part of the subject building (including material, labor, overhead and builder's profit) is multiplied by the number of units of that component part in the subject building. Most components will be measured in square feet although certain items, such as plumbing fixtures, will be estimated as complete units.
4. *Quantity survey method.* The itemized costs of erecting or installing all of the component parts of a new building are added. Indirect costs (building permit, land survey, overhead expenses such as insurance and payroll taxes, and builder's profit) are totaled, as well as direct costs (site preparation and all phases of building construction, including fixtures).

The quantity survey method is the one generally used by cost estimators, contractors and builders because it yields the most accurate cost estimate, since *all* of the building's components are analyzed. This method, as well as the unit-in-place method, can be quite accurate when used by qualified cost estimators although both are more time consuming than the square foot method. The index method is rarely used alone because it fails to take into account the many specific differences between structures; however, it may be useful for double-checking a figure arrived at by one of the other methods.

Index Method

Although the *index method* of finding reproduction cost is rarely accurate enough to be used alone, it may serve as a useful way of verifying cost figures arrived at by one of the other methods if the original construction cost of the improvements is known. Cost reporting or indexing services keep records of building cost changes over time, and sometimes from area to area. All dollar amounts are given a numerical factor relative to whatever base year is being used. By comparing the current cost index with the cost index at the time construction took place and then applying that factor to the original construction cost, an estimate of current cost can be derived. The formula used is:

$$\frac{\text{Present Index}}{\text{Index at Time of Construction}} \times \text{Original Cost} = \text{Present Cost}$$

EXAMPLE: An office building constructed in 1978 for $149,000 had a cost index at that time of 177. The present cost index is 354. Using the formula:

$$\frac{354}{177} \times \$149{,}000 = \$298{,}000$$

In the example above, $298,000 is the estimated reproduction cost of the subject building. Using cost indexes successfully obviously requires that the building cost of the subject property be fairly typical; any additions or changes to the original structure would have to be taken into consideration. If a building or one of its components is fairly standard, however, the method can be useful.

Exercise 6.2

The Jones residence cost $39,000 to construct in 1975. A cost index published at that time was 158.2. The current cost index from the same cost reporting service is 537.8. What is the current reproduction cost of the Jones residence?

Check your answer against the one given in the Answer Key at the back of the book.

Square Foot Method

To begin the *square foot method* of estimating reproduction cost, the appraiser must find the dimensions of the subject building to compute the number of square feet of ground area the building covers. In collecting cost data for the square foot method, the appraiser must find the cost of comparable new buildings. The appraiser may also rely on *cost manuals* (such as those published by Boeckh Publications, F. W. Dodge Corporation, Marshall and Swift Publication Company and R. S. Means Company) for basic construction costs. Cost manuals, which give building specifications and typical construction costs, are usually updated quarterly, sometimes even monthly. Some cost estimating services make their data available on computer software for ease and efficiency of use. Some even offer direct computer linkup to their data base via telephone modem.

A sample page from a cost manual is reproduced in Figure 6.1. The type of building is specified (in Figure 6.1, the building includes both factory and office space), and its dimensions are given. Construction features are itemized, with utilities (mechanical features) listed separately. Because office and factory spaces have dissimilar features (such as windows and wall height), their costs have been listed separately. Because the appraiser is interested only in the cost per square foot of a particular type and construction of building, the total cost of the example building is not given. If the closest example in the cost manual still has significant differences from the subject building, a cost differential could be added to (or subtracted from) the cost per square foot given in the cost manual. Although cost estimates of high-ceilinged structures may utilize the *cubic foot method* of estimating reproduction cost, a height adjustment made to the figure arrived at by the square foot method is usually sufficient.

EXAMPLE: The following floor plan is that of a factory building with contiguous office space that approximates the example building shown in Figure 6.1. There are no significant differences between the buildings.

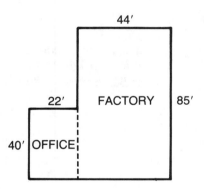

The area of the office space is 22' × 40', or 880 square feet; the area of the factory space is 44' × 85', or 3,740 square feet. Approximately 20% of floor area is thus office space, making this building comparable to the example, which has 22% office space. The reproduction cost of the office space is 880 square feet × $70.65 or $62,172. The reproduction cost of the factory space is 3,740 square feet × $38.05, or $142,307. The total estimate of the reproduction cost for the subject building is $62,172 + $142,307, or $204,479. If this building differed from the base building in the manual, height, perimeter or other extra adjustments to the estimate of reproduction cost would be necessary.

Regional multipliers.   Even with frequent updating, there may be a considerable time lapse between the appraisal date of a property and the publication date of a cost manual; therefore, the appraiser using the cost manual should keep informed of price increases in the area. Some cost manuals meant for national use have *regional multipliers,* so that a given example can be used for any area of the coun-

FIGURE 6.1   Typical Page from a Cost Manual

FACTORY AND OFFICE

One Story Brick and Concrete Block Building. Size—50′ × 79′

FOUNDATION—Concrete walls, footings and piers.

WALLS—158 L/F 8″ concrete block, 10′ high, continuous steel sash windows, 8′ high, including gutters and downspouts.

100 L/F 8″ concrete block, 20′ high, including 50 L/F 4″ brick veneer front, 10′ high, stone coping.

FLOOR—Concrete.

ROOF—Flat, tar and gravel roofing, insulated, steel decking, steel bar joists, beams and columns.

MECHANICAL FEATURES

Electric—Pipe conduit wiring, metal reflectors.

Heating—Gas unit heaters.

Plumbing—3 water closets, 3 lavatories, 1 urinal, 1 water heater.

Sprinkler—None.

OTHER FEATURES—Miscellaneous steel crane girders on building columns. One Story Brick Office Addition—22′ × 50′ × 10′ high.

Office—Cost per Square Foot of Ground Area $70.65
Factory—Cost per Square Foot of Ground Area $38.05

try, provided the cost estimate obtained is multiplied by the adjustment factor for that locality.

Residential appraisals.   The widespread use of the appraisal report forms prepared by the Federal Home Loan Mortgage Corporation (FHLMC) and Federal National Mortgage Association (FNMA) has made the square foot method of calculating reproduction cost a commonly used technique for residences. The Uniform Residential Appraisal Report (URAR) form appears on pages 238 and 239.

With the URAR form, gross living area (derived by using the outside measurements of the house, less nonliving areas) is multiplied by cost per square foot. That figure is then added to the cost of nonliving areas and other improvements, such as garage and patio, to arrive at the total estimated cost new of all improvements.

EXAMPLE: The Smith residence is being appraised. The house has 1,800 square feet of living area, based on exterior building measurements. Current construction cost is $73 per square foot. Garage space of 550 square feet has a current construction cost of $25 per square foot. The house has a patio valued at $1,500. Other site improvements, including a driveway and landscaping, are valued at $8,500. What is the reproduction cost of the Smith property?

The improvements have a present reproduction cost new of $131,400 (1,800 × $73) plus $13,750 (550 × $25) plus $1,500 plus $8,500, for a total of $155,150.

Exercise 6.3

The drawing below shows the perimeter of a residence you are appraising.

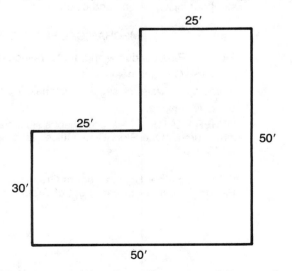

A residence of similar construction, 45 feet by 50 feet and in the same area, was recently completed at a cost of $184,500. What is your cost estimate of the subject building?

Check your answer against the one given in the Answer Key at the back of the book.

Unit-in-Place Method

In the *unit-in-place method* of estimating building reproduction cost, the costs of the various components of the subject building are estimated separately, then added together to find the total building cost. All of the components are itemized, each is measured where necessary and the current construction cost per unit of measure of each component is multiplied by the number of measured units of that component in the subject building.

The unit-in-place method provides a much more detailed breakdown of the type of building being appraised than does the square foot method. As such, it is much more time consuming but likely to be more accurate than the square foot method. As with the square foot method, the unit-in-place method relies on cost manuals, with some allowances made (if necessary) for regional differences or recent cost increases.

A detailed breakdown of residential building costs (such as that provided in the publications of the Marshall and Swift Company) typically will include the following building components:

foundation	interior construction
floor structure	heating and cooling system
floor covering	electrical system
exterior walls	plumbing
gable roof	fireplace(s)
ceiling	appliances
roof structure and covering	stairway
roof dormers	

If the costs for an industrial building were to be found in a cost manual, they might be given as shown in Table 6.1. Appendix C also shows how cost figures may be broken down. *Note: Prices shown are for illustration purposes only.*

EXAMPLE: Using the cost data in Table 6.1, we will compute the reproduction cost of the industrial building shown on the next page with adjacent 50′ × 125′ parking area. The following items will be costed separately, then totaled to find the reproduction cost of the subject building: concrete, foundation, roof, exterior walls, building frame, interior construction, floor, electrical, heating and A/C, plumbing and parking area. *Later in this chapter, you will be asked to analyze and appraise a similar type of property, so study this example carefully.*

Foundation: The measured unit used for computing the construction cost of the foundation is the *linear foot,* which is a measurement of length, in this case the perimeter of the building. So,

$$100' + 125' + 100' + 125' = 450'$$

Since the cost is $30.70 per linear foot,

$$450 \text{ ft.} \times \$30.70 = \$13,815$$

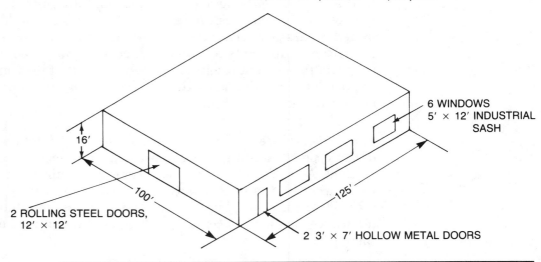

6 WINDOWS
5' × 12' INDUSTRIAL
SASH

16'

100'

125'

2 ROLLING STEEL DOORS,
12' × 12'

2 3' × 7' HOLLOW METAL DOORS

TABLE 6.1   Cost Data

Component	Cost Per Measured Unit
Foundation 12″ concrete wall and footings	$ 30.70 per linear foot
Floor Construction 8″ reinforced concrete	3.60 per sq. ft. of floor area
Framing 14′ steel columns, beams and purlins	4.50 per sq. ft. of support area

Roof Construction
    sheathing, 2″ polystyrene insulation,
    4-ply asphalt and gravel covering
	3.70 per sq. ft.

Exterior Walls 12″ concrete block backup	10.20 per sq. ft.
Windows industrial sash, steel, 50% vented	14.20 per sq. ft.

Doors
    hollow metal, 3′ × 7′
    rolling steel, chain hoist operated, 12′ × 12′
	355.00 per door
	1,435.00 per door

Interior painting	.35 per sq. ft.
Electrical wiring and fixtures	3.10 per sq. ft. of building area
Heating and A/C	5.30 per sq. ft. of building area
Plumbing including fixtures	2.25 per sq. ft. of building area
Parking Area 3″ asphalt on 3″ stone base	7.20 per sq. yd.

Frame: The space occupied by the steel frame is measured in square feet of support area. The subject building has bearing walls without steel columns, which support part of the roof area, so that part must be subtracted from the total roof area. The roof area supported by bearing walls is considered to be halfway to the nearest frame columns. The frame columns of the subject building, as shown in the following illustration, are 25 feet apart; thus 12½ feet will be subtracted from each side dimension to find the roof area supported by the frame columns. In the illustration, the area supported by bearing walls is shaded, and the area supported by the steel frame is not shaded.

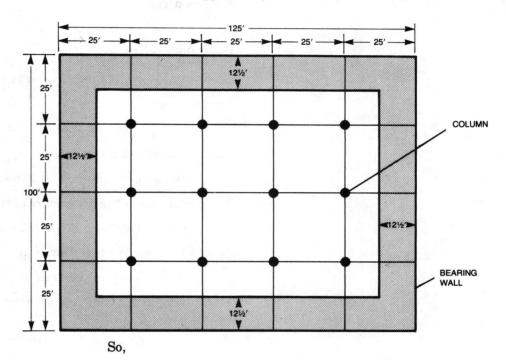

So,

$$100' - (12\tfrac{1}{2}' + 12\tfrac{1}{2}') = 100' - 25' = 75'$$
$$125' - (12\tfrac{1}{2}' + 12\tfrac{1}{2}') = 125' - 25' = 100'$$
$$75' \times 100' = 7{,}500 \text{ sq. ft.}$$

The area supported by frame columns is multiplied by the cost of the steel frame, which is $4.50 per square foot.

$$7{,}500 \times \$4.50 = \$33{,}750$$

Floor: The floor is measured in square feet, so

$$100' \times 125' = 12{,}500 \text{ sq. ft.}$$

Since the cost is $3.60 per square foot,

$$12{,}500 \text{ sq. ft.} \times \$3.60 = \$45{,}000$$

Roof: The roof is to be measured in square feet, so

$$100' \times 125' = 12{,}500 \text{ sq. ft.}$$

Since the cost is $3.70 per square foot,

$$12{,}500 \text{ sq. ft.} \times \$3.70 = \$46{,}250$$

Exterior Walls: The walls are measured in square feet, but window and door areas must be subtracted. Per window,

$$5' \times 12' = 60 \text{ sq. ft.}$$

For six windows,

$$60 \text{ sq. ft.} \times 6 = 360 \text{ sq. ft.}$$

Per hollow metal door,

$$3' \times 7' = 21 \text{ sq. ft.}$$

For two doors,

$$21 \text{ sq. ft.} \times 2 = 42 \text{ sq. ft.}$$

Per rolling steel door,

$$12' \times 12' = 144 \text{ sq. ft.}$$

For two doors,

$$144 \text{ sq. ft.} \times 2 = 288 \text{ sq. ft.}$$

Total window and door area is

$$360 \text{ sq. ft.} + 42 \text{ sq. ft.} + 288 \text{ sq. ft.} = 690 \text{ sq. ft.}$$

Total area within the perimeters of the walls is

$$(16' \times 100' \times 2 \text{ walls}) + (16' \times 125' \times 2 \text{ walls}) = 7,200 \text{ sq. ft.}$$

Subtracting window and door areas,

$$7,200 \text{ sq. ft.} - 690 \text{ sq. ft.} = 6,510 \text{ sq. ft.}$$

Multiplying the remaining area by the cost of $10.20 per square foot,

$$6,510 \text{ sq. ft.} \times \$10.20 = \$66,402$$

Windows: Total window area, as computed above, is 360 square feet. At $14.20 per square foot,

$$360 \text{ sq. ft.} \times \$14.20 = \$5,112$$

Doors: There are two $3' \times 7'$ hollow metal doors. At $355 per door,

$$2 \text{ doors} \times \$355 = \$710$$

There are two $12' \times 12'$ rolling steel doors. At $1,425 per door,

$$2 \text{ doors} \times \$1,425 = \$2,850$$

Total cost, for all doors, is

$$\$710 + \$2,850 = \$3,560$$

Interior: Interior wall space, subtracting door and window areas, would be the same as exterior wall space, or 6,510 square feet. At a cost of $.35 per square foot for painting,

$$6,510 \text{ sq. ft.} \times \$.35 = \$2,279$$

Electrical: Necessary electrical wiring and lighting fixtures for standard industrial illumination are measured per square foot of floor space. Since there are 12,500 square feet of floor space (as measured earlier), at $3.10 per square foot.

$$12,500 \text{ sq. ft.} \times \$3.10 = \$38,750$$

Heating and A/C: Measured per square foot of area served, in this case, the entire floor area. At $5.30 per square foot,

$$12,500 \text{ sq. ft.} \times \$5.30 = \$66,250$$

Plumbing: The cost of plumbing, including standard fixtures, is measured in square feet of building area. At $2.25 per square foot,

$$12,500 \text{ sq. ft.} \times \$2.25 = \$28,125$$

Parking Area: The parking area adjacent to the building is illustrated below.

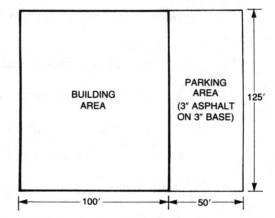

The cost of asphalt paving is measured in square yards, so,

$$125' \times 50' = 6,250 \text{ sq. ft.}$$
$$6,250 \text{ sq. ft.} \div 9 = 694.4 \text{ sq. yd.}$$

At a cost of $7.20 per square yard for 3″ asphalt paving on a 3″ stone base,

$$694.4 \text{ sq. yd.} \times \$7.20 = \$5,000$$

In our example cost analysis, no adjustments are necessary to allow for price increases since the cost data were compiled. Add all costs to arrive at the total reproduction cost of all improvements:

Foundation	$ 13,815
Frame	33,750
Floor	45,000
Roof	46,250
Exterior Walls	66,402
Windows	5,112
Doors	3,560
Interior	2,279
Electrical	38,750
Heating and A/C	66,250
Plumbing	28,125
Parking Area	5,000
	$354,293

The reproduction cost of the improvements on the subject property is $354,293. If this problem were to be carried through to find the market value estimate by the cost approach, the value of any depreciation on the improvements would have to be subtracted from the reproduction cost and the resultant figure added to the land value.

Exercise 6.4

Based on the following unit-in-place costs, what is the reproduction cost estimate of a rectangular warehouse, 125′ by 250′?

Foundation: concrete walls and footings at $37.30 per linear foot

Floor: reinforced concrete at $3.10 per sq. ft.

Roof: built-up tar and gravel at $2.40 per sq. ft.; roof sheathing at $.65 per sq. ft.; fiberboard insulation at $.55 per sq. ft.

Interior construction: painting and some partitions, at total cost of $4,500

Front exterior wall: common brick on concrete block, 125′ long by 15′ high, at $9.50 per sq. ft.; 2 windows, each 6′ by 12′, at $15.30 per sq. ft.; 10′ by 12′ drive-in door at a total cost of $1,300

Rear exterior wall: same as front wall with drive-in door, but no windows

Side exterior walls: concrete block, 250′ long by 15′ high, at $7.10 per sq. ft.; windows covering about 20 percent of wall area at $14.20 per sq. ft.

Steel framing: area supported by frame, 100′ by 225′; with 14′ eave height, at $4.50 per sq. ft.

Electrical: $3.25 per sq. ft. of floor area

Heating: $2.75 per sq. ft. of floor area

Plumbing: $1.60 per sq. ft. of floor area

Check your answer against the one given in the Answer Key at the back of the book.

Quantity Survey Method

A builder or contractor estimating construction cost will need precise, up-to-date cost figures. Such an estimate usually is made by the *quantity survey method,* which necessitates a thorough itemization of all the costs expected in the construction of the building. *Direct* costs (those related to materials and labor) are computed much more precisely than in the unit-in-place method. Every stage of construction is broken down into separate costs for materials and labor. The required expenditure for the electrical system, for instance, will take into account both the cost of materials at an estimated price per unit and the cost of labor for the required number of hours at the going rate per hour. Thus the appraiser must be able to estimate material unit quantities and costs as well as work times and labor rates. *Indirect* costs (those involved in necessary, but not construction-related expenses, such as surveys, payroll taxes and profit) are also added. A typical cost itemization for a 14-unit apartment building, using the quantity survey method, could include the following totals for the separate building components:

Direct Costs

Clearing the land	$ 723
Rough and fine grading	16,753
Footings	8,760
Slabs	8,341
Entrance and stoops	4,200
Balconies	12,350
Interior stairs	575
Dampproofing	938
Rough and finished carpentry	127,390
Furring	3,480
Doors	3,560
Rough and finished hardware	11,722
Kitchen cabinets	14,250
Flooring	18,764
Refrigerators	11,920
Disposals	2,330
Gas ranges	7,386
Venetian blinds	4,800
Bathroom tile	7,297
Painting	13,750
Insulation	1,070
Glazing	2,483
Structural steel and lintels	4,747
Ornamental iron	8,190
Masonry	79,423
Drywall	35,961
Heating and air-conditioning	39,467
Plumbing	44,200
Electrical wiring	21,870

Water mains	4,102
Water and sewer connections	790
Roofing and sheet metal	6,200
Incidentals	9,340
Cleaning, general and contract	5,900
Landscaping	7,450
Fence	1,800
Temporary utilities	4,728
Temporary roads and structures	2,857
Streets, parking area, sidewalks, curbs and gutters	33,689
Sanitary and storm sewers	15,042
Supervision and time-keeping	21,785
	$630,383

Indirect Costs

Permit	$ 35
Survey	1,980
Layout	465
Payroll taxes and insurance	8,570
Builder's overhead and profit	64,000
	$ 75,050
Total Cost	$705,433

An appraiser using the quantity survey method obviously needs a much more comprehensive knowledge of building construction than he or she would using the square foot or unit-in-place method. The appraiser must know every facet of building construction—almost as well as the builder.

Accrued Depreciation

In the second part of the cost approach equation, depreciation is subtracted from building reproduction or replacement cost.

Depreciation may be defined as any loss in value from original construction cost. The loss in value may come from wear and tear or the presence of features that are deficient, excessive or simply currently undesirable. There also may be external factors that cause a loss in value. *Accrued depreciation* is the total depreciation from time of construction to the date of appraisal due to all causes.

Generally, there are three categories of depreciation. A particular item of depreciation could fit within two categories, and more than one form of depreciation may be present in the same building. The three categories of depreciation are:

1. *Physical deterioration*. This is the physical wearing out of the structure, usually the most obvious form of depreciation. If a building needs painting or tuckpointing or has broken windows, cracked

plaster or water-damaged walls from a leaky roof, these are all the ordinary effects of wear and tear.

2. *Functional obsolescence.* This results when layout, design or other features are undesirable in comparison with features designed for the same functions in newer property. Functional obsolescence can be the result of a deficiency, the presence of a feature that should be replaced or modernized, or the presence of a feature that is superfluous (superadequate) for the building's intended purpose. A two-story, five-bedroom house with one bathroom and only one of the bedrooms on the first floor and no bathroom on the second floor, would be functionally undesirable; the same house might still be functionally undesirable if it had a second bathroom on the first floor and none on the second floor. Functional obsolescence depends on the changing requirements of homebuyers. When family rooms came into great demand, many homes were built with little or no dining room space, to allow for a family room at no major cost increase. In some areas, however, dining rooms and family rooms are both desirable, and a "formal" (separate) dining room may be a valuable feature.

3. *External obsolescence* (also called *environmental, economic* or *locational obsolescence*). This is loss of value from causes outside the property itself. Zoning changes, proximity to nuisances, changes in land use and market conditions can all be causes of external obsolescence. If a drive-in restaurant is constructed on a vacant lot, an adjacent residential property will probably lose value because of the increased noise and traffic.

Depreciation is the most difficult part of the cost approach equation to compute accurately. The older the building, the more likely it is to have deteriorated to a marked degree, often in ways not easily observable (such as corroded plumbing lines or cracked plaster hidden by wallpaper or paneling). Physical deterioration begins the moment a building is constructed and continues until the building is no longer usable.

Every building has an *economic life,* also called its *useful life,* during which it will be functionally useful for its original intended purpose. When a building no longer can be used, it ceases to serve any profitable purpose. At that point, the value of the building site is no higher *with* the building than it would be without it. In some cases, the existence of a building may make a site *less* valuable because the cost of demolition and removal of the structure must be taken into account.

A building's economic life may or may not coincide with its *physical life,* which is the length of time it could physically exist if allowed to remain standing. Most buildings that are torn down are not totally derelict but have instead become uneconomic (unprofitable) in terms of the highest and best use of the site they occupy.

A building's *effective age* reflects the quality of its construction and the degree of maintenance it has received. Any building will suffer some physical defect eventually, whether from the elements or from the way in which it is used. Those defects will have a greater effect on a poorly constructed building. If necessary maintenance and repairs are not accomplished, the process of deterioration is enhanced, and the physical life of the building is shortened. On the other hand, a well-constructed and well-maintained building will benefit from a prolonged physical life.

Effective age will be greater or less than chronological age when the building's condition differs significantly from that of average buildings in the area. This is often the case with single-family residences, where maintenance (or the lack of it) can be conspicuous.

EXAMPLE: The Smith residence was constructed 20 years ago. The Smiths have maintained their home in excellent condition, including repainting the exterior several times and remodeling the kitchen. The average home in the Smiths' neighborhood is adequately maintained but not as well as the Smith home. The Smith residence thus has an effective age of only 15 years.

The *remaining economic life* of a building is the period from the date of appraisal during which it can be expected to remain useful for its original intended purpose. In determining that period, the appraiser must consider not only the present condition of the building but also other known factors that might affect its future use or desirability, such as the use or condition of nearby property. The houses adjacent to a shopping mall may suffer from increased traffic noise, fumes and congestion. Over time, those houses may be sold more frequently and receive less investment in upkeep and repairs than others in the same neighborhood but not as close to the shopping area.

By depreciating a building's cost, the appraiser takes into account the probable past and future effects of the building's economic life, considering both its condition and outside factors.

Depreciation can be measured either directly or indirectly. The economic age-life method and observed condition method measure depreciation directly. The capitalized value and sales comparison methods measure depreciation indirectly.

Economic Age-Life Method

The *economic age-life* method of computing depreciation (also called the *straight-line* method) is the simplest to understand and use. It is based on the assumption that depreciation occurs at an even rate throughout the economic life of a building. The economic life of the building is first estimated. If a graph is constructed with a building's cost as one axis and its years of economic life as the other axis, the line connecting the two would be a straight line. Any point on the line would indicate the building's remaining value after the given number of years have elapsed. After 30 years, for instance, the graph shown as Figure 6.2 indicates that the building's remaining value is $40,000; thus the building has depreciated $40,000 ($80,000 − $40,000), or $1,333 per year ($40,000 ÷ 30 years).

The appraiser does not have to draw a graph to find the given depreciation for any one year, however. The yearly percentage of cost lost through accrued depreciation is found by dividing, as shown below.

$$\frac{1}{\text{Number of Years of Economic Life}}$$

FIGURE 6.2   Economic Age-Life Depreciation

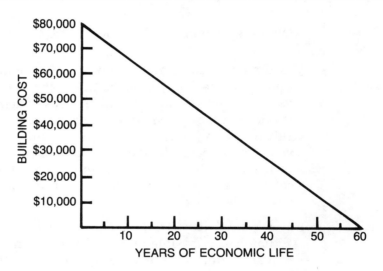

A decimal figure, which may be converted to a percentage, results from this equation. This percentage is the *accrued depreciation rate*. The depreciation rate is multiplied by the effective age of the building in years to find the total percentage of past or accrued depreciation. The building cost is multiplied by this percentage to find the dollar amount of depreciation, which then can be applied to the cost approach formula.

EXAMPLE: The reproduction cost of a commercial building is estimated to be $800,000. The building should have an economic life of 60 years, and it is now five years old, which is also its effective age. What is its rate of depreciation, and what is its value by the cost approach (exclusive of land value)?

Using the formula for finding the depreciation rate, the building is depreciating at a rate of 1.7 percent (1/60) per year. The reproduction cost of the building multiplied by the rate of depreciation equals $13,600 per year ($800,000 × 1.7%). Since the building is five years old, it has depreciated by $68,000 ($13,600 × 5). The building is now worth $732,000 ($800,000 − $68,000).

Exercise 6.5

A company bought a building for $450,000 and estimated its economic life at 25 years. Compute the amount of the building's total depreciation under the economic age-life method after seven years.

Check your answer against the one given in the Answer Key at the back of the book.

Observed Condition Method

In the *observed condition* method of computing depreciation (also known as the *breakdown* method), the appraiser estimates the loss in value for curable and incurable items of depreciation. A *curable* item is one that can be easily and economically restored or replaced, resulting in an immediate increase in appraised value. An item that would be impossible, too expensive or not cost-effective to replace is *incurable*. Following are examples in each of the three depreciation categories (physical deterioration, functional obsolescence and external obsolescence).

1. *Physical deterioration—curable.* This includes repairs that are economically feasible and would result in an increase in appraised value equal to or exceeding their cost. Items of routine maintenance fall into this category, as do simple improvements that can add far more than their cost to the value of the property. Fixtures and appliances should be in good working order, broken windows replaced and landscaping tended. Exterior and interior painting very often will return more than their cost by improving the overall appearance of a building, particularly a residence.

   The loss in value due to curable physical deterioration is the cost to cure the item(s) of depreciation.

   Physical deterioration—incurable. This includes the separate physical components of a building, which do not deteriorate at the same rate. If roof, foundation, electrical system, and so on, did deteriorate at the same rate, the economic life of a building would simply be the economic life of its components. Unfortunately (or fortunately), the foundation of a building typically will last far longer than its roofing material, and other items will need replacing at other times.

   Generally, the individual building components can be divided into *short-lived* items and *long-lived* items of incurable physical deterioration. Short-lived items are those that may be replaced or repaired once or more over the economic life of the building. These include roof, gutters, wall coverings, cabinets and other finishing materials. Painting and decorating could be included here or under curable physical deterioration. Loss in value due to depreciation of these items can be estimated on an individual basis or by assigning an average percentage of depreciation to the total value of all items.

Long-lived items are those that should last as long as the building's remaining economic life. Foundation, framework, walls, ceilings and masonry would fall within this category.

Loss in value for items of incurable physical deterioration can be based on a percentage reflecting the ratio of effective age to the number of years of total physical life when new. All long-lived items are treated as a group, but short-lived items are depreciated individually.

2. *Functional obsolescence—curable.* This includes physical or design features that are inadequate or no longer considered desirable by property buyers, or that are not necessary for the structure's intended use but could be added, replaced, redesigned or removed economically (at a cost no greater than the resulting increase in value). Outmoded plumbing fixtures are usually easily replaced. Room function might be redefined at no cost if the basic room layout allowed for it, such as converting a bedroom adjacent to the kitchen to a family room. A closet converted to a darkroom might be easily converted back into a closet.

Loss in value from an item of curable functional obsolescence takes into account the fact that an item of remodeling or repair is more expensive when done separately than when work of the same design and specifications is performed as part of an entire building's construction. Thus loss in value is the difference between the increase in total reproduction cost that would cure the item and what it would cost to cure only that item. If a kitchen suffers from lack of modern cabinets and appliances, its depreciated value is the difference between the addition to reproduction cost represented by a modernized kitchen and the cost to modernize the kitchen separately. If a modern kitchen would add $9,000 to reproduction cost, and the cost as of the same date to modernize the existing kitchen by remodeling is $10,500, then $1,500 is the loss in value due to an out-of-date kitchen. Remodeling an existing building to cure a defect is more expensive with regard to that defect than if an entirely new building could be constructed without the defect.

If replacement, rather than reproduction, cost is used, physical or design features that exceed current requirements (a superadequacy) represent a loss in value equal to the cost to remove them; their initial construction cost and degree of physical deterioration are not considered.

Functional obsolescence—incurable. This includes currently undesirable physical or design features that could not be easily or economically remedied. The feature might be the result of a deficiency, a lack of modernization or a superadequacy. Many older multistory industrial buildings are considered less suitable than one-story buildings. Older apartments with large rooms and high ceilings might not bring as high a rent per cubic foot of space as smaller, newer apartments. The cost to correct these deficiencies is not justified. The single-family house with three or more bedrooms but only one bathroom clearly suffers from functional obsolescence that is not readily cured.

The loss in value caused by incurable functional obsolescence could be estimated by comparing either the selling prices or rents of similar buildings with and without the defect.

3. *External obsolescence—incurable only.* This is caused by factors not on the subject property, so this type of obsolescence cannot be considered curable. Proximity of a residence to a nuisance, such as a factory, would be an unchangeable factor that could not be assumed to be curable by the owner of the subject property. A depressed real estate market could also have a significant effect on market value. The appraiser's market analysis should be thorough enough to reveal any economic or other factors likely to affect market value.

Loss in value due to external obsolescence could be measured by comparing the selling prices or rents of similar properties, including some that are and some that are not affected by this type of depreciation. This may not be possible in a depressed market, where comparable sales may be few or nonexistent.

When estimating accrued depreciation by the observed condition method, the appraiser must decide on the amount of value lost through applicable depreciation in each of the categories described above. The appraiser must be careful not to depreciate the same item more than once.

Exercise 6.6

Determine the depreciation category of each of the following items as specifically as you can.

1. residential location on heavily traveled highway

2. severe termite damage throughout a structure

3. need for tuckpointing on house in overall good condition

4. office space adjacent to extremely noisy factory

5. newer split-level house in good condition but with potholes in asphalt driveway

6. dry rot in attic beams

7. 1940-built major commercial airport, with runways too short for modern jet planes

8. three-bedroom house with one bathroom

9. hot water–radiator heating system

10. 20,000-seat sports arena with no drinking fountains

Check your answers against those given in the Answer Key at the back of the book.

Capitalized Value Method

The *capitalized value* method of determining depreciation, also referred to as the *rent loss* method, is an indirect method of computing depreciation. In this method, known rental values of properties comparable to the subject property are analyzed to determine the loss in rental value attributable to the depreciated item. It is necessary to have comparable properties that also possess the same defect, and some that do not, to isolate the difference in rental value due solely to that cause. The loss in rental value is then capitalized by applying a *gross rental multiplier* to determine the effect on total property value of that loss in rent.

EXAMPLE: The Moran residence has four bedrooms and one-and-one-half bathrooms. Comparable homes with the same number of bathrooms rent for $695 per month, while comparable homes with two full bathrooms rent for $725 per month.

The monthly difference in rent attributable to the lack of two full bathrooms is $30. That number is multiplied by a factor of 135, which is the monthly gross rent multiplier for the area. The resulting figure of $4,050 is the loss in value to the reproduction cost of the subject property that is attributable to one item of incurable functional obsolescence.

Exercise 6.7

A building with an obsolete floor plan is being appraised. A comparable building with the same floor plan rents for $980 per month. A comparable building with a more desirable floor plan rents for $1,100 per month. If the monthly rental multiplier is 125, what is the loss in value caused by the obsolete floor plan?

Check your answer against the one given in the Answer Key at the back of the book.

Sales Comparison Method

The *sales comparison* method, also referred to as the *market comparison* method, is another indirect method of computing depreciation. This method uses the sales prices of comparable properties to derive the value of a depreciating feature. Sales prices of recently sold properties comparable to the subject property, some with and some without the defect, are analyzed.

EXAMPLE: The Moran house has four bedrooms but only one-and-one-half bathrooms. Comparable properties with one-and-one-half bathrooms have recently sold for $91,000. Comparable properties with two full bathrooms have recently sold for $95,000. The deduction from reproduction cost attributable to the lack of two full bathrooms is $4,000.

Exercise 6.8

A building with an obsolete floor plan is being appraised. A comparable building with the same floor plan recently sold for $142,000. A comparable building with a more desirable floor plan recently sold for $156,000. What is the loss in value attributable to the floor plan?

Check your answer against the one given in the Answer Key at the back of the book.

Itemizing Accrued Depreciation

To make the most accurate and thorough use of the cost approach, the appraiser must compute applicable depreciation in each category (physical deterioration, functional obsolescence and external obsolescence), then subtract those figures from the building reproduction or replacement cost. The appraiser does so by listing all items within a category and determining the amount of depreciation attributable to each.

While one of the indirect methods of calculating depreciation (capitalized value or sales comparison) may be the only available method for some types of depreciation or property, in general the better approach is to estimate a percentage of depreciation for each feature. Those percentages can be computed and the resulting figures added to find the total loss in reproduction cost. Remember, a given item should not be depreciated more than once; that is, it should not appear in more than one category.

EXAMPLE: The following chart gives the items of curable and short-lived incurable physical deterioration found in a one-story house, as well as the reproduction cost of each item. What amount will be subtracted from the house's reproduction cost of $92,750 as curable physical deterioration, the first step in the observed condition method of determining depreciation?

Item	Reproduction Cost	Percent Depreciation	Amount of Depreciation
Exterior Painting	$1,400	60%	$840
Carpeting	2,600	20%	520
Air Conditioner Compressor	1,400	70%	980
Water Heater	350	100%	350

Total reproduction cost of items of short-lived incurable physical deterioration is $5,750 ($1,400 + $2,600 + $1,400 + $350).

Total amount of short-lived incurable physical deterioration is $2,690 ($840 + $520 + $980 + $350).

Because long-lived incurable physical deterioration is usually based on general wear and tear of items not separately measured by the appraiser, the economic age–life method of computing depreciation is applied to the reproduction cost remaining *after* the full value of other items of physical deterioration has been subtracted.

EXAMPLE: In the previous example, the building is ten years old (also its effective age) and has an estimated remaining economic life of 40 years. The appraiser has determined that the amount of long-lived incurable physical deterioration is $^{10}/_{50}$, or 20% of the building's remaining reproduction cost. After the full value of all items of physical deterioration is subtracted, the remaining reproduction cost is $87,000 ($92,750 − $5,750). The amount attributable to long-lived incurable physical deterioration is $17,400 ($^{1}/_{5}$ of $87,000). Total depreciation due to physical deterioration is $20,090 ($2,690 + $17,400).

The next categories, functional and external obsolescence, may be derived by one of the methods outlined in this chapter. When all categories of depreciation have been applied to the reproduction cost, the land value of the property being appraised is added to the depreciated value to determine the final market value estimate by the cost approach.

EXAMPLE: There is no functional obsolescence in the house described in the examples above. External obsolescence due to location too close to a highway is estimated by the sales comparison method at $7,000. Land value is estimated at $44,000. Therefore:

Reproduction cost	$ 92,750
Physical deterioration	− 20,090
Functional obsolescence	N/A
External obsolescence	− 7,000
Depreciated building cost	$ 65,660
Site value	44,000
Property value estimate by cost approach	$109,660

Exercise 6.9

You are estimating the market value of a lot with a one-story industrial building that is 12 years old and has a remaining economic life of 48 years. You believe that 20 percent is an adequate depreciation deduction for everything except the following:

	Reproduction Cost	Observed Depreciation
heating system	$12,800	60%
plumbing	15,200	30
electric and power	23,000	40
floors	18,200	45
roof	16,500	55

Additional information: The building is 125' by 160'. You estimate that it would cost $55 per square foot to reproduce the building. You estimate site value at $180,000.

What is your estimate of the property's market value?

Check your answer against the one given in the Answer Key at the back of the book.

Conclusion

In the cost approach, the reproduction cost of a structure establishes its upper limit of value. However, there often is a significant difference between the current cost to reproduce a structure and its actual value in the market. For example, any property on which the improvements are not new requires an estimate of accrued depreciation. In the appraisal of older buildings in particular, measuring depreciation accurately and convincingly may be impossible. In such a case, greater emphasis should be placed on the sales comparison and/or income capitalization approaches.

The cost approach is especially useful when a value estimate using either the income capitalization approach or the sales comparison approach is impractical. For example, in appraising special-purpose properties, such as churches, schools, museums and libraries, there are no income figures available and few, if any, comparable sales.

A cost approach estimate is also needed in establishing value for insurance purposes. Insurance payments are based on the cost of restoration, or reimbursement for loss, as determined by the appraised insurance value; therefore, an insurance appraiser is mainly concerned with reproduction cost. Condemnation proceedings and real estate tax assessments are other instances in which a cost approach estimate is necessary.

Achievement Examination 6

You will now have the opportunity to apply what you have learned in this chapter. You will be guided through a detailed simulation of an industrial appraisal problem, in which you will have to perform cost and depreciation analyses to arrive at an estimate of property value by the cost approach. You will estimate reproduction cost, depreciation, land value and total property value.

Each computation you must record is numbered so that you can check your answer in the Answer Key at the back of the book. To make the best use of this case problem, you should check each answer as it is derived, rather than waiting until you have reached your final estimate of value.

You will be using the following data in this problem.

Identification of Property:

The subject property is located at the corner of Parker Avenue and Plymouth Road (see Exhibit A on page 152) and is improved with a one-story office and factory building, approximately 20 years old. The lot is rectangular. The building is on the west section of the lot, with parking space to the east.

Neighborhood:

The neighborhood is located approximately four miles from the center of a small city. The immediate area is developed with various types of industrial and commercial properties, such as auto showrooms, gas stations, tool and die factories, and photographic and instrument manufacturers. The subject property is accessible to both employee automobile and truck traffic.

Public Utilities and Zoning:

All the public utilities are installed and in service. These include gas, electricity, sewers, telephone and water. The zoning is light industrial.

Land Value:

On the land comparison table in Exhibit F (see page 156), there are four plots of land that are reliable indications of value for the subject property. Adjustments were made for size, location, date of sale and desirability. In estimating land value for this type of property, the square foot rate is the most practical measurement used in this area.

Exterior Construction:

foundation—12″ concrete wall and footings
floor—6″ reinforced concrete
exterior walls—12″ common brick with block backup; jumbo face brick veneer
framing—steel frame with 14′ eave height
roof—sheathing, 1⅞″ fiberglass insulation, four-ply tar and gravel covering
windows—industrial sash, aluminum, 50 percent vented.
doors—six 3′ × 7′ hollow metal; one rolling steel 12′ × 12′, chain hoist–operated

Interior Construction:

   walls—painted drywall on 8' wood stud partitions in office; perimeter walls in
      office are painted at a cost of $.25 per square foot of wall area; 12" concrete
      block dividing wall (14' high) separating factory area from office area
   floor covering—vinyl tile in office
   ceiling—suspended mineral fiber acoustic tile
   doors—six 3' × 7' hollow metal within office; one 3' × 7' hollow metal leading
      from office to factory
   interior of factory—unfinished
   electrical fixtures—fluorescent lights, normal lighting requirements
   plumbing—standard fixtures
   heating and air conditioning—both office and factory
   miscellaneous—3" asphalt paving on 3" stone base

Physical Deterioration (Curable)—none

Physical Deterioration (Short-Lived Incurable):

   brickwork—40%
   roof (asphalt and gravel)—60%
   exterior doors—75%
   floor covering (vinyl tile)—55%
   acoustic tile ceiling—45%
   electric—35%
   plumbing—30%
   heating and air-conditioning—30%
   asphalt paving—40%

Depreciation Deduction for Balance of Building—Physical Deterioration (Long-
   Lived Incurable)—25%

Functional Obsolescence (Curable)—none

Functional Obsolescence (Incurable)—5% of net value after physical deterioration

External Obsolescence—none

EXHIBIT A: PLAT PLAN AND BUILDING LAYOUT

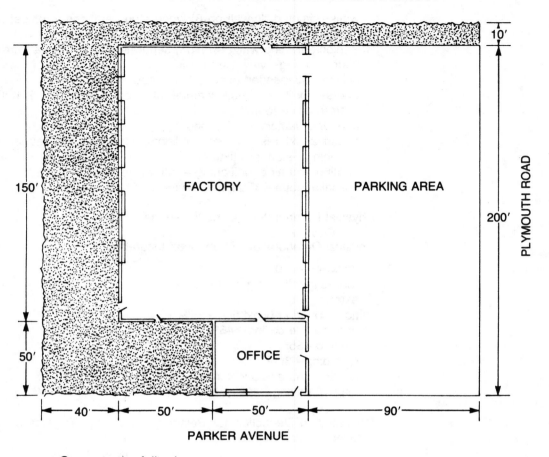

Compute the following:

1. total factory area   _____

2. total office area   _____

3. total building area   _____

4. building perimeter (including foundation wall
    between factory and office areas)   _____

5. total parking area   _____

EXHIBIT B: EXTERIOR WALL AREA

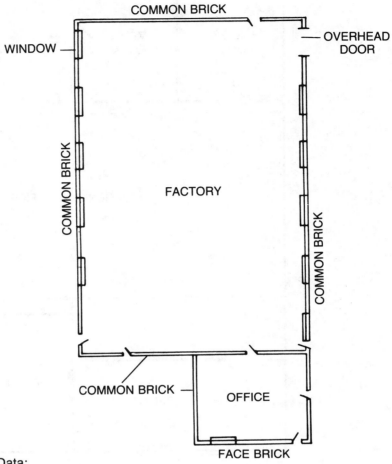

Data:

Factory height is 14'.
Office height is 10'.
Overhead door is 12' × 12'.
All other exterior doors are 3' × 7'.
All windows are 6' × 12'.

Compute the following:

6. total area covered by common brick   _____
    (including factory area above office roof and side walls)

7. total area covered by face brick   _____

CAUTION: Door and window areas must be deducted.

EXHIBIT C: INTERIOR WALL AREA (Excluding perimeter of office)

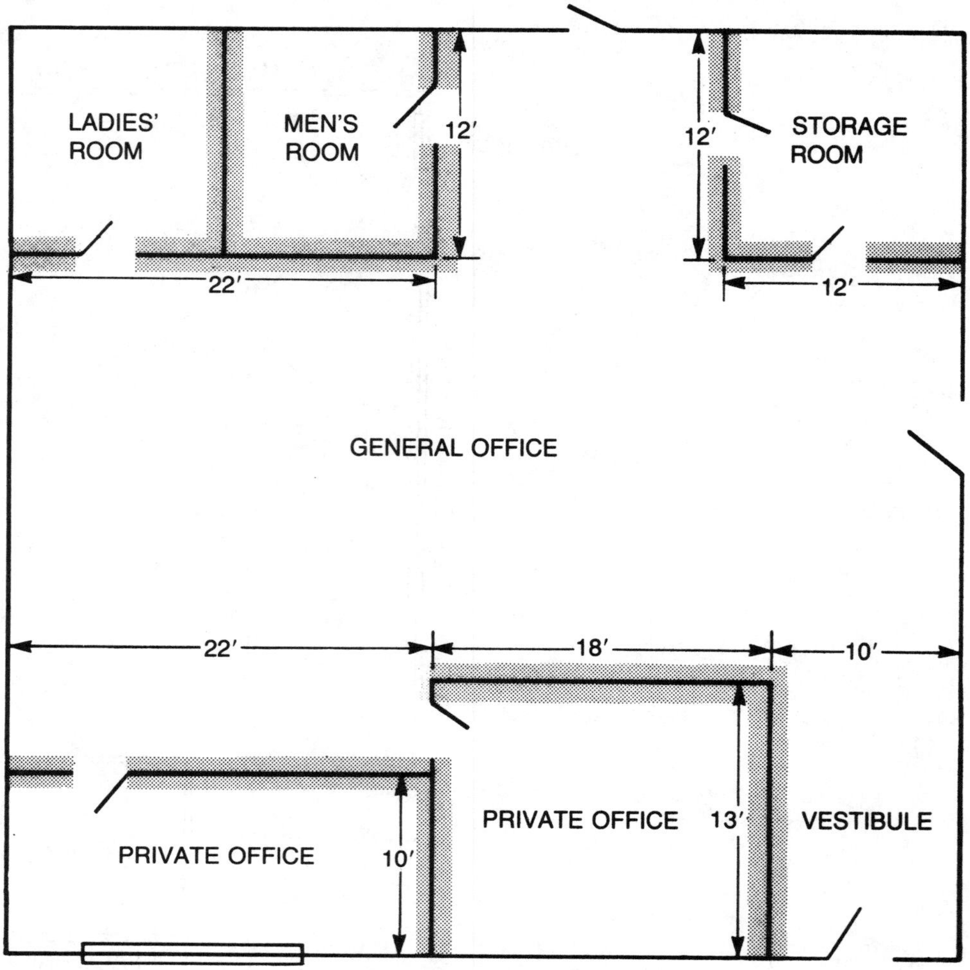

Data:

Ceiling height is 8'.
Doors are 3' × 7'.
Construction is drywall on wood studs.

8. Compute the interior wall area for the office portion of the building. _____

CAUTION: Both sides of a wall and door opening must be accounted for.

EXHIBIT D: INTERIOR WALL AREA (Perimeter of office)

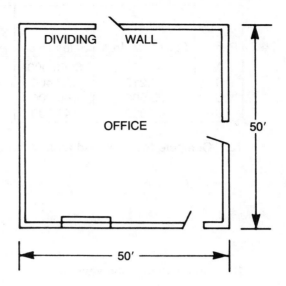

Data:

Dividing wall height is 14′.
Ceiling height is 8′.
Doors are 3′ × 7′.
Window is 6′ × 12′.

9. Compute the total wall area (perimeter of office only).   _____

10. Compute area of concrete block dividing wall.   _____

EXHIBIT E: FRAME SUPPORT

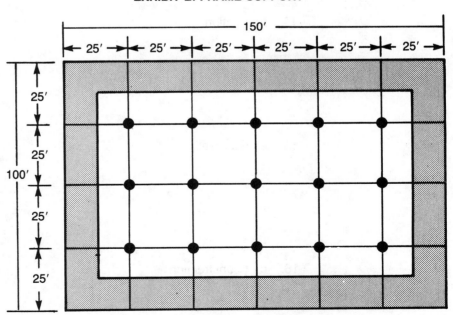

Shaded area is supported by bearing walls.
Unshaded area is supported by steel frame.

11. Compute the area supported by the steel frame.   _____

EXHIBIT F: LAND COMPARISONS

Parcel	Sq. Ft. of Area	Sales Price	Sales Price per sq. Ft.	Adjustments	Adjusted Sales Price per Sq. Ft.
A	45,000	$ 90,000	$2.00	+ 10%	$2.20
B	46,217	129,400	2.80	− 20%	2.24
C	25,900	60,900	2.35	− 15%	2.00
D	47,829	143,500	3.00	− 25%	2.25

12. Compute the total land area of the subject property.   _____

13. Compute the land value.   _____

Using the cost data in Appendix C, compute your cost estimate for each building component listed on this and the next two pages. Where a cost range is given, use the highest estimate. Round off all of your answers to the nearest dollar.

14. foundation

15. exterior walls

16. roof construction

17. framing

18. floor construction

19. windows

20. exterior doors

21. interior construction

22. electric

23. plumbing

24. heating and air-conditioning

25. miscellaneous

26. Enter and total your reproduction cost figures in the list below.

REPRODUCTION COSTS

Exterior Construction:

Foundation	_____
Floor Construction	_____
Exterior Walls	_____
Framing	_____
Roof Construction	_____
Windows	_____
Doors	_____

Interior Construction:

Walls	_____
Floor Covering	_____
Ceiling	_____
Doors	_____
Electric	_____
Plumbing	_____
Heating and Air-Conditioning	_____
Miscellaneous	_____
Total Reproduction Cost	_____

27. Observed depreciation:

brickwork

roof

exterior doors

floor covering

acoustic tile ceiling

electrical

plumbing

heating

air-conditioning

asphalt paving

Depreciation deduction for balance of building:

Deduction for incurable functional obsolescence:

28.   Use the list below to determine a total property value.

COST VALUATION

Reproduction Cost   _____

Depreciation:
  Deterioration—Curable   _____
                Short-Lived Incurable   _____
                Long-Lived Incurable   _____
  Functional Obsolescence—Curable   _____
                          Incurable   _____
  External Obsolescence   _____

  Total Accrued Depreciation   _____

Building Value Estimate   _____

Land Value Estimate   _____

Total Property Value Indicated by Cost Approach   _____

_____

Check your solution to the case problem with the one given in the Answer Key at the back of the book.

CHAPTER 7

The Income Capitalization Approach

The income capitalization approach is based on the premise that there is a relationship between the income a property can earn and the property's value.

Many commercial properties are purchased to be leased to other parties. The future net income the property is capable of earning is the main benefit to the owner. For this reason, the worth of the property to a prospective buyer is based largely on its earning capacity. The income approach to value translates the estimated future income of a property into a present value by the use of certain data and mathematical computations.

The usefulness of the income capitalization approach depends on the type of property under appraisal and the data available. Obviously, it is most useful for income-producing investment properties. But there is also another technique called the *gross income multiplier* method, sometimes included as part of the sales comparison approach because it compares rents of similar properties to their selling prices to arrive at an estimate of value for the subject property. Gross income multipliers frequently are used to estimate the value of properties such as single-family residences. Although these may never be rented, they have rental income potential, which is particularly important when inflated prices and high mortgage interest rates result in a weak resale market.

The *income capitalization approach formula* for single-family residential properties is:

Potential Gross Income × Gross Income Multiplier (GIM) = Value

The basic *income capitalization approach formula* for income-producing investment properties is:

$$\frac{\text{Net Operating Income}}{\text{Capitalization Rate}} = \text{Value}$$

The four categories of data needed for an appraisal by the income capitalization approach are thus:

1. The *potential gross income* from the property, which includes the annual income from all sources.
2. The amount of the expected annual *effective gross income* from the property, estimated by subtracting anticipated vacancy and collection losses from potential gross income.
3. The *net operating income,* found by deducting normal annual operating and other expenses from the effective gross income.
4. *The capitalization rate* for the property; that is, the rate that can be applied to the property's net annual income, the result being the appraiser's estimate of the property's value.

This chapter is divided into five sections, one for each of the four categories of data described above and the last for the capitalization techniques by which the appraiser makes an estimate of value. The student who wishes to study the income approach in greater depth after covering the material in this chapter is referred to Appendix D, which details the techniques of annuity capitalization, and Appendix E, which describes how lease interests are valued.

Potential Gross Income

The appraiser must first estimate the property's *gross income,* which may be defined as a property's total potential income from all sources during a specified period of time, usually a year. This income typically includes rent and also any nonrent income, such as income from vending machines, laundry services and parking.

Rent

Rent is the major source of income from most real estate. When an appraiser gathers data for an appraisal using the income capitalization approach, he or she will need to know the amount of the property's *market rent.* Market rent is an estimate of a property's rent potential—what an investor can expect to receive in rental income. To find market rent, the appraiser must know what rent tenants have paid, and are currently paying, on both the subject and comparable properties. By comparing present and past performances of the subject and similar properties, the appraiser should be able to recognize what the subject property's rent potential is and whether the property is living up to that potential.

Scheduled rent. Rent currently being paid by agreement between the user and the owner is called *scheduled rent* or *contract rent.* Scheduled rent is usually computed per square foot per year on income properties such as stores, offices and warehouses. The usual practice in determining apartment rents is to compute scheduled rent per room per year.

Some sources of scheduled rent data are:

1. The *lessee,* the person or company renting or leasing the property.
2. The *lessor,* the owner of the property.
3. The real estate agent, if the property has been recently sold or is managed by an agent.

Historical rent.   Scheduled rent paid in past years is called *historical rent.* Historical rent information can serve as a check on the validity of current scheduled rent data. Past periodic rent increases for the subject and similar properties may indicate a trend that current scheduled rents should follow. For instance, rents in a given area may be increasing at the rate of 8 percent yearly. If the current scheduled rent of either the subject or comparable properties is not in line with the trend, the appraiser should find the reason for the discrepancy to justify his or her estimate of the rental value the property could command on the current market. Recent rental trends, of course, should be emphasized in estimating the current market rental income for the appraised property.

The needed data on comparable properties for estimating market rental can be provided by owners, lessees, real estate agents and brokers in the area, or perhaps by previous appraisals. The following example shows how to develop and use comparable property data in determining market rental for a property to be appraised by the income capitalization approach.

EXAMPLE: Data for Finding Market Rent

Subject Property	Use Size Scheduled Rent	Hardware store 90′ × 95′ (one floor) $12,850
Property 1	Use Size Scheduled Rent	Clothing store 70′ × 100′ (two floors) $21,700
Property 2	Use Size Scheduled Rent	Drugstore 85′ × 100′ (one floor) $18,105
Property 3	Use Size Scheduled Rent	Cleaners 105′ × 120′ (one floor) $20,500
Property 4	Use Size Scheduled Rent	Grocery store 90′ × 100′ (one floor) $18,450

The information above can be converted into like units of measurement to make the comparative data more meaningful.

	Use	Square Feet	Scheduled Rent	Rent per Square Foot per Year
Subject	Hardware	8,550	$12,850	$1.50
Property 1	Clothing	14,000	21,700	1.55
Property 2	Drugstore	8,500	18,105	2.13
Property 3	Cleaners	12,600	20,500	1.63
Property 4	Grocery	9,000	18,450	2.05

Properties 2 and 4 are roughly the same size as the subject; both are one-floor structures, and the rents are close. Properties 1 and 3 probably don't apply because of the big differences in size.

Property 2 rents for $2.13 per square foot, and property 4 rents for $2.05 per square foot. This suggests that the market (potential) rent of the subject property may be higher than the current scheduled rent of $1.50 per square foot.

In an actual appraisal, other factors of similarity and/or dissimilarity for selecting comparable properties must be considered. Factors to be considered include location, construction of the building, its age and condition, parking facilities, front footage, air-conditioning and responsibilities of the tenant. If comparable properties rent for more or less than the subject, the appraiser must search for clues as to why there are rental differences. Another important factor that should be considered is the age of the leases. Although the properties may be similar, an old lease could reflect a rental level lower than prevailing rentals.

Exercise 7.1

You are asked to appraise a six-unit apartment building. Each apartment has one bath and five rooms: living room, dining room, kitchen and two bedrooms. Each apartment is presently leased at $900 per room per year. For this problem, historical rent will be ignored. There are three other six-unit apartment buildings in the area, of similar room size and construction:

Property 1—contains two-bedroom apartments with living room, dining room, kitchen and bath, renting for $1,260 per room per year.

Property 2—contains three-bedroom apartments with living room, dining room, kitchen and bath, renting for $1,440 per room per year.

Property 3—contains two-bedroom apartments with living room, dining room, kitchen and bath, renting for $1,176 per room per year.

What is the scheduled rent for the subject property?

What is the expected (market) rent for the subject property?

Check your answers against those given in the Answer Key at the back of the book.

Outside Economic Factors

Various national, regional and local factors might also have to be analyzed in deriving market rent. For example, suppose the country had been in a period of recession for the year prior to the date of an appraisal. Historical rental data might have indicated a 10% increase per year over the preceding five years, but this rate of increase would be too high for the present year. Thus, the appraiser must keep informed of economic trends at all levels.

Or assume that a factory, which will employ hundreds of people, is being built close to a town. If no new construction has begun on housing facilities, rent for dwelling space in that area would most likely increase because of the relatively low supply of, and high demand for, housing. The appraiser should be aware of this factor and take it into consideration when estimating market rent.

Using both historical and scheduled rent information for the subject and similar properties, the appraiser can derive the subject property's market rent, the amount for which the competitive rental market indicates the property should rent. This figure may be the same as, higher than, or lower than the property's present rent. The appraiser will base the potential gross income estimate on market rent added to any other income derived from the property during a one-year period.

Other Income

Not all income may be from rents. In even the smallest apartment building, the owner may have coin-operated laundry facilities for the tenants' use. Or the owner of an office or apartment building may keep vending machines on the premises for the convenience of the tenants and for the income they produce.

In making up a statement of potential gross income, market rent and other forms of income would usually be itemized separately, then totaled to reflect the productivity of the property.

EXAMPLE: An appraisal for ABC Office Management, Inc., estimates the potential gross income from one of its buildings as $230,000 in scheduled rent, $8,600 from food vending machines and $400 from newspaper sales. Show the building's income in an itemized statement.

Potential Gross Income		
Scheduled rent	$230,000	
Vending machines	8,600	
Newspaper sales	400	$239,000

The total potential gross income for the building under appraisal is $239,000.

A number of items under the potential gross income category often are reported improperly by owners and accountants. Among the more important errors are these:

1. Leaving out any percentage income that may be paid if the lease is on a minimum-plus-percentage basis. This type of lease is most often found with retail stores. The lessee pays a stipulated minimum rent plus a percentage of the gross business income over a stated amount. This percentage may increase automatically as gross sales (or business) income rises. For instance, the rent may be $6,000 per year plus 8 percent of annual gross sales over $50,000 and 6 percent of gross sales over $80,000.
2. Reporting only the actual income for a year and not the total potential gross income.
3. Leaving out equivalent rents for owner-occupied areas and/or caretaker's quarters. These can materially affect the capitalized value of the property if the owner and/or the caretaker occupy substantial space.
4. Leaving out any "other" income *not* derived from rents, such as income from parking garages or lots and from the resale of electricity, heat or air-conditioning to the tenant.

The appraiser should not accept figures and statements without verifying them by questioning either the tenants or the real estate broker or rental agent involved.

Exercise 7.2

You are appraising a six-unit residential property, and the only information available is the yearly income and expense data below. List the income information in statement form, then compute the estimated potential gross income.

Apartment rental income is $32,000. Outlay for janitorial service is $2,700, with another $700 for supplies. Utilities are $4,800, and maintenance and repairs amount to about $1,000. Taxes are $2,700. Income from washers and dryers is $900. Building depreciation is estimated at $2,500 per year. Rental spaces in the adjacent parking lot bring in $1,000 per year.

Check your answers against those given in the Answer Key at the back of the book.

Gross Income Multiplier

As mentioned earlier in this chapter, certain properties are not purchased primarily for income. As a substitute for the income capitalization approach, the *gross income multiplier* method is frequently used, particularly in appraising single-family residences. Gross income in such a case usually includes only gross rent, so it may also be called a *gross rent multiplier*. Gross rent multipliers are simply numbers that express the ratio between the sales price of a residential property and its gross monthly unfurnished rental.

Because they are subject to essentially the same market influences, rental prices and sales prices tend to move in the same direction and in the same proportion. If rental prices go up or down, sales prices will usually follow suit, and to the same degree. The relationship between the sales price and rental price can be expressed as a factor or ratio, which is the gross income or rent multiplier. The ratio is:

$$\frac{\text{Sales Price}}{\text{Gross Income}} = \text{GIM} \quad \text{or} \quad \frac{\text{Sales Price}}{\text{Gross Rent}} = \text{GRM}$$

Generally, annual gross income multipliers are used in appraising industrial and commercial properties, while monthly gross rent multipliers (GRM) are used for residential properties. This distinction is made because some types of income earned by industrial and commercial properties may come from sources other than rent.

EXAMPLE: A commercial property sold a month ago for $261,000. The annual gross income was $29,000. What is the gross income multiplier for the property?

Because the property is commercial, the annual gross income is used in the formula for finding the gross income multiplier:

$$\frac{\$261,000}{\$29,000} = 9, \text{ the gross income multiplier for this property}$$

To establish a reasonably accurate gross income multiplier, the appraiser should have recent sales and income data from at least four similar properties that have sold in the same market area and were rented at the time of sale. The resulting gross income multiplier (GIM) could then be applied to the actual or projected rental of the subject property to estimate its market value. The formula would then be:

$$\text{Gross Income} \times \text{GIM} = \text{Market Value}$$

EXAMPLE: Estimate of Market Value via Gross Income Multiplier Analysis

Sale No.	Market Value	Annual Gross Income	Gross Income Multiplier
1	$100,000	$10,000	10.0
2	153,000	17,000	9.0
3	123,500	13,000	9.5
4	187,000	22,000	8.5
5	114,000	12,000	9.5
Subject	?	11,000	?

The range of gross income multipliers applied to the subject's gross income gives:

$$\$11,000 \times 8.5 = \$93,500$$
$$\$11,000 \times 10 = \$110,000$$

These comparisons bracket the estimate of value within reasonable limits. By using sales 1, 3 and 5 as most comparable, the appraiser concludes that the subject property's gross income multiplier should be 9.5. Therefore:

$$\$11,000 \times 9.5 = \$104,500, \text{ the estimated value of the}$$
$$\text{subject property}$$

The gross income multiplier is a quick way to check the validity of a property value obtained by the three accepted appraisal methods: sales comparison, cost and income.

Because the multiplier converts gross, rather than net, income into value, the result can be misleading. For example, consider two very similar properties, each with an asking price of eight times gross income, but one property netting $10,000 per year and the other netting only $5,000 per year. (The lower net income could be caused by excessive operating expenses.) According to the GIM method, the investor ought to pay the same price for either property. This is not actually the case, however. The property with the larger net income is certainly more valuable than the other. The length of the lease term may also be a significant factor. A property nearing the end of a five-year lease term in a period of high inflation may well be generating less income than it might if the lease had been renegotiated during that period.

In the income approach, the multiplier concept is refined by considering not only gross rent but also the lease term, as well as the operating expenses incurred. It is important to use comparable properties that have similar operating expense ratios.

Exercise 7.3

The subject has a gross income of $18,000 per year. Information on comparable properties is listed below, with adjustment factors indicated.

Sale No.	Adjustment	Sales Price	Gross Income	GIM
1	new, long-term lease	$167,000	$18,750	
2	high operating expenses	125,000	11,500	
3	old lease	195,600	11,500	
4	low operating expenses	144,000	13,400	
5	customized property	147,000	28,000	

Compute the GIM for each property. Then, estimate the GIM for the subject property, taking into account the adjustment factors that indicate that a GIM should be raised or lowered to reflect special circumstances. Finally, estimate the value of the subject property.

Check your answers against those given in the Answer Key at the back of the book.

Effective Gross Income

As discussed earlier, the appraiser's estimate of potential gross income is based on a combination of market rent plus all other income earned by the property. But it is reasonable to assume that some properties will not be fully rented all the time. Normally, and especially during times of economic recession or overbuilt markets, many properties have vacancies. Vacancies, as well as instances of nonpayment of rent, can significantly reduce a property's income. Vacancy and collection loss allowance is usually estimated as a percentage of potential gross income.

For example, assume that the potential gross income of an apartment building that derives all of its income from rent is $250,000. Historically, the subject property has had 10 percent vacancies. If the rate of vacancies in the current year, based on market data analysis, does not differ from past years, the real or *effective gross income* of the property would be $225,000. To calculate the effective gross income for a property, the appraiser first determines the potential market rent, then adds any nonrent income. Finally, the appraiser reduces the resulting estimated potential gross income by the percentage of market rent that probably will be lost due to vacancies, collection losses or both.

EXAMPLE: An eight-unit apartment building historically has a 4 percent vacancy rate and a 4 percent collection loss rate. A current survey of the local market also supports these vacancy estimates. The projected income for the building over the next year is $46,400 market rent, $2,000 parking income, $1,300 from vending machine income and $800 income from laundry facilities. What is the property's effective gross income?

The effective gross income can be found most easily by first making an itemized statement of potential gross income.

Potential Gross Income		
Market rent	$46,400	
Parking	2,000	
Vending machines	1,300	
Laundry facilities	800	$50,500

Next, vacancy and collection losses based on rental income can be computed and subtracted from potential gross income to arrive at effective gross income.

Potential Gross Income		
Market rent	$46,400	
Parking	2,000	
Vending machines	1,300	
Laundry facilities	800	$50,500
Vacancy and Collection Losses @ 8% of Potential Gross Income		4,040
Effective Gross Income		$46,460

The effective gross income of the subject property is $46,460.

Many factors may influence the percentage of vacancy and collection losses selected, including:

1. the present and past rental losses of the subject property;
2. competitive conditions in the area (rental levels for the subject property and other competitive buildings in the neighborhood);
3. the estimate of future area population and economic trends;
4. the quality of the tenants; and
5. the length of the leases.

Although an allowance of 5 percent to 10 percent is often set up for vacancy and collection losses, each appraisal assignment requires that this allowance be derived from pertinent market facts.

Exercise 7.4

Using the income and expense information given in Exercise 7.2, draw up an effective gross income statement for the subject property. The effective gross income will be based on the following vacancy and rental losses:

The apartment units are vacant for an average of one week of each year. There has also been a total rental loss of 3 percent for each of the past three years.

Check your answers against those given in the Answer Key at the back of the book.

Net Operating Income

The value of an income-producing property is measured by the *net operating income* it can be expected to earn during its remaining economic life or forecast income period. Net operating income is calculated by deducting the *operating expenses* of owning a property from its effective gross income. Operating expenses are the periodic expenditures needed to maintain the property and continue the production of the effective gross income. Expenses include the cost of all goods and services used or consumed in the process of obtaining and maintaining rental income.

The expenses incurred depend on the property and the services provided by the owner. Apartment buildings may require a doorman, hallway lighting and a gardener, in addition to maintenance, insurance, property taxes and management. Some owners of retail store properties provide the real estate and pay for the exterior maintenance of the building, insurance and property taxes. All of the utilities and inside maintenance and repairs may be the responsibility of the tenant.

Classification of Operating Expenses

Operating expenses are usually grouped according to the nature of the cost incurred. Expenses may be classified as follows:

1. *Variable expenses* are the out-of-pocket costs incurred for management, wages and benefits of building employees, fuel, utility services, decorating, repairs and other items required to operate the property. These expenses tend to vary according to the occupancy level of the property.
2. *Fixed expenses* are those costs that are more or less permanent and do not vary according to occupancy, such as real estate taxes and insurance for fire, theft and hazards.
3. *Reserves for replacement* are allowances set up for replacement of building and equipment items that have a relatively short life expectancy. For example, reserves should be set up for heating systems, roof replacements, elevators, air conditioners, ranges, refrigerators, carpeting and other items that routinely wear out and have to be replaced during the economic life of the building. The appraiser provides for the replacement of an item by estimating its *replacement cost* and its *remaining economic life*. The annual charge is the cost of the item divided by the number of years of economic life.

Expenses for Accounting Purposes Versus Expenses for Appraisal Purposes

Operating expenses for appraisal purposes do not include expenditures that are beyond the direct operation of an income-producing property. There are four types of expenses to the owner that are *not* operating expenses of real estate:

1. *Financing costs.* Property is appraised without considering available or probable financing, except under the mortgage equity capitalization method.
2. *Income tax payments.* Income taxes are a powerful force and exert an influence on investment behavior, but they relate to the owner and not the property. Personal income tax depends on the total income of a person, personal expenses, age, health, size of family and so on, and are not treated as expenses of the property for appraisal purposes.
3. *Depreciation charges on buildings or other improvements.* An annual depreciation charge is an accounting method of recovering the cost of an investment over a period of time. The process of capitalization, which will be explained later, automatically provides for the recovery of the investment.
4. *Capital improvements.* Although payments may have been made for capital improvements, such as new refrigerators, ranges or storm windows, the payments themselves are not treated as operating expenses but are taken from the replacement reserve monies.

Reconstructing the Operating Statement

Current expenses may be adjusted if the appraiser's study indicates that they are out of line for comparable properties. The process of eliminating the inapplicable expenses and adjusting the remaining valid expenses, if necessary, is *reconstruction* of the operating statement. An operating statement for a multistory, self-service, elevator apartment building appears below. The first column of figures was prepared by the owner's accountant. The second column was reconstructed by the appraiser (rounding amounts to the nearest $100).

OPERATING STATEMENT

		Accountant's Figures	Appraiser's Adjusted Estimate
①	Gross Income (Rent)	$56,000.00	$58,700
②	Allowance for Vacancies and Bad Debts	——	2,900
	Effective Gross Income	——	55,800
	Operating Expenses		
VARIABLE EXPENSES	Salaries and wages	6,000.50	6,000
	Employees' benefits	519.20	500
	Electricity	900.12	900
	Gas	3,014.60	3,000
	Water	400.10	400
	Painting and decorating	1,000.00	1,000
	Supplies	525.56	500
	Repairs	2,024.30	2,000
	Management	3,000.00	3,000
	Legal and accounting fees	800.00	800
	Miscellaneous expenses	400.00	400
FIXED EXPENSES	Insurance (three-year policy)	1,500.00	500
	Real estate taxes	5,100.00	5,100
RESERVES FOR REPLACEMENT	Reserves—		
	③ Roof replacement	——	500
	④ Plumbing and electrical	——	1,000
⑤	Payments on air-conditioners	1,200.00	——
⑥	Principal on mortgage	1,500.00	——
⑦	Interest on mortgage	10,000.00	——
⑧	Depreciation—building	8,000.00	——
	Total Expenses	$45,884.38	$25,600
	Net Income	$10,115.62	$30,200

The circled numbers in the operating statement refer to the following bracketed information.

[1] Income was adjusted upward to reflect the rental value of an apartment occupied by the owner.
[2] Vacancy and collection losses, based on an area study, typically amount to 5 percent of gross rental income.
[3] Roof replacement is expected every 20 years at a cost of $10,000, or $500 per year ($10,000 ÷ 20).

[4] Plumbing and electrical replacements are based on a 20-year service life for fixtures costing $20,000, or $1,000 per year ($20,000 ÷ 20).

[5] Payments for capital improvements such as air conditioners are not operating expenses.

[6] [7] Principal and mortgage interest payments are personal income deductions, not property expenses, when appraising on a "free and clear basis."

[8] Depreciation is included in the accountant's figures as the owner's expense to allow for the loss of income that will result when the property reaches the end of its useful life. (For more information on how accrued depreciation is estimated in judging the value of a property, see Chapter 6.)

Exercise 7.5

You are gathering data for the appraisal of a 32-unit apartment building. Using the form on page 175, list the yearly income and expense data given in the accountant's summary below. Then, compute the property's effective gross income, total expenses and net operating income. Gas rates are expected to increase, perhaps by 25 percent. Because of a general increase in the tax rate, taxes should be increased by about 20 percent. Round off all figures to the nearest $100.

Property address: 759 Fourteenth Street

Rental Income	$210,000.00
Vacancy and Collection Losses	9,850.00
Salaries—Janitor	9,248.17
Employee Benefits	612.00
Management	6,000.00
Natural Gas	12,375.00
Water	3,845.67
Electricity	8,674.32
Property Taxes	6,000.00
Janitorial Supplies	673.00
Redecorating	2,000.00
Reserves for Building Replacements	2,500.00
Legal and Accounting Fees	2,400.00

Check your form against the completed one in the Answer Key at the back of the book.

Operating Statement

Potential Gross Income   _____

   Allowance for Vacancy and Collection Losses   _____

Effective Gross Income   _____

Operating Expenses

   Variable Expenses   _____

                         _____

                         _____

                         _____

                         _____

                         _____

                         _____

                         _____

                         _____

   Fixed Expenses   _____

   Reserves for Replacement   _____

Total Operating Expenses   _____

Net Operating Income   _____

Capitalization Rate

Income-producing property is usually bought as an investment. The rate of return the investor receives is the *capitalization rate* (also called the *overall capitalization rate*), which can be expressed as a relationship between the annual net income a property produces and its value. Put into equation form:

$$\frac{\text{Net Operating Income}}{\text{Value}} = \text{Capitalization Rate, or } \frac{I}{V} = R$$

EXAMPLE: An investor paid $500,000 for a building that earns a net income of $50,000 per year. What is the capitalization rate of the investment?

Using the formula $\frac{I}{V} = R$, the capitalization rate is

$$\frac{\$50,000}{\$500,000}, \text{ or } 10\%$$

The formula for the capitalization rate is useful for appraisal purposes because of its two corollaries:

Capitalization Rate $\times$ Value = Net Operating Income, or R $\times$ V = I

$$\frac{\text{Net Operating Income}}{\text{Capitalization Rate}} = \text{Value, or} \qquad \frac{I}{R} = V$$

By dividing the estimated net income of a property by the appropriate capitalization ("cap") rate, the property's value may be estimated.

There are several ways an appraiser can find a property's capitalization rate. The appraiser can study comparable properties that have recently sold and assume that the capitalization rate of a comparable would be approximately the same as that of the subject. Or the appraiser can analyze the component parts of a capitalization rate and structure one for the subject property.

In earlier sections we have seen that the appraiser must analyze income and operating expense data to accurately estimate a property's potential gross income and compute its net operating income. Using these two types of data, the appraiser compiles information from even more sources to arrive at the property's capitalization rate. In the rest of this section, the types of data needed to formulate a property's capitalization rate will be discussed.

Direct Capitalization

A capitalization rate may be developed by evaluating net income figures and sales prices of comparable properties in a process called *direct capitalization*.

EXAMPLE: An appraiser has determined the annual net operating income of the subject property to be $13,000. By screening the market data the appraiser has compiled, a comparable property is located with a net operating income of $12,800 a year that sold recently for $182,000. Using this comparable alone, what is the capitalization rate of the subject property?

The overall capitalization rate of the comparable property is $\frac{I}{V}$, which is $\frac{\$12,800}{\$182,000}$, or 7%. The net operating income for the subject property is $13,000, so its value is $\frac{I}{R}$, which is $\frac{\$13,000}{.07}$, or $185,700.

Of course, the appraisal would be more reliable if several comparable properties were used to derive the capitalization rate.

By definition, comparable properties should have comparable capitalization rates. If a property the appraiser thought was comparable has a capitalization rate significantly higher or lower than that of other comparable properties, the appraiser should consider discarding that sample. Closer examination of the property or sales transaction would probably reveal extenuating circumstances (such as a transaction between related companies) that should have kept the property from consideration as a comparable.

When the capitalization of the subject property is being estimated, even a slight difference in the assigned capitalization rate will have a serious effect on the estimate of property value. If a property was assigned a capitalization rate of 9 percent and its net operating income was $18,000, its value would be estimated at $\frac{\$18,000}{.09}$, or $200,000. If the capitalization rate assigned was 8 percent, the value estimate would be $\frac{\$18,000}{.08}$, or $225,000.

One percentage point difference in the capitalization rate would make a 12½ percent difference in the value estimate. By discarding extremes, the appraiser should have a narrow range of capitalization rates from which the subject property's capitalization rate can be estimated; the appraiser must use judgment in selecting a capitalization rate that is reflective of the most comparable properties.

Exercise 7.6

You are appraising an industrial building with a net operating income of $17,000. You have previously appraised or studied the comparable properties listed below. Use all of the information you have on hand to find a suitable capitalization rate for the subject, and its value. Round your answer to the nearest $100.

Property	Selling Price	Net Operating Income	Capitalization Rate
A	$136,000	$14,800	
B	94,000	11,000	
C	127,000	15,000	
D	110,500	12,600	
E	150,000	32,000	

Check your answers against those given in the Answer Key at the back of the book.

Yield Capitalization

The second way of determining a capitalization rate for the subject property, called *yield capitalization*, is by analyzing the capitalization rate's component parts and estimating each of those components for the subject property. The two basic components of the capitalization rate are the recapture rate and the discount rate, which will be discussed throughout the rest of this chapter.

An investor who purchases an income-producing property expects two things:

1. Return *of* the investment. This is the right to get back the purchase price at the end of the term of ownership and is ordinarily expressed as an annual rate. Appraisers refer to this as capital *recapture.*
2. Return *on* the investment. This return is the investor's profit on the money used to purchase the property and is expressed as a *discount rate.* The discount rate is also referred to as the *interest rate, risk rate* or *return on* rate.

Because land usually does not depreciate, its sales price at the end of the investor's period of ownership is considered adequate compensation. Buildings depreciate, however, and the investor has an asset of continually decreasing value. This anticipated future depreciation is provided for in the recapture part of the capitalization rate.

These two investment objectives can be illustrated by the following example.

EXAMPLE: The ABC Corporation owns a lot on which it builds an office building for $100,000. The building has an economic life of 20 years. The company expects to receive an annual net operating income of 10 percent from the building during its economic life and also expects to have the building investment repaid over that period of time. To achieve these two objectives, the net operating income of the property would have to be as follows:

$100,000 × .10   = $10,000 Discount (Return on Investment)
$100,000 ÷ 20   = $5,000 Annual Recapture (Return of Investment)
$10,000 + $5,000 = $15,000 Annual Net Operating Income

In the above example, with a net operating income of $15,000 and a value of $100,000, the building capitalization rate is $\frac{I}{V}$, or $\frac{\$15,000}{\$100,000}$, or 15%. The return *on* the investment (discount) makes up 10 percent of the capitalization rate, and the return *of* the investment (recapture) makes up 5 percent of the total capitalization rate of 15 percent.

By analyzing the factors that comprise the interest and recapture rates, the appraiser can determine a property's capitalization rate and use that and the property's net income to find its value. The recapture and discount rates are discussed next.

Selecting the Rate for Capital Recapture

Every good investment provides for a return *on* the invested capital, called the *discount* or *interest,* and a return *of* the invested capital, called *recapture*. In processing income produced by land only, a recapture provision is usually unnecessary. The assumption is that land will not depreciate, and recapture can therefore be accomplished entirely through resale. A building, however, does depreciate. That is, its value decreases with the passing of time. The appraiser, therefore, must add to the interest rate a percentage that will provide for the recapture of the investment in the building.

Straight-line method of recapture.   The simplest and most widely used method of computing the recapture rate is the *straight-line* method. Under this method, total accrued depreciation is spread over the useful life of a building in equal annual amounts. Thus, when the building is 100 percent depreciated and presumably economically useless, all of the investment will have been returned to the investor. To find the recapture rate by the straight-line method, divide the total accrued depreciation (100 percent) by the estimated economic life of the building.

$$\frac{100\%}{\text{Economic Life}} = \text{Annual Recapture Rate}$$

If, for example, a building has a remaining economic life of 20 years, 5% of the building's value should be returned annually out of net operating income: $\frac{100\%}{20}$ = 5% recapture rate.

The straight-line method of recapture requires a good deal of knowledge about the useful life of a given type of property. As a starting point, the appraiser may refer to tables, contained in various cost manuals, that deal with the useful lives of buildings by type. Then, the appraiser must consider the factors unique to the subject property, such as its age, its condition and the neighborhood in which it is located.

A building most frequently becomes useless through external or functional obsolescence, rather than physical deterioration; that is, more buildings are torn down in still-usable condition than fall down from deterioration. For this reason, the recapture period is often referred to as *estimated remaining economic life*. An appraiser estimates the remaining economic life of a property after considering the physical, functional and environmental factors involved.

Selecting the Discount Rate

There are two principal methods of developing an interest or discount rate. The first is the *market extraction* method. The second is the *band of investment* method.

Market extraction method.   In this method, the appraiser finds the discount rate of a comparable property by subtracting the portion of the property's net operating income attributable to building recapture from total net operating income, and dividing the remainder by the selling price of the property.

EXAMPLE: Property X sold for $200,000. The site is valued at $50,000, and the building has a remaining economic life of 40 years. Total net operating income is $30,000.

The building value is $150,000 ($200,000 − $50,000), and the recapture rate is .025 (1 ÷ 40 years), so:

$$\$150,000 \times .025 = \$3,750$$

The net operating income available for building recapture is $3,750, leaving $26,250 ($30,000 − $3,750) as net operating income available for the property. Dividing that amount by the property's sales price:

$$\frac{\$26,250}{\$200,000} = 0.13125$$

The discount rate for property X is thus 13%.

Exercise 7.7

Construct a discount rate for a recently sold commercial property with the following known facts: The selling price was $435,000. The site value is $125,000, and the building's estimated remaining economic life is 25 years. Total net operating income is $57,000.

Check your answer against the one given in the Answer Key at the back of the book.

Band of investment method.   Another method commonly used to build a discount rate is the *band of investment* method. This method takes into account everyone who has an interest in the real estate being appraised. Not every investor will be satisfied with the same rate of return on an investment. For example, the owner may regard his or her position as riskier than that of the first or second mortgage holders. Each mortgage creates a lien on the property. If the owner defaults, the property may be sold to pay such liens, and the owner receives only those proceeds that may remain from the sale of the property. Since the owner's interest is generally considered inferior to those of lien holders, the owner may require a higher return on the investment.

The discount rate developed by the band of investment method is based on (1) the rate of mortgage interest available and (2) the rate of return required on equity. For example, assume a case in which a first mortgage covering 70 percent of the value of the property can be obtained at 10 percent interest, and the buyer requires a return of 12 percent on the equity portion (the 30 percent of the value of the property the buyer will invest). Using the band of investment method, the discount rate could be developed as follows:

	Percent of Property's Total Value	Return Required		Product
First Mortgage	70%	× 10%	=	7.0%
Equity	30%	× 12%	=	3.6%
Total	100%			10.6%

Thus, the discount rate on 100 percent of value is 10.6 percent. The procedure for secondary financing is the same as that just described. For example, suppose a first mortgage of 70 percent is obtainable at 10.5 percent, a second mortgage of 15 percent is obtainable at 12 percent, and the equity of 15 percent requires a 15 percent return. The discount rate would be developed as follows:

	Percent of Property's Total Value	Return Required		Product
First Mortgage	70%	× 10.5%	=	7.35%
Second Mortgage	15%	× 12%	=	1.80%
Equity	15%	× 15%	=	2.25%
Total	100%			11.40%

In the band of investment method of finding the discount rate, each portion of the property's ownership or interest is multiplied by the rate of return required to attract money into that type of ownership position.

Relationship of Capitalization Rate and Risk

From the examples discussed thus far, several generalizations about the capitalization rate and the risk of an investment can be drawn.

High Risk = High Capitalization Rate
Low Risk = Low Capitalization Rate

Because high risk implies a high possibility of investment loss, a property with a high risk will have a lower selling price or value than one with a relatively low risk factor. The generalization can be carried one step further.

High Risk = High Capitalization Rate = Low Value
Low Risk = Low Capitalization Rate = High Value

Exercise 7.8

Assuming the following data, what capitalization rate would you use in appraising the subject property?

A first mortgage covering 65 percent of the property can be obtained from a bank at 10 percent.

A second mortgage of 20 percent can be obtained from a private lender at 13 percent.

Equity for this type of property requires a 14 percent return.

The remaining economic life of the building is estimated at 25 years.

Check your answer against the one given in the Answer Key at the back of the book.

Selecting the Capitalization Technique

There are three physical techniques by which net operating income can be capitalized into value: (1) the building residual technique, (2) the land residual technique, and (3) the property residual technique. In appraising, a residual is the income remaining after all deductions have been made. It may refer to:

1. the net operating income remaining to the *building* after return on land value has been deducted (building residual technique);
2. the net operating income remaining to the *land* after return on and recapture of the building value have been deducted (land residual technique); or
3. the net operating income remaining to the *property as a whole* (property residual technique).

In estimating the value of real estate, each technique will produce approximately the same answer—provided the return (discount rate) and recapture assumptions remain the same for each technique.

Building Residual Technique

To use the *building residual* technique, the appraiser must know the value of the land, which is usually found by analyzing comparable sales.

First, the appraiser deducts the amount of net operating income that must be earned by the land to justify its value. The balance of the net operating income must be earned by the building. This building income is then capitalized at the discount rate *plus* the rate of recapture to arrive at the building's value.

EXAMPLE: A commercial property is being appraised. The land value has been estimated at $80,000, and the typical rate of return is 12 percent, so the land itself must earn $9,600 ($80,000 × .12) if it is to justify its purchase price. The property should yield a total net operating income of $37,000 yearly. The residual income to the building, therefore, is $27,400 ($37,000 − $9,600).

The capitalization rate for the building will be based on the discount rate of 12 percent (already applied to the land value) and a recapture rate of 5 percent based on an estimated remaining economic life of 20 years (100% ÷ 20 years = 5% per year). The building capitalization rate, therefore, is 17 percent (12% + 5%). The estimated building value is $27,400 ÷ .17 or $161,200 (rounded to the nearest hundred dollars).

Finally, the value of the building is added to the value of the land to arrive at the total property value, which is $241,200 ($161,200 + $80,000).

All of the information in this example problem could be itemized as follows:

Estimated Land Value		$ 80,000
Net Operating Income	$37,000	
Discount on Land Value ($80,000 × .12)	−9,600	
Residual Income to Building	$27,400	
Capitalization Rate for Building		
Discount Rate	12%	
Recapture Rate	+ 5%	
	17%	
Building Value ($27,400 ÷ .17)		161,200
Total Property Value		$241,200

The building residual technique is most useful when land values are stable and can be easily determined by recent sales of similar sites. This technique is also used when the construction cost of the building and the amount of accrued depreciation are difficult to measure accurately because of the building's age or unusual design.

Exercise 7.9

The property under appraisal is a 25-year-old apartment building producing a net operating income of $50,000 a year. Compute the value of the property, assuming a remaining economic life of 40 years for the building, a 10½ percent discount rate, and land value estimated at $100,000.

Check your answer against the one given in the Answer Key at the back of the book.

Land Residual Technique

The land residual technique follows the same procedure as the building residual technique—but with the building and land calculations reversed.

EXAMPLE: Assume that the net operating income for a commercial property is $45,000 annually, and the value of the building has been estimated at $225,000. The appropriate discount rate for the building is 11⅞ percent and the estimated recapture rate is 4 percent. What is the value of the property to the nearest $100?

Assumed Building Value		$225,000
Net Operating Income	$45,000	
Capitalization Rate for Building		
Discount Rate 11.875%		
Recapture Rate 4.000%		
Total 15.875%		
Discount and Recapture on Building		
Value ($225,000 × .15875)	− 35,700	
Residual Income to Land	$ 9,300	
Land Value ($9,300 ÷ .11875)		78,300
Total Property Value		$303,300

In this example, the value of land and building together is $303,300.

The land residual technique is used (1) when the land value cannot be estimated from comparable sales or (2) when the building is new or in its early life and represents the highest and best use of the land. When a building is new, value usually is assumed to be equal to reproduction cost.

Exercise 7.10

A new office building valued at $300,000 produces an annual net operating income of $53,000. A first mortgage of 60 percent can be obtained from a bank at 10¼ percent. Equity for this type of property requires a 12 percent return, and the building's remaining economic life is estimated at 50 years. Estimate the total property value by the land residual technique.

Check your answer against the one given in the Answer Key at the back of the book.

Property Residual Technique

In the *property residual* technique, the land and building are valued as a single unit, rather than as separate units. This technique is used when the building is very old or when it is difficult to make reliable estimates of either the land or the building value.

The property residual technique is applied by either of two methods. In one method, the appraiser makes use of annuity (yearly increment) tables, which are discussed in Appendix D. The other method is one that has already been discussed—direct capitalization. The appraiser analyzes sales of comparable properties and develops a net operating income for each property.

Then, using the formula for the capitalization rate, $\frac{I}{V} = R$, the appraiser computes a range of overall rates from which a rate appropriate to the subject property can be selected.

For example, if a comparable property producing a net operating income of $12,000 sold for $100,000, by dividing $12,000 by $100,000, an overall rate of 12 percent is derived. This rate includes both discount and recapture. Now, if several additional properties comparable to the subject were also producing net operating incomes which, when divided by their selling prices, indicated a yield of approximately 12 percent, it would seem reasonable to capitalize the net operating income of the subject property at the same overall rate—12 percent. Then, if the net operating income of the subject were $10,000, its value by direct capitalization would be $10,000 ÷ .12, or approximately $83,000.

Exercise 7.11

You have been asked to appraise an income-producing property in an area where it is difficult to substantiate either building or land values. You have obtained the following income and selling price data on comparable properties:

	Net Operating Income	Selling Price
Property 1	$15,000	$115,400
Property 2	20,000	166,700
Property 3	12,500	100,000
Property 4	18,000	140,600
Subject	16,000	

Because all properties above are highly comparable, you feel that an average cap rate will probably be applicable to the subject. What is your estimate of value for the subject property?

Check your answer against the one given in the Answer Key at the back of the book.

Conclusion

Under the income capitalization approach, the value of a property is estimated by the annual income it is expected to produce. The process requires accurate income and expense estimation and the selection of a capitalization rate and technique to process the net operating income into value.

The primary advantage of the income capitalization approach is that it approximates the thinking of the typical investor, who is interested in the dollar return realized through income-producing real estate.

The disadvantages of the income capitalization approach stem from the fact that a large number of estimates must be made and, in most cases, a complex set of relationships must be developed. In addition, the complexities of yield capitalization tend to confuse nonappraisers. Despite these difficulties, the income capitalization approach is an important valuation tool and must be understood by every real estate appraiser.

Achievement Examination 7

1. To arrive at net operating income, expenses are deducted from:

   a. operating profit
   b. gross income

   c. effective gross income
   d. none of these

2. In income property investments:

   a. low risk = low cap rate = high value
   b. low risk = low cap rate = low value
   c. low risk = high cap rate = low value
   d. low risk = high cap rate = high value

3. All other factors being equal, as the location of an income property becomes less desirable, the cap rate used will be:

   a. lower
   b. higher

   c. less reliable
   d. unaffected

4. Recapture generally applies to:

   a. wasting assets, such as buildings
   b. nonwasting assets, such as land

   c. both a and b
   d. neither a nor b

5. In the land residual technique, the appraiser starts with an assumption of:

   a. replacement cost
   b. building value

   c. net capitalization
   d. land value

6. In the building residual technique, the appraiser starts with an assumption of:

   a. replacement cost
   b. building value

   c. net capitalization
   d. land value

7. In the list below, check each item that is NOT an expense from an appraiser's point of view.

   a. gas and electric
   b. depreciation on building
   c. water
   d. real estate taxes
   e. building insurance
   f. income tax
   g. supplies
   h. payments on air conditioners
   i. janitor's salary
   j. management fees
   k. maintenance and repairs
   l. legal and accounting fees
   m. social security tax
   n. principal and interest on mortgage
   o. advertising

    p.   painting and decorating
    q.   depreciation on equipment
    r.   value of janitor's apartment (rent free)
    s.   water and sewer tax
    t.   salaries and wages of employees
    u.   reserves for replacement
    v.   payments on stoves and refrigerators

8. Name the two component rates that are inherent in every capitalization rate.

9. Using the following data, compute value by (a) the building residual technique and (b) the land residual technique. Round your figures to the nearest $100.

   Net operating income is $40,000.

   Land value is $50,000.

   65 percent of the value of the property can be borrowed at 11 percent, and equity capital for this type of investment requires a 12 percent return.

   The building's remaining economic life is 25 years.

10. In this case problem, you will estimate the market value of a property by the income capitalization approach. Round all figures to the nearest $1.

You have been asked to appraise a one-story commercial building located in a small neighborhood shopping center. The building is about 20 years old and is divided into four separate stores, all of equal size. Each store pays a yearly rental of $10,200, which is well in line with comparable properties analyzed.

The owner of the subject property lists the following items of expense for the previous year:

real estate taxes—$4,000

insurance—three-year policy—$3,000

repairs and maintenance—$2,800

mortgage payments—$8,400

legal and accounting fees—$550

miscellaneous expenses—$500

In addition to the above expense listing, you obtain the following information:

Tenants pay for their own water, heating, electricity and garbage removal.

Repairs and general maintenance should be based on 12 percent of effective gross income.

Miscellaneous expenses should be increased to 2 percent of potential gross income.

The records of property managers indicate that vacancy and collection losses in the area run about 4 percent.

A new roof, costing $2,000 and having an average life of 20 years, was installed last year.

The gas furnace in each store can be replaced for $950 and will carry a 10-year guarantee.

Recent land sales in the area indicate that the land value of the subject property should be estimated at $55,000.

You have determined from banks in the area that 75 percent of the value of the property can be borrowed at 11 percent interest, and equity money for this type of investment requires a 13 percent return.

The building is 20 years old and appears to have depreciated about one-third.

a. On the basis of the information on the previous page, reconstruct the operating statement.

b.   Determine the appropriate capitalization rate.

c.   Estimate the total property value.

CHAPTER 8

Reconciliation and the Appraisal Report

The last step in the appraisal process is the reconciliation of the values indicated by each of the three approaches to appraising. In the *cost approach,* the cost of reproducing or replacing the structure less depreciation plus the site value has been calculated. In the *income capitalization approach,* value has been based on the income the property should be capable of earning. Using the *sales comparison approach,* the sales prices of recently sold similar properties have been adjusted to derive an estimate of value for the appraised property.

Many appraisers believe that all three approaches to value should be used in every appraisal assignment—if the right kinds of data are available. Other appraisers feel that only one or two of the approaches are really necessary in typical assignments. For instance, it may be argued that the income capitalization approach does not lend itself to valuing single-family residences, since such properties are not typically bought for their income-producing capacities. The sales comparison approach would not be appropriate in valuing a special-purpose property, such as a public library or zoo, because there would not be any useful comparable sales information available. The cost approach cannot be used to value vacant land. In reaching a decision as to which approach or approaches to use, the appraiser must first understand the nature of the property and purpose of the assignment.

In this chapter on reconciling the indicated values and the appraisal report, we will use all three approaches.

Reconciliation

In theory, the value estimates by the different approaches should all be exactly the same; that is, if the appraiser had all of the relevant data and had carried out each step in each approach without error, each value indication would be the same. In actual practice, this seldom happens. In almost every case, the application of the three approaches will result in three different estimates of value. In the value reconciliation process, the validity of the methods and result of each approach are weighed objectively to arrive at the single best and most supportable conclusion of value. This is also called *correlation*.

In reconciling, or correlating, the appraiser reviews his or her work and considers at least four factors, including the:

1. definition of value sought;
2. amount and reliability of the data collected in each approach;
3. inherent strengths and weaknesses of each approach; and
4. relevance of each approach to the subject property and market behavior.

The appraiser never averages differing value estimates. After the factors listed above are considered, the most relevant approach—cost, sales comparison or income—receives the greatest weight in determining the value estimate that most accurately reflects the value sought. In addition, each approach serves as a check against the others.

Review of the Three Approaches

To begin the reconciliation process, the appraiser verifies the steps followed in each approach. In reviewing the sales comparison approach, the appraiser should check:

1. that properties selected as comparables are sufficiently similar to the subject property;
2. amount and reliability of sales data;
3. factors used in comparison;
4. logic of the adjustments made between comparable sale properties and the subject property;
5. soundness of the value estimate drawn from the adjusted sales prices of comparable properties; and
6. mathematical accuracy of the adjustment computations.

In reviewing the cost approach, the appraiser should check:

1. that sites used as comparables are, in fact, similar to the subject site;
2. amount and reliability of the comparable sales data collected;
3. appropriateness of the factors used in comparison;
4. logic of the adjustments made between comparable sale sites and the subject site;
5. soundness of the value estimate drawn from the adjusted sales prices of comparable sites;
6. mathematical accuracy of the adjustment computations;
7. appropriateness of the method of estimating reproduction or replacement cost;
8. appropriateness of the unit cost factor;
9. accuracy of the reproduction or replacement cost computations;
10. market values assigned to accrued depreciation charges; and
11. for double-counting and/or omissions in making accrued depreciation charges.

In reviewing the income capitalization approach, the appraiser should check the logic and mathematical accuracy of the:

1. market rents;
2. potential gross income estimate;
3. allowance for vacancy and collection losses;
4. operating expense estimate, including reserves for replacement;
5. net income estimate;
6. estimate of remaining economic life; and
7. capitalization rate and method of capitalizing.

Weighing the Choices

Once the appraiser is assured of the validity of the three value estimates, he or she must decide which is the most reliable, in terms of the value sought, for the subject property. Inherent factors may make a particular method automatically more significant for certain kinds of property (such as the income approach for investment properties). But other factors, of which the appraiser should be aware, may negate part of that significance. An unstable neighborhood, for instance, may make any structure virtually worthless. If the appraiser is trying to arrive at an estimate of market value, and if the market for property in a certain neighborhood is likely to be extremely small, this fact should be reflected in the appraiser's final value estimate.

EXAMPLE: An appraiser estimating the market value of a six-unit apartment building in a neighborhood composed predominantly of two- to eight-unit apartment buildings, arrived at the following initial estimates:

Sales Comparison Approach	$222,500
Cost Approach	228,500
Income Capitalization Approach	226,850

Based on these indications of value, the range is from $222,500 to $228,500, a difference of $6,000 between the lowest indication of value and the highest. This relatively narrow range suggests that the information gathered and analyzed is both a reasonable and reliable representation of the market.

In reviewing the data collected for the sales comparison approach and the results drawn, the appraiser realized that this value estimate should be very reliable. Other buildings in the same general condition, and with the same types of improvements, were selling from $216,000 to $228,000. However, because all comparable sales used in the analysis required considerable adjusting, less weight was given to the sales comparison approach than would normally be expected. After allowing for specific differences, an indicated value of $222,500 was determined for the subject property by the sales comparison approach.

Next, the appraiser analyzed the information collected and the result obtained using the cost approach. The cost approach tends to set an upper limit of value when the property is new, without functional or external obsolescence and at its highest and best use. However, the older a property becomes, the more difficult it is to accurately estimate the proper amount of accrued depreciation. The fact that the subject building is only a few years old strengthens the $228,500 estimate of value by the cost approach.

Finally, the appraiser considered the market value derived from the income capitalization approach. For several reasons, this approach seemed to have the most validity for this particular property. First, none of the apartments was owner occupied, and the tenants were only 16 months through three-year leases. The rents charged were comparable to those for similar apartments when the leases were first signed. Since then, however, rents of other properties have risen as much as 20 percent and will probably keep rising for the next 20 months, when the leases will expire. The appraiser allowed for this in arriving at the income approach estimate. The property's current income indicates a market value of $226,850.

Even though the sales prices of comparable buildings suggest a market value of $222,500 for the subject, the building's utility as an income-producing property allows for a market value of $226,850.

Because a prudent investor for property of this type would very likely give highest consideration to an analysis of income and expenses, and because the cost approach strongly supports the income capitalization approach, the appraiser's estimate of market value is $227,000.

Summary

The reconciliation process can be summarized best by a discussion of what it is *not*. Value reconciliation is *not* the correction of errors in thinking and technique. Any corrections to be made are actually part of the review process that precedes the final conclusion of value. The appraiser reconsiders the reasons for the various choices that were made throughout the appraisal framework as they affect the value estimates reached by the three approaches.

There is no formula for reconciling the various indicated values. Rather, it involves the application of careful analysis and judgment for which no mathematical or mechanical formula can be substituted.

Reconciliation is also not merely a matter of averaging the three value estimates. A simple arithmetical average implies that the data and logic applied in each of the three approaches are equally reliable and should therefore be given equal weight. Certain approaches obviously are more valid and reliable with some kinds of properties than with others. But even if the appraiser multiplied each value estimate by a different factor, judgment and analysis still would be replaced by mechanical formula.

Finally, value reconciliation is not a narrowing of the range of value estimates. The value estimates developed from each approach are never changed—unless an error is found. Reconciliation is the final statement of reasoning and weighing of the relative importance of the facts, results and conclusions of each of the approaches that culminates in a fully justified final estimate of market value.

Types of Appraisal Reports

After the three approaches have been reconciled, the resulting opinion of value will be presented by the appraiser in the form requested by the client. While the appraiser must *always* fully document the research and reasoning leading to the conclusion of value, all of that background information may not be presented in the report to the client.

A certificate or *letter of opinion* states only the appraiser's conclusion of value or, often, a range of value; because it provides neither supporting data nor the appraiser's analysis to the client, it is of limited use. A *form report* makes use of a standard form to provide, in a few pages, a synopsis of the data supporting the conclusion of value. The type of property as well as the definition of value sought will determine the exact form used. The purpose of the *narrative report* is to give the client not only the facts about the property but also the reasoning the appraiser used to develop the estimate of value.

The remainder of this chapter examines the requirements of the narrative appraisal report and a typical form report.

Narrative Report

A narrative appraisal report presents the most complete documentation of the data supporting the appraiser's final estimate of value to the client. Because there is no one way to prepare a narrative report, a state, governmental agency, institution or appraisal organization may impose particular requirements. A narrative appraisal report ordinarily will contain most or all of the sections described below. As you read each description, find the corresponding section in the sample appraisal report on a single-family residence, which begins on page 202.

Title page.   An identifying label, or title page, gives the name of the appraiser and the client, the date of appraisal and the type of property and its address.

Letter of transmittal.   Page one of a narrative appraisal report is the letter of transmittal, which formally presents the report to the person for whom the appraisal was made. The letter should be addressed to the client and contain the following information: street address and a complete and accurate legal description of the subject property, property rights to be appraised, type of value sought (most often, market value), appraiser's value estimate, effective date of the appraisal and appraiser's signature.

Table of contents.   A complete listing of the separate parts of the appraisal and all appendixes will be of great help to both the client and the appraiser and will provide an overview of the appraisal process.

Purpose of the appraisal.   The purpose of an appraisal is its objective, which is usually to estimate market value as of a specified date. Although market value has been the main subject of this book, the content and result of the appraisal can vary greatly with its purpose. For example, in appraisals for inheritance tax, condemnation or the sale of property, the sales comparison approach is important. For certain mortgage loan purposes, the income-producing capacity of the property would be stressed. For life insurance purposes, reproduction or replacement cost data and construction features and materials would be most significant.

Definition of value.   Because the word *value* can have many interpretations, the type of value sought should always be given in the report so the client fully understands the basis for the reported value.

Property rights.   In most cases, the property rights to be appraised will be a fee simple interest. The appraiser, however, may be asked to estimate the value of fractional interests or to estimate the effect on value of a change in zoning or a deed restriction, and so on. Whatever property rights are involved, they must be given in exact detail.

Highest and best use.   Most appraisals are based on the highest and best use to which the subject property can be put. Overimprovements or underimprovements are a part of the highest and best use concept, as is use of the site, whether proper or improper. It is not enough simply to say that the existing improvements reflect the highest and best use of the site. Some explanation or justification must be given. Remember, this is a highest and best use *analysis*—not simply an unsupported statement.

Summary of important facts and conclusions.   The summary page highlights the important facts and conclusions of the report. This section should include the estimate of land value and highest and best use, the reproduction or replacement cost estimate per square foot or cubic foot, the age of the improvement(s) and their depreciated value(s), the gross rental value on a stated occupancy basis, the net income expectancy, the estimate of the value by each of the three approaches and the final estimate of value.

National, regional and city data. In a typical appraisal, most of the general data about the nation, region and city will be gathered initially from office files or previous appraisal reports. Such information should be included in the appraisal report only if it is useful in measuring the future marketability of the property—its economic life, the stability of its location, area trends and so on. For this reason, national and regional data are generally not included in the appraisal report. Any relevant maps should be included in an appendix to help describe the region or city. When necessary, the body of the report should contain cross-references to such exhibits.

Neighborhood data. Neighborhood data provides important background information that may influence value. Cross-references to photographs and maps can be helpful here, too. Factors such as distance to schools, public transportation and shopping and business areas may affect property values. Such information is especially useful if the report is to be submitted to someone unfamiliar with the area. If any form of external obsolescence exists, it should be described in some detail, since it must be measured later in the report.

Financing. The report should include a brief statement about financing available in the area.

Site data. A factual presentation of site data is needed, with cross-references to the plat map, also included in an appendix. A description of the site, including its shape, area, contour, soil and subsoil, must be given. Census tract identification should be included when available to the appraiser.

Utilities. The important site utilities, their capacities and how adequately they serve the present or proposed highest and best use(s) should be inventoried.

Zoning. A statement about current zoning regulations is not enough. The report should indicate whether zoning regulations are strictly enforced or a change could be easily effected. Information about the uses permitted and to what extent they conform under the present zoning should also be included. This would have an important bearing on both highest and best use and value.

Amenities. This section should contain community features, such as schools, places of worship, shopping facilities and public services.

Description of improvements. Among the items this section should contain are construction details and finishing, including quality, floor plan, dimensions, design and layout, age and condition, list of equipment or fixtures and needed repairs or deferred maintenance. If physical deterioration or functional obsolescence exists, it should be described in some detail, since it will have to be valued later.

Taxes. Current assessed value, tax rate, taxes and the likelihood of tax changes and their effects should be included.

Each approach to value should be developed separately and in enough detail for the reader to understand the basis for the appraiser's final conclusion of value.

The cost approach. The basic unit cost used to arrive at reproduction or replacement cost must be explained. Two buildings are seldom if ever identical, so a square foot cost or a cubic foot cost taken from known cost data is almost always subject to some adjustment. The measurement of depreciation resulting from physical wear and tear, layout and design and neighborhood defects must also be explained.

The sales comparison approach. In the sales comparison approach, the selling prices of properties considered comparable are used to arrive at the value of the appraised property. These comparable properties must be described in detail to illustrate the points of comparison and convince the reader that the appraiser's choices are valid comparables.

Usually it is possible to list the comparable properties on one page, bringing out both the similarities and differences. A second page might show the adjustments the appraiser has developed, with a third page explaining the adjustments. Sometimes an adjustment grid showing the required adjustments is followed by a description of each comparable sale and an explanation of the adjustments made. Very large adjustments suggest that the properties are not comparable.

The income capitalization approach. In the income capitalization approach, the value of the property is based on the income it produces. Rent and expense schedules of comparable properties should be included in this section to support the appraiser's net income estimate. When available, the income history of the subject property should be listed, along with some explanation of vacancy expectations and anticipated changes in expense items.

Reconciliation of indicated values. Reconciliation of the value estimates derived under the sales comparison, cost and income approaches to value is presented. The reasons for emphasizing one estimate over another should be explained clearly.

Statement of assumptions and limiting conditions. The appraiser must make certain assumptions: (1) the legal description of the property as stated in the appraisal is correct, (2) the named owner of the property is indeed its true owner and (3) there is no legal impediment to the marketability of the property (no "cloud on the title"). The appraiser must also use information provided by other sources, including legal descriptions, surveys and other data, which may turn out to be in error. A statement in the appraisal report, that the value estimate is dependent on the assumptions specified and the correctness of various facts or information provided by other persons, will protect both the appraiser and the client making use of the report. *Such* *a statement does not relieve the appraiser of the responsibility to independently verify certain data, as discussed in this book, and to follow generally accepted appraisal methods and techniques.*

Certificate of appraisal.   The appraiser's certification is a guarantee that the appraiser or the appraiser's agent has personally inspected the property, has no present or contemplated interest in the property, and that the statements contained in the report are correct to the best of his or her knowledge.

Qualifications of appraiser.   The reader of the report will be interested in knowing the qualifications of the appraiser, because experience and sound judgment are essential in the appraisal estimate. For this reason, a description of the appraiser's education, professional background and appraisal experience is needed. It serves no purpose to include civic and social offices held or other extraneous information.

Appendix.   The appendix usually includes tables of supporting data, maps, photographs, plat and floor plans, and résumés of leases, deeds, contracts or other items that influenced the appraiser in reaching the final conclusion of value.

Exhibits must be neat, uncluttered and professionally executed. An area or neighborhood plan, if included, should clearly indicate the important aspects of the area or neighborhood. When plot plans and floor plans are included in the appendix, such plans should be drawn to scale and, as in the case of other exhibits, should have a professional appearance.

A P P R A I S A L   R E P O R T

OF

A SINGLE-FAMILY RESIDENCE

LOCATED AT:

9999 BOWLING GREEN ROAD
HOMEWOOD, ILLINOIS
60430

PREPARED FOR:

MARTIN J. KLEIN
619 CHERRY DRIVE
HOMEWOOD, ILLINOIS
60430

AS OF:

MAY 29, 1989

BY:

ALVIN L. WAGNER, JR., S.R.A., R.M.
2709 FLOSSMOOR ROAD
FLOSSMOOR, ILLINOIS
60422

APPRAISAL CERTIFICATE

I hereby certify that upon application for valuation by:

MARTIN J. KLEIN
619 CHERRY DRIVE
HOMEWOOD, ILLINOIS
60430

the undersigned personally inspected the following described property:

Lot 480 in Block 6 in Homewood Terrace Unit #1, being a subdivision of part of the Southeast ¼ of Section 5, Township 35
North, Range 14, East of the Third Principal Meridian, according to the plat thereof registered in the Office of the Registrar of Titles of Cook County, Illinois, on January 18, 1961, as
Document #1960782, and commonly known as:

9999 BOWLING GREEN ROAD
HOMEWOOD, ILLINOIS
60430

and to the best of my knowledge and belief the statements contained in this
report are true and correct, and that neither the employment to make
this appraisal nor the compensation is contingent upon the value reported,
and that in my opinion the MARKET VALUE as of the 29th day of May,
1989, is:

ONE HUNDRED FOURTEEN THOUSAND AND NO/100 DOLLARS

($114,000.00)

The property was appraised as a whole, owned in fee simple title and
unencumbered, subject to the contingent and limiting conditions outlined herein.

ALVIN L. WAGNER, JR., S.R.A., R.M.

TABLE OF CONTENTS

APPENDIX

PURPOSE OF THE APPRAISAL

The purpose of this appraisal is to estimate the market value of the subject property in fee simple title unencumbered as of May 29, 1989.

DEFINITION OF MARKET VALUE

Market value, as used in this report, is defined as:

> The most probable price, in terms of money, which a property should bring in a competitive and open market under all conditions requisite to a fair sale, with the buyer and seller each acting prudently and knowledgeably, and assuming the price is not affected by undue stimulus.

PROPERTY RIGHTS

The property rights being appraised are fee simple. Fee simple is defined as:

> The maximum possible estate one can possess in real property. A fee simple estate is the least limited interest and the most complete and absolute ownership in land; it is of indefinite duration, freely transferable, and inheritable.

HIGHEST AND BEST USE

Highest and best use is defined by **The Appraisal of Real Estate**, published by the American Institute of Real Estate Appraisers, as: "The use that, at the time of appraisal, is the most profitable likely use." It may also be defined as: "The available use and program of future utilization that produces the highest present land value."

However, elements affecting value that depend upon events or a combination of occurrences which, while within the realm of possibility, are not fairly shown to be reasonably probable, should be excluded from consideration. Also, if the intended use is dependent on an uncertain act of another person, the intention cannot be considered.

Based on the above definition and after seeing the site, neighborhood, and area, it is my opinion that the present use of the subject property is its highest and best use.

SUMMARY OF IMPORTANT CONCLUSIONS

The estimate of value applies as of May 29, 1989.

Reproduction Cost Estimate per Square Foot	$ 65.25
Depreciated Value of the Improvement	$ 83,800.00
Depreciated Value of Landscaping, Driveway, Fencing, and other extras	$ 2,400.00
Estimated Land Value	$ 29,900.00
Value Indicated by:	
Cost Approach	$116,100.00
Sales Comparison Approach	$114,000.00
Income Approach	$112,600.00
Final Estimate of Value	$114,000.00
Gross Monthly Rental Value	$ 810.00

-4-

VILLAGE DATA

HOMEWOOD

The Village of Homewood, 24 miles south of Chicago's Loop, was incorporated in 1893, has a population exceeding 20,000, and encompasses an area of 4.7 square miles. The village median age is 34, and the median income is $26,758.

IN GENERAL ... Homewood speaks of itself as a "sturdy middle-class community." Zoning restricts the village to various areas of business, residences, one racetrack and light manufacturing. No heavy industry can be found in town. This and the neighboring village of Flossmoor provide one of the most desirable living locations in Chicago's south suburbs. In both villages, there are some 80 civic and service organizations and clubs. Homewood celebrated its diamond jubilee in 1968.

HOUSING ... All types of homes are available and are priced from $85,000 to $175,000. Some new homes can also be found in town, and are priced from about $110,000. Homewood has some 800 rental units renting from $400 to $950 per month.

SCHOOLS ... Public: five elementary and one junior high. Pupil-teacher ratio is 20:1, with $1,471 spent annually per pupil. The two-campus Homewood-Flossmoor High School (which has an exceptionally high percentage of graduates going on to college) also serves the community. Parochial: one Catholic and one Lutheran elementary school are in town.

CHURCHES ... The 11 churches include two Community, and one each: Baptist, Catholic, Christian Science, Evangelical Lutheran, Lutheran, Presbyterian, Reformed, Reorganized Church of Jesus Christ of Latter Day Saints and United Methodist.

TRANSPORTATION ... The Illinois Central Gulf Railroad provides 35-minute express service to the Loop from Homewood, with local service taking about 50 minutes for the trip. All through Amtrak passenger trains also stop in town. South Suburban Safeway Lines serve the village with buses to Chicago (1½ hours). The Calumet Expressway is 5 miles east of town and provides free automobile access to the Loop, while an entrance to the Tri-State Tollway, which parallels Homewood's northern boundary, is at 171st and Halsted.

-5-

<u>VILLAGE DATA</u>   (Continued)

<u>HOMEWOOD</u>

MEDICAL ... South Suburban (122 beds) and St. James Hospitals (394 beds) are "next door" in Hazel Crest and Chicago Heights, while Ingalls Memorial Hospital (334 beds) is five miles away, in Harvey. Some 34 doctors and 27 dentists practice in town in several medical center buildings.

SHOPPING ... Downtown Homewood offers a wide variety of stores. The Southgate shopping area and the Cherry Creek shopping center are handy for all residents, and the Woolco shopping center and Washington Park Plaza Mall are on the east side of town. The Park Forest shopping center, offering over 70 stores, and the Lincoln Mall Regional Shopping Center, located in Matteson, are approximately four miles south of Homewood.

RECREATION ... An active park district offers supervised recreation programs. 14 parks are located on 80 acres in town, and have complete playgrounds, which add to the play facilities found at the schools. Little League, Pony League, and American Legion baseball teams function in town. The high school swimming pool, a Lions pool, and the Dolphin Club (operated by the park district) offer swimming facilities for those interested. The Isaac Walton League maintains a nearby area stocked for fishing, and ice skating is available at several of the parks in the winter. There are four tennis courts plus a membership fee indoor tennis club, and basketball facilities available. The Washington Park racetrack is one of the main attractions in this area. In addition, Flossmoor, Olympia Fields, Idlewild, Cherry Hills, Ravisloe, Calumet Hills, and Chicago Heights country clubs are all nearby.

SUMMARY ... Homewood has enjoyed a steady, stable growth. It has had a very capable and forward Village Government which has provided an orderly growth of various types of commercial, apartment, industrial, and residential developments. An excellent tax base to support the amenities has been provided. This upward trend should continue for many years into the future.

-6-

NEIGHBORHOOD DATA

The subject property is located in the Homewood Terrace subdivision in the central eastern section of the Village of Homewood. This area was developed by a single developer, commencing twelve years ago with single-family residences, currently ranging in value from $85,000 to $120,000.

The subject's subdivision is bounded on the east by the Village of Glenwood, on the south by 187th Street, to the west by Center Street, and to the north by land owned by the Homewood Park District and the U.S. Government. The neighborhoods surrounding the subject neighborhood are newer residential communities with homes ranging in value from $100,000 to $150,000.

The majority of the people living in the subject's neighborhood are professional or white collar workers, with median incomes from $28,000 to $50,000. The neighborhood is within walking distance of public grade schools, shopping and transportation, and offers several nearby parks and playgrounds.

Pride of ownership is evident throughout the subject's neighborhood. There has been a strong demand for housing in this neighborhood, with a constant uptrend in values during the past several years. This trend should continue in the future.

FINANCING

Typical financing in the area is through assumptions of existing loans, at interest rates generally less than 11½% with cash payments of 20% or more. Conventional mortgages are available, with up to 80% being financed, at interest rates ranging from 10% to 12%.

SITE DATA

STREET NUMBER: 9999 Bowling Green Road

CITY: Homewood   COUNTY: Cook   STATE: Illinois

LOCATED ON THE: North   SIDE OF: Bowling Green Road

BETWEEN: Morgan Avenue   AND: Queens Road

LOT SIZE: 71' × 115'; or 8,165 square feet

OFF-STREET DRIVEWAY: Asphalt

ALLEY: None

STREET PAVING: Asphalt   CURBS: Concrete   SIDEWALKS: Concrete

SEWERS: Sanitary and storm   WATER: City supplied

ELECTRICITY: Public utility   GAS: Public utility

LANDSCAPING: Typical of the neighborhood, with a sodded lawn, shrubs, and trees

FENCING: 4-foot chain link fenced rear yard

ZONING

The subject property is located in an area zoned "R-2, single-family residential." The subject conforms to the zoning ordinance.

AMENITIES

DISTANCE TO:

DOWNTOWN: Chicago--24 miles   LOCAL SHOPPING: 4 blocks

GRADE SCHOOL: 3 blocks   HIGH SCHOOL: Homewood-Flossmoor
Bus--2 miles

TRANSPORTATION: ICRR--2 miles   EXPRESSWAY
ACCESS: Tri-State--2 miles
I-57   --4 miles

DETRIMENTAL INFLUENCES:

Properties are well maintained throughout the neighborhood.

-8-

<u>DESCRIPTION OF IMPROVEMENTS</u>

<u>GENERAL DESCRIPTION</u>:	A single-family residence containing 9½ rooms, 4 bedrooms and 2½ baths
<u>NO. OF STORIES</u>:	split level
<u>AGE</u>:	13 years
<u>CONDITION</u>:	
Exterior:	Good
Interior:	Average
<u>ROOMS</u>:	
Lower Level:	Family room and 2-car garage
1st Floor:	"L" living room and dining room, kitchen and dinette, ½ bath and 1 closet
2nd Floor:	4 bedrooms, 2 baths and 6 closets
Basement:	Sub-basement, underneath the living room, dining room, and kitchen, containing a finished recreation room
<u>EXTERIOR</u>:	
Foundation:	Concrete
Walls:	70% brick veneer and 30% aluminum
Sash:	Wood casement and thermopane
Gutters:	Galvanized; painted
Roof:	Hip and gable, asphalt shingle
Storms and Screens:	Combination aluminum
<u>INTERIOR--PRINCIPAL ROOMS</u>:	
Flooring:	Vinyl tile, oak, and carpet
Walls:	Drywall taped and painted/papered
Ceilings:	Drywall taped and painted
Trim:	Painted pine
<u>KITCHEN</u>:	Modern; original
Cabinets:	Birch
Counters:	Formica
Walls:	Metal, ceramic tile, and drywall
Flooring:	Vinyl with carpet in dinette
Sink:	Double bowl porcelain
Exhaust Fan:	Hood type
Pantry:	None
Equipment:	Built-in gas oven and range, garbage disposal (new) and refrigerator

-9-

<u>DESCRIPTION OF IMPROVEMENTS</u> (Continued)

BATHROOMS:	1st Floor Off Kitchen Hall:	2nd Floor Off Hall:	2nd Floor Off Master Bedroom:
Number:	½	One	One
Flooring:	Carpet	Carpet	Ceramic tile with rug
Walls:	Ceramic tile	Ceramic tile	Ceramic tile
Bathtub:	None	Built-in with shower	Shower
Lavatory:	Single bowl wall hung	Single bowl vanity	Single bowl wall hung
Water Closet:	2-piece	2-piece	2-piece
Medicine Cabinet:	Built-in, mirrored	Built-in, mirrored	Built-in, mirrored
Miscellaneous:	Fan	None	None

<u>CONSTRUCTION</u>:

Floor:	Plywood sub-flooring covered with oak or tile
Joists:	2″ × 10″
Beams:	Steel
Columns:	Steel
Plumbing:	Galvanized pipes

<u>BASEMENT</u>:   Lower level area with an additional sub-basement that is ½ finished with carpeted, drywalled recreation room, and ½ partitioned into a furnace room and playroom (paneled walls and acoustical ceiling), all with asphalt tile floors

<u>HEATING</u>:   Gas fired, forced warm air Bryant furnace with a 190,000 BTU input and an Aprilaire humidifier

<u>COOLING</u>:   3-ton Bryant central air conditioner with a 190,000 BTU input

<u>HOT WATER HEATER</u>:   1-year-old, 40-gallon, gas-fired, Sears hot water heater

<u>ELECTRIC</u>:   100 AMPS, 220-volt system containing 12 circuitbreakers

<u>PORCH</u>:   There are sliding glass doors off the family room that open onto a concrete patio

DESCRIPTION OF IMPROVEMENTS (Continued)

GARAGE: 2 car built-in

    Size: 22¼′ × 23¾′
    Walls: Brick veneer
    Roof: 2nd floor
    Floor: Concrete
    Doors: Wood overhead
    Interior: Drywall
    Miscellaneous   Electric door opener

MISCELLANEOUS AND EXTRAS:

    The foyer of the home has a slate floor and a cathedral ceiling. It was noted that the glass above the front door is effectively screened by a diagonal shade. There is wall-to-wall pile carpeting in the living room, dining room, hall and stairs, with wall-to-wall shag carpeting in the master bedroom. The dinette has wall-to-wall indoor/outdoor carpeting. The family room features a brick raised hearth fireplace, wall-to-wall carpeting, and sliding glass doors leading to a rear concrete patio. There is a walk-in closet in the master bedroom.

    The exterior of the home has six-month-old aluminum siding. There is a gaslight in the front yard, and a basketball backboard and hoop at the patio area.

GENERAL CONDITION:

    The home is in good condition on the exterior, and in average condition on the interior. There are some items that detract from the initial good impression of the house. On the exterior, the patio has settled and has a large crack running through the middle. The fence post nearest the house has concrete broken away from it. These are minor items, but ones which detract from the appearance of the home.

    To bring the highest sale price, the appraiser would recommend curing the following deferred maintenance:

        The trim and gutters around the home show some peeling and are in need of paint. On the interior, the family room ceiling is in need of paint, and one taped seam of the drywall ceiling has come loose and

-11-

<u>DESCRIPTION OF IMPROVEMENTS</u> (Continued)

should be replaced. One upstairs bedroom is painted a lavender color, which is attractive, however, most buyers prefer neutral colors. It is suggested that the bedroom be painted a lighter color. Some of the wallpaper was nonprofessionally installed and detracts from a home in this price range.

The above items should be corrected before offering the home for sale.

<u>FLOOD HAZARD INSURANCE</u>:

FIA Flood Hazard Boundary Map No. H-02, special flood hazard area identification date June 21, 1978, indicates the subject is not located in a special flood hazard area.

<u>FINANCING</u>:

The owners' mortgage, which has a remaining principal balance of $67,500, bearing an interest rate of 10¼%, and with a remaining term of 20 years is assumable.

<u>1988 REAL ESTATE TAXES</u>

VOLUME	TOWN	PERMANENT REAL ESTATE INDEX NUMBER	VALUATION ASSESSED	EQUALIZED
11	2218	32-06-406-028	$22,592.00	$29,372.60

TAX RATE: $7.950   TOTAL TAXES: $2,335.12

The real estate taxes are favorable and probably do not reflect the finishing of the sub-basement.

THE COST APPROACH

The cost approach may be defined as the reproduction cost of the improvements in new condition, less accrued depreciation, plus the value of the land.

Your appraiser has gathered current costs from local contractors actively engaged in building similar properties in the area, and compared these costs to known costs published by current cost manuals.

Since the subject is thirteen years old, and has a remaining economic life of 37 years, physical depreciation due to general deterioration has been estimated at 26%. There is no indication of functional or external depreciation.

REPRODUCTION COST   ALL FIGURES ROUNDED TO NEAREST $100

   *1,736 square feet @ $65.25 per square foot $113,300

LESS DEPRECIATION OF THE STRUCTURE

Physical	$29,500
Functional	-0-
External	-0-

TOTAL DEPRECIATION OF THE STRUCTURE $ 29,500

DEPRECIATED VALUE OF THE STRUCTURE $ 83,800

EXTRAS: DEPRECIATED VALUE

Walks, drive and patio	$ 600
Landscaping	$ 800
Wall-to-wall carpeting	$ 500
Refrigerator	$ 100
Fence	$ 400

TOTAL DEPRECIATED VALUE OF THE EXTRAS $ 2,400

VALUE OF THE LAND BY COMPARISON $ 29,900

   (71 front feet × $421 per front foot)

ESTIMATED VALUE OF THE PROPERTY BY THE COST APPROACH $116,100

   *Base area including built-in garage. Living area including finished sub-basement is 2,445 square feet.

-13-

INCOME APPROACH TO VALUE

The income approach is the second approach used to estimate market value. It is most effectively used with properties that are intended to produce income.

Since single-family residences are not normally built or purchased to obtain income, the income approach is not a reliable method. The typical purchaser of a residence is not looking for a return on the investment in a monetary way, rather, he or she is interested in the amenities or intangibles the investment may bring.

In order to apply this approach to single-family residences, we consider the gross monthly rent unfurnished in relation to the sales price and arrive at a factor called the "gross rent multiplier." This multiplier is abstracted from the market by taking rented properties that have sold and dividing the sales price by the monthly rent. The individual multipliers are analyzed and correlated to give an indication of the gross rent multiplier for houses within a specific price range for a specified area.

The market rent of the subject must now be estimated. This market rent is estimated by comparison with other comparable rented properties. The gross rent multiplier is then multiplied by the estimated market rent of the subject property to arrive at a value estimate for the subject.

Information was secured from four rented properties in the same neighborhood as the property being appraised. All have recently been sold. The following is a resume of these sales.

COMPARABLE PROPERTIES	RENTAL	SALES PRICE	GRM
316 Delta Road	$810	$112,900	139
211 Royal Road	$790	$111,700	141
368 Delta Road	$865	$116,900	135
423 Coach Road	$810	$111,900	138

All of the above data was taken from the same subdivision as the subject. The data indicates a rental value of the subject of $810 per month.

The computed gross rent multipliers range from 135 to 141. It is judged that 139 is the multiplier which is most applicable for the subject property. Therefore, the estimated rental value of $810 multiplied by the gross rent multiple of 139 indicates a value of:

ONE HUNDRED TWELVE THOUSAND SIX HUNDRED DOLLARS ($112,600)

THE SALES COMPARISON APPROACH

In the sales comparison approach, the appraiser's objective is to find the probable market value of the subject property by interpreting data on sales of similar properties. Each comparable sale is compared with the subject property. Typically the elements of comparison include <u>date of sale</u>, <u>location</u>, <u>physical characteristics</u>, <u>terms of financing</u>, and <u>conditions of sale</u>. Adjustments are made to the comparable sales prices to arrive at an indication of what the subject property would sell for if offered in the market.

Following are four sales which are similar to the property being appraised. The information is then summarized on the Comparable Sales Analysis form on page 18 of this report.

<u>SALE NO. 1</u>:

Location: 164 May Street, Homewood, Illinois
Date of Sale: May 15, 1989
Sales Price: $112,900
Type: A 13-year-old brick and frame split level, same model as sub-
               ject, containing 9-½ rooms, 4 bedrooms, 2½ baths, and a
               2-car built-in garage, on a 71′ × 115′ lot. Extras include cen-
               tral air-conditioning, wall-to-wall carpeting in seven rooms,
               fireplace, finished family room, built-in oven and range, dish-
               washer, disposal, intercom, and patio. The sub-basement was
               finished and included a bar. It was reported to your appraiser
               that the home was in average condition at the time of sale
               and was originally listed on March 21, 1989 for $115,100. The
               sellers' mortgage (10½% interest for 22 years with $71,000
               remaining balance) was assumed by the buyers.

<u>THE SALES COMPARISON APPROACH</u> (Continued)

<u>SALE NO. 2</u>

Location:	186 May Street, Homewood, Illinois
Date of Sale:	February 26, 1989
Sales Price:	$115,000
Type:	A 12-year-old brick and frame split level, same model as subject, containing 9½ rooms, 4 bedrooms, 2½ baths, and a 2-car built-in garage, on a 119′ × 143′ × 130′ × 75′ corner lot. Extras included wall-to-wall carpeting in three rooms, drapes in four rooms, built-in oven and range, central air-conditioning, artificial fireplace, patio, privacy stockade fence and a recreation room in the sub-basement. It was reported to your appraiser that the home was in good condition at the time of sale and was originally listed on December 5, 1988 for $119,800. Buyers assumed sellers' mortgage (10½% interest for 21 years on $69,000).

<u>SALE NO. 3</u>

Location:	149 Coach Road, Homewood, Illinois
Date of Sale:	November 23, 1988
Sales Price:	$115,000
Type:	A 12-year-old brick and frame split level, same model as subject, containing 9½ rooms, 4 bedrooms, 2½ baths, and a 2-car built-in garage, on a 70′ × 200′ × 70′ × 175′ lot. Extras included central air conditioning, fireplace, wall-to-wall carpeting, patio, gas grill, oven and range, dishwasher, disposal and a humidifier. This home was originally listed on September 15, 1988, and offered for sale at $117,500. The sellers' mortgage (10¼% interest for 18 years with $63,000 remaining balance) was assumed by the buyers.

THE SALES COMPARISON APPROACH (Continued)

SALE NO. 4

Location: 153 May Street, Homewood, Illinois
Date of Sale: December 15, 1988
Sales price: $106,800
Type: A 12-year-old brick and frame split level, same model as sub-
                 ject, containing 8½ rooms, 4 bedrooms, 2½ baths, and a 2-car
                 built-in garage, on a 74′ × 165′ × 147′ lot. Extras included
                 wall-to-wall carpeting, oven and range, central air-conditioning,
                 family room with beamed ceiling, tiled sub-basement floor
                 and electric garage door opener. This home was offered for sale
                 with three brokers, and was on the market for 1½ years,
                 with an original asking price of $112,300. Because the sell-
                 ers' mortgage was not assumable, and they did not want to
                 help finance the sale, the buyers obtained a conventional
                 mortgage with a 10¾% interest rate on $85,000 of the pur-
                 chase price.

COMPARABLE SALES ANALYSIS

	SUBJECT PROPERTY	SALE NUMBER 1	*Adj.	SALE NUMBER 2	Adj.	SALE NUMBER 3	Adj.	SALE NUMBER 4	Adj.
ADDRESS	9999 Bowling Green Rd. Homewood	164 May Homewood		186 May Homewood		149 Coach Homewood		153 May Homewood	
PROXIMITY TO SUBJECT		4 blocks		3 blocks		4 blocks		4 blocks	
DESCRIPTION OF IMPROVEMENTS	Split Level	Same		Same		Same		Same	
Rms.	9½	9½		9½		9½		8½	
Bdrms.	4	4		4		4		4	
Bths.	2½	2½		2½		2½		2½	
Other Rms.	Sub-Bsmt.	Fin/Bar	-.5	Same		Unfin	+1.0	Unfin	+1.0
LOCATION		Same		Same		Same		Same	
HOUSE SIZE	Base/1736SF	1736SF		1736SF		1736SF		1736SF	
AGE	13 years	13 yrs.		12 yrs.	-.5	12 yrs.	-.5	12 yrs.	-.5
CONDITION	Average	Avg.		Good	-1.5	Exc.	-2.0	Avg.	
QUALITY OF CONST.	Average	Avg.		Avg.		Avg.		Avg.	
LOT SIZE	71' × 115'	70' × 115'		+Corner	-1.0	+Lrger	-.5	74' × 165'	-1.0
FINANCING	Assumable	Assump.		Assump.		Assump.		Conv.	+3.5
UTILITY	Very Good	V. Good		V. Good		V. Good		V. Good	
Air Conditioning	Central	Central		Central		Central		Central	
Fireplace	Yes	Yes		Artif.	+1.0	Yes		None	+1.5
W/W Carpeting	Yes	Same		Same		New	-.5	Same	
Misc. Extras	Bis, Patio, etc.	Same		Same		New	-.5	Same	
DESC. & ADJ. FOR CHG.									
MKT. COND. SINCE LAST SALE	Purchased new	None		Strong Upward Market	+1,000	Strong Upward Market	+1,500	Strong Upward Market	+1,500
DATE OF SALE	N/A	5-15-89		2-26-89		11-23-88		12-15-88	
SALES PRICE		$112,900		$115,000		$115,000		$106,500	
TERMS OF SALE		Assump.		Assump.		Assump.		Conv.	
TOTAL ADJUSTMENT			-500		-1,000		-1,500		+6,000
INDICATED VALUE OF SUBJECT		$112,400		$114,000		$113,500		$112,500	

*Adjustments stated in $1,000 amounts; that is, 1.0 = $1,000.

THE SALES COMPARISON APPROACH (Continued)

The four sales produced a range of adjusted sales prices from $112,400 to $114,000, a very close range. It was concluded that the upper end of this range best reflected the appraised property's value because of the strong demand for and current shortage of homes offered for sale in the subject's neighborhood. The subject also has a large, assumable loan, at a rate lower than prevailing market rates, so that financing should be no impediment to a sale.

Based on these four sales and considering other available sales on the market, it is this appraiser's opinion that the indicated market value of the subject property is:

ONE HUNDRED FOURTEEN THOUSAND DOLLARS ($114,000)

VALUE RECONCILIATION

Reconciliation is the bringing into harmony of ideas or indications. The different indications of value derived in this appraisal report follow:

Value Indicated by Cost Approach	$116,100
Value Indicated by Income Approach	$112,600
Value Indicated by Sales Comparison Approach	$114,000

All these approaches were utilized to make the final value estimate. I have carefully reexamined each step in each method, and I believe the conclusions accurately reflect the attitude of typical purchasers of residential property in this neighborhood. It is my belief that this reexamination has confirmed the original conclusions.

The Cost Approach will result in an excellent estimate if all elements are figured accurately, because no prudent person will pay more for a property than the cost to produce a substitute property with equal desirability and utility. Purchasers of the type of dwelling typical of the subject property are more concerned with amenities than with hypothetical replacement of the property. The value of the cost approach is not disregarded, but given less weight because more errors of judgment can be made in this approach.

The Income Approach, for the most part, is the least reliable of the three approaches to value for this type of property, since the typical purchaser is more interested in the amenities and benefits that will be received than the income such properties will produce. It has been used primarily in this appraisal as a check on the other two approaches and tends to support the conclusions found by the cost and sales comparison approaches.

The Sales Comparison Approach was based on several recent sales of properties similar to that of the subject, all of which are located in the same general area. The adjusted sales prices are most consistent under comparison. This approach is the most reliable because it reflects the reactions of typical buyers and sellers in the market.

CONCLUSION

   All three approaches indicate close values. After careful consideration
of the three approaches, it is this appraiser's judgment that the greatest
weight should be given to the value found in the sales comparison approach. This approach is the one that best reflects the emotions and de-
sires of the buying public and for which the greatest amount of reliable data
was available.

   As a result of this appraisal and analysis, it is concluded that the market value of the subject property in its present condition in fee simple
interest unencumbered as of May 29, 1989, is:

   ONE HUNDRED FOURTEEN THOUSAND DOLLARS ($114,000)

UNDERLYING ASSUMPTIONS AND LIMITING CONDITIONS APPLICABLE TO THIS APPRAISAL

1.   I assume no responsibility for matters legal in nature, nor do I render any opinion as to the title, which is assumed to be marketable. The property is appraised as though under responsible ownership.

2.   The legal description used herein is assumed, but is not guaranteed to be correct.

3.   I have made no survey of the property, and the boundaries are taken from records believed to be reliable. The sketches in this report are included to assist the reader in visualizing the property, and I assume no responsibility for their accuracy.

4.   I am not required to testify or appear in court on matters contained herein, unless previous arrangements have been made.

5.   The distribution of the total valuation in this report between land and improvements applies only under the existing program of utilization. The separate valuations for land and building must not be used in conjunction with any other appraisal and are invalid if so used.

6.   I assume that there are no hidden or unapparent conditions of the property, subsoil or structures which would render it more or less valuable. I assume no responsibility for such conditions or for engineering which might be required to discover such factors.

7.   The information, estimates, and opinions furnished to me and contained in this report were obtained from sources considered reliable and believed to be true and accurate. However, no responsibility for accuracy can be assumed by me.

8.   This report is to be used in its entirety and only for the purpose for which it was rendered.

9.   Neither all nor any part of the contents of this report (especially any conclusions as to value, the identity of the appraiser or the firm with which he is connected, or any reference to the American Institute of Real Estate Appraisers and the Society of Real Estate Appraisers or to the R.M. or S.R.A. designation) shall be reproduced, published, or disseminated to the public through advertising media, public relations media, news media, sales media, or any other public means of communication, without the prior written consent and approval of the appraiser.

<u>CERTIFICATE OF APPRAISAL</u>

This appraiser hereby certifies that:

1. I have no present or contemplated future interest in the subject property.

2. I have no personal interest or bias with respect to the subject matter of this appraisal report or the parties involved. My findings are not based on the employment to make the appraisal or the compensation expected.

3. To the best of my knowledge and belief, the statements of fact contained in this appraisal report, upon which the analyses, opinions and conclusions expressed herein are based, are true and correct.

4. This appraisal report sets forth all of the limiting conditions (imposed by the terms of my assignment or by the undersigned) affecting the analyses, opinions and conclusions contained in this report.

5. This appraisal report has been made in conformity with and is subject to the requirements of the Code of Professional Ethics and Standards of Professional Conduct of the appraisal organizations with which the appraiser is affiliated.

6. No one other than the undersigned prepared the analyses, conclusions and opinions concerning real estate that are set forth in this appraisal report.

7. Based upon the information contained in this report and upon my general experience as an appraiser, it is my opinion that the Market Value as defined herein, of the subject property, as of May 29, 1989 is:

ONE HUNDRED FOURTEEN THOUSAND DOLLARS ($114,000)

ALVIN L. WAGNER, JR., S.R.A., R.M.

QUALIFICATIONS OF APPRAISER--ALVIN L. WAGNER, JR.

EDUCATION

Graduated: Drake University, Des Moines, Iowa, BA in Economics. Appraisal Courses I, II, and VIII given by the American Institute of Real Estate Appraisers; Courses I, II, and III of the Real Estate Institute, Chicago

PROFESSIONAL MEMBERSHIPS

Member: American Institute of Real Estate Appraisers, R.M.; Society of Real Estate Appraisers, S.R.A.; Chicago Board of Realtors; Illinois Association of Realtors; National Association of Realtors; Homewood-Flossmoor Board of Realtors; Licensed Real Estate Broker--State of Illinois

EXPERIENCE

Owner: A.L. Wagner and Company, Real Estate Appraiser and Consultant; 1969-Present C.A. Bruckner and Associates--Chicago; Real Estate Appraiser 1967-69; Real Estate Loan Officer and Chief Appraiser, Beverly Bank, Chicago, 1963-67; Staff Appraiser, Oak Park Federal, part-time, Oak Park, Illinois, 1955-60; Current instructor of Real Estate Appraisal Courses I and II and member Advisory Committee, Prairie State College, Chicago Heights, Illinois; Rich Township Quadrennial Assessors Committee; Instructor of Course VIII and member of Governing Council 1974-75 of American Institute of Real Estate Appraisers

APPRAISAL EXPERIENCE AND CLIENTS

Appraisals for purposes of mortgage loans, buyers, sellers, estates, employee transfers, vacant land, special purpose, apartments, industrial, and foreclosures have been made for the following partial list of clients in the States of Illinois and Indiana:

Government: Federal National Mortgage Association (FNMA); Federal Savings and Loan Insurance Corporation; Federal Deposit Insurance Corporation; Federal Home Loan Bank; Village of Homewood; City of Palos Heights

Financial Institutions: Beverly Bank; Continental Bank; Northern Trust Company; Lakeside Bank--Chicago; Matteson-Richton Bank--Matteson; Bank of Park Forest; Park Forest Savings and Loan; Bank of Homewood; Homewood Federal Savings and Loan; Union Federal Savings and Loan; 1st Savings and Loan of Hegewisch; Chicago Heights Federal Savings and Loan

-24-

<u>QUALIFICATIONS OF APPRAISER--ALVIN L. WAGNER, JR.</u> (Continued)

Insurance   Equitable Life Assurance Society; C.N.A. Insurance; Prudential In-
Companies: surance Company; Aetna Life and Casualty Company; Continen-
                 tal Casualty Company; Investors Mortgage Insurance Company--
                 Boston

Corporations: Sherwin-Williams; Interlake Inc.; Ford Motor; Eaton Corp.; Gen-
                 eral Foods Corp.; Honeywell; Kraft Foods; Abbott Labs; R.R.
                 Donnelley and Sons; Desoto Chemical; Youngstown Sheet and Tube;
                 F.M.C. Corp.; Park Forest Properties; Illinois Bell Telephone; In-
                 land Steel; General Electric; Atlantic Richfield; U.S. Steel; Dow
                 Chemical; IBM; Xerox; Upjohn Co.; G.A.F. Corp.; Illinois Central;
                 Penn Central; Martin Oil Service Inc.; Humble Oil and Refining;
                 Cities Service Oil; Phillips Petroleum; Homequity, Inc.; Employee
                 Transfer Corporation; T-I Home Transfer; Previews, Inc.; Vulcan
                 Materials

Attorneys and Individuals

EXHIBIT "A"

PHOTOGRAPHS OF SUBJECT PROPERTY
TAKEN ON MAY 1, 1989

FRONT VIEW LOOKING NORTHEAST

REAR VIEW LOOKING SOUTHEAST

-26-

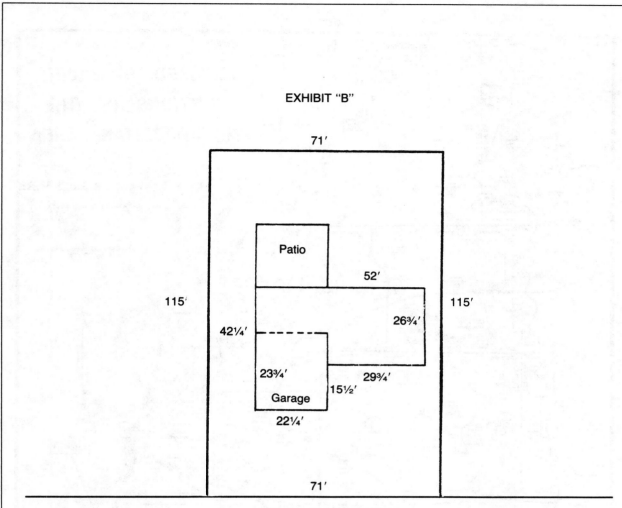

EXHIBIT "B"

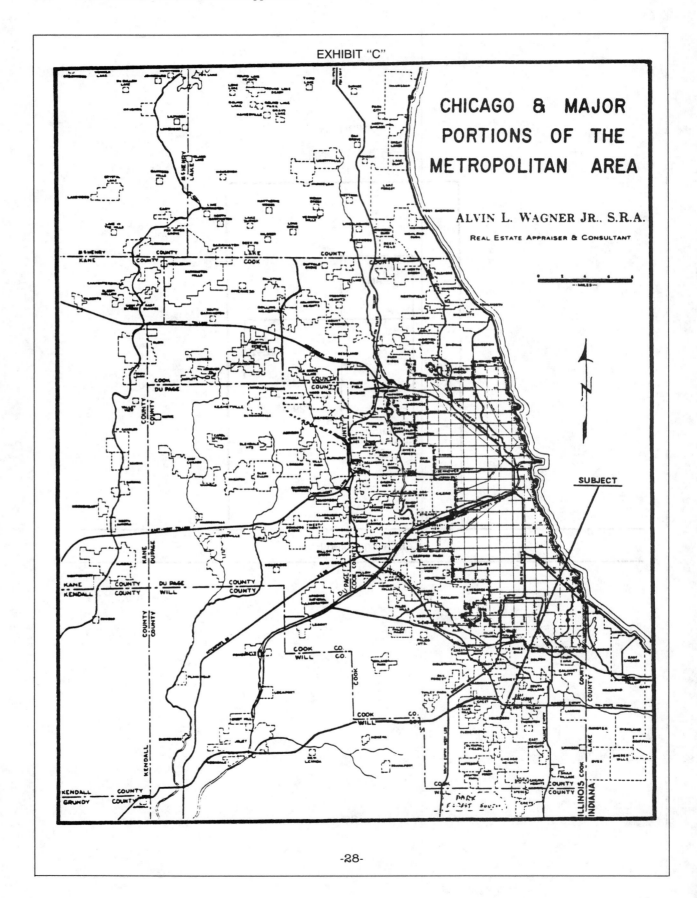

EXHIBIT "C"

CHICAGO & MAJOR PORTIONS OF THE METROPOLITAN AREA

ALVIN L. WAGNER JR., S.R.A.
REAL ESTATE APPRAISER & CONSULTANT

EXHIBIT "D"

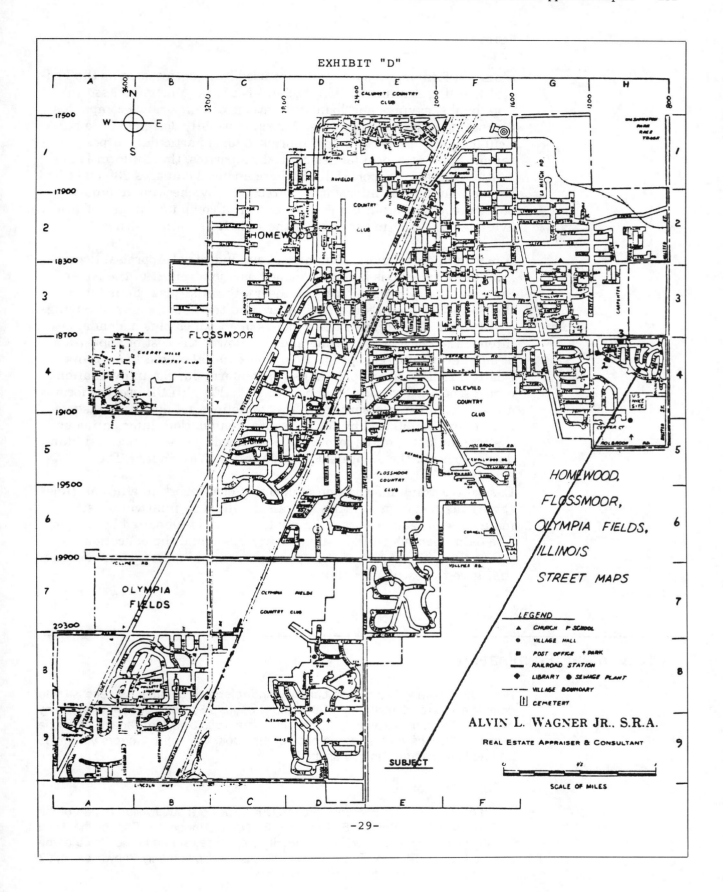

HOMEWOOD,
FLOSSMOOR,
OLYMPIA FIELDS,
ILLINOIS
STREET MAPS

LEGEND
▲ CHURCH ⌐ SCHOOL
● VILLAGE HALL
■ POST OFFICE + PARK
▬ RAILROAD STATION
◆ LIBRARY ● SEWAGE PLANT
— ·· — VILLAGE BOUNDARY
[†] CEMETERY

ALVIN L. WAGNER JR., S.R.A.
REAL ESTATE APPRAISER & CONSULTANT

SUBJECT

SCALE OF MILES

Form Report

Standard form appraisal reports are used by agencies such as the Federal Housing Administration, Federal National Mortgage Association, banks, savings and loan associations and insurance companies for routine property appraisals. A form is usually designed for a particular type of property being appraised for a particular purpose. A sample appraisal form for residential properties, the Uniform Residential Appraisal Report (URAR), is reproduced on pages 238 and 239. Notice that specific information is recorded by checking appropriate boxes and/or filling in blanks. A number of computer programs are available to assist in completing the URAR and other forms.

A new form, the Uniform Commercial and Industrial Appraisal Report—Existing Property, is being developed as a joint effort of the American Institute of Real Estate Appraisers, the Appraisal Foundation, the Society of Real Estate Appraisers and the U.S. League of Savings Institutions. The form, which consists of 13 pages plus addenda, is intended to cut down the time and thus lower the cost of appraisals of smaller commercial properties. The Federal Home Loan Bank Board (FHLBB) has approved use of the form during an evaluation period scheduled to end December 31, 1989. For FHLBB use, the form must be completed according to the guidelines set out in an instruction manual published by the Appraisal Foundation. Information on the current status of the form can be obtained from the Appraisal Standards Board of the Appraisal Foundation in Washington, D.C.

Ease of recording information makes the form report an efficient, time-saving method of presenting appraisal data. The final value estimate does not gain accuracy simply because it is supported by a report. The data upon which the estimates are based and the education, experience and judgment of the appraiser are the important elements that give the estimate validity.

Achievement Examination 8

Read the following information carefully and refer to it as often as necessary to complete the residential appraisal form on pages 238 and 239. Fill in as many items on the form as you can, then compare your own form against the one shown in the Answer Key at the back of the book. Correct any errors you made and add any information you omitted.

Legal Description:

Lot 31 in Block 4 in Hickory Gardens Unit 1, being a subdivision of part of the Southeast ¼ of Section 5, Township 30 North, Range 15, East of the Third Principal Meridian, according to the plat thereof registered in the Office of the Registrar of Titles of Cook County, Illinois, and commonly known as: 4807 Catalpa Road, Woodview, Illinois 60000.

Purpose of the Appraisal:

To estimate the fair market value of the subject property, held in fee simple, for possible sale purposes.

Real Estate Taxes:

The subject property is assessed for ad valorem tax purposes at $29,092. The tax rate is $7.828 per $100 of assessed value, which compares favorably with comparable suburban areas.

Neighborhood Data:

The subject property is located in a desirable subdivision in the Central Eastern section of the Village of Woodview. The seven-year-old neighborhood is 100 percent developed with single-family residences currently ranging in value from $90,000 to $120,000. Most are valued at about $110,000, and virtually all are owner occupied.

The subject's subdivision is bounded on the East by the Village of Willow; on the South by 40th Street; to the West by Grand Street; and to the North by Park District land. The surrounding neighborhoods are newer residential communities with homes ranging in value from $100,000 to $160,000.

The occupants of the subject's area are mostly white-collar workers, with median incomes ranging from $22,000 to $38,000. Employment opportunities in this area have historically been better than the national average. The neighborhood is within walking distance of public grade schools of good reputation, shopping and transportation and offers several nearby parks and playgrounds. Police and fire protection have been above average. Pride of ownership is evident throughout the subject's neighborhood and there has been a strong demand for housing, with a steady uptrend in values during the past several years. Most houses are sold within three months of being put on the market.

Amenities:

Downtown Chicago is 30 miles away, accessible by car, bus and train; local shopping, six blocks; grade school, two blocks; high school, one mile, but accessible by bus; commuter railroad station, four blocks; expressway, two miles.

There are no detrimental influences.

Site Data:

The site is at 4807 Catalpa Road in Woodview, Cook County, Illinois 60000. The site is on the north side of Catalpa between Salem and Third. The lot is a rectangle, 65′ × 130′ or 8,450 square feet, providing a large rear yard. There is an asphalt driveway but no alley. The street paving is also asphalt; the sidewalks and curbs are concrete. The site is an inside lot, level and with a good view of the tree-lined street, typical of the area.

Sanitary and storm sewers are maintained by the city. Drainage is very good, and there is no danger of flooding. A review of the applicable flood-zone map indicates that the subject property is not located in a flood hazard area. Water is city supplied; public utility companies provide electricity and gas. There have been no major fuel supply problems in this area, and none are foreseen. Streetlights are city maintained. Electric and telephone lines are underground.

Landscaping is typical of the neighborhood, with a sodded lawn, shrubs and trees. The rear yard has a six-foot redwood fence.

Zoning:

The subject property is zoned "R-2, Single-Family Residence District." The subject conforms to the zoning ordinance.

Highest and Best Use:

The subject property conforms to existing zoning regulations and constitutes the highest and best use of the site.

Easements and Encroachments:

There are no easements or encroachments affecting this property, either of record or as noted by visual inspection.

Description of Improvements:

general description—a single-family residence, ranch style, containing seven rooms, three bedrooms and two baths; contemporary open floor plan and typical room layout and dimensions

age—seven years (effective age seven years); remaining economic life, 43 to 48 years

condition—exterior, good; interior, good

rooms—living room, dining room, family room, kitchen, three bedrooms, two baths, six closets and two-car garage

exterior—concrete foundation, 100 percent brick veneer walls, wood-framed, double-hung windows with thermopane glass, galvanized and painted gutters, hip and gable roof with asphalt shingles, and aluminum combination storms and screens.

Interior (principal rooms)—vinyl tile in kitchen and bathrooms, finished oak flooring covered with wall-to-wall carpeting in other rooms; wall covering of drywall, taped and painted or papered; ceilings of drywall, taped and painted; average trim of painted pine.

kitchen—modern, with maple cabinets, formica counters, vinyl flooring with carpet in dinette, double-bowl porcelain sink, hood-type exhaust fan, built-in gas oven and range, garbage disposal (new), dishwasher and refrigerator; no pantry

bathrooms—two full baths, each with ceramic tile floor and wainscoting, built-in tub with shower, single-bowl vanity lavatory with mirrored medicine cabinet and a two-piece built-in water closet

construction—plywood subflooring covered with oak or tile, 2″ × 10″ joists, steel beams and columns; galvanized pipes in good condition

basement—crawl space

heating—very good, gas-fired, forced warm air furnace with adequate 190,000 BTU output

cooling—very good three-ton central air conditioner with adequate 190,000 BTU output

hot water heater—one-year-old, 40-gallon, gas-fired hot water heater

electrical wiring—100-amp, 220-volt system containing 12 circuit breakers

insulation—six inches above ceilings and behind drywall

garage—two-car detached, 20′ × 25′ with frame walls, asphalt roof, concrete floor and wood overhead door.

Miscellaneous and Extras:

The foyer of the home has a ceramic tile floor. There is wall-to-wall plush carpeting of good quality in the living room, dining room, hall, stairs and bedrooms. The dinette and family room have wall-to-wall indoor/outdoor carpeting. The family room has a masonry fireplace. A low attic accessible by drop-stair could be used for storage, but is not floored or heated.

General Condition:

Overall, the house and garage are in good condition, with normal wear and tear. Materials and finish are somewhat better than average, but comparable to other homes in this area.

Current Market Conditions:

The current housing market is strong, reflecting a healthy local economy. Typical financing in the area is through conventional mortgages, with up to 80 percent financed at interest rates ranging from 10¾ percent to 11¼ percent, depending on the down payment. Mortgage funds are readily available.

Cost Data:

house	$65 per square foot
extra insulation	$600
garage	$20 per square foot
landscaping, driveway, fencing	$5,400
land value by allocation	$35,000

depreciation factors (to date)		
garage	physical	10%
	functional	0
	external	0
house	physical	10%
	functional	0
	external	0
other improvements	physical	10%

Market Data:

Adjustment value of fireplace is $2,000.
Adjustment value of finished basement is $5,000.

The subject has an assumable mortgage.

Income Data:

House like subject, but without fireplace, rents for $1,050
House like subject, but without garage, rents for $1,025
House like subject, but without garage and fireplace, rents for $1,000

Typical Sales and Rental Statistics:

House (A) sold for $140,000 and rented for $950.
House (B) sold for $146,550 and rented for $1,000
House (C) sold for $153,500 and rented for $1,050

The square footage of the house may be computed by using the figures indicated in the diagram below.

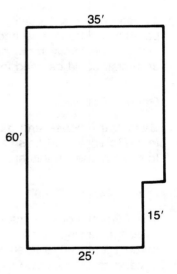

Check your completed appraisal report form against the one given in the Answer Key at the back of the book.

SALES PRICE ADJUSTMENT CHART

COMPARABLES

	1140 CENTRAL PARK	25 JACKSON	4310 W. GLADYS	3846 W. MONROE	316 IOWA
SALES PRICE	$142,000	$151,000	$158,000	$159,500	$167,250
FINANCING	CASH	CONV.	CONV.	CONV.	CONV.
DATE OF SALE	4 WKS. AGO	1 YR. AGO	6 WKS. AGO	3 WKS. AGO	6 WKS. AGO
LOCATION	QUIET RESID.	QUIET RESID.	QUIET RESID.	QUIET RESID.	QUIET RESID.
SITE/VIEW	GOOD	GOOD	GOOD	GOOD	GOOD
SIZE OF LOT	65'X130'	65'X130'	65'X130'	65'X130'	65'X130'
DESIGN AND APPEAL	RANCH/GOOD	RANCH/GOOD	RANCH/GOOD	RANCH/GOOD	RANCH/GOOD
CONSTRUCTION	GOOD	GOOD	GOOD	GOOD	GOOD
AGE	7 YRS.	7 YRS.	7 YRS.	7 YRS.	7 YRS.
CONDITION	FAIR	GOOD	GOOD	GOOD	GOOD
NO. OF RMS./BEDRMS./BATHS	7/3/2	7/3/2	7/3/2	7/3/2	7/3/2
SQ. FT. OF LIVING SPACE	1,950	2,300	1,975	1,950	1,940
OTHER SPACE (BASEMENT)	CRAWL SP.	CRAWL SP.	CRAWL SP.	CRAWL SP.	FINISHED BASEMENT
FUNCTIONAL UTILITY	ADEQUATE	ADEQUATE	ADEQUATE	ADEQUATE	ADEQUATE
HEATING/COOLING	CENTRAL H/A	CENTRAL H/A	CENTRAL H/A	CENTRAL H/A	CENTRAL H/A
GARAGE/CARPORT	NONE	2-CAR DET.	2-CAR DET.	2-CAR DET.	2-CAR DET.
OTHER EXT. IMPROVEMENTS	NONE	NONE	NONE	NONE	NONE
SPECIAL ENERGY EFFICIENT ITEMS	EXTRA INSULATION	EXTRA INSULATION	EXTRA INSULATION	EXTRA INSULATION	EXTRA INSULATION
FIREPLACE(S)	ONE, MASONRY	ONE, MASONRY	NONE	ONE, MASONRY	ONE, MASONRY
OTHER INT. IMPROVEMENTS	NONE	NONE	NONE	NONE	NONE
TYPICAL HOUSE VALUE					
VARIABLE FEATURE					
ADJUSTMENT VALUE OF VARIABLE					

Property Description & Analysis   **UNIFORM RESIDENTIAL APPRAISAL REPORT**   File No. _____

SUBJECT

Property Address	Census Tract	**LENDER DISCRETIONARY USE**
City ___ County ___ State ___	Zip Code	Sale Price $ _____
Legal Description		Date _____
Owner/Occupant	Map Reference	Mortgage Amount $ _____
Sale Price $ ___ Date of Sale	PROPERTY RIGHTS APPRAISED	Mortgage Type _____
Loan charges/concessions to be paid by seller $	☐ Fee Simple	Discount Points and Other Concessions
R.E. Taxes $ ___ Tax Year ___ HOA $/Mo.	☐ Leasehold	Paid by Seller $ _____
Lender/Client	☐ Condominium (HUD/VA)	
	☐ De Minimis PUD	Source

NEIGHBORHOOD

LOCATION	☐ Urban	☐ Suburban	☐ Rural	NEIGHBORHOOD ANALYSIS	Good	Avg.	Fair	Poor
BUILT UP	☐ Over 75%	☐ 25-75%	☐ Under 25%	Employment Stability	☐	☐	☐	☐
GROWTH RATE	☐ Rapid	☐ Stable	☐ Slow	Convenience to Employment	☐	☐	☐	☐
PROPERTY VALUES	☐ Increasing	☐ Stable	☐ Declining	Convenience to Shopping	☐	☐	☐	☐
DEMAND/SUPPLY	☐ Shortage	☐ In Balance	☐ Over Supply	Convenience to Schools	☐	☐	☐	☐
MARKETING TIME	☐ Under 3 Mos.	☐ 3-6 Mos.	☐ Over 6 Mos.	Adequacy of Public Transportation	☐	☐	☐	☐

PRESENT LAND USE %	LAND USE CHANGE	PREDOMINANT OCCUPANCY	SINGLE FAMILY HOUSING PRICE $ (000) / AGE (yrs)					
Single Family ___	Not Likely ☐	Owner ☐		Recreation Facilities	☐	☐	☐	☐
2-4 Family ___	Likely ☐	Tenant ☐		Adequacy of Utilities	☐	☐	☐	☐
Multi-family ___	In process ☐	Vacant (0-5%) ☐	Low	Property Compatibility	☐	☐	☐	☐
Commercial ___	To: ___	Vacant (over 5%) ☐	High	Protection from Detrimental Cond.	☐	☐	☐	☐
Industrial ___			Predominant	Police & Fire Protection	☐	☐	☐	☐
Vacant ___			—	General Appearance of Properties	☐	☐	☐	☐
				Appeal to Market	☐	☐	☐	☐

Note: Race or the racial composition of the neighborhood are not considered reliable appraisal factors.

COMMENTS: _____

SITE

Dimensions ___		Topography ___
Site Area ___	Corner Lot ___	Size ___
Zoning Classification ___	Zoning Compliance ___	Shape ___
HIGHEST & BEST USE: Present Use ___	Other Use ___	Drainage ___

UTILITIES	Public	Other	SITE IMPROVEMENTS	Type	Public	Private		
Electricity	☐		Street		☐	☐	View	___
Gas	☐		Curb/Gutter		☐	☐	Landscaping	___
Water	☐		Sidewalk		☐	☐	Driveway	___
Sanitary Sewer	☐		Street Lights		☐	☐	Apparent Easements	___
Storm Sewer	☐		Alley		☐	☐	FEMA Flood Hazard Yes* ___ No ___
							FEMA* Map/Zone	___

COMMENTS (Apparent adverse easements, encroachments, special assessments, slide areas, etc.): _____

IMPROVEMENTS

GENERAL DESCRIPTION	EXTERIOR DESCRIPTION	FOUNDATION	BASEMENT	INSULATION	
Units ___	Foundation ___	Slab ___	Area Sq. Ft. ___	Roof	☐
Stories ___	Exterior Walls ___	Crawl Space ___	% Finished ___	Ceiling	☐
Type (Det./Att.) ___	Roof Surface ___	Basement ___	Ceiling ___	Walls	☐
Design (Style) ___	Gutters & Dwnspts. ___	Sump Pump ___	Walls ___	Floor	☐
Existing ___	Window Type ___	Dampness ___	Floor ___	None	☐
Proposed ___	Storm Sash ___	Settlement ___	Outside Entry ___	Adequacy	☐
Under Construction ___	Screens ___	Infestation ___		Energy Efficient Items:
Age (Yrs.) ___	Manufactured House ___			
Effective Age (Yrs.) ___				

ROOM LIST

ROOMS	Foyer	Living	Dining	Kitchen	Den	Family Rm.	Rec. Rm.	Bedrooms	# Baths	Laundry	Other	Area Sq. Ft.
Basement												
Level 1												
Level 2												

Finished area **above** grade contains: ___ Rooms; ___ Bedroom(s); ___ Bath(s); ___ Square Feet of Gross Living Area

INTERIOR

SURFACES	Materials/Condition	HEATING	KITCHEN EQUIP.	ATTIC	IMPROVEMENT ANALYSIS	Good	Avg.	Fair	Poor
Floors	___	Type ___	Refrigerator ☐	None ☐	Quality of Construction	☐	☐	☐	☐
Walls	___	Fuel ___	Range/Oven ☐	Stairs ☐	Condition of Improvements	☐	☐	☐	☐
Trim/Finish	___	Condition ___	Disposal ☐	Drop Stair ☐	Room Sizes/Layout	☐	☐	☐	☐
Bath Floor	___	Adequacy ___	Dishwasher ☐	Scuttle ☐	Closets and Storage	☐	☐	☐	☐
Bath Wainscot	___	COOLING	Fan/Hood ☐	Floor ☐	Energy Efficiency	☐	☐	☐	☐
Doors	___	Central ___	Compactor ☐	Heated ☐	Plumbing-Adequacy & Condition	☐	☐	☐	☐
		Other ___	Washer/Dryer ☐	Finished ☐	Electrical-Adequacy & Condition	☐	☐	☐	☐
		Condition ___	Microwave ☐		Kitchen Cabinets-Adequacy & Cond.	☐	☐	☐	☐
Fireplace(s) # ___		Adequacy ___	Intercom ☐		Compatibility to Neighborhood	☐	☐	☐	☐

AUTOS

CAR STORAGE:	Garage	☐ Attached	☐ Adequate	House Entry ☐	Appeal & Marketability	☐	☐	☐	☐
No. Cars ___	Carport	☐ Detached	☐ Inadequate	Outside Entry ☐	Estimated Remaining Economic Life ___ Yrs.
Condition ___	None	☐ Built-In	☐ Electric Door	Basement Entry ☐	Estimated Remaining Physical Life ___ Yrs.

Additional features: _____

COMMENTS

Depreciation (Physical, functional and external inadequacies, repairs needed, modernization, etc.): _____

General market conditions and prevalence and impact in subject/market area regarding loan discounts, interest buydowns and concessions: _____

Valuation Section

UNIFORM RESIDENTIAL APPRAISAL REPORT   File No. _____

Purpose of Appraisal is to estimate Market Value as defined in the Certification & Statement of Limiting Conditions.

COST APPROACH

BUILDING SKETCH (SHOW GROSS LIVING AREA ABOVE GRADE)
If for Freddie Mac or Fannie Mae, show only square foot calculations and cost approach comments in this space

ESTIMATED REPRODUCTION COST – NEW – OF IMPROVEMENTS:

Dwelling _____ Sq. Ft. @ $ _____ = $ _____
_____ Sq. Ft. @ $ _____ = _____
Extras _____ = _____
_____ =
Special Energy Efficient Items _____ = _____
Porches, Patios, etc. _____ = _____
Garage/Carport _____ Sq. Ft. @ $ _____ = _____
Total Estimated Cost New .... = $ _____

	Physical	Functional	External
Less			

Depreciation _____ = $ _____
Depreciated Value of Improvements .... = $ _____
Site Imp. "as is" (driveway, landscaping, etc.) = $ _____
ESTIMATED SITE VALUE .... = $ _____
(If leasehold, show only leasehold value.)
INDICATED VALUE BY COST APPROACH .... = $ _____

(Not Required by Freddie Mac and Fannie Mae)
Does property conform to applicable HUD/VA property standards? ☐ Yes ☐ No
If No, explain: _____

Construction Warranty ☐ Yes ☐ No
Name of Warranty Program _____
Warranty Coverage Expires _____

SALES COMPARISON ANALYSIS

The undersigned has recited three recent sales of properties most similar and proximate to subject and has considered these in the market analysis. The description includes a dollar adjustment, reflecting market reaction to those items of significant variation between the subject and comparable properties. If a significant item in the comparable property is superior to, or more favorable than, the subject property, a minus (–) adjustment is made, thus reducing the indicated value of subject; if a significant item in the comparable is inferior to, or less favorable than, the subject property, a plus (+) adjustment is made, thus increasing the indicated value of the subject.

ITEM	SUBJECT	COMPARABLE NO. 1		COMPARABLE NO. 2		COMPARABLE NO. 3	
Address							
Proximity to Subject							
Sales Price	$	$		$		$	
Price/Gross Liv. Area	$ ☐	$ ☐		$ ☐		$ ☐	
Data Source							
VALUE ADJUSTMENTS	DESCRIPTION	DESCRIPTION	+ (–) $ Adjustment	DESCRIPTION	+ (–) $ Adjustment	DESCRIPTION	+ (–) $ Adjustment
Sales or Financing Concessions							
Date of Sale/Time							
Location							
Site/View							
Design and Appeal							
Quality of Construction							
Age							
Condition							
Above Grade Room Count	Total : Bdrms : Baths	Total : Bdrms : Baths		Total : Bdrms : Baths		Total : Bdrms : Baths	
Gross Living Area	Sq. Ft.	Sq. Ft.		Sq. Ft.		Sq. Ft.	
Basement & Finished Rooms Below Grade							
Functional Utility							
Heating/Cooling							
Garage/Carport							
Porches, Patio, Pools, etc.							
Special Energy Efficient Items							
Fireplace(s)							
Other (e.g. kitchen equip., remodeling)							
Net Adj. (total)		☐ + ☐ – $		☐ + ☐ – $		☐ + ☐ – $	
Indicated Value of Subject		$		$		$	

Comments on Sales Comparison: _____

INDICATED VALUE BY SALES COMPARISON APPROACH .... $ _____
INDICATED VALUE BY INCOME APPROACH (If Applicable) Estimated Market Rent $ _____ /Mo. x Gross Rent Multiplier _____ = $ _____
This appraisal is made ☐ "as is" ☐ subject to the repairs, alterations, inspections or conditions listed below ☐ completion per plans and specifications.
Comments and Conditions of Appraisal: _____

RECONCILIATION

Final Reconciliation: _____

This appraisal is based upon the above requirements, the certification, contingent and limiting conditions, and Market Value definition that are stated in
☐ FmHA, HUD &/or VA instructions.
☐ Freddie Mac Form 439 (Rev. 7/86)/Fannie Mae Form 1004B (Rev. 7/86) filed with client _____ 19 ____ ☐ attached.
I (WE) ESTIMATE THE MARKET VALUE, AS DEFINED, OF THE SUBJECT PROPERTY AS OF _____ 19 ____ to be $ _____
I (We) certify: that to the best of my (our) knowledge and belief the facts and data used herein are true and correct; that I (we) personally inspected the subject property, both inside and out, and have made an exterior inspection of all comparable sales cited in this report; and that I (we) have no undisclosed interest, present or prospective therein.

Appraiser(s) SIGNATURE _____
NAME _____

Review Appraiser SIGNATURE _____
(if applicable) NAME _____
☐ Did ☐ Did Not Inspect Property

Freddie Mac Form 70 10/86 10CH USF#10110C   Fannie Mae Form 1004 10/86

Data Bank

Source List

1. Personal inspection
2. Seller
3. Buyer
4. Broker
5. Salesperson
6. Register of deeds
7. Title reports
8. Transfer maps or books
9. Leases
10. Mortgages
11. Banks, savings and loans, and other lending institutions
12. City hall or county courthouse
13. Assessor's office
14. Published information on transfers, leases or assessed valuation
15. Property managers or owners
16. Building and architectural plans
17. Accountants
18. Financial statements
19. Building architects, contractors and engineers
20. County or city engineering commission
21. Regional or county government officials
22. Area planning commissions
23. Highway commissioner's office, road commission
24. Newspaper advertisements
25. Multiple-listing systems
26. Cost manuals (state, local, private)
27. Local material suppliers
28. Public utility companies
29. United States Bureau of the Census
30. Department of Commerce
31. Federal Housing Administration
32. Local chamber of commerce
33. Government councils
34. Local board of REALTORS®
35. National, state or local Association of Home Builders

36. Public transportation officials
37. Other appraisers
38. Professional journals
39. Railroad and transit authorities or companies
40. Labor organizations
41. Employment agencies
42. Plats
43. Neighbors
44. Area maps (topographic, soil)
45. Airlines and bus lines, moving companies
46.
47.
48.
49.
50.

A. REGIONAL DATA

Types of Information	Sources
Topography	44
Natural resources	32, 44
Climate	32
Public transportation: Air Rail	 32, 45 32, 39
Expressways	23, 44
Population trends	22, 29, 33
Political organization and policies	21
Employment level	33, 40
Level of business activity and growth	11, 32
Average family income	22, 32
New building (amount and kind)	30
Percentage of home ownership	29
Electrical power consumption and new hookups	28

B. CITY DATA

Types of Information	Sources
Topography	1, 44
Natural resources	1, 44
Climate	32
Public transportation: Air Rail Bus Subway	 32, 45 39, 45 36, 45 36, 45

Types of Information (continued)	**Sources** (continued)
Expressways	23, 44
Traffic patterns	12, 20, 23
Population trends	22, 29, 33
Family size	22
Zoning	12, 22
Building codes	12, 19, 20
Political organization, policies and personnel	12
Employment level	32, 33, 40
Professions, trades or skills required	32
Level of business activity and growth	11, 32
Average family income	22, 32
Rental rates	15, 34
Percentage of vacancies	4, 31, 34
New building (amount and kind)	15, 34, 35
Building permits issued	12, 20
Bank deposits and loans	11, 32
Percentage of home ownership	4, 29, 34
Tax structure	12, 13
Electrical power consumption and new hookups	28

C. NEIGHBORHOOD DATA

All references are for residential, commercial and industrial properties. Additional references for each are called out by letter: R (residential), C (commercial) or I (industrial).

Types of Information	**Sources**
Topography	1, 44
Boundaries	1, 4, 12, 42
Public transportation:	
Bus	36
Subway	36
Frequency of service	36; C, I, 32
Distance to boarding point	1, 36; C, I, 32
Distance and time to reach central business district	1, 36; C, I, 32
Traffic patterns	1, 22, 33, 36; C, I, 32
Family size	R, 4, 22
Population density	C, I, 32, 44

Types of Information (continued)	**Sources (continued)**
Population trend	32, 33
Zoning, codes or regulations	12, 20, 22
Employment level	R, 4, 11; C, I, 32
Professions and trades	R, 4, 43; C, I, 32
Average family income	R, 29, 30, 32, 40
Percentage of home ownership	R, 11, 34, 29
Rents and lease features	4, 9; R, 34
Percentage of vacancies	R, 4, 34
Level of business activity and growth	C, I, 11, 32
New building (amount and kind)	R, 19, 27
Building permits issued	12, 20
Assessments	R, 12, 13
Utilities or improvements available (streets, curbs, sidewalks; water; electricity; telephone; gas; sewers)	12, 28
Percent built up	R, 12, 34
Predominant type of building	1, 13, 22; C, I, 19
Typical age of buildings	1, 13; R, 15; C, I, 19
Condition of buildings	1, 22, 33, 37
Price range of typical properties	4; R, 7, 31, 34; C, 15
Marketability	4; C, I, 15
Life cycle	4, 37
Land value trend	4, 13, 37
Location of facilities:	
Churches	R, 1, 22, 44
Schools	R, 1, 22, 44
Shopping	R, C, 1, 22, 44
Recreational, cultural	R, 1, 22, 44
Avenues of approach	1, 20
Types of services offered	R, 28
Availability of personnel	C, I, 22, 32
Employee amenities (shopping, eating and banking facilities)	I, 1
Marketing area	C, 22, 32
Competition	C, I, 1, 32
Types of industry (light, heavy)	I, 32
Sources of raw materials	I, 32
Hazards and nuisances	1; R, 43
Deed restrictions	6, 7
Taxes	12, 13
Changing use of area	4

D. SITE DATA

Types of Information	Sources
Legal description	6
Dimensions and area	1, 6, 42
Street frontage	1, 6, 42
Location in block	6, 42
Topography	6, 44
Topsoil and drainage	19, 44
Landscaping	1
Improvements:	
Streets, curbs, sidewalks	1, 12, 20
Water	28
Electricity	28
Telephone	28
Gas	28
Sewers	1, 12, 20
Tax rates and assessed valuation	13
Liens and special assessments	7, 13
Zoning, codes or regulations	12, 22
Easements and encroachments	6
Status of title	7

E. BUILDING DATA

Types of Information	Sources
Architectural style	1
Date of construction and additions	6, 13, 20
Placement of building on land	1, 20, 44
Dimensions and floor area	16, 42
Floor plan(s)	16, 20
Construction materials used (exterior and interior)	16, 19, 27
Utilities available	1, 28, 32
Interior utility and other installations:	1, 13, 16
Heating and air-conditioning	
Plumbing	
Wiring	
Special equipment, such as elevators	
Exceptions to zoning, codes or regulations	6, 20, 22
Status of title	7
Mortgages and liens	6, 11
Condition of building	1, 13, 22

F. SALES DATA

Types of Information	Sources
Date of sale	1 to 6, 25
Sales price	1 to 6, 25
Name of buyer and seller	1 to 6, 25
Deed book and page	6, 8, 37
Reasons for sale and purchase	2 to 5

G. COST DATA

Types of Information	Sources
Building reproduction cost	19, 26, 27, 40
Building replacement cost	19, 26, 27, 40
Depreciation factors:	
Physical deterioration	1, 19, 26
Functional obsolescence	1, 16, 19, 26
External obsolescence	1, 19, 22, 26

H. INCOME AND EXPENSE DATA

Types of Information	Sources
Income data (both subject and comparable properties):	
Annual income	18
Current lease terms	1, 15
Occupancy history	15, 18
Collection loss history	15, 18
Fixed expense data (both subject and comparable properties):	13, 15, 18, 38
Real estate taxes	
Insurance	
Operating expense data (both subject and comparable properties):	13, 15, 18, 38
Management	
Payroll	
Legal and accounting	
Maintenance	
Repairs	
Supplies	
Painting and decorating	
Fuel	
Electricity	
Miscellaneous	
Reserves for replacement	1, 18, 26

Area and Volume*

Many mathematical computations occur throughout the appraisal of either the simplest one-room warehouse or the most complex apartment or office building. The appraiser must find the square footage of the appraised site, the number of square feet of usable building space and the total square feet of the ground area the building covers. In addition, one of the methods used in the cost approach to appraisal requires the measurement of cubic feet of building space.

The appraiser should know how to compute the area (and volume, where applicable) of any shape. Property boundaries, particularly those measured by the method known as *metes and bounds* (also called *courses and distances*) often are not regularly shaped, and buildings usually are not.

Readers will have varying levels of knowledge and experience in area and volume computations. The Achievement Examination at the end of this appendix may be taken to review such computations and determine whether all of the material in this part of the book should be studied.

Area of Squares and Rectangles

To review some basics about shapes and measurements:

The space inside a 2-dimensional shape is called its *area*.

---

*The material in this appendix is adapted from *Mastering Real Estate Mathematics,* 5th Edition, by Ventolo, Allaway and Irby (Chicago: Real Estate Education Company, 1989).

A *right angle* is the angle formed by one-fourth of a circle. Since a full circle is 360 degrees and one-fourth of 360 degrees is 90 degrees, a right angle is a 90-degree angle.

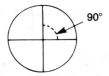

A *rectangle* is a closed figure with four sides that are at right angles to each other.

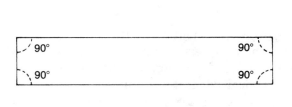

A *square* is a rectangle with four sides of equal length. A square with four sides, each one inch long, is a *square inch*. A square with four sides, each one foot long, is a *square foot*.

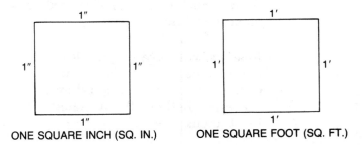

ONE SQUARE INCH (SQ. IN.)   ONE SQUARE FOOT (SQ. FT.)

Note:
The symbol for *inch* is ".
The symbol for *foot* is '.
The abbreviations are *in.* and *ft.*

The following formula may be used to compute the area of any rectangle.

$$\text{area} = \text{length} \times \text{width}$$
$$A = L \times W$$

The area of the following rectangle, using the formula, is 5" × 6", or 30 square inches.

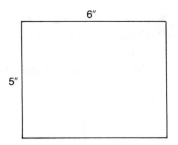

The term *30 inches* refers to a straight line 30 inches long. The term *30 square inches* refers to the area of a specific figure. When inches are multiplied by inches, the answer will be in square inches. Likewise, when feet are multiplied by feet, the answer will be in square feet.

Square feet are sometimes expressed by using the *exponent,* two; for example, 10^2 is read 10 feet squared and means 10×10, or 100 square feet.

The exponent[2] indicates how many times the number, or unit of measurement, is multiplied by itself. This is called *power* of the number or unit of measurement. The exponent is indicated at the upper right of the original number or unit of measurement.

The area of the rectangle at the left, below, is $4' \times 6'$, or 24 square feet. The area of the square at the right, below, is 5 yards $\times$ 5 yards, or 25 square yards.

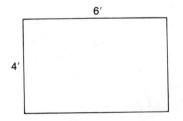   

EXAMPLE: Mr. Blair has leased a vacant lot that measures 60 feet by 160 feet. How much rent will he pay per year, if the lot rents for $.35 per square foot per year?

In order to solve this problem, first the area of the lot must be computed.

$$A = L \times W = 160' \times 60' = 9{,}600 \text{ sq. ft.}$$

The number of square feet is then multiplied by the price per square foot to get the total rent.

$$9{,}600 \times \$.35 = \$3{,}360$$

Front Foot Versus Area

In certain situations, a tract of land may be priced at \$X per *front foot.* Typically, this occurs where the land faces something desirable, such as a main street, a river or lake, thus making the frontage the major element of value.

For example, consider a tract of land facing (or fronting on) a lake:

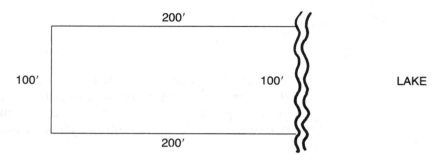

The area of the lot is 20,000 square feet (100′ × 200′). If this lot sells for $100,000, its price could be shown as $5 per square foot ($100,000 ÷ 20,000 square feet), or $1,000 per front foot ($100,000 ÷ 100 front feet).

Conversions—Using Like Measures for Area

When area is computed, all dimensions used must be given in the *same kind of units*. When a formula is used to find an area, units of the same kind must be used for each element of the formula, with the answer as square units of that kind. So, inches must be multiplied by inches to arrive at square inches, feet must be multiplied by

12 inches = 1 foot
36 inches = 1 yard
3 feet   = 1 yard

To convert *feet* to *inches*,
multiply the number of feet by 12.   (*ft.* × 12 = in.)

To convert *inches* to *feet*,
divide the number of inches by 12.   (*in.* ÷ 12 = ft.)

To convert *yards* to *feet*,
multiply the number of yards by 3.   (*yd.* × 3 = ft.)

To convert *feet* to *yards*,
divide the number of feet by 3.   (*ft.* ÷ 3 = yd.)

To convert *yards* to *inches*,
multiply the number of yards by 36.   (*yd.* × 36 = in.)

To convert *inches* to *yards*,
divide the number of inches by 36.   (*in.* ÷ 36 = yd.)

feet to arrive at square feet and yards must be multiplied by yards to arrive at square yards.

If the two dimensions to be multiplied are in different units of measure, one of the units of measure must be converted to the other. The chart on page 250 shows how to convert one unit of measure to another.

Exercise B.1

Solve the following problems.

1. 12″ × 3′ = _____ square feet or _____ square inches

2. 15″ × 1.5′ = _____ square feet or _____ square inches

3. 72″ × 7′ = _____ square feet or _____ square inches

4. What is the area of the square below in square inches?

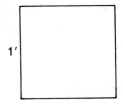

1′

5. 1,512 square inches = _____ square feet.

6. Mr. Johnson's house is on a lot that is 75 feet by 125 feet. What is the area of his lot?

Check your answers against those given in the Answer Key at the back of the book.

To convert square inches, square feet and square yards, use the following chart.

To convert *square feet* to *square inches, multiply the number of square feet by 144.*	*(sq. ft.* × 144 = sq. in.)
To convert *square inches* to *square feet, divide the number of square inches by 144.*	*(sq. in.* ÷ 144 = sq. ft.)
To convert *square yards* to *square feet, multiply the number of square yards by 9.*	*(sq. yd.* × 9 = sq. ft.)
To convert *square feet* to *square yards, divide the number of square feet by 9.*	*(sq. ft.* ÷ 9 = sq. yd.)
To convert *square yards* to *square inches, multiply the number of square yards by 1,296.*	*(sq. yd.* × 1,296 = sq. in.)
To convert *square inches* to *square yards, divide the number of square inches by 1,296.*	*(sq. in.* ÷ 1,296 = sq. yd.)

Area of Triangles

A *triangle* is a closed figure with three straight sides and three angles. *Tri* means three.

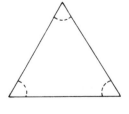 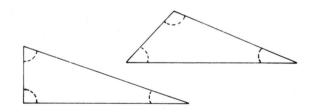

The square inch figure at the top left on page 253 has been cut in half by a straight line drawn through its opposite corners, to make two equal triangles. When one of the triangles is placed on a square-inch grid, it is seen to contain ½ sq. in. + ½ sq. in. + 1 sq. in., or 2 sq. in.

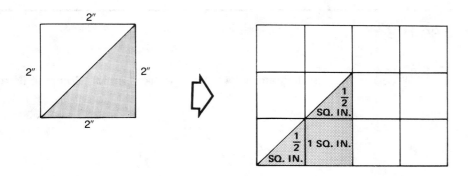

The area of the triangle below is 4.5 sq. ft.

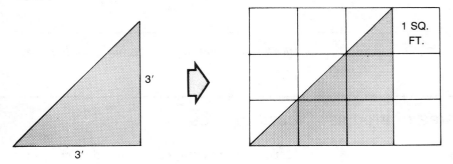

The square-unit grid is too cumbersome for computing large areas. It is more convenient to use a formula for finding the area of a triangle.

> area of a triangle = ½ (base × height)
> A = ½ (BH)

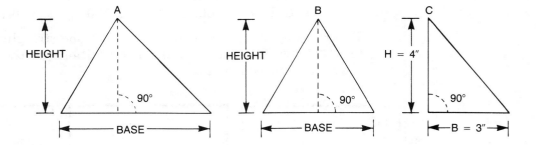

The *base* is the side on which the triangle sits. The *height* is the straight line distance from the tip of the uppermost angle to the base. The height line must form a 90-degree angle to the base. The area of triangle C above is:

A = ½(BH) = ½(3″ × 4″) = ½(12 sq. in.) = 6 sq. in.

Exercise B.2

The diagram below shows a lakefront lot. Compute its area.

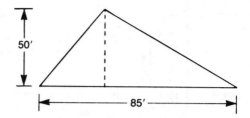

Check your answer against the one given in the Answer Key at the back of the book.

Area of Irregular Closed Figures

Here is a drawing of two neighboring lots:

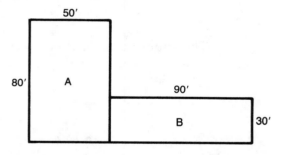

To find the total area of both lots:

lot A = 50′ × 80′ = 4,000 sq. ft.
lot B = 90′ × 30′ = 2,700 sq. ft.
both lots = 4,000 sq. ft. + 2,700 sq. ft. = 6,700 sq. ft.

Two rectangles can be made by drawing one straight line inside figure 1, below. There are two possible positions for the added line, as shown in figures 2 and 3.

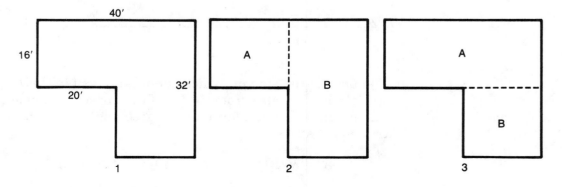

Using the measurements given in figure 1, the total area of the figure may be computed in one of two ways:

area of A = 20' × 16' = 320 sq. ft.
area of B = 32' × (40' − 20') = 32' × 20' = 640 sq. ft.
total area = 320 sq. ft. + 640 sq. ft. = 960 sq. ft.

Or:

area of A = 40' × 16' = 640 sq. ft.
area of B = (40' − 20') × (32' − 16') = 20' × 16' = 320 sq. ft.
total area = 640 sq. ft. + 320 sq. ft. = 960 sq. ft.

The area of an irregular figure can be found by dividing it into regular figures, computing the area of each regular figure and adding all of the areas together to obtain the total area.

Exercise B.3

a. This figure has been divided into rectangles, as shown by the broken lines. Compute the area of the figure.

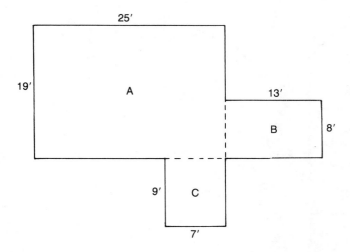

b. Make a rectangle and a triangle by drawing a single line through the figure below, then compute the area of the figure.

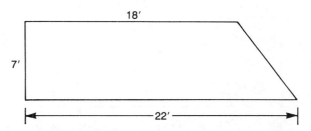

c. Compute the area of each section of the figure below. Then, compute the total area.

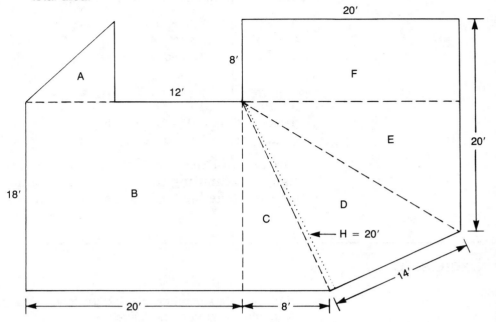

Living Area Calculations

Real estate appraisers frequently must compute the amount of living area in a house.

> The living area of a house is the area enclosed by the outside dimensions of the heated and air-conditioned portions of the house. This excludes open porches, garages, and such.

When measuring a house in preparation for calculating the living area, these steps should be followed:

1. Draw a sketch of the foundation.
2. Measure *all* outside walls.
3. If the house has an attached garage, treat the inside garage walls that are common to the house as outside walls of the house.
4. Measure the garage.
5. Convert inches to tenths of a foot (so that the same units of measurement are used in the calculations).
6. Before leaving the house, check to see that net dimensions of opposite sides are equal. If not, remeasure.
7. Section off your sketch into rectangles.
8. Calculate the area of each rectangle.
9. Add up the areas, being careful to *subtract* the area of the garage, *if necessary.*
10. Before leaving the house, you should *always* recheck the dimensions.

Exercise B.4

What is the living area of the house shown in the sketch below? Follow the steps above and remember to compute each area separately.

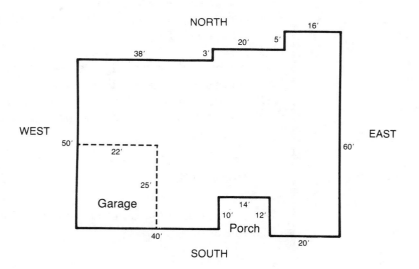

Check your answer against the one given in the Answer Key at the back of the book.

Volume

When a shape has more than one side and encloses a space, the shape has *volume*.

> The space that a three-dimensional object occupies is called its *volume*.

Of the following shapes A, C and E have volume; B, D and F have area only.

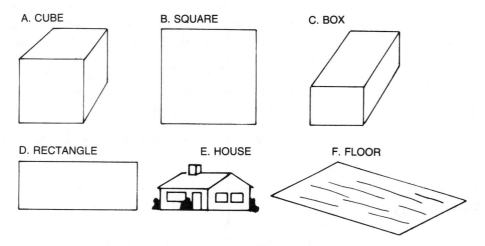

Flat shapes—squares, rectangles, triangles and so on—do not have *volume*. Flat shapes have two dimensions (length and width or height), and shapes with volume have three dimensions (length, width and height).

Technically speaking, each shape with three dimensions can also be measured in terms of its surface area. For example, a bedroom has volume because it has three dimensions—length, width and height; however, *one wall* can be measured as *surface area,* or: area = length × width.

Cubic Units

A *cube* is made up of six squares. Look at the six sides of the following cube.

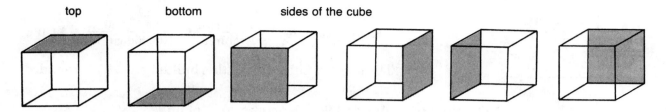

top   bottom   sides of the cube

Volume is measured in *cubic* units. In the following cube, each side measures one inch. The figure represents *one cubic inch,* abbreviated *1 cu. in.*

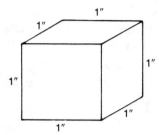

There are four cubic feet in the figure below. The exponent three may also be used to express cubic feet; that is, 1^3 is one cubic foot.

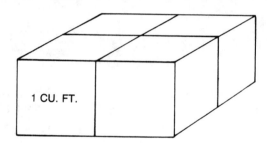

1 CU. FT.

Using the formula for computing volume,

$$V \text{ (volume)} = L \text{ (length)} \times W \text{ (width)} \times H \text{ (height)}$$

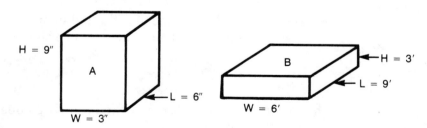

volume of box A = L × W × H = 6″ × 3″ × 9″ = 162 cu. in.

volume of box B = L × W × H = 9′ × 6′ × 3′ = 162 cu. ft.

EXAMPLE: A building's construction cost was $450,000. The building is 60 feet long, 45 feet wide and 40 feet high, including the basement. What was the cost of this building per cubic foot?

V = L × W × H = 60′ × 45′ × 40′ = 108,000 cu. ft.

$$\text{cost per cubic foot} = \frac{\text{total cost}}{\text{volume}} = \frac{\$450,000}{108,000 \text{ cu. ft.}} = \$4.166$$

The cost per cubic foot of this building is \$4.17 (rounded).

Conversions—Using Like Measures for Volume

To convert cubic inches, cubic feet and cubic yards, use the following chart.

To convert *cubic feet* to *cubic inches, multiply the number of cubic feet by 1,728.*	(cu. ft. × 1,728 = cu. in.)
To convert *cubic inches* to *cubic feet, divide the number of cubic inches by 1,728.*	(cu. in. ÷ 1,728 = cu. ft.)
To convert *cubic yards* to *cubic feet, multiply the number of cubic yards by 27.*	(cu. yd. × 27 = cu. ft.)
To convert *cubic feet* to *cubic yards, divide the number of cubic feet by 27.*	(cu. ft. ÷ 27 = cu. yd.)
To convert *cubic yards* to *cubic inches, multiply the number of cubic yards by 46,656.*	(cu. yd. × 46,656 = cu. in.)
To convert *cubic inches* to *cubic yards, divide the number of cubic inches by 46,656.*	(cu. in. ÷ 46,656 = cu. yd.)

EXAMPLE: How many cubic yards of space are there in a flat-roofed house that is 30 feet long, 18 feet wide and 10 feet high?

$$V = L \times W \times H = 30' \times 18' \times 10' = 5,400 \text{ cu. ft.}$$

$$\text{cu. yd.} = \text{cu. ft.} \div 27 = 5,400 \text{ cu. ft.} \div 27 = 200 \text{ cu. yd.}$$

Volume of Triangular Prisms

To compute the volume of a three-dimensional triangular figure, called a *prism* (e.g., an A-frame house), use the following formula:

$$\text{volume} = \tfrac{1}{2}(B \times H \times W)$$

To compute the volume of the following house, first divide the house into two shapes, S and T.

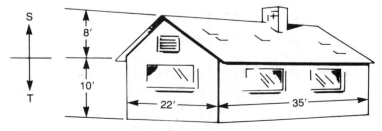

Find the volume of S.

$$V = \tfrac{1}{2}(B \times H \times W) = \tfrac{1}{2}(22' \times 8' \times 35') = \tfrac{1}{2}(6,160 \text{ cu. ft.}) = 3,080 \text{ cu. ft.}$$

Find the volume of T.

$$V = 22' \times 35' \times 10' = 7,700 \text{ cu. ft.}$$

Total volumes S and T.

$$3,080 \text{ cu. ft.} + 7,700 \text{ cu ft.} = 10,780 \text{ cu. ft.}$$

Exercise B.5

Complete the following problems.

1. 8′ × 7′ = _____ sq. ft. = _____ sq. in. = _____ sq. yd.

    9′ × 3′ × 2′ = _____ cu. ft. = _____ cu. in. = _____ cu. yd.

2. Find the total ground area covered by a building with the perimeter measurements shown below.

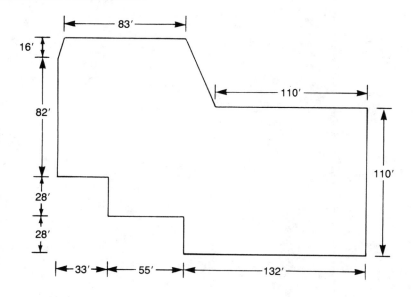

3.   The building below has a construction cost of $45 per cubic yard. What is the total cost of this building?

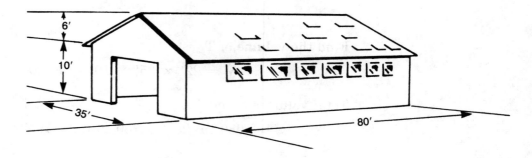

Achievement Examination Appendix B

1. Find the total area of the figure below.

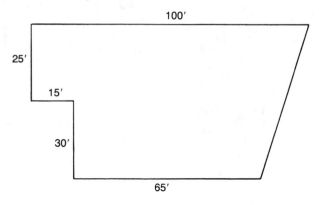

2. The house below would cost $2.75 per cubic foot to build. What would be the total cost, at that price?

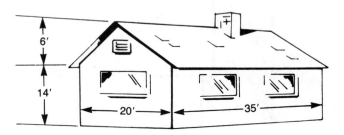

3. What is the total area of the figure below in square feet?

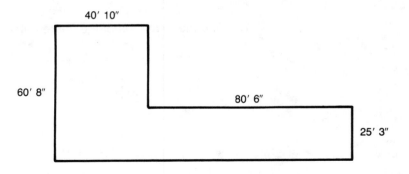

4. What is the living area of the house shown in the sketch below?

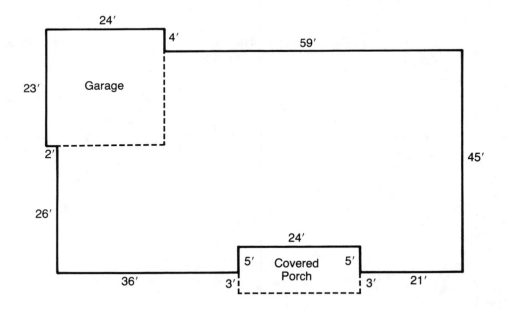

_____

Check your answers against those given in the Answer Key at the back of the book.

Cost Data

	Material	Specification	Cost Per Unit of Measurement*
FOUNDATION	Concrete wall and footing, 4' deep, incl. excavation	8" wide 12" 16"	$20.50 per linear foot of wall 30.70 37.30
FLOOR CONSTRUCTION	Reinforced concrete, poured in place, including forms and reinforcing	4" 6" 8"	$ 2.50 per sq. ft. of floor 3.10 3.60
FLOOR COVERING	Nylon carpet Vinyl tile		$12.00 per sq. yd. 1.90 per sq. ft.
FRAMING	Steel frame, with steel columns, beams and purlins	10' eave height 14' 20'	$ 3.70 per sq. ft. of support area 4.50 5.60

ROOF CONSTRUCTION	Wood deck
	  Sheathing
	  Fiberboard R-2.78
	  Fiberglass R-7.7
	  Polystyrene R-8
		
		½" thick
		1"
		1⅞"
		2"
			
			$ .65 per sq. ft.
			.55
			1.10
			.52

ROOF COVERING	Asphalt and gravel Polyurethane spray-on	3-ply 4-ply 1" thick 3"	$ 2.10 per sq. ft. 2.40 1.35 2.50
EXTERIOR WALLS	Common brick facing with block backup	8" thick 12"	$ 9.50 per sq. ft. of wall area 10.20
	Jumbo face brick veneer		3.80
	Roman brick veneer		7.50
	Ribbed aluminum siding, 4" profile	.040" thick	2.40 per sq. ft.
	Steel siding, beveled, vinyl coated	8" wide	1.25 per sq. ft.

*The figures given here are for purposes of illustration only.

	Material	Specification	Cost Per Unit of Measurement*
DOORS	Hollow metal, 3′ × 7′, including frame, lockset and hinges	exterior interior	$ 355 each 275
	Rolling steel, chain hoist operated	8′ × 8′ 10′ × 10′ 12′ × 12′ 20′ × 16′	$ 840 each 1,175 1,425 3,200
	Pine, 3′ × 7′, including frame, lockset and hinges	exterior interior	$ 290 each (incl. storm & screen) 95
	Oak, including frame, lockset and hinges	3′ × 7′ × 1¾″	$ 245 each

WINDOWS	Industrial sash
	  steel, fixed
	  steel, 50% vented
	  aluminum, fixed
	  aluminum, 50% vented
			$11.40 per sq. ft. of window area
			14.20
			17.50
			20.10

INTERIOR WALLS AND PARTITIONS	Concrete block	4″ 6″ 8″ 12″	$3.20 per sq. ft. of wall area 3.70 4.05 4.40
	Drywall on wood studs, including two coats of paint		$3.15 per sq. ft. of wall area
	Drywall on metal studs, including two coats of paint		2.70
CEILING	Mineral fiber acoustic tile, including suspension system		$1.65 per sq. ft. of ceiling area
ELECTRICAL WIRING	Fluorescent fixtures, normal lighting requirements		$3.10 per sq. ft. of building area
HEATING AND COOLING	Heating and central air-conditioning with ducts and controls		$3.70–5.75 per sq. ft. of building area
PLUMBING	Plumbing, including fixtures		$1.75–2.75 per sq. ft. of building area
MISC.	Asphalt paving on 3″ stone base	1½″ thick 3″	$4.25 per sq. yd. 7.20

*The figures given here are for purposes of illustration only.

Annuity Capitalization

The various methods of income capitalization may include the use of present worth tables to find values for various investment yields over a given period of time. An investor intending to buy an income-producing property wants to know what should be paid for the income-producing ability of the property. An investor planning to obtain a mortgage loan to help pay for the property will also want to know how the mortgage payments will affect income from the property.

The tables discussed in this section can be used to make such calculations, but only after the appraiser has made a thorough analysis of the subject property and the degree of risk it carries as an investment. The permanence of the investment is considered; that is, the length of the lease term coupled with the reliability of the tenant. The capitalization method chosen by the appraiser will depend on the potential stability of the income stream. Generally, the tables included here assume a relatively long-term lease and a very reliable tenant.

The discussion that follows includes the use of the *Inwood annuity table* and the reversion table, as well as the contributions of L. W. Ellwood, who explained how the various tables can be used in real estate appraisals.

In this appendix, you will learn the two basic ways of using an annuity table to find property value: the *building residual* technique and the *property residual* technique. You will also learn how a reversion table can be used to determine the present worth of any land value that will remain at the end of the projected income stream.

Finally, you will learn the differing effects on value when capitalization is computed using a straight-line method of recapture or, alternatively, an annuity table.

Annuity Method of Capitalization

An *annuity* is a fixed yearly return on an investment. It may be for any number of years, if the investment is high enough to provide the return desired. The return may also be paid weekly, monthly or quarterly, rather than yearly.

An investor who wants a return of $1,120 on a one-year investment that will pay 12 percent interest would have to invest $1,000. The $1,000 would be returned to the investor at the end of the year, along with interest of $120 ($1,000 × 12%), making a total of $1,120. A total return of $1,000 at 12 percent interest for one year would require an investment of $893. The investor would receive interest income of $107.16. In effect, the investor would be paying $893 for the right to receive income of $107.16 and have the amount of original investment returned.

As shown above, the mathematics of computing investment amounts for one year is very simple. The total return is 100 percent of the original investment plus the interest for the time period involved (in the example above, 12 percent); thus, the total return is 112 percent of the original investment. Most income properties, however, are expected to yield income for more than one year. Tables have been developed that take into account the number of years an investment will be expected to produce income and the estimated yearly rate of return. One such table may be used to find the discounted, present worth of an annuity of one dollar at a stipulated interest rate for a given number of years. Such an *annuity factors table* (frequently called the *Inwood table*) provides a factor to be multiplied by the desired level of yearly income (based on the interest rate and length of time of the investment) to find the present worth of the investment, that is, what the investor should pay.

An annuity table that may be used for investment periods from one to forty years, and from 10 percent to 18 percent interest, is shown on page 270. Such tables are available on a monthly, quarterly and semiannual basis as well. By matching the projected length of the investment with the interest rate it is expected to produce, the factor to be multiplied by the desired level of yearly income can be found.

EXAMPLE: An investor wishes to receive an annual income of $6,000 for four years by making an investment earning 10 percent. What should be the amount of the original investment?

The annuity factor for an interest rate of 10 percent over an investment period of four years is 3.170. Multiplied by the annual income sought ($6,000 × 3.170), an initial investment figure of $19,020 is derived. In other words, a $19,020 investment for four years at 10 percent interest will yield yearly income of $6,000. At the end of the four years, the entire amount invested, plus all interest earned, will have been returned to the investor.

As stated earlier, annuity table factors may not be applied to every investment in real estate. The investment should be a stable one. Even though it would be impossible to predict the reliability of tenants or possible changes in market usage *exactly,* the investment should have certain indicators of the stability of the income to be produced. The sound financial status of the tenant and a long-term lease should indicate a reliable income stream.

In the use of annuity tables, the number of years that the investment will be expected to yield income will be based on the typical holding period for the investment, which may not coincide with the length of the lease term.

Building Residual Technique

Ideally, then, the income stream over the remaining economic life of the property will be ensured by a lease signed by a reliable client. In such a case, if land value can be estimated, the total property value can be found by using the *building residual* technique.

EXAMPLE: An appraiser is analyzing the current market value of an investment property with a land value of $100,000 (estimated by analyzing comparable sales). The retail store on the land is being leased by a major supermarket chain, which has been financially successful for 20 years and should remain so. The lease, as of the date of appraisal, will run for another 23 years. The discount rate on land and building has been calculated at 13 percent. The property provides an annual net operating income of $36,000. What is its current market value?

The interest on the land value of $100,000 is $13,000 ($100,000 × 13%). When $13,000 is subtracted from the total annual net operating income of $36,000, a *net income residual* of $23,000 ($36,000 − $13,000) may be used to derive the building value. Using the annuity table, a 13 percent interest rate over 23 years provides a factor of 7.230. The building value is the building income multiplied by the annuity factor, or:

$$\$23,000 \times 7.230 = \$166,290$$

The value of the building is $166,290. The total property value, then, is $166,290 plus the land value of $100,000, or $266,290.

The appraiser in the preceding example would have recorded the information shown on page 271.

APPENDIX D: Annuity Factors Table

Interest Rate

Year	10%	11%	12%	13%	14%	15%	16%	17%	18%
1	.909	.901	.893	.885	.887	.870	.862	.855	.847
2	1.736	1.713	1.690	1.668	1.647	1.626	1.605	1.585	1.566
3	2.487	2.444	2.402	2.361	2.322	2.283	2.246	2.210	2.174
4	3.170	3.102	3.037	2.974	2.914	2.855	2.798	2.743	2.690
5	3.791	3.696	3.605	3.517	3.433	3.352	3.274	3.199	3.127
6	4.355	4.231	4.111	3.998	3.889	3.784	3.685	3.589	3.498
7	4.868	4.712	4.564	4.423	4.288	4.160	4.039	3.922	3.812
8	5.335	5.146	4.968	4.799	4.639	4.487	4.344	4.207	4.078
9	5.759	5.537	5.328	5.132	4.946	4.772	4.607	4.451	4.303
10	6.145	5.889	5.650	5.426	5.216	5.019	4.833	4.659	4.494
11	6.495	6.207	5.938	5.687	5.453	5.234	5.029	4.836	4.656
12	6.814	6.492	6.194	5.918	5.660	5.421	5.197	4.988	4.793
13	7.103	6.750	6.424	6.122	5.842	5.583	5.342	5.118	4.910
14	7.367	6.982	6.628	6.302	6.002	5.724	5.468	5.229	5.008
15	7.606	7.191	6.811	6.462	6.142	5.847	5.575	5.324	5.092
16	7.824	7.379	6.974	6.604	6.265	5.954	5.668	5.405	5.162
17	8.022	7.549	7.120	6.729	6.373	6.047	5.749	5.475	5.222
18	8.201	7.702	7.250	6.840	6.467	6.128	5.818	5.534	5.273
19	8.365	7.839	7.366	6.938	6.550	6.198	5.877	5.584	5.316
20	8.514	7.963	7.469	7.025	6.623	6.259	5.929	5.628	5.353
21	8.649	8.075	7.562	7.102	6.687	6.312	5.973	5.665	5.384
22	8.772	8.176	7.645	7.170	6.743	6.359	6.011	5.696	5.410
23	8.883	8.266	7.718	7.230	6.792	6.399	6.044	5.723	5.432
24	8.985	8.348	7.784	7.283	6.835	6.434	6.073	5.746	5.451
25	9.077	8.422	7.843	7.330	6.873	6.464	6.097	5.766	5.467
26	9.161	8.488	7.896	7.372	6.906	6.491	6.118	5.783	5.480
27	9.237	8.548	7.943	7.409	6.935	6.514	6.136	5.798	5.492
28	9.307	8.602	7.984	7.441	6.961	6.534	6.152	5.810	5.502
29	9.370	8.650	8.022	7.470	6.983	6.551	6.166	5.820	5.510
30	9.427	8.694	8.055	7.496	7.003	6.566	6.177	5.829	5.517
31	9.479	8.733	8.085	7.518	7.020	6.579	6.187	5.837	5.523
32	9.526	8.679	8.112	7.538	7.035	6.591	6.196	5.844	5.528
33	9.569	8.801	8.135	7.556	7.048	6.600	6.203	5.849	5.532
34	9.609	8.829	8.157	7.572	7.060	6.609	6.210	5.854	5.536
35	9.644	8.855	8.176	7.586	7.070	6.617	6.215	5.858	5.539
36	9.677	8.879	8.192	7.598	7.079	6.623	6.220	5.862	5.541
37	9.706	8.900	8.208	7.609	7.087	6.629	6.224	5.865	5.543
38	9.733	8.919	8.221	7.618	7.094	6.634	6.228	5.867	5.545
39	9.757	8.936	8.233	7.627	7.100	6.638	6.231	5.869	5.547
40	9.779	8.951	8.244	7.634	7.105	6.642	6.233	5.871	5.548

Estimated Land Value		$100,000
Annual Net Operating Income before		
Recapture of Building	$ 36,000	
Discount on Estimated Land Value		
(@ 13% per year on $100,000)	13,000	
Annual Residual Income to Building	$ 23,000	
Annuity Factor (based on 13% interest		
over 23 years is 7.230)		
Building Value ($23,000 × 7.230)		$166,290
Total Property Value		$266,290

Rounded to $266,000

Exercise D.1

Use the building residual technique and the annuity table to estimate the value of a property that produces a net operating income before recapture of $26,400 per year. The land is valued at $75,000, discount rate on land and building is calculated at 11 percent per year, and the current tenant has 30 years remaining on the lease.

Check your answer against the one given in the Answer Key at the back of the book.

Property Residual Technique

An annuity table also may be used to estimate value by the *property residual* technique as well as the land residual technique. If the property used to explain the building residual technique in the preceding example were to be treated as a whole (both land and building), the present worth of the property, with an income stream of $36,000 and an annuity factor of 7.230, would be estimated at $260,280. Or,

Total Annual Net Operating Income	$36,000
Annuity Factor (23 years at 13%)	7.230
Present Worth of Net Operating Income	$260,280

At the end of the income stream of 23 years, however, the land will revert back to the owner. That is, although the building will have reached the end of its economic life, the land will still be valuable. The present worth of the whole property will be what the investor is willing to pay for the specified income stream, plus the right to the reversionary value of the land at the end of the income-producing period.

The amount that the investor should pay for the land's future value is computed by applying a reversion factor to its present estimated value. The *reversion table* on the next page lists the computed factors at specified interest rates for an investment term of one to forty years. In the example problem introduced on page 269, an investment valued at 13 percent interest for 23 years gives a reversion factor of .060. Since the present (and assumed future) value of the land was estimated at $100,000, the value of the reversion at the end of 23 years is $6,000 ($100,000 × .060). When the present worth of the reversion ($6,000) is added to the present worth of the net income stream ($260,280), the resulting property value is $266,280. This value is almost exactly that reached by the building residual technique. The slight discrepancy results from the rounding off of the annuity and reversion factors. Even this discrepancy would be reduced if the factors were carried out to more decimal places.

Exercise D.2

Using the property residual technique and the annuity and reversion tables, estimate the value of the following. (Record your computations below.)

The property is a two-acre site with an industrial warehouse leased to a major auto parts manufacturer at an annual rental of $30,000, which is also the net operating income. The lease term will expire in 25 years, which is the estimated remaining economic life of the building. The value of the site in 25 years is expected to be $75,000 per acre. The investment should yield an income stream at 12 percent interest.

Check your answer against the one given in the Answer Key at the back of the book.

APPENDIX D: Reversion Table

Interest Rate

Year	10%	11%	12%	13%	14%	15%	16%	17%	18%
1	.909	.901	.893	.885	.877	.870	.862	.855	.847
2	.826	.812	.797	.783	.769	.756	.743	.731	.718
3	.751	.731	.712	.693	.675	.658	.641	.624	.609
4	.683	.659	.636	.613	.592	.572	.552	.534	.516
5	.621	.593	.567	.543	.519	.497	.476	.456	.437
6	.564	.535	.507	.480	.456	.432	.410	.390	.370
7	.513	.482	.452	.425	.400	.376	.354	.333	.314
8	.467	.434	.404	.376	.351	.327	.305	.285	.266
9	.424	.391	.361	.333	.308	.284	.263	.243	.225
10	.386	.352	.322	.295	.270	.247	.227	.208	.191
11	.350	.317	.287	.261	.237	.215	.195	.178	.162
12	.319	.286	.257	.231	.208	.187	.168	.152	.137
13	.290	.258	.229	.204	.182	.163	.145	.130	.116
14	.263	.232	.205	.181	.160	.141	.125	.111	.099
15	.239	.209	.183	.160	.140	.123	.108	.095	.084
16	.218	.188	.163	.141	.123	.107	.093	.081	.071
17	.198	.170	.146	.125	.108	.093	.080	.069	.060
18	.180	.153	.130	.111	.095	.081	.069	.059	.051
19	.164	.138	.116	.098	.083	.070	.060	.051	.043
20	.149	.124	.104	.087	.073	.061	.051	.043	.037
21	.135	.112	.093	.077	.064	.053	.044	.037	.031
22	.123	.101	.083	.068	.056	.046	.038	.032	.026
23	.112	.091	.074	.060	.049	.040	.033	.027	.022
24	.102	.082	.066	.053	.043	.035	.028	.023	.019
25	.092	.074	.059	.047	.038	.030	.024	.020	.016
26	.084	.066	.053	.042	.033	.026	.021	.017	.014
27	.076	.060	.047	.037	.029	.023	.018	.014	.011
28	.069	.054	.042	.033	.026	.020	.016	.012	.010
29	.063	.048	.037	.029	.022	.017	.014	.011	.008
30	.057	.044	.033	.026	.020	.015	.012	.009	.007
31	.052	.039	.030	.023	.017	.013	.010	.008	.0059
32	.047	.035	.027	.020	.015	.011	.009	.007	.0050
33	.043	.032	.024	.018	.013	.010	.007	.006	.0042
34	.039	.029	.021	.016	.012	.009	.0064	.005	.0036
35	.036	.026	.019	.014	.010	.008	.0055	.004	.0030
36	.032	.023	.017	.012	.009	.007	.0048	.0035	.0026
37	.029	.021	.015	.011	.008	.006	.0041	.0030	.0022
38	.027	.019	.013	.010	.007	.005	.0036	.0026	.0019
39	.024	.017	.012	.009	.006	.0043	.0031	.0022	.0016
40	.022	.015	.011	.008	.005	.0037	.0026	.0019	.0013

Recapture Rates

Annuity tables do not assume a static (unchanging from year to year) recapture rate. Slow changes in building value are assumed in the early years of the investment term, with greater changes in the last years of the investment. In the straight-line method of recapture, however, the same recapture rate is assumed for each year of the investment. The following figures show the difference in value that cán result after a 25-year investment term, using the straight-line method of recapture and the annuity table. The subject property is the one used in the example on page 269.

BUILDING RESIDUAL TECHNIQUE
After 25 Years

Straight-Line Method		Annuity Method	
Total Net Operating Income	$ 36,000	Total Net Operating Income	$ 36,000
Return on Land Value ($100,000 × 13%)	13,000	Return on Land Value ($100,000 × 13%)	13,000
Residual Income to Building	$ 23,000	Residual Income to Building	$ 23,000
Capitalization Rate: Return 13% Recapture 4% Total 17%			
Building Value ($23,000 ÷ 17%)	$135,294	Building Value ($23,000 × 7.330)	$168,590
Plus Land Value	100,000	Plus Land Value	100,000
Total Property Value	$235,294	Total Property Value	$268,590

The land value of $100,000 in both methods is the same, since the sales comparison approach was used. Building value differs, however, because the annuity method allows for a slower decrease in building value over the early years of the building's life, providing a higher value in later years. The straight-line method, on the other hand, applies an equal decrease in value to be recaptured for every year of the building's economic life.

From this discussion, we can summarize the assumptions and effects of the annuity and straight-line recapture methods on income, interest and recapture.

Under the annuity method:

1. The income stream does not vary but remains constant for each year of the building's economic life.

2. Interest accrues each year on the decreasing principal.
3. Recapture accounts for an increasing share of income each year.

Under the straight-line method:

1. Income decreases each year by the same amount.
2. Interest accrues each year on the decreasing property value.
3. Recapture remains constant for each year.

The following chart compares the effects of the straight-line and annuity recapture methods on income, interest and recapture.

	Straight-Line	*Annuity*
Income	decreases	constant
Interest	decreases	decreases
Recapture	constant	increases

Exercise D.3

Which of the two capitalization methods discussed in this chapter—straight-line or annuity—is appropriate in each of the following examples?

1. An office building leased by a major oil company is being appraised. The lease will run for another 22 years.

2. A building with a 20-year lease is being appraised. The lessee has hinted to the appraiser that, if the building is to be sold, he will expect to renegotiate his lease with the new owner, since the rent is more than he can really afford.

Check your answers against those given in the Answer Key at the back of the book.

Ellwood Tables

The late L. W. Ellwood compiled the best-known appraising tables and offered his interpretation of how they work and when they may be used. These explanations and tables are given in *Ellwood Tables for*

Real Estate Appraising and Financing, Fourth Edition (© Copyright 1977 by American Institute of Real Estate Appraisers of the National Association of REALTORS®).

Among the topics Ellwood covered are common formulas, their symbols, the mortgage coefficient method of finding an investment yield and capitalization rate, other equity techniques, and purchase and leaseback problems, in addition to tables for all techniques at varying interest rates.

Many of the areas explained by Ellwood, such as the Inwood annuity table and reversion table, have already been touched on in this book. For more detailed explanations of these as well as other subjects mentioned, refer to the Ellwood book and to *American Institute of Real Estate Appraisers Financial Tables,* edited and compiled by James J. Mason (American Institute of Real Estate Appraisers, Chicago, 1981), and *Basic Income Property Appraisal* by James H. Boykin and Donald R. Epley (Addison-Wesley Publishing Co., Reading, Mass., 1982).

Achievement Examination D

1. You are appraising a property by the building and property residual techniques and the annuity method of recapture. What would be the effect of the two residual techniques on your estimate of value?

2. Under which method are the recapture installments lowest in the earlier years?

    a. annuity   b. straight-line

3. Under which method are the installments highest?

    a. annuity   b. straight-line

4. Of the two recapture approaches, which would yield:

    a. the highest value?   b. the lowest value?

5. Which recapture method suggests the greatest reduction in risk?

    a. annuity   b. straight-line

6. You are appraising a commercial building earning an annual net operating income before recapture of $50,000. Based on supportable information, the interest rate has been established at 15 percent. Land value has been estimated at $100,000 and the building's remaining economic life at 25 years.

    Determine the estimated value of the property in each case below.

    a. The property has year-to-year tenants of average credit risk.

    b. The property is leased for the entire 25 years to a national concern with an excellent credit rating.

Check your answers against those given in the Answer Key at the back of the book.

Appraising Lease Interests

In previous chapters we have referred to the owner of income-producing property as the *lessor* and the person who leases the property as the *lessee*. When the scheduled rent the lessee pays is the same as the market rent, or economic potential of the property, both parties receive full value for their lease and investment dollar. If the scheduled rent is lower or higher than market rent, however, one party gains and the other loses the amount of the difference. How the lessor's and lessee's interests are defined and evaluated is discussed in this section.

Definition of Terms

Leased Fee

An owner who leases property for a given period of time creates a *leased fee*, which represents the lessor's interest and rights in the real estate. In return for the lease permitting the tenant to occupy and use the property, the lessor receives a stipulated fee or rental and retains the right to repossess the property at the termination of the lease. The value of the rental payments plus the remaining property value at the end of the lease period, known as the reversion, make up the lessor's interest in the property. This leased fee interest may be sold or mortgaged, subject to the rights of the tenant.

Leasehold Estate

A second interest created by a lease belongs to the tenant. It is referred to as the *leasehold estate,* or the lessee's interest and rights in the real estate. Because the lessee is obligated under the terms of the lease to pay rent, the lessee's interest in the property can have value only if the agreed-on scheduled rent is less than the prevailing market rental, or economic rent.

Sandwich Lease

When a tenant has a leasehold estate of value, the tenant may sublet that interest. By doing so, the tenant creates what is known as a *sandwich lease,* and the value of the property is then divided among three interests: the lessor's, the original or prime lessee's and the sublessee's.

Creation of Lease Interests

Because changing conditions affect the value of real estate, leases made prior to the current period may be for amounts above or below the current market figures. If market rent exceeds scheduled rent, the property owner is, in effect, transferring part of the property interest to the tenant, thus creating a positive leasehold interest. On the other hand, if scheduled rent exceeds market rent, a negative leasehold interest exists and the unfavorable lease, in a sense, is a liability of the lessee. If the difference between scheduled rent and market rent becomes too great in the owner's favor, the tenant may try to renegotiate the terms of the lease or perhaps even default. If scheduled rent and market rent are the same, the tenant's interest in the property is of zero value.

The principle involved in the valuation of lease interests is similar to that of capitalized income valuation under the annuity or Inwood method. The value of the lessor's and the lessee's interests is found by capitalizing the present value of the income each receives and adding the reversionary value of the land, or land and building, at the expiration of the lease term. Ordinarily, it is the lessor who receives the reversionary value of the property. But some leases provide for payments to the lessee by the lessor for any improvements made by the lessee that will ultimately revert to the lessor.

Exercise E.1

Explain how a leasehold estate of value is created.

Check your answer against the one given in the Answer Key at the back of the book.

Leased Fee and Leasehold Valuations

In valuing lease interests, the appraiser must first carefully study the detailed provisions of the lease to determine the rights and obligations of the owner and tenant. Then, the valuation of leased fee and leasehold interests is basically a matter of dividing the value of the property into separate values attributable to each of the various interests. The total of the various interests in the property may exceed the value of the property under free and clear ownership.

The examples in this appendix give leased property situations and suggested methods of appraisal. The first example illustrates the valuation of an investment property free and clear of any lease interests.

EXAMPLE: A property earning a net operating income of $48,000 per year is rented on an annual basis to one tenant. The remaining economic life of the building is 25 years and the current market value of the land is estimated at $100,000. The rate of interest for similar investments is 14 percent. Based on these facts, the value of the property is obtained using the building residual technique.

Estimated Land Value		$100,000
Net Operating Income	$48,000	
Land Income ($100,000 × 14%)	14,000	
Residual Income to Building	$34,000	
Capitalization Rate for Building:		
Discount Rate	14%	
Recapture Rate	+4%	
	18%	
Building Value ($34,000 ÷ 18%)		188,889
Total Property Value		$288,900 (rounded)

To illustrate the valuation of leased fee and leasehold interests, a series of examples, all based on the same hypothetical property but with varying conditions as to term of lease and amount of rent under the lease, will be presented.

EXAMPLE: Assume that the property described in the previous example is now leased to a nationally known company on a 25-year lease at the same net annual rent of $48,000, which is equal to market rent. The building is considered of no value at the end of the lease term. Because of the increased security, and therefore the decreased risk, in having the property leased for a long period of time by a national company, the discount rate (sometimes called *risk* rate) has been lowered from 14 percent to 12 percent. The interest rate applicable to reversion is assumed to be 14 percent.

Based on these facts, and using the Inwood method of capitalization, the value of the leased fee is derived as follows:

Net Operating Income	$ 48,000
*Annuity Factor (25 yrs. @ 12%)	7.843
Present Worth of Net Income	$376,500 (rounded)
**Present Worth of Reversion	
(25 yrs. @ 14%)	
($100,000 × .038 reversion factor)	3,800
Total Property Value	$380,300

In the above example, the lower risk rate of 12 percent results in an increase in the value of the investment (from $288,900 to $380,300).

EXAMPLE: The property is leased to a nationally known company on a 25-year lease, but the net operating income is only $40,000, which is $8,000 below the market rent. The appraiser in this instance must estimate the value of the two affected interests— leased fee and leasehold. Because of the greatly reduced risk brought on by the long lease to a national company at a scheduled rent well below the market rent, the discount rate has been lowered to 11 percent. The interest rate applicable to reversion is unchanged at the 14 percent rate assumed above as appropriate for the type of property, however.

The leased fee interest can be computed as follows:

Net Operating Income	$ 40,000
*Annuity Factor (25 yrs. @ 11%)	8.422
Present Worth of Net Income	$336,900 (rounded)
**Present Worth of Reversion	
(25 yrs. @ 14%)	
($100,000 × .038 reversion factor)	$ 3,800
Value of the Leased Fee Interest	$340,700

The leasehold interest can be computed as follows:

Market Rent	$ 48,000
Scheduled Rent	40,000
Excess Rent	$ 8,000
Present Worth of Excess Rent	
Discounted @ 15%	6.464
Value of Leasehold Interest	$ 51,700 (rounded)
Total Value of Leased Fee and Leasehold	
Interests ($340,700 + $51,700)	$392,400

In the example above, the lessee has an interest in the property that can be valued in terms of the difference between the rental value of the property today and the actual rent paid to the landlord. This is the value of the lessee's interest if a sandwich lease were to be created, with (under these facts) the sublessee's scheduled rent equal to the market rent. To measure the lessee's leasehold interest, the ex-

*See page 270 (Annuity Factors Table).
**See page 273 (Reversion Table).

cess rent must be capitalized over the term of the lease. Since the excess rent arises out of a leasehold interest, it is subject to the covenants and conditions of the lease and is less secure; therefore, the interest rate used (15 percent) is higher than the 14 percent rate used to value the property under free and clear ownership.

EXAMPLE: The scheduled rent is $52,000 per year, or $4,000 higher than the current market rent. A higher interest rate (15 percent) will be applied to the excess rent portion of the total income, because it may not continue for the length of the lease.

The leased fee interest can be computed as follows:

Present Value of Market Rent (from page 282)	$376,500
Value of Reversion	3,800
	$380,300
Excess Rent Discounted @ 15% ($4,000 × 6.464 annuity factor)	25,900 (rounded)
Value of Leased Fee Interest	$406,200

When scheduled rent is higher than market rent, as in the last example, the value of the lessor's interest increases. This happens even though the excess rent is capitalized at a higher rate because the tenant may default if he or she is paying more rent than may ordinarily be expected.

Exercise E.2

Using the figures given in the example above, what is the value of the leased fee interest if scheduled rent is $54,000? If scheduled rent is $50,000?

Check your answers against those given in the Answer Key at the back of the book.

Conclusion

Because the annuity method of capitalization is based on the premise that income will remain scheduled and predictable throughout the term of a long lease, it is almost always used in valuing leased fee and leasehold interests.

A leasehold interest can have value only if the scheduled rent under the lease is less than the market rent value of the property free of lease. In a sense, a leasehold interest has many of the characteristics of first mortgage equity. If there is a sublessee who also has an interest (which may occur when scheduled rent is less than market rent), the middleman (the prime lessee) is referred to as a sandwich lessee. The sublessee's interest will have risk characteristics similar to a second mortgage. Thus, the capitalization of either the prime lessee's interest or the sublessee's interest normally will warrant a higher capitalization rate than that of the lessor's interest.

The sum of the values of the various lease interests may be more than the value of the property under free and clear ownership, such as when scheduled rent paid by a reliable lessee exceeds market rent.

Achievement Examination Appendix E

An industrial property with a 30-year lease to a highly rated tenant calls for an annual rental of $36,000. Data on comparative properties indicate that the market rent of the subject property is $45,000 per year.

The lessor is virtually assured of receiving the rent, as long as it remains below market rent. In the opinion of the appraiser, an appropriate rate of interest for a low-risk investment of this type is 11 percent. The lessee, on the other hand, has an interest that is subject to variation in value. If market conditions change and the per year rental value is no longer a favorable one, the value of the leasehold estate will be reduced considerably, or even eliminated. To reflect the lessee's risk, the appraiser estimates the leasehold rate at 14 percent. The annuity factor for 30 years at 14 percent is 7.003.

If land value at the expiration of the lease is estimated to be $150,000 and the building assumed to be worthless at the time, what is the value of the leased fee interest?

What is the value of the leasehold interest?

Appraisal Glossary

AACI. Accredited Appraiser Canadian Institute.

AAE. Accredited Assessment Evaluator, International Association of Assessing Officers.

AAR. Accredited in Appraisal Review, Accredited Review Appraisers Council.

ABATEMENT. Stopping or reducing of amount or value, such as when assessments for ad valorem taxation are abated after the initial assessment has been made.

ABSENTEE LANDLORD. An owner of an interest in income-producing property who does not reside on the premises and who may rely on a property manager to oversee the investment.

ABSOLUTE FEE SIMPLE TITLE. A title that is unqualified. Fee simple is the best title that can be obtained. (See FEE SIMPLE.)

ACCESS. A way to enter and leave a tract of land, sometimes by easement over land owned by another. (See INGRESS and EGRESS.)

ACCESSIBILITY. The relative ease of entrance to a property by various means, a factor that will contribute to the probable most profitable use of a site.

ACCESSORY BUILDINGS. Structures on a property, such as sheds and garages, that are secondary to the main building.

ACCRETION. Land buildup resulting from the deposit by natural action of sand or soil washed up from a river, lake or sea.

ACCRUED DEPRECIATION. (1) For accounting purposes, total depreciation taken on an asset from the time of its acquisition. (2) For appraisal purposes, the difference between reproduction or replacement cost and the appraised value as of the date of appraisal.

ACCRUED EXPENSES. Expenses incurred that are not yet payable. In a closing statement, the accrued expenses of the seller typically are credited to the purchaser (taxes, wages, interest, etc.).

ACQUISITION APPRAISAL. A market value appraisal of property condemned or otherwise acquired for public use, to establish the compensation to be paid to the owner.

ACRE. A measure of land, 208.71 by 208.71 feet in area, being 43,560 square feet, or 160 square rods or 4,840 square yards.

ACTUAL AGE. The number of years elapsed since the original structure was built. Sometimes referred to as historical or chronological age.

ADJUSTMENT. Decrease or increase in the sales price of a comparable property to account for a feature that the property has or does not have in comparison to the subject property.

AD VALOREM. According to value (Latin); generally used to refer to real estate taxes that are based on assessed property value.

AESTHETIC VALUE. Relating to beauty, rather than to functional considerations.

AFA. Association of Federal Appraisers.

AIA. American Institute of Architects.

AIC. Appraisal Institute of Canada.

AIREA. American Institute of Real Estate Appraisers.

AIR RIGHTS. The right to use the open space above the physical surface of the land, generally allowing the surface to be used for some other purpose.

ALLOCATION METHOD. The allocation of the appraised total value of the property between land and building. The allocation may be accomplished either on a ratio basis or by subtracting a figure representing building value from the total appraised value of the property.

ALLOWANCE FOR VACANCY AND COLLECTION LOSSES. The percentage of potential gross income that will be lost due to vacant units, collection losses or both.

AMENITIES. The qualities and state of being pleasant and agreeable; in appraising, those qualities that are attached to a property and from which the owner derives benefits other than monetary; satisfaction of possession and use arising from architectural excellence, scenic beauty and social environment.

AMORTIZED MORTGAGE. A mortgage loan in which the principal and interest are payable in periodic installments during the term of the loan so that at the completion of all payments there is a zero balance.

ANNUITY. A fixed, regular return on an investment.

ANNUITY METHOD. A method of capitalization that treats income from real property as a fixed, regular return on an investment. For the annuity method to be applied, the lessee must be reliable and the lease must be long term.

ANTICIPATION, PRINCIPLE OF. The principle that the purchase price of property is affected by the expectation of its future appeal and value.

APPRAISAL. An estimate of quantity, quality or value; the process through which conclusions of property value are obtained; also refers to the report setting forth the process of estimating value. (See APPRAISAL PROCESS.)

APPRAISAL METHODS. The approaches used in the appraisal of real property. (See COST APPROACH, INCOME CAPITALIZATION APPROACH, SALES COMPARISON APPROACH.)

APPRAISAL PROCESS. A systematic analysis of the factors that bear on the value of real estate; an orderly program by which the problem is defined, the work necessary to solve the problem is planned, the data involved are acquired, classified, analyzed and interpreted into an estimate of value and the value estimate is presented in the form requested by the client.

APPRAISAL REPORT. An appraiser's written opinion to a client of the value of the subject property sought as of the date of appraisal, giving all details of the appraisal process.

APPRAISED VALUE.   An estimate by an appraiser of the amount of a particular value, such as assessed value, salvage value or market value, based on the particular assignment.

APPRAISER.   One who estimates value.

APPRECIATION.   Permanent or temporary increase in monetary value over time due to economic or related causes.

APPROACHES TO VALUE.   Any of the following three methods used to estimate the value of real estate: cost approach, income capitalization approach and sales comparison approach.

APPURTENANCE.   Anything used with land for its benefit, either affixed to land or used with it, that will pass with the conveyance of the land.

ARM'S-LENGTH TRANSACTION.   A transaction in which both buyer and seller act willingly and under no pressure, with knowledge of the present conditions and future potential of the property, and in which the property has been offered on the open market for a reasonable length of time and there are no unusual circumstances.

ASA.   American Society of Appraisers.

ASR.   Senior Residential Member, American Society of Appraisers.

ASSESSED VALUE.   The value placed on land and buildings by a government unit (assessor) for use in levying real property taxes.

ASSESSMENT.   The imposition of a tax, charge or levy, usually according to established rates. (See SPECIAL ASSESSMENT.)

ASSESSOR.   One who determines property values for the purpose of ad valorem taxation.

ASSET.   Property that is owned and has value, such as cash or real or personal property.

BAND OF INVESTMENT.   A method of developing the discount rate portion of a capitalization rate based on (1) the rate of mortgage interest available, (2) the rate of return required on equity and (3) the debt and equity share in the property.

BASE LINE.   A reference survey line of the government or rectangular survey, being an imaginary line extending east and west and crossing a principal meridian at a definite point.

BASE RENT.   The minimum rent payable under a percentage lease.

BENCH MARK.   A permanent reference mark (PRM) used by surveyors in measuring differences in elevation.

BENCHMARK.   The standard or base from which specific estimates are made.

BOOK VALUE.   The value of a property as an asset on the books of account; usually, reproduction or replacement cost, plus additions to capital and less reserves for depreciation.

BUILDING CAPITALIZATION RATE.   The sum of the discount and capital recapture rates for a building.

BUILDING CODES.   Rules of local, municipal or state governments specifying minimum building and construction standards for the protection of public safety and health.

BUILDING RESIDUAL TECHNIQUE.   A method of capitalization using the net income remaining to the building after interest on land value has been deducted.

BUNDLE OF RIGHTS. A term often applied to the rights of ownership of real estate, including the rights of using, renting, selling or giving away the real estate, or *not* taking any of these actions.

CAE. Certified Assessment Evaluator, International Association of Assessing Officers.

CAO. Certified Appraisal Organization, National Association of Master Appraisers.

CAPITAL. Money and/or property comprising the wealth owned or used by a person or business enterprise.

CAPITALIZATION. The process employed in estimating the value of a property by the use of the appropriate capitalization rate and the annual net operating income expected to be produced by the property, the formula being expressed as:

$$\frac{\text{Income}}{\text{Rate}} = \text{Value}$$

CAPITALIZATION RATE. The percentage rate applied to the income a property is expected to produce to derive an estimate of the property's value; includes both an acceptable rate of return on the amount invested (yield) and return of the actual amount invested (recapture).

CAPITAL RECAPTURE. The return of an investment; the right of the investor to get back the amount invested at the end of the term of ownership or over the productive life of the improvements.

CAPITALIZED VALUE METHOD OF DEPRECIATION. A method of computing depreciation by determining loss in rental value attributable to a depreciated item and applying a gross rent multiplier to that figure.

CASH EQUIVALENCY TECHNIQUE. Mechanical method of assisting in determining the adjustment to a sales price necessary to reflect the effect on value of assumption or procurement by buyer of a loan at an interest rate lower than the prevailing market rate.

CCRA. Certified Commercial Real Estate Appraiser, American Society of Professional Appraisers.

CHAIN. A surveyor's unit of measurement equal to four rods or 66 feet, consisting of 100 links of 7.92 inches each; ten square chains of land are equal to one acre.

CHANGE, PRINCIPLE OF. The principle that no physical or economic condition ever remains constant.

CHATTELS. Tangible personal property items.

CLIENT. One who hires another person as a representative or agent for a fee.

CLOSING STATEMENT. The computation of financial adjustments required to close a real estate transaction, computed as of the day of closing the sale; used to determine the net amount of money the buyer must pay to the seller to complete the transaction, as well as amounts to be paid to other parties, such as the broker or escrow holder. (See SETTLEMENT.)

CMDA. Certified Market Data Analyst, National Residential Appraisers Institute.

CODE OF ETHICS. Rules of ethical conduct, such as those that govern the actions of members of a professional group.

COMPARABLES. Properties that are substantially equivalent to the subject property.

COMPARISON METHOD.   (See SALES COMPARISON APPROACH.)

COMPETITION, PRINCIPLE OF.   The principle that a successful business attracts other such businesses, which may dilute profits.

COMPOUND INTEREST.   Interest paid on both the original investment and accrued interest.

CONDEMNATION.   Taking private property for public use through court action, under the right of eminent domain, with compensation to the owner.

CONDITIONS, COVENANTS AND RESTRICTIONS (CC&Rs).   Private limitations on property use placed in the deed received by a property owner, typically by reference to a Declaration of Restrictions.

CONDOMINIUM.   An estate in real property consisting of the absolute ownership of an apartment or a commercial unit, generally in a multiunit building, with a legal description of the airspace that the unit actually occupies, plus an undivided interest in the ownership of the common elements owned jointly with the other condominium unit owners.

> **PARCEL.**   The entire tract of real estate included in a condominium development; also referred to as a development parcel.

> **UNIT.**   One ownership space in a condominium building or a part of a property intended for independent use and having lawful access to a public way. Ownership of one unit also includes a definite undivided interest in the common elements.

COMMON ELEMENTS.   All portions of the land, property and space comprising a condominium property including land, all improvements and structures, and all easements, rights and appurtenances, excluding all space comprising individual units. Each unit owner owns a definite percentage of undivided interest in the common elements.

CONFORMITY, PRINCIPLE OF.   The principle that buildings should be similar in design, construction and age to other buildings in the neighborhood to enhance appeal and value.

CONTIGUOUS.   Adjacent; in actual contact; touching.

CONTRACT.   An agreement entered into by two or more legally competent parties who, for a consideration, undertake to do or to refrain from doing some legal act or acts.

CONTRACT RENT.   (See SCHEDULED RENT.)

CONTRIBUTION, PRINCIPLE OF.   The principle that any improvement to a property, whether to vacant land or a building, is worth only what it adds to the property's market value, regardless of the improvement's actual cost.

CONVENTIONAL LOAN.   A loan, made with real estate as security, that is neither insured by the FHA nor guaranteed by the VA.

CONVEYANCE.   A written instrument, such as a deed or lease, by which title or an interest in real estate is transferred.

COOPERATIVE.   A multiunit residential building with title in a trust or corporation that is owned by and operated for the benefit of persons living within it, who are the beneficial owners of the trust or the stockholders of the corporation, each possessing a proprietary lease granting occupancy of a specific unit in the building.

CORRECTION LINES.   A system of compensating for inaccuracies in the rectangular survey system due to the curvature of the earth. Every fourth township line (24-mile intervals) is used as a correction line on which the intervals between the north and south range lines are remeasured and corrected to a full six miles.

CORRELATION. (See RECONCILIATION.)

COST APPROACH. The process of estimating the value of a property by adding the appraiser's estimate of the reproduction or replacement cost of property improvements, less depreciation, to the estimated land value.

COST INDEX. Figure representing construction cost at a particular time in relation to construction cost at an earlier time, prepared by a cost reporting or indexing service.

COVENANT. An agreement written into deeds and other instruments promising performance or nonperformance of certain acts or stipulating certain uses or nonuses of property.

CPE. Certified Personalty Evaluator, International Association of Assessing Officers.

CRA. Canadian Residential Appraiser, Appraisal Institute of Canada; Certified Review Appraiser, National Association of Review Appraisers and Mortgage Underwriters.

CREA. Certified Real Estate Appraiser, National Association of Real Estate Appraisers.

CRRA. Certified Residential Real Estate Appraiser, American Society of Professional Appraisers.

CUBIC FOOT METHOD. A method of estimating reproduction cost by multiplying the number of cubic feet of space a building encloses by the construction cost per cubic foot.

CURABLE DEPRECIATION. A depreciated item that can be restored or replaced economically. (See PHYSICAL DETERIORATION—CURABLE and FUNCTIONAL OBSOLESCENCE—CURABLE.)

DATA. Information pertinent to a specific appraisal assignment. Data may be *general* (relating to the economic background, the region, the city and the neighborhood) or *specific* (relating to the subject property and comparable properties in the market).

DATUM. A horizontal plane from which heights and depths are measured.

DECREASING RETURNS, LAW OF. The situation in which property improvements no longer bring a corresponding increase in property income or value.

DEED. A written instrument that conveys title to or an interest in real estate when properly executed and delivered.

DEED RESTRICTIONS. Provisions in a deed limiting the future uses of the property. Deed restrictions may take many forms; they may limit the density of buildings, dictate the types of structures that can be erected and prevent buildings from being used for specific purposes or used at all. Deed restrictions may impose a myriad of limitations and conditions affecting the property rights appraised.

DEFAULT. Failure to perform a duty or meet a contractual obligation.

DEMISED PREMISES. Property conveyed for a certain number of years, most often by a lease.

DEPRECIATED COST. For appraisal purposes, the reproduction or replacement cost of a building, less accrued depreciation to the time of appraisal.

DEPRECIATION. For appraisal purposes, loss in value due to any cause, including physical deterioration, functional obsolescence and external obsolescence. (See OBSOLESCENCE.)

DEPTH FACTOR. An adjustment factor applied to the value per front foot of lots that vary from the standard depth.

DEVELOPMENT.   (See NEIGHBORHOOD LIFE CYCLE.)

DIRECT CAPITALIZATION.   Method used to estimate value from annual net operating income by applying a capitalization rate derived by analyzing sales of comparable properties and applying the formula $\frac{I}{V} = R$ to each.

DIRECT COSTS.   Costs in erecting a new building involved with either site preparation or building construction, including fixtures.

DIRECT MARKET COMPARISON APPROACH.   (See SALES COMPARISON APPROACH.)

DISCOUNT RATE.   (See INTEREST RATE.)

DISINTEGRATION.   (See NEIGHBORHOOD LIFE CYCLE.)

EASEMENT.   A right to use the land of another for a specific purpose, such as a right of way or for utilities; a nonpossessory interest in land. An *easement appurtenant* passes with the land when conveyed.

ECONOMIC AGE-LIFE METHOD OF DEPRECIATION.   A method of computing accrued depreciation in which the cost of a building is depreciated at a fixed annual percentage rate; also called the straight-line method.

ECONOMIC LIFE.   The period of time during which a structure may reasonably be expected to perform the function for which it was designed or intended.

ECONOMIC OBSOLESCENCE.   (See EXTERNAL OBSOLESCENCE.)

EFFECTIVE AGE.   The age of a building based on the actual wear and tear and maintenance, or lack of it, that the building has received.

EFFECTIVE GROSS INCOME.   Estimated potential gross income of a rental property from all sources, less anticipated vacancy and collection losses.

EGRESS.   A way to leave a tract of land; the opposite of ingress. (See ACCESS.)

ELLWOOD, L. W.   Author of *Ellwood Tables for Real Estate Appraising and Financing,* Fourth Edition (American Institute of Real Estate Appraisers, National Association of REALTORS®, 1977), based on principles of mortgage equity capitalization.

EMINENT DOMAIN.   The right of a federal, state or local government or public corporation, utility or service corporation to acquire private property for public use, through a court action called condemnation in which the court determines whether the use is a necessary one and what the compensation to the owner should be.

ENCROACHMENT.   A building, wall or fence that extends beyond the land of the owner and illegally intrudes on land of an adjoining owner or a street or alley.

ENCUMBRANCE.   Any lien (such as a mortgage, tax lien or judgment lien), easement, restriction on the use of land, outstanding dower right or other interest that may diminish the value of property to its owner.

ENVIRONMENTAL OBSOLESCENCE.   (See EXTERNAL OBSOLESCENCE.)

EQUALIZATION.   The raising or lowering of assessed values for tax purposes in a particular county or taxing district to make them equal to assessments in other counties or districts.

EQUILIBRIUM.   (See NEIGHBORHOOD LIFE CYCLE.)

EQUITY.   The interest or value that an owner has in real estate over and above any mortgage or other lien or charge against it.

ESCALATOR CLAUSE. A clause in a contract, lease or mortgage providing for increases in wages, rent or interest, based on fluctuations in certain economic indexes, costs or taxes.

ESCHEAT. The reversion of property of a decedent who died intestate (without a will) and without heirs to the state or county as provided by state law.

ESCROW. The closing of a transaction through a disinterested third person called an escrow agent or escrow holder, who holds funds and/or documents for delivery upon the performance of certain conditions.

ESTATE. The degree, quantity, nature and extent of ownership interest that a person has in real property.

EXCESS INCOME. (See EXCESS RENT.)

EXCESS RENT. The difference between market rent and scheduled rent when market rent is lower.

EXTERNAL OBSOLESCENCE. Loss of value from forces outside the building or property, such as changes in optimum land use, legislative enactments that restrict or impair property rights and changes in supply-demand relationships.

EXTERNALITIES. The principle that outside influences may have a positive or negative effect on property value.

FEE SIMPLE. The greatest possible estate or right of ownership of real property, continuing without time limitation. Sometimes called fee or fee simple absolute.

FHA. The Federal Housing Administration. Insures loans made by approved lenders in accordance with its regulations.

FINAL VALUE ESTIMATE. The appraiser's estimate of the defined value of the subject property, arrived at by reconciling (correlating) the estimates of values derived from the sales comparison, cost and income approaches.

FIRST MORTGAGE. A mortgage that has priority as a lien over all other mortgages.

FIXED EXPENSES. Those costs that are more or less permanent and do not vary in relation to the property's occupancy or income, such as real estate taxes and insurance for fire, theft and hazards.

FIXTURE. Anything affixed to land, including personal property attached permanently to a building or to land so that it becomes part of the real estate.

FORECLOSURE. A court action initiated by a mortgagee or lienor for the purpose of having the court order that the debtor's real estate be sold to pay the mortgage or other lien (mechanic's lien or judgment).

FORM APPRAISAL REPORT. Any of the relatively brief standard forms prepared by agencies such as the Federal Home Loan Mortgage Corporation and Federal National Mortgage Association and others for routine property appraisals.

FREEHOLD. An estate in land in which ownership is for an indeterminate length of time.

FRONT FOOT. A standard of measurement, being a strip of land one foot wide fronting on the street or waterfront and extending the depth of the lot. Value may be quoted per front foot.

FUNCTIONAL OBSOLESCENCE. Defects in a building or structure that detract from its value or marketability, usually the result of layout, design or other features that are less desirable than features designed for the same functions in newer property.

FUNCTIONAL OBSOLESCENCE—CURABLE. Physical or design features that are no longer considered desirable by property buyers but could be replaced or redesigned at relatively low cost.

FUNCTIONAL OBSOLESCENCE—INCURABLE. Currently undesirable physical or design features that are not easily remedied or economically justified.

GSA. Graduate Senior Appraiser, National Residential Appraisers Institute.

GROSS INCOME. (See POTENTIAL GROSS INCOME.)

GROSS INCOME MULTIPLIER. A figure used as a multiplier of the gross income of a property to produce an estimate of the property's value.

GROSS LEASE. A lease of property under the terms of which the lessee pays a fixed rent and the lessor pays all property charges regularly incurred through ownership (repairs, taxes, insurance and operating expenses).

GROSS RENT MULTIPLIER. (See GROSS INCOME MULTIPLIER.)

GROUND LEASE. A lease of *land only* on which the lessee usually owns the building or is required to build as specified by the lease. Such leases are usually long-term net leases; the lessee's rights and obligations continue until the lease expires or is terminated for default.

HIGHEST AND BEST USE. The legally and physically possible use of land that is likely to produce the highest land (or property) value. It considers the balance between site and improvements as well as the intensity and length of uses.

HISTORICAL COST. Actual cost of a property at the time it was constructed.

HISTORICAL RENT. Scheduled rent paid in past years.

HOSKOLD SINKING FUND TABLE. A table that supplies a factor by which a property's annual net income may be multiplied to find the present worth of the property over a given period at a given rate of interest.

HUD. Department of Housing and Urban Development.

IAAO. International Association of Assessing Officers.

IFA. Member, National Association of Independent Fee Appraisers, Inc.

IMPROVED LAND. Real property made suitable for building by the addition of utilities and publicly owned structures, such as a curb, sidewalk, street-lighting system and/or sewer.

IMPROVEMENTS. Structures of whatever nature, usually privately rather than publicly owned, erected on a site to enable its utilization, e.g., buildings, fences, driveways and retaining walls.

INCOME CAPITALIZATION APPROACH. The process of estimating the value of an income-producing property by capitalization of the annual net operating income expected to be produced by the property during its remaining economic life.

INCREASING RETURNS, LAW OF. The situation in which property improvements increase property income or value.

INCURABLE DEPRECIATION. A depreciated item that would be impossible or relatively too expensive to restore or replace.

INDEPENDENT CONTRACTOR. A person who contracts to do work for another by using his or her own methods and without being under the control of the other person regarding how the work should be done. Unlike an employee, an independent contractor pays for all of his or her expenses, personally pays income and social security taxes and receives no employee benefits. Many real estate salespeople are independent contractors.

INDIRECT COSTS. Costs in erecting a new building not involved with either site preparation or building construction; for example, building permit, land survey, overhead expenses such as insurance and payroll taxes, and builder's profit.

INDUSTRIAL DISTRICT OR PARK. A controlled development zoned for industrial use and designed to accommodate specific types of industry, providing public utilities, streets, railroad sidings, water and sewage facilities.

INGRESS. The way to enter a tract of land. Often used interchangeably with access. (See ACCESS.)

INSTALLMENT CONTRACT. A contract for the sale of real estate by which the purchase price is paid in installments over an extended period of time by the purchaser, who is in possession, with the title retained by the seller until a certain number of payments are made. The purchaser's payments may be forfeited upon default.

INTEREST. A percentage of the principal amount of a loan charged by a lender for its use, usually expressed as an annual rate.

INTEREST RATE. Discount rate; return on an investment; an interest rate is composed of four component rates—safe rate, risk rate, nonliquidity rate and management rate.

> **SAFE RATE.** The interest rate paid by investments of maximum security, highest liquidity and minimum risk.

> **RISK RATE.** An addition to the safe rate to compensate for the hazards that accompany investments in real estate.

> **NONLIQUIDITY RATE.** A penalty charged for the time needed to convert real estate into cash.

> **MANAGEMENT RATE.** Compensation to the owner for the work involved in managing an investment and reinvesting the funds received from the property.

INTESTATE. Dying without a will or without having made a valid will. Title to property owned by someone who dies intestate will pass to his or her heirs, as provided in the law of descent of the state in which the property is located.

INWOOD ANNUITY TABLE. A table that supplies a factor to be multiplied by the desired yearly income (based on the interest rate and length of time of the investment) to find the present worth of the investment.

LAND. The earth's surface in its natural condition, extending down to the center of the globe, its surface and all things affixed to it, and the airspace above the surface.

LAND CAPITALIZATION RATE. The rate of return, including interest, on land only.

LANDLOCKED PARCEL. A parcel of land without any access to a public road or way.

LANDLORD. One who owns property and leases it to a tenant.

LAND RESIDUAL TECHNIQUE. A method of capitalization using the net income remaining to the land after return on and recapture of the building value have been deducted.

LATENT DEFECT. Physical deficiencies or construction defects not readily ascertainable from a reasonable inspection of the property, such as a defective septic tank or underground sewage system, or improper plumbing or electrical wiring.

LEASE.   A written or oral contract for the possession and use of real property for a stipulated period of time, in consideration for the payment of rent. Leases for more than one year generally must be in writing.

LEASED FEE.   The lessor's interest and rights in the real estate being leased.

LEASEHOLD ESTATE.   The lessee's right to possess and use real estate during the term of a lease. This is generally considered a personal property interest.

LEGAL DESCRIPTION.   A statement identifying land by a system prescribed by law.

LESSEE.   The person to whom property is leased by another; also called a tenant.

LESSEE'S INTEREST.   An interest having value only if the agreed-on rent is less than the market rent.

LESSOR.   The person who leases property to another; also called a landlord.

LESSOR'S INTEREST.   The value of lease rental payments plus the remaining property value at the end of the lease period.

LEVY.   To impose or assess a tax on a person or property; the amount of taxes to be imposed in a given district.

MAI.   Member of the Appraisal Institute, American Institute of Real Estate Appraisers.

MAINTENANCE EXPENSES.   Costs incurred for day-to-day upkeep, such as management, wages and benefits of building employees, fuel, utility services, decorating and repairs.

MARKET COMPARISON APPROACH.   (See SALES COMPARISON APPROACH.)

MARKET COMPARISON METHOD OF DEPRECIATION.   (See SALES COMPARISON METHOD OF DEPRECIATION.)

MARKET DATA APPROACH.   (See SALES COMPARISON APPROACH.)

MARKET PRICE.   (See SALES PRICE.)

MARKET RENT.   The amount for which the competitive rental market indicates property should rent.

MARKET VALUE.   The most probable price real estate should bring in a sale occurring under normal market conditions.

MECHANIC'S LIEN.   A lien created by statute that exists in favor of contractors, laborers or materialmen who have performed work or furnished materials in the erection or repair of a building.

MFLA.   Master Farm and Land Appraiser, National Association of Master Appraisers.

MILE.   A measurement of distance, being 1,760 yards or 5,280 feet.

MORTGAGE.   A conditional transfer or pledge of real property as security for the payment of a debt; also, the document used to create a mortgage lien.

MORTGAGEE.   The lender in a loan transaction secured by a mortgage.

MORTGAGOR.   An owner of real estate who borrows money and conveys his or her property as security for the loan.

MRA.   Master Residential Appraiser, National Association of Master Appraisers.

MREA. Master Real Estate Appraiser, National Society of Real Estate Appraisers, Inc.

MSA. Master Senior Appraiser, National Association of Master Appraisers.

NAHB. National Association of Home Builders of the United States.

NAIFA. National Association of Independent Fee Appraisers, Inc.

NAR. National Association of REALTORS®.

NARAMU. National Association of Review Appraisers and Mortgage Underwriters.

NAREA. National Association of Real Estate Appraisers.

NARRATIVE APPRAISAL REPORT. A detailed written presentation of the facts and reasoning behind an appraiser's estimate of value.

NEIGHBORHOOD. A residential or commercial area with similar types of properties, buildings of similar value or age, predominant land-use activities, and natural or fabricated geographic boundaries, such as highways or rivers.

NEIGHBORHOOD LIFE CYCLE. The period during which most of the properties in a neighborhood undergo the stages of development, equilibrium and decline.

> **DEVELOPMENT (growth).** Improvements are made, and properties experience a rising demand.

> **EQUILIBRIUM.** Properties undergo little change; also called stability.

> **DECLINE.** Properties require an increasing amount of upkeep to retain their original utility and become less desirable.

NET LEASE. A lease requiring the tenant to pay rent and all costs of maintenance including taxes, insurance, repairs and other expenses of ownership. Sometimes known as an absolute net lease or triple net lease.

NET OPERATING INCOME. Income remaining after operating expenses are deducted from effective gross income.

NONCONFORMING USE. A once lawful property use that is permitted to continue after a zoning ordinance prohibiting it has been established for the area; a use that differs sharply from the prevailing uses in a neighborhood.

OBSERVED CONDITION DEPRECIATION. A method of computing depreciation in which the appraiser estimates the loss in value for all items of depreciation. (See CURABLE DEPRECIATION and INCURABLE DEPRECIATION.)

OBSOLESCENCE. Lessening of value from out-of-date features as a result of current changes in property design, construction or use; an element of depreciation. (See EXTERNAL OBSOLESCENCE and FUNCTIONAL OBSOLESCENCE.)

OCCUPANCY. Possession and use of property as owner or tenant.

OCCUPANCY RATE. The percentage of total rental units occupied and producing income.

OPERATING EXPENSES. The cost of all goods and services used or consumed in the process of obtaining and maintaining income. (See MAINTENANCE EXPENSES, FIXED EXPENSES and RESERVES FOR REPLACEMENT.)

OPERATING STATEMENT. The written record of a business's gross income, expenses and resultant net income.

OPTION. A right given for a valuable consideration to purchase or lease property at a future date, for a specified price and terms. The right may or may not be exercised at the option holder's (optionee's) discretion.

ORIENTATION.   Positioning a structure on its lot with regard to exposure to the sun, prevailing winds, privacy and protection from noise.

OVERALL RATE.   The direct ratio between a property's annual net income and its sales price.

OVERIMPROVEMENT.   An improvement to property that is more than warranted by the property's highest and best use and thus not likely to contribute its cost to the total market value of the property.

PERCENTAGE LEASE.   A lease commonly used for commercial property that provides for a rental based on the tenant's gross sales at the premises. It generally stipulates a base monthly rental, plus a percentage of any gross sales exceeding a certain amount.

PERSONAL PROPERTY.   Items that are tangible and movable and do not fit the definition of realty; chattels.

PHYSICAL DETERIORATION—CURABLE.   Loss of value due to neglected repairs or maintenance that are economically feasible and, if performed, would result in an increase in appraised value equal to or exceeding their cost.

PHYSICAL DETERIORATION—INCURABLE.   Loss of value due to neglected repairs or maintenance of short-lived or long-lived building components that would not contribute comparable value to a building if performed.

PHYSICAL LIFE.   The length of time a structure can be considered habitable, without regard to its economic use.

PLAT.   A map representing a parcel of land subdivided into lots, showing streets and other details or a single site.

PLOTTAGE VALUE.   The subsequent increase in the unit value of a group of adjacent properties when they are combined into one property in a process called assemblage.

POLICE POWER.   The right of the government to impose laws, statutes and ordinances to protect the public health, safety and welfare. Includes zoning ordinances and building codes.

POSSESSION.   The right of the owner to occupy property. When property is occupied by a tenant, the owner has constructive possession by right of title.

POTENTIAL GROSS INCOME.   A property's total potential income from all sources during a specified period of time.

PREPAID ITEMS OF EXPENSE.   Expense items, such as insurance premiums and tax reserves, that have been paid in advance of the time that the expense is incurred. Prepaid expenses typically are prorated and credited to the seller in the preparation of a closing statement.

PRICE.   The amount of money set or paid as the consideration in the sale of an item at a particular time.

PRINCIPAL.   (1) A sum lent or employed as a fund or investment—as distinguished from its income or profits; (2) the original amount (as of a loan) of the total due and payable at a certain date; or (3) a party to a transaction—as distinguished from an agent.

PRINCIPAL MERIDIAN.   One of 35 north and south survey lines established and defined as part of the rectangular survey system.

PROFIT-AND-LOSS STATEMENT.   (See OPERATING STATEMENT.)

PROPERTY RESIDUAL TECHNIQUE.   A method of capitalization using the net income remaining to the property as a whole.

PRORATIONS. The adjustment of taxes, interest, insurance and/or other costs on a pro rata basis as of the closing of a sale. (See CLOSING STATEMENT.)

PURCHASE MONEY MORTGAGE. A note secured by a mortgage or trust deed given by the buyer, as mortgagor, to the seller, as mortgagee, as part of the purchase price of real estate.

QUANTITY SURVEY METHOD. A method for finding the reproduction cost of a building in which the costs of erecting or installing all of the component parts of a new building, including both direct and indirect costs, are added.

QUITCLAIM DEED. A conveyance by which the grantor transfers whatever interest he or she has in the land, without warranties or obligations.

RA. Residential Appraiser, National Society of Real Estate Appraisers, Inc.

REAL ESTATE. Land; a portion of the earth's surface extending downward to the center of the earth and upward into space including fixtures permanently attached thereto by nature or by man, anything incidental or appurtenant to land and anything immovable by law; freehold estate in land.

REAL ESTATE BROKER. Any person, partnership, association or corporation who, for a compensation or valuable consideration, sells or offers for sale, buys or offers to buy, or negotiates the purchase, sale or exchange of real estate, or who leases or offers to lease, or rents or offers for rent any real estate or the improvement thereon for others. Such a broker must secure a state license. For a license to be issued to a firm, it is usually required that all active partners or officers be licensed real estate brokers.

REAL ESTATE SALESPERSON. Any person who, for a compensation or valuable consideration, is employed either directly or indirectly by a real estate broker to sell or offer to sell, or to buy or offer to buy, or negotiate the purchase, sale or exchange of real estate, or to lease, rent or offer for rent any real estate, or to negotiate leases thereof or improvements thereon. Such a salesperson must secure a state license.

REAL PROPERTY. The rights of ownership of real estate; often called the *bundle of rights,* for all practical purposes, synonymous with real estate.

REALTOR®. A registered trademark term reserved for the sole use of active members of local boards of REALTORS® affiliated with the National Association of REALTORS®.

RECAPTURE RATE. The percentage of a property's original cost that is returned to the owner as income during the remaining economic life of the investment.

RECONCILIATION. The final step in the appraisal process, in which the appraiser reconciles the estimates of value received from the sales comparison, cost and income capitalization approaches to arrive at a final estimate of market value for the subject property.

RECONSTRUCTION OF THE OPERATING STATEMENT. The process of eliminating the inapplicable expense items for appraisal purposes and adjusting the remaining valid expenses, if necessary.

RECTANGULAR SURVEY SYSTEM. A system, established in 1785 by the federal government, that provides for the surveying and describing of land by reference to principal meridians and base lines; also called the U.S. government survey system and the section and township system.

REGIONAL MULTIPLIERS. Adjustment factors by which standard cost figures can be multiplied to allow for regional price differences.

REMAINDER. The remnant of an estate that has been conveyed to take effect and be enjoyed after the termination of a prior estate; for instance, when an owner conveys a life estate to one party and the remainder to another. (For the case in which the owner retains the residual estate, see REVERSION.)

REMAINING ECONOMIC LIFE. The number of years of useful life left to a building from the date of appraisal.

RENT LOSS METHOD OF DEPRECIATION. (See CAPITALIZED VALUE METHOD.)

REPLACEMENT COST. The current construction cost of a building having exactly the same utility as the subject property.

REPRODUCTION COST. The current construction cost of an exact duplicate of the subject building.

RES. Residential Evaluation Specialist, International Association of Assessing Officers.

RESERVES FOR REPLACEMENT. Allowances set up for replacement of building and equipment items that have a relatively short life expectancy.

RESIDUAL. In appraising, the value remaining after all deductions have been made.

REVERSION. The remnant of an estate that the grantor (as opposed to a third party) holds after he or she has granted a limited estate such as a leasehold or life estate to another person, and which will return or revert back to the grantor. (See REMAINDER.)

RIGHT-OF-WAY. The right that one has to travel over the land of another; an easement.

RIPARIAN RIGHTS. Rights of an owner of land that borders on or includes a stream, river, lake or sea. These rights include definition of (and limitations on) access to and use of the water, ownership of streambed, navigable water and uninterrupted flow and drainage. (See ACCRETION.)

RISK RATE. (See INTEREST RATE.)

RM. Residential Member, American Institute of Real Estate Appraisers.

ROD. A measure of length, 16½ feet.

RRA. Registered Review Appraiser (Canada), National Association of Review Appraisers and Mortgage Underwriters.

SAFE RATE. (See INTEREST RATE.)

SALES COMPARISON APPROACH. The process of estimating the value of property through examination and comparison of actual sales of comparable properties; also called the direct market comparison or market data approach.

SALES COMPARISON METHOD OF DEPRECIATION. Way of estimating loss in value through depreciation by using sales prices of comparable properties to derive the value of a depreciated item.

SALESPERSON. (See REAL ESTATE SALESPERSON.)

SALES PRICE. The actual price that a buyer pays for a property.

SANDWICH LEASE. The ownership interest of a sublessee.

SCA. Senior Certified Appraiser, National Residential Appraisers Institute.

SCHEDULED RENT. Rent paid by agreement between lessor and lessee; also called contract rent.

SECOND MORTGAGE. A mortgage loan secured by real estate that has previously been made security for an existing mortgage loan. Also called a junior mortgage or junior lien.

SELLING PRICE.   The actual price that a buyer pays for a property.

SETTLEMENT.   The process of closing a real estate transaction by adjusting and prorating the required credits and charges.

SINKING FUND METHOD.   Use of a factor by which a property's annual net income may be multiplied to find the present worth of the property over a given period at a given rate of interest.

SIR.   Society of Industrial REALTORS®.

SITE.   Land suitable for building purposes, usually improved by the addition of utilities or other services.

SPECIAL ASSESSMENT.   A charge against real estate made by a unit of government to cover the proportionate cost of an improvement, such as a street or sewer.

SPECIAL-PURPOSE PROPERTY.   Property that has unique usage requirements, such as a church or a museum, making it difficult to convert to other uses.

SQUARE FOOT METHOD.   A method for finding the reproduction cost of a building in which the cost per square foot of a recently built comparable structure is multiplied by the number of square feet in the subject property.

SRA.   Senior Residential Appraiser, Society of Real Estate Appraisers.

SREA.   Senior Real Estate Analyst, Society of Real Estate Appraisers.

SRPA.   Senior Real Property Appraiser, Society of Real Estate Appraisers.

SR/WA.   Member designation, International Right of Way Association.

STRAIGHT-LINE METHOD OF DEPRECIATION.   Another name for the age-life method of computing accrued depreciation.

STRAIGHT-LINE RECAPTURE.   A method of capital recapture in which total accrued depreciation is spread over the useful life of a building in equal amounts.

SUBDIVISION.   A tract of land divided by the owner into blocks, building lots and streets by a recorded subdivision plat. Compliance with local regulations is required.

SUBLETTING.   The leasing of premises by a lessee to a third party for a part of the lessee's remaining term.

SUBSTITUTION, PRINCIPLE OF.   The basic appraisal premise that the market value of real estate is influenced by the cost of acquiring a substitute or comparable property.

SUMMATION METHOD.   Another name for the cost approach to appraising.

SUPPLY AND DEMAND, PRINCIPLE OF.   A principle that the value of a commodity will rise as demand increases and/or supply decreases.

SURVEY.   The process of measuring land to determine its size, location and physical description; also, the map or plat showing the results of a survey.

TENANT.   One who has possession of real estate; an occupant, not necessarily a renter; the lessee under a lease. The estate or interest held is called a tenancy.

TIME-SHARE.   Estate or use interest in real property for a designated time period each year.

TITLE.   The evidence of a person's right to the ownership and possession of land.

TOPOGRAPHY.   Surface features of land; elevation, ridges, slope, contour.

TRADE FIXTURES. Articles of personal property installed by a commercial tenant under the terms of a lease. Trade fixtures are removable by the tenant before the lease expires and are not true fixtures.

UNDERIMPROVEMENT. An improvement that is less than a property's highest and best use.

UNIT-IN-PLACE METHOD. A method for finding the reproduction cost of a building in which the construction cost per square foot of each component part of the subject building (including material, labor, overhead and builder's profit) is multiplied by the number of square feet of the component part in the subject building.

USEFUL LIFE. (See ECONOMIC LIFE.)

USE VALUE. The value of a property designed to fit the specific requirements of the owner but which would have little or no use to another owner. Also referred to as value-in-use.

USURY. Charging interest in excess of the maximum legal rate.

VACANCY AND COLLECTION LOSSES. (See ALLOWANCE FOR VACANCY AND COLLECTION LOSSES.)

VALUATION PRINCIPLES. Factors that affect market value, such as the principle of substitution, highest and best use, supply and demand, conformity, contribution, increasing and decreasing returns, competition, change, stage of life cycle, anticipation and externalities.

VALUE. The power of a good or service to command other goods or services in exchange; the present worth of future rights to income and benefits arising from ownership.

VA MORTGAGE. A mortgage loan on approved property made to a qualified veteran by an authorized lender and guaranteed by the Veterans Administration to limit possible loss by the lender.

VENDEE. Buyer.

VENDOR. Seller.

YIELD. Income produced by an investment. Usually used to refer to equity investments.

YIELD CAPITALIZATION. Method used to estimate value from annual net operating income by applying a capitalization rate derived by analyzing each of the rate's component parts, providing both return on and return of the investment.

ZONING ORDINANCE. Regulation of the character and use of property by a municipality or other governmental entity through the exercise of its police power.

Construction Glossary*

ACOUSTICAL MATERIAL. Sound-absorbing materials, such as tile or fiberboard, which are applied to walls and/or ceilings.

ADDITION. Any construction that increases a building's size or significantly adds to it. For example, constructing a second floor on top of a one-level structure would be an addition.

AIRWAY. A space between roof insulation and roof boards for the movement of air.

ANCHOR BOLT. A bolt that secures the *sill* of the house to the *foundation wall*.

ASH DUMP. A container under a fireplace where ashes are temporarily deposited. Ashes can be removed later through a *cleanout door*.

ATTIC. Accessible space located between the top of a ceiling and the underside of a roof. Inaccessible spaces are considered structural cavities.

ATTIC VENTILATORS. Openings in the roof or in gables to allow for air circulation.

BACKFILL. The earth or gravel used to fill in the space around a building wall after the foundation is completed.

BALLOON FRAMING. A type of framing in which the studs extend from the top of the *foundation sill* to the roof. Support for the second floor is provided by a horizontal ribbon or ledge board and by joists that are nailed to the studs.

BALUSTER. One of a string of small poles used to support the handrail of a stairway.

BAND OR BOX SILL. In pier and beam foundations, the two horizontal members that connect the pier to the *floor joist*. The boards are joined to create a right angle, and the joist is placed perpendicular to the upright angle. This prependicular placement provides the foundation with the necessary rigidity.

BASEBOARD. A board running around the bottom of the wall next to the floor. A baseboard covers the gap between the floor and the wall, protects the wall from scuffs and provides a decorative accent.

---

*The material in this glossary is taken in part from *The Language of Real Estate*, 3rd ed., by John W. Reilly (Chicago: Real Estate Education Company, 1989).

BASEMENT. A space of full-story height below the first floor, and wholly or partly below the exterior grade, that is not used primarily for living accommodations. Space partly below grade used primarily for living accommodations or commercial use is not defined by FHA as basement space.

BASE SHOE. Molding used at the junction of the *baseboard* and the floor. Also called a *carpet strip*.

BASE TOP MOLDING. A thin strip placed on top of the *baseboard* and perpendicular to the wall to cover gaps between the wall and the baseboard and give the molding a finished appearance.

BATTEN. Narrow strips of wood or metal used to cover joints either on the interior or the exterior; used for decorative effect.

BAY WINDOW. A window that forms a bay in a room, projects outward from the wall and is supported by its own foundation.

BEAM. A structural member that transversely supports a load.

BEARING WALL. A wall that supports any vertical load in addition to its own weight.

BEDROCK. The solid rock underlying soils and other superficial formations.

BLACKTOP. Asphalt paving used in streets and driveways.

BLUEPRINT. A working plan used on a construction job by tradespeople; an architectural drafting or drawing that is transferred to chemically treated paper by exposure to strong light, causing the paper to turn blue, thus reproducing the drawing in white.

BOARD AND BATTEN. A type of vertical siding composed of wide boards and narrow battens. The boards are nailed to the sheathing with a space left between them. The battens are then nailed over the spaces.

BOARD FOOT. A measure of lumber one foot square by one inch thick; 144 cubic inches = 1′ × 1′ × 1′.

BRACING. Framing lumber nailed at an angle to provide rigidity.

BRICK VENEER. See VENEER.

BRIDGING. Small wood or metal pieces placed diagonally between the *floor joists*. Bridgings disburse weight on the floor over adjacent joists, thus increasing the floor's load capacity.

BROWNSTONE. A dark-colored red sandstone, often used as facing for row houses.

BTU. British Thermal Unit. One BTU is the amount of heat required to raise one pound of water 1° in temperature.

BUILDING PAPER. Fiber-reinforced, waterproof paper treated with bitumen, a natural asphalt from coal, petroleum or some other water-resistant compound. Building paper is placed between *siding* and *wall sheathing*, around door and window frames, and in other areas to insulate the house and keep out moisture.

BUILDING STANDARDS. The specific elements of construction that the owner/developer uses throughout a building. The building standard offered an office tenant, for example, would relate to the type of partitions, doors, ceiling tile, light fixtures, carpet, draperies and like items.

BUILT-UP ROOF. A roof composed of three to five layers of asphalt felt laminated with coal tar, pitch, or asphalt and coated with gravel. Generally used on flat or low-pitched roofs.

BX. Electrical cable consisting of a flexible metal covering enclosing two or more wires.

CARPORT.   A roofed space having at least one side open to the weather. A carport is often made by extending the house roof to one side and is primarily designed to store motor vehicles. The term *carport* is usually related to small one- and two-family dwellings. In multifamily properties, a *garage* may have one or more sides open to the weather.

CASEMENT WINDOW.   A type of window having a sash with hinges on the side and opening outward.

CASING.   A frame, as of a window or door.

CESSPOOL.   Part of a waste disposal system that functions like a septic tank; a covered cistern of stone, brick or concrete block. The liquid seeps out through the walls directly into the surrounding earth.

CHIMNEY.   A stack of brick or other masonry that extends above the surface of the roof and carries the smoke to the outside. The smoke is carried inside the chimney through the *flue*.

CHIMNEY CAP.   Ornamental stone or concrete edging around the top of the chimney stack that helps protect the masonry from the elements and improves the draft in the chimney.

CHIMNEY FLASHING.   A strip of material, usually metal, placed over the junction of the chimney and the roof to make the joint watertight. Flashings are used wherever the slope of the roof is broken up by a vertical structure.

CHIMNEY POT.   A fire clay or terra cotta pipe projecting from the top of the chimney stack. The chimney pot is decorative and also increases the draft of the chimney.

CINDER FILL.   A layer of cinders placed between the ground and the basement floor or between the ground and the *foundation walls* to aid in water drainage.

CISTERN.   An artificial reservoir or tank, often underground, for the storing of rainwater collected from a roof.

CLAPBOARD.   Siding of narrow boards, thicker at one edge, used as exterior finish for frame houses.

CLEANOUT DOOR.   An exterior door located at the base of the chimney for convenient removal of the ashes that were put through the *ash dump*.

CLEAR SPAN.   The condition within a building wherein a given floor area is free of posts, support columns or *shear walls*.

COLLAR BEAM.   A horizontal beam connecting pairs of opposite roof *rafters*. It helps stiffen the roof structure.

COLLECTOR.   A device used to collect solar radiation and convert it into heat.

COMBED (STRIATED) PLYWOOD.   Common building material in modern homes, particularly for interior finish. The exposed surface is combed in parallel grooves.

COMPACTION.   Matted down or compressed extra soil that may be added to a lot to fill in the low areas or raise the level of the parcel.

CONCRETE BASEMENT FLOOR.   A floor generally constructed on concrete, reinforced with steel bars within the concrete. The basement floor, along with the *foundation walls* and the *piers,* provides the support for the structure. Concrete is used because it is moisture-proof and inexpensive.

CONDUIT.   A metal pipe in which electric wiring is installed.

CORNICE.   A horizontal projection or molding at the top of the exterior walls under the *eaves*. The cornice is decorative and aids in water drainage;

any molded projection at the top of an interior or exterior wall, in the enclosure at the roof eaves or at the rake of the roof.

COVE MOLDING.   A molding with a concave face used as trim or as finish around interior corners.

CROWN MOLDING.   Molding that is installed between the top of the wall and the ceiling.

DAMPER.   An adjustable valve at the top of a fireplace that regulates the flow of heated gases into the chimney.

DECK.   An open porch usually on the roof of a ground-floor porch or wing; a paved or hard surface area contiguous to a swimming pool.

DISPOSAL FIELD.   A drainage area, not close to the water supply, where waste from a septic tank is dispersed. The waste is drained into the ground through tile and gravel.

DOORSTOP.   A device attached to the wall or floor to prevent a door from opening too far and damaging the wall.

DORMER.   A projection built out from the slope of a roof, used to provide house windows on the upper floor and additional headroom. Common types of dormers are the gable dormer and the shed dormer.

DOUBLE CORNER STUD OR POST.   Two vertical *studs* jointed at right angles to form the corner of the frame. The double studs are heavier than regular to give greater support.

DOUBLE PLATE.   Two horizontal boards on top of and connecting the *studs*. The plate serves as a foundation for the *rafters*.

DOUBLE WINDOW HEADER.   Two boards laid on edge that form the upper portion of a door or window.

DOWNSPOUT.   A vertical pipe made of cement, metal, clay or plastic that carries rainwater from the eaves through to the ground.

DRAIN TILE.   A pipe, usually clay, placed next to the foundation footing to aid in water drainage.

DRY ROT.   Fungus-caused decay in timber, which reduces the wood to a fine powder.

DRYWALL CONSTRUCTION.   Any type of interior wall construction not using plaster as finish material. Wood paneling, plywood, plasterboard, gypsum board or other types of wallboard are usually used for drywall.

DUCT.   A tube, pipe or channel for conveying or carrying fluids, cables, wires or tempered air. Under-floor duct systems are commonly used to provide for telephone and electrical lines.

EAVE.   The overhang of a sloping roof that extends beyond the walls of the house. Also called *roof projection*.

EAVE TROUGH OR GUTTER.   A channel, usually metal pipe, placed at the ends of the *eaves* to carry rainwater to the *downspout*.

FELT JOINT COVER.   A covering of tightly woven wool treated with a bitumen tar derivative that prevents seepage at the joints of plumbing pipes.

FENESTRATION.   The arrangement and design of doors and windows in a wall.

FINISH FLOORING.   The visible interior floor surface, which is usually made of a decorative hardwood such as oak. The finish flooring may be laid in strips or in a block design such as parquet.

FIRE BRICK.   A clay brick capable of resisting high temperatures; used to line heating chambers and fireplaces.

FIRE STOP. Short boards placed horizontally between the *studs* or *joists* that decrease drafts and thus help retard fires.

FLASHING. Sheet metal or other impervious material used in roof and wall construction to protect a building from seepage of water.

FLOOR JOIST. Horizontal board or joists laid on edge, resting on the beams that provide the main support for the floor. The *subflooring* is nailed directly to the joists. Joists are also found in ceilings.

FLUE. An enclosed passage in a chimney or any duct or pipe through which smoke, hot air and gases pass upward. Flues are usually made of fire clay or terra cotta pipe.

FOOTING. A concrete support under a foundation, chimney or column that usually rests on solid ground and is wider than the structure being supported. Footings are designed to distribute the weight of the structure over the ground.

FORMICA. A trade name for a plastic material used primarily for countertops but also for wall covering, as a *veneer* for plywood panels or as a wallboard where a fire-resistant material is desired. Similar and competitive materials are produced under other trade names.

FOUNDATION DRAIN TILE. A pipe, usually clay, placed next to the foundation *footing* to aid in water runoff.

FOUNDATION WALL. The masonry or concrete walls below ground level that serve as the main support for the frame structure. Foundation walls form the side walls of the basement.

FRAME CONSTRUCTION. Construction in which the structural parts are of wood or depend on a wood frame for support.

FRIEZE BOARD. A horizontal exterior band or molding, often decorated with sculpture, resting directly below the *cornice*.

FROSTLINE. The depth of frost penetration in the soil. The frostline varies throughout the United States, and footings should be placed below this depth to prevent movement of the structure.

FURRING. Thin strips of wood used to level up a wall and provide airspace between the wall and the plaster. Furring is often used to give the wall a thicker appearance.

GABLE END OF ROOF. The triangular portion of an end wall rising from the level top wall under the inverted *V* of a sloping roof. The gable can be made of weatherboard, tile or masonry and can extend above the *rafters*. The gable aids in water drainage.

GAMBREL ROOF. A variation of the gable roof, having a steep lower slope and a flatter one above, as seen in Dutch colonial architecture.

GIRDER. A heavy wooden or steel beam supporting the *floor joists*. The girder provides the main horizontal support for the floor.

GRADIENT. The slope, or rate of increase or decrease in elevation, of a surface, road or pipe. Gradient is expressed in inches of rise or fall per horizontal linear foot of ascent or descent.

HEAD CASING. The strip of molding placed above a door or window frame.

HEARTH. The floor of the fireplace. The front hearth, which extends out into the room, may be made of brick or decorative stone. The back hearth inside the fireplace is usually made of fire brick.

HEIGHT, BUILDING. Vertical distance measured from curb or grade level, whichever is the higher, to the highest level of a flat roof or to the average height of a pitched roof, excluding penthouse or other roof appendages occupying less than 30 percent of the roof area.

HIP ROOF.   A pitched roof with sloping sides and ends.

INDIRECT LIGHTING.   The light that is reflected from the ceiling or other object external to the fixture.

INSULATION.   Pieces of plasterboard, fire-proofed sheeting, compressed wood-wool, fiberboard or other material placed between inner and outer surfaces, such as walls and ceilings, to protect the interior from heat loss. Insulation works by breaking up and dissipating air currents.

JALOUSIES.   Adjustable glass *louvers* in doors or windows used to regulate light and air or exclude rain.

JAMB.   A vertical surface lining the opening in the wall left for a door or window.

JOINT.   The point where two surfaces join or meet.

JOIST.   A heavy piece of horizontal timber to which the boards of a floor, or the lath of a ceiling, are nailed. Joists are laid edgewise to form the floor support.

KITCHENETTE.   Space, less than 60 square feet in area, used for cooking and preparation of food.

KNOCKDOWN.   Prepared construction materials that are delivered to the building site complete but unassembled and ready to be assembled and installed.

LANAI.   A popular term in the western and southern states for a balcony, veranda, porch or covered patio.

LATH.   Thin strips of wood or metal nailed to *rafters,* ceiling *joists* or wall *studs* to form a groundwork for slates, tiles, shingles or plaster.

LEACHING CESSPOOL.   In plumbing, any cesspool that is not watertight and permits waste liquids to pass into the surrounding soil by percolation.

LINTEL.   A horizontal board that supports the load over an opening such as a door or window.

LIVABILITY SPACE RATIO (LSR).   For purposes of site planning, the minimum square feet of nonvehicular outdoor area that is provided for each square foot of total floor area.

LOAD.   Weight supported by a structural part such as a load-bearing wall.

LOFT.   An atticlike space below the roof of a house or barn; any of the upper stories of a warehouse or factory.

LOUVER.   Slats or fins over an opening, pitched so as to keep out rain or snow yet still permit ventilation; a finned sunshade on a building; the diffusion grille in fluorescent light fixtures. Also spelled *louvre.*

MANSARD ROOF.   A roof with two slopes or pitches on each of the four sides, with the lower slope steeper than the upper.

MANTEL.   The decorative facing placed around a fireplace. Mantels are usually made of ornamental wood and topped by a shelf.

MASONRY.   Anything constructed of brick, stone, tile, cement, concrete or similar materials.

MASTER SWITCH.   An electrical wall switch that controls more than one fixture or outlet in a room.

MITER.   In carpentry terminology, the ends of any two pieces of board or corresponding form cut off at an angle and fitted together in an angular shape.

MOLD.   The cornice; wood molding applied to cover the junction of roof boards and outside wall. On the interior, the picture mold is where a wall joins a ceiling.

MUD ROOM.   A vestibule or small room used as the entrance from a playyard or alley. The mud room frequently contains a washer and dryer.

MULLION.   Thin vertical strips inside the *window sash* that divide the window glass into panes.

MUNTIN.   The narrow vertical strip that separates two adjacent *window sashes*.

NOSING.   The rounded outer face of a stair *tread*.

O.C. (ON CENTER).   The measurement of spacing for studs, rafters, joists and similar members in a building from the center of one member to the center of the next.

ORIENTATION.   The direction a house faces.

OVERHANG.   The part of a roof that extends beyond the exterior wall.

PARAPET.   The part of the wall of a house that rises above the roofline.

PARQUET FLOOR.   A finished floor constructed of wood blocks laid in rectangular or square patterns.

PIER.   A column, usually of steel-reinforced concrete, evenly spaced under a structure to support its weight. In a house, foundation piers are formed by drilling holes in the earth to a prescribed depth and pouring concrete into them. Foundation piers that support some structures, such as bridges, may be above the ground. Pier may also refer to the part of a wall between windows or other openings that bear the wall weight.

PILASTER.   An upright, architectural member of vertical projection from a wall, on either one or both sides, used to strengthen the wall by adding support or preventing buckling.

PLANK AND BEAM FRAMING.   A type of frame construction that uses heavier structural members spaced farther apart than other framing, with the supporting posts, roof beams and roof deck left exposed to the interior as part of the decor.

PLASTER FINISH.   The last thin layer of fine-grain plaster applied as a decorative finish over several coats of coarse plaster on the lath base. Finishing plaster usually has a high ratio of lime to sand, while coarser plasters have more sand. Plaster is pasty when applied to the wall but hardens as it dries. In new buildings plasterboard or gypsum board often is used instead of plaster because it does not have to harden.

PLATE.   A horizontal piece that forms a base for supports. The *sill* or sole plate rests on the foundation and forms the base for the *studs*. The wall plate is laid along the tip of the wall studs and forms a support base for the *rafters*.

PLATFORM (WESTERN) FRAME.   A type of framing in which *floor joists* of each story rest on the top plates of the story below (or on the foundation sill for the first story). The *bearing walls* and partitions rest on the *subfloor* of each story.

PREFABRICATION.   The manufacture and assembly of construction materials and parts into component structural units such as floor, wall, and roof panels, which are later erected or installed at the construction site.

QUARTER-ROUND.   A molding whose shape forms a quarter of a circle.

RAFTER.   One of a series of sloping beams that extend from the exterior wall to a center *ridgeboard* and provide the main support for the roof.

RENDERING.   A term used in perspective drawing meaning to finish with ink or color to bring out the effect of the design, as in an architect's rendering of a proposed project.

RETAINING WALL.   Any wall erected to hold back or support a bank of earth; any enclosing wall built to resist the lateral pressure of internal loads.

RIDGEBOARD.   A heavy horizontal board set on edge at the apex of the roof. The rafters are attached to it.

RISER.   The vertical face of the step that supports the *tread*. As you walk upstairs, the riser is the part of the step facing you.

ROOF BOARDS.   Boards nailed to the top of the *rafters*, usually touching each other, to tie the roof together and form a base for the roofing material. The boards, or roof sheathing, can also be constructed of sheets of plywood.

ROOFING FELT.   Sheets of felt or other closely woven, heavy material placed on top of the *roof boards* to insulate and waterproof the roof. Like building paper, roofing felt is treated with bitumen or some other tar derivative to increase its water resistance. Roofing felt is applied either with a bonding and sealing compound or with intense heat, which softens the tar and causes it to adhere to the roof.

ROW HOUSE.   One of a series of individual houses having architectural unity and a common wall between each unit.

SHEAR WALL.   A permanent structural wall used to provide lateral stability.

SHEATHING.   Plywood or boards nailed to the *studs* and roof *rafters* on the exterior of a house as a foundation for the finished siding and roofing.

SHINGLE.   A roof-covering or wall-covering material usually made of asphalt, wood, slate or tile applied in overlapping layers.

SHOE MOLDING.   A thin strip of wood placed at the junction of the *baseboard* and the floor boards to conceal the joint. The shoe molding improves the aesthetics of the room and helps seal out drafts.

SHORING.   The use of timbers to prevent the sliding of earth adjoining an excavation; the timbers used as bracing against a wall for temporary support of loads during construction.

SIDING.   Boards nailed horizontally to the vertical *studs,* with or without intervening *sheathing,* to form the exposed wood surface of the outside walls of the building. Siding may be made of wood, metal or mineral sheets.

SILL.   The lowest horizontal member of the house frame. It rests on the top of the foundation wall and forms a base for the *studs;* the lowest horizontal member in the frame for a window or door.

SLAB.   A flat, horizontal reinforced concrete area, usually the interior floor of a building but also an exterior or roof area.

SLEEPERS.   Strips of wood laid over rough concrete floors so a finished wood floor can be applied over them.

SOFFIT.   Usually the underside of an overhanging cornice.

SOLAR HEATING.   A system that gathers the heat from the sun's rays with one or more solar collectors. Water or air is forced through a series of pipes in the solar collector to be heated by the sun. The hot air or water is then stored in a heavily insulated tank until it is needed to heat the house.

SPLIT-LEVEL.   A house in which two or more floors are usually located directly above one another and one or more additional floors, adjacent to them, are placed at a different level.

STRINGER.   One of the sloping enclosed sides of a staircase that supports the *treads* and *risers;* a horizontal beam that connects the uprights in a frame.

STUCCO.   A cement or plaster wall covering that is installed wet and dries into a hard surface coating.

STUD.   In wall framing, a vertical member to which horizontal pieces are attached. Studs are placed between 16 inches and 24 inches apart and serve as the main support for the roof and/or the second floor.

SUBFLOORING.   Boards or plywood sheets nailed directly to the *floor joists*, serving as a base for the *finishing flooring*. Subflooring is usually made of rough boards, although some houses have concrete subflooring.

SUMP.   A pit or reservoir used for collecting and holding water (or some other liquid), which is subsequently disposed of, usually by a pump.

SUPERSTRUCTURE.   That part of the structure above the ground or above the top of the *foundation walls*.

SUSPENDED CEILING.   A ceiling system that derives its support from the overhead structural framing.

TERMITE SHIELD.   A metal sheet laid into the exterior walls of a house near ground level, usually under the *sill,* to prevent termites from entering the house. Termite shields should be affixed to all exterior wood in the house and around pipes entering the building. Shields are generally constructed with an overhanging lip to allow for water runoff.

TONGUE AND GROOVE.   A method of joining two pieces of board wherein one has a tongue cut in the edge and the other board has a groove cut to receive the corresponding tongue. The method is used to modify any material prepared for joining in this fashion, as tongue-and-groove lumber.

TREAD.   The horizontal surface of a stair step resting on the *riser*. The tread is the part on which you step.

TRIM.   Wood or metal interior finishing pieces such as door and window *casings,* moldings and hardware.

TRUSS.   A type of roof construction employing a rigid framework of beams or members, which supports the roof load and usually makes possible relatively wide spans between its supports.

VALLEY.   The internal angle formed by the junction of two sloping sides of a roof.

VAPOR BARRIER.   Material used to keep moisture from penetrating walls or floors.

VENEER.   A layer of material covering a base of another substance, such as mahogany veneer over other less valuable wood, or brick exterior finish over wood framing.

VENT.   A small opening to allow the passage of air through any space in a building, as for ventilation of an attic or the unexcavated area under a first-floor construction.

VESTIBULE.   A small entrance hall to a building or to a room.

WAINSCOTING.   Wood lining of an interior wall; the lower part of a wall when finished differently from the wall above.

WALLBOARD.   A board used as the finishing covering for an interior wall or ceiling. Wallboard can be made of plastic laminated plywood, cement sheeting, plywood, molded gypsum, plasterboard or other materials. Wallboard is applied in thin sheets over the insulation. It is often used today as a substitute for plaster walls but can also serve as a base for plaster.

WALL SHEATHING.   Sheets of plywood, gypsum board or other material nailed to the outside face of the *wall studs* to form a base for the *exterior siding*.

WALL STUD.   See STUD.

WASTE LINE.   A pipe that carries waste from a bathtub, shower, lavatory or any fixture or appliance except a toilet.

WEATHERSTRIP.   A thin strip of material, such as metal, felt or wood, used around doors and windows to keep out air, water, moisture or dust.

WESTERN FRAME.   See PLATFORM FRAME.

WET COLUMN.   A column containing plumbing lines facilitating the installation of sinks, drinking fountains and like things.

WINDOW JAMB TRIM.   A thin vertical strip of molding covering the junction of the vertical members of the window frame and the *jamb*.

WINDOW SASH.   The movable frame that holds the window glass. Sash windows move vertically and may be single, in which only the lower half of the window opens, or double, in which both the upper and lower portions are movable.

X-BRACING.   Cross bracing in a partition.

Answer Key

Chapter 1

Exercise 1.1
Real estate: 1, 3, 4, 5, 6, 9
Real property: 10
Personal property: 2, 7, 8

Likely to prevent an arm's-length transaction: 11, 13, 15

16. If an item were personal property, it could not be considered in estimating the value of real property. On the other hand, if the item were real estate, then its contribution to the value of the real property would have to be estimated.

Exercise 1.2
1. Highest and best use, change, conformity
2. Progression
3. Contribution, law of increasing and decreasing returns
4. Competition, contribution
5. Law of increasing and decreasing returns, contribution
6. Externalities

Exercise 1.3
Sales comparison approach: $78,000 − $7,000 = $71,000 (Value of house X)
Cost approach: $130,000 − (30% × $130,000) + $52,000 = Property value
$130,000 − $39,000 + $52,000 = $143,000

Income capitalization approach: $14,500 ÷ 15% = $96,667 (rounded to nearest dollar)

Exercise 1.4
1. Cost
2. Income capitalization
3. Cost
4. Sales comparison
5. Income capitalization
6. Sales comparison
7. Income capitalization
8. Sales comparison
9. Cost
10. Income capitalization

Achievement Examination 1
1. b
2. c
3. a. Sales comparison   b. Income capitalization   c. Cost
4. Real estate is the land itself and all things permanently attached to it. Real property refers to the right of ownership of the physical real estate.
5. Market value is the most probable price property should bring in a sale occurring under normal market conditions—an arm's-length transaction. Sales price is the actual selling price of a property.
6. Value property B: $80,000 − $6,000 = $74,000
7. $425,000 − (40% × $425,000) + $175,000 = Property value
$425,000 − $170,000 + $175,000 = $430,000
8. $24,000 ÷ 13% = $184,615 (rounded to nearest dollar)
9. Conformity
10. Substitution
11. Anticipation
12. Highest and best use
13. Highest and best use
14. Supply and demand
15. Contribution

Chapter 2

Exercise 2.1
1. (1) Personal inspection
   (6) Register of deeds
   (42) Plats

2. Residential only: (19) Building architects, contractors and engineers
                     (27) Local material suppliers
   All properties: (12) City hall
                     (20) County or city engineering commission

3. (12) City hall
   (20) County or city engineering commission
   (22) Area planning commissions

4. Regional and city: (22) Area planning commissions
                           (29) United States Bureau of the Census
                           (33) Government councils

   Neighborhood: (32) Local chamber of commerce
                           (33) Government councils

5. Residential: (1) Personal inspection
                           (22) Area planning commissions
                           (44) Area maps

6. Residential, commercial: (1) Personal inspection
                             (22) Area planning commissions
                             (32) Local chamber of commerce
                             (44) Area maps

   Residential only: (28) Public utility companies
   Income: (1) Personal inspection

7. (12) City hall
    (20) County or city engineering commission
    (22) Area planning commissions

8. (6) Register of deeds
    (7) Title reports

9. (7) Title reports
    (12) City hall
    (13) Assessor's office

Exercise 2.2

colonial style

1½ stories (or one story plus attic)

stone veneer

side drive

two-car detached garage with attic

well-landscaped lawn with trees and shrubs

lightpost

gable roof

small front porch

picture window

single- or double-hung, four-paned windows

side entry

asphalt roofing

general appearance very good

Achievement Examination 2 (See page 318.)

Chapter 3

Exercise 3.1

One-and-a-half-story house: there is economy in cost per cubic foot of habitable space and built-in expandability.

Two-story house: plumbing can be lined up; winter heating is utilized to the best advantage (heat rises); more house can be built on a smaller piece of property.

Split-entry house: the square footage of the house is doubled at a modest cost increase by finishing the rooms on the lower level.

If a house is oriented with the main living areas facing south, it can result in savings in heating and air-conditioning costs. Orientation also contributes to the enjoyment of a house if it takes advantage of a natural view and the maximum amount of land is allocated for private use.

Circulation areas should provide for well-regulated traffic that allows people to get directly from one room to another.

The kitchen should be centrally located, afford direct access to the dining area and the front entrance and be close to the garage or the back entrance.

The living room should be close to the front entrance, away from sleeping areas and next to the dining room.

The sleeping zone should be in a quiet section, on the cool side of the house and out of sight from the entrance door and living area.

Storage space should include a linen closet, a guest closet near the front door, a closet four feet wide by two feet deep for each person in the house, stor-

Achievement Examination 2

SALES PRICE ADJUSTMENT CHART

COMPARABLES

SALES PRICE												
FINANCING												
DATE OF SALE												
LOCATION												
SITE/VIEW												
SIZE OF LOT												
DESIGN AND APPEAL												
CONSTRUCTION												
AGE												
CONDITION												
NO. OF RMS./BEDRMS./BATHS												
SQ. FT. OF LIVING SPACE												
OTHER SPACE (BASEMENT)												
FUNCTIONAL UTILITY												
HEATING/COOLING												
GARAGE/CARPORT												
OTHER EXT. IMPROVEMENTS												
SPECIAL ENERGY EFFICIENT ITEMS												
FIREPLACE(S)												
OTHER INT. IMPROVEMENTS												
TYPICAL HOUSE VALUE												
VARIABLE FEATURE												
ADJUSTMENT VALUE OF VARIABLE												

age for games, toys and books, large spaces (garage or basement) for outdoor and sports equipment, and easy-to-reach cabinets in the kitchen.

Exercise 3.2
Solid cores are generally preferred for exterior doors because they provide better heat and sound insulation and are more resistant to warping. Hollow-core doors are about a third as heavy as the solid-core type and are commonly used for interior locations where heat and sound insulation are not as critical.

The *water supply system* brings water to the house from a well or city main and distributes hot and cold water through two sets of pipes. The *vent piping system* carries out of the house all sewer gases from drainage lines.

The main drawback to the heat pump is its initial cost. Once installed, however, the heat pump operates very economically and requires little maintenance.

1. *Safety*—The system must meet all NEC requirements.
2. *Capacity*—The system must meet the home's existing needs and have the capacity to accommodate room additions and new appliances.
3. *Convenience*—There should be enough switches, lights and outlets and they should be located so that occupants will not have to walk in the dark or use extension cords.

Balloon construction differs from the *platform* method in that the studs are continuous, extending to the ceiling of the second floor, rather than shorter lengths, extending the length of one floor at a time.

The platform method is usually preferred.

firestopping: Boards or blocks nailed between studs or joists to stop drafts and retard the spread of fire.

circuit breaker box: The distribution panel for the many electrical circuits in the house. If a circuit is overloaded, the heat generated by the additional flow of electrical power will cause the circuit breaker to open at the breaker box. By removing the overload and allowing the breaker to cool, the switch in the circuit breaker box may be turned to "on" and electrical service restored.

ridge: The top horizontal edge or peak of a roof that aligns and receives the rafters.

monolithic slab: Concrete slab forming foundation area of structure. Monolithic concrete is poured in a continuous process so there are no separations due to different setting times.

sills: The horizontal members of the foundation that are secured to the piers by the anchor bolts to prevent the house from sliding from its foundation.

Achievement Examination 3
1. monolithic concrete slab
2. balloon frame
3. wood sheathing covered with building paper, and siding (probably wood)

4. plaster over wallboard
5. could be either single or double hung
6. conventional, gable
7. boards covered with roofing felt and shingles
8. finished wood on first floor; unfinished concrete in basement

---

Chapter 4

Exercise 4.1

The property being appraised is the single-family residence located at 2130 West Franklin Street, Lakeside, Illinois. Fee simple property rights are to be appraised. The purpose of the appraisal is to estimate market value, which is the most probable price the property should bring in a sale occurring under normal market conditions. The date of valuation is the date of the report.

Exercise 4.5

1. records on previous appraisals; county clerk's office; principals involved; brokers or salespeople

2. Sale 2 should be dropped from consideration because of its age. Sale 5 should be dropped because it has three more rooms than the subject; if the only difference was its having only one bathroom, it could still be considered as comparable.

Exercise 4.6 (See chart on page 324.)

Construction: Aluminum siding
  $121,000 - $115,000 = $6,000

No. of Bedrooms: 4 (1 extra)
  $126,000 - 121,000 = $5,000

No. of Baths: extra ½ bath
  $124,000 - $121,000 = $3,000

Exercise 4.7 (See chart on page 325.)

No. All properties are similar to the subject and should be considered in this appraisal.

Exercise 4.10

Since the value range (excluding comparable 2) is close, and comparable 5 required no adjustment, it can be assumed that the subject property has a market value of $125,000.

Achievement Examination 4 (See pages 328–330.)

3. $116,300 is the indicated market value of the subject property by the sales comparison approach.

Exercise 4.2

NEIGHBORHOOD DATA FORM

BOUNDARIES: ADJACENT TO:

NORTH ____Cedar Street____   Business district and moderately priced apartments

SOUTH ____Parkside Boulevard____   Park District land

EAST ____Ellis Avenue____   Commercial area

WEST ____Lombard Avenue____   Expensive high-rise apartments

TOPOGRAPHY: __flat; park land gently rolling__   ☒ URBAN   ☐ SUBURBAN   ☐ RURAL

STAGE OF LIFE CYCLE OF NEIGHBORHOOD: ☐ GROWTH   ☒ EQUILIBRIUM   ☐ DECLINE

% BUILT UP: __99%+__ GROWTH RATE: ☐ RAPID   ☒ SLOW   ☐ STEADY

AVERAGE MARKETING TIME: __4 months__ PROPERTY VALUES: ☒ INCREASING ☐ DECREASING ☐ STABLE

SUPPLY/DEMAND: ☐ OVERSUPPLY   ☐ UNDERSUPPLY   ☒ BALANCED

CHANGE IN PRESENT LAND USE: ____None anticipated____

POPULATION: ☐ INCREASING   ☐ DECREASING   ☒ STABLE   AVERAGE FAMILY SIZE: __4.2__

AVERAGE FAMILY INCOME: __$25,000 to $35,000__   INCOME LEVEL: ☒ INCREASING   ☐ DECREASING

PREDOMINANT OCCUPATIONS: __white collar, skilled trades, some self-employed business people__

TYPICAL PROPERTIES:	% OF	AGE	PRICE RANGE	% OWNER OCCUPIED	% RENTALS
VACANT LOTS	1				
SINGLE-FAMILY RESIDENCES	98	8 yrs.	$110,000—$140,000	98	2
2–6-UNIT APARTMENTS	1	20 yrs.	$185,000—$275,000		
OVER 6-UNIT APARTMENTS					
NONRESIDENTIAL PROPERTIES					

TAX RATE: __$5 per $100 of assessed valuation__ ☐ HIGHER ☐ LOWER ☒ SAME AS COMPETING AREAS

SPECIAL ASSESSMENTS OUTSTANDING: __None__   EXPECTED: __None__

SERVICES: ☒ POLICE   ☒ FIRE   ☒ GARBAGE COLLECTION   OTHER: _____

DISTANCE AND DIRECTION FROM

BUSINESS AREA: __within 2 miles__

COMMERCIAL AREA: __within 2 miles__

PUBLIC ELEMENTARY AND HIGH SCHOOLS: __both within ¾ mile__

PRIVATE ELEMENTARY AND HIGH SCHOOLS: __elementary 1 mile; high school 2 miles__

RECREATIONAL AND CULTURAL AREAS: __within 2 miles__

CHURCHES AND SYNAGOGUES: __Presbyterian, Episcopal, Roman Catholic, Jewish Synagogue__

EXPRESSWAY INTERCHANGE: __within 2 miles, in business area__

PUBLIC TRANSPORTATION: __bus—excellent service__

TIME TO REACH BUSINESS AREA: __15 min.__   COMMERCIAL AREA: __15 min.__

EMERGENCY MEDICAL SERVICE: __15 min.__

GENERAL TRAFFIC CONDITIONS: __good__

PROXIMITY TO HAZARDS (AIRPORT, CHEMICAL STORAGE, ETC.): __none nearby__

PROXIMITY TO NUISANCES (SMOKE, NOISE, ETC.): __none nearby__

Exercise 4.3

SITE DATA FORM

ADDRESS: _2130 West Franklin Street, Lakeside, Illinois_

LEGAL DESCRIPTION: _Lot 114 in Block 2 of Gunderson Subdivision, being part of the_
Northwest ¼ of the Southeast ¼ of Section 4, Township 37 North,
Range 18, East of The Third Principal Meridian as recorded in the
Office of the Registrar of Titles of Grove County, Illinois, on April 27, 1970.

DIMENSIONS: _50′ × 200′_

SHAPE: _Rectangular_   SQUARE FEET: _10,000_

TOPOGRAPHY: _Level_   VIEW: _Parkway_

NATURAL HAZARDS: _None_

☒ INSIDE LOT   ☐ CORNER LOT   FRONTAGE: _50′_

ZONING: _Residential_   ADJACENT AREAS: _bus., park, comm., other res._

UTILITIES: ☒ ELECTRICITY   ☒ GAS   ☒ WATER   ☒ TELEPHONE
☒ SANITARY SEWER   ☒ STORM SEWER

IMPROVEMENTS: DRIVEWAY: _asphalt_   STREET: _asphalt_
SIDEWALK: _concrete_   CURB/GUTTER: _concrete_   ALLEY: _no_
STREETLIGHTS: _yes_

LANDSCAPING: _nicely done with evergreen shrubbery & fruit trees_

TOPSOIL: _good_   DRAINAGE: _good_

EASEMENTS: _easement line running across rear 10 ft. of property_

DEED RESTRICTIONS: _10 ft. to side property lines, 30 ft. to street, 50 ft. to rear property line._

SITE PLAT:

Exercise 4.4

BUILDING DATA FORM

ADDRESS: 2130 WEST FRANKLIN STREET

NO. OF UNITS 1   NO. OF STORIES 1   ORIENTATION: N S E W

TYPE: SINGLE FAMILY DESIGN: RANCH   AGE: 6 YEARS   SQUARE FEET: 1,300

	GOOD	AVERAGE	FAIR	POOR
GENERAL CONDITION OF EXTERIOR	✓			
FOUNDATION TYPE ~~CONCRETE~~ (BSMT)/CRAWL SP./SLAB	✓			
EXTERIOR WALLS: (BRICK)/BLOCK/VENEER/STUCCO/	✓			
WOOD/ALUMINUM/VINYL				
WINDOW FRAMES: METAL/(WOOD)	✓			
STORM WINDOWS ALUM. SCREENS: ALUM.	✓			
GARAGE BRICK (ATTACHED)/DETACHED	✓			
NUMBER OF CARS: 2				
☐ PORCH ☐ DECK ☐ PATIO ☐ SHED				
OTHER _____				
GENERAL CONDITION OF INTERIOR	✓			
INTERIOR WALLS: (DRY WALL)/PLASTER/WOOD	✓			
CEILINGS: DRY WALL	✓			
FLOORS: (WOOD)/CONCRETE/(TILE)/(CARPET)	✓			
ELECTRICAL WIRING AND SERVICE: 220 VOLT	✓			
HEATING PLANT: 100,000 BTU FORCED AIR AGE: 6 YRS.	✓			
(GAS)/OIL/WOOD/ELECTRIC				
CENTRAL AIR-CONDITIONING: YES AIR FILTRATION: ___	✓			
NUMBER OF FIREPLACES: _____ TYPE: _____				
OTHER _____				
BATHROOM: FLOOR VINYL TILE WALLS CER.TILE PAINT FIXTURES BUILT-IN TUB/SHOWER VANITY. TOILET	✓			
BATHROOM: FLOOR SAME WALLS SAME FIXTURES SAME AS ABOVE	✓			
BATHROOM: FLOOR SAME WALLS PAINT FIXTURES VANITY, TOILET	✓			
KITCHEN: FLOOR VINYL TILE WALLS _____ CABINETS 12 FEET, WOOD	✓			
FIXTURES DOUBLE BASIN STAINLESS STEEL SINK DISHWASHER, RANGE W/ HOOD & EXHAUST, REF.	✓			

ROOM SIZES	LIVING ROOM	DINING ROOM	KITCHEN	BEDROOM	BATH	CLOSETS	FAMILY ROOM
BASEMENT							
1ST FLOOR	16' X 18'	9' X 14'	12'X13'	12'X16' 10'X10' 9½'X12'	6'X8' 6'X8' 4'X7'	1½'X2' 2'X4' 2'X4'	10½' X 17'
2ND FLOOR							
ATTIC						2'X5' 2'X8'	

DEPRECIATION (DESCRIBE):

   PHYSICAL DETERIORATION HOUSE IS 6 YEARS OLD

   FUNCTIONAL OBSOLESCENCE NONE

   EXTERNAL OBSOLESCENCE NONE

Exercise 4.6

SALES PRICE ADJUSTMENT CHART

COMPARABLES

	A	B	C	D	E	F	G	H	I	J
SALES PRICE	$121,000	$115,000	$122,000	$124,000	$120,500	$112,000	$136,000	$111,000	$126,000	$121,000
FINANCING	75% assump.	70% assump.	75% assump.	75% assump.	70% assump.	75% assump.	70% assump.	70 or 75% assump.	70% assump.	70% assump.
DATE OF SALE	6 wks.	2 mos.	3 wks.	5 wks.	6 wks.	5 wks.	3 wks.	1 yr.	5 wks.	11 wks.
LOCATION	resid.	resid.	resid.	resid.	resid.	highway	commercial	resid.	resid.	resid.
SITE/VIEW	good	good	good	good	good	good	good	good	good	good
SIZE OF LOT	50' × 200'	50' × 200'	50' × 200'	50' × 200'	50' × 200'	50' × 200'	50' × 200'	50' × 200'	50' × 200'	50' × 200'
DESIGN AND APPEAL	good	good	good	good	good	good	good	good	good	good
CONSTRUCTION	brick	aluminum siding	brick	brick	brick	brick	brick	brick	brick	brick
AGE	8 yrs.	7 yrs.	8 yrs.	6 yrs.	6 yrs.	7 yrs.	6 yrs.	7 yrs.	6 yrs.	7 yrs.
CONDITION	good	good	good	good	good	good	good	good	good	good
NO. OF RMS./BEDRMS./BATHS	7/3/2	7/3/2	7/3/2	7/3/2½	7/3/2	7/3/2	7/3/2	7/3/2	8/4/2	7/3/2
SQ. FT. OF LIVING SPACE	1,275	1,300	1,290	1,300	1,300	1,325	1,300	1,350	1,400	1,300
OTHER SPACE (BASEMENT)	full basement	full basement	full basement	full basement	full basement	full basement	full basement	full basement	full basement	full basement
FUNCTIONAL UTILITY	adequate	adequate	adequate	adequate	adequate	adequate	adequate	adequate	adequate	adequate
HEATING/COOLING	central heat/air	central heat/air	central heat/air	central heat/air	central heat/air	central heat/air	central heat/air	central heat/air	central heat/air	central heat/air
GARAGE/CARPORT	2-car att.	2-car att.	2-car att.	2-car att.	2-car att.	2-car att.	2-car att.	2-car att.	2-car att.	2-car att.
OTHER EXT. IMPROVEMENTS	patio	patio	patio	patio	patio	patio	patio	patio	patio	patio
SPECIAL ENERGY EFFICIENT ITEMS	none	none	none	none	none	none	none	none	none	none
FIREPLACE(S)	one	one	one	one	one	one	one	one	one	one
OTHER INT. IMPROVEMENTS	none	none	none	none	none	none	none	none	none	none
TYPICAL HOUSE VALUE	$121,000	$121,000	$121,000	$121,000	$121,000	$121,000	$121,000	$121,000	$121,000	$121,000
VARIABLE FEATURE	aluminum siding	aluminum siding		extra half bath		poor location	commercial area	year-old sale	4th bedroom	
ADJUSTMENT VALUE OF VARIABLE	$6,000	$6,000		$3,000		$9,000	$15,000	$10,000	$5,000	

Exercise 4.7

COMPARABLE SALES CHART

	SUBJECT	COMPARABLE NO. 1	COMPARABLE NO. 2	COMPARABLE NO. 3	COMPARABLE NO. 4	COMPARABLE NO. 5
Address	2130 W. Franklin	2017 Parkside Blvd.	2135 HASTINGS AVE.	2209 MADISON AVE.	2320 PLEASANT BLVD.	2003 FRANKLIN ST.
Proximity to Subject		within half-mile	WITHIN HALF-MILE	WITHIN HALF-MILE	WITHIN HALF-MILE	WITHIN HALF-MILE
Sales Price		$113,000	$119,000	$117,500	$127,500	$125,000
Data Source	owner	sales agent	SALES AGENT	SALES AGENT	SALES AGENT	SALES AGENT
VALUE ADJUSTMENTS	DESCRIPTION	DESCRIPTION / +(-)$ Adjustment	DESCRIPTION / +(-)$ Adjustment	DESCRIPTION / +(-)$ Adjustment	DESCRIPTION / +(-)$ Adjustment	DESCRIPTION / +(-)$ Adjustment
Sales or Financing Concessions	n/a	none / $	NONE / $	NONE / $	NONE / $	NONE / $
Date of Sale/Time	n/a	6 wks. ago / $	1 YR. AGO / $	2 MOS. AGO / $	5 WKS. AGO / $	5 WKS. AGO / $
Location	quiet st.	heavy traf.	QUIET ST.	QUIET ST.	QUIET ST.	QUIET ST.
Site/View	50 × 200 gd.	50 × 200 gd.	50 × 200 GD.	50 × 200 GD.	50 × 200 GD.	50 × 200 GD.
Design and Appeal	ranch/good	ranch/good	RANCH/GOOD	RANCH/GOOD	RANCH/GOOD	RANCH/GOOD
Quality of Construction	good	good	GOOD	GD./ALUM.SD.	GOOD	GOOD
Age	6 yrs.	8 yrs.	7 YRS.	8 YRS.	6 YRS.	7 YRS.
Condition	good	good	GOOD	GOOD	GOOD	GOOD
Above Grade Room Count (Total / Bdrms / Baths)	7 / 3 / 2½	7 / 3 / 2	7 / 3 / 2	7 / 3 / 2	8 / 4 / 2	7 / 3 / 2½
Gross Living Area (Sq. Ft.)	1,300	1,275	1,350	1,300	1,400	1,300
Basement & Finished Rooms Below Grade	full basement	full basement	FULL BSMT.	FULL BSMT.	FULL BSMT.	FULL BSMT.
Functional Utility	adequate	adequate	ADEQUATE	ADEQUATE	ADEQUATE	ADEQUATE
Heating/Cooling	central h/a	central h/a	CENTRAL H/A	CENTRAL H/A	CENTRAL H/A	CENTRAL H/A
Garage/Carport	2-car att.	2-car att.	2-CAR ATT.	2-CAR ATT.	2-CAR ATT.	2-CAR ATT.
Other Ext. Improvements	none	none	NONE	NONE	NONE	NONE
Special Energy Efficient Items	none	none	NONE	NONE	NONE	NONE
Fireplace(s)	none	none	NONE	NONE	NONE	NONE
Other Int. Improvements	none	none	NONE	NONE	NONE	NONE
Add'l Adj.		□+ □- $	□+ □- $	□+ □- $	□+ □- $	□+ □- $
Adjusted Value		$	$	$	$	$

Exercise 4.8

COMPARABLE SALES CHART

	SUBJECT	COMPARABLE NO. 1		COMPARABLE NO. 2		COMPARABLE NO. 3		COMPARABLE NO. 4		COMPARABLE NO. 5	
Address	2130 W.Franklin	2017 Parkside Blvd.		2135 Hastings Ave.		2209 Madison Ave.		2320 Pleasant Blvd.		2003 Franklin St.	
Proximity to Subject		within half-mile		within half-mile		within half-mile		within half-mile		within half-mile	
Sales Price		$113,000		$119,000		$117,500		$127,500		$125,000	
Data Source	owner	sales agent		sales agent		sales agent		sales agent		sales agent	
VALUE ADJUSTMENTS	DESCRIPTION	DESCRIPTION	+(-)$ Adjustment	DESCRIPTION	+(-)$ Adjustment	DESCRIPTION	+(-)$ Adjustment	DESCRIPTION	+(-)$ Adjustment	DESCRIPTION	+(-)$ Adjustment
Sales or Financing Concessions	n/a	none		none		none		none		none	
Adjusted Value			$		$		$		$		$
Date of Sale/Time	n/a	6 wks. ago		1 yr. ago	+10,700 (ROUNDED)	2 mos. ago		5 wks. ago		5 wks. ago	
Adjusted Value			$		$		$		$		$
Location	quiet st.	heavy traf.	+9,000	quiet st.		quiet st.		quiet st.		quiet st.	
Site/View	50×200 gd.	50×200 gd.		50×200 gd.		50×200 gd.		50×200 gd.		50×200 gd.	
Design and Appeal	ranch/good	ranch/good		ranch/good		ranch/good		ranch/good		ranch/good	
Quality of Construction	good	good		good		gd/alum sd.	+6,000	good		good	
Age	6 yrs.	8 yrs.		7 yrs.		8 yrs.		6 yrs.		7 yrs.	
Condition	good	good		good		good		good		good	
Above Grade Room Count	Total 7 / Bdrms 3 / Baths 2½	Total 7 / Bdrms 3 / (Baths) 2	+3,000	Total 7 / Bdrms 3 / (Baths) 2	+3,000	Total 7 / Bdrms 3 / (Baths) 2	+3,000	Total 8 / (Bdrms) 4 / (Baths) 2	-5,000 +3,000	Total 7 / Bdrms 3 / Baths 2½	
Gross Living Area	1,300 Sq. Ft.	1,275 Sq. Ft.		1,350 Sq. Ft.		1,300 Sq. Ft.		1,400 Sq. Ft.		1,300 Sq. Ft.	
Basement & Finished Rooms Below Grade	full basement	full basement		full basement		full basement		full basement		full basement	
Functional Utility	adequate	adequate		adequate		adequate		adequate		adequate	
Heating/Cooling	central h/a	central h/a		central h/a		central h/a		central h/a		central h/a	
Garage/Carport	2-car att.	2-car att.		2-car att.		2-car att.		2-car att.		2-car att.	
Other Ext. Improvements	none	none		none		none		none		none	
Special Energy Efficient Items	none	none		none		none		none		none	
Fireplace(s)	none	none		none		none		none		none	
Other Int. Improvements	none	none		none		none		none		none	
Add'l Adj.		□+ □-	$	□+ □-	$	□+ □-	$	□+ □-	$	□+ □-	$
Adjusted Value			$		$		$		$		$

Exercise 4.9

COMPARABLE SALES CHART

	SUBJECT	COMPARABLE NO. 1		COMPARABLE NO. 2		COMPARABLE NO. 3		COMPARABLE NO. 4		COMPARABLE NO. 5	
Address	2130 W. Franklin	2017 Parkside Blvd.		2135 Hastings Ave.		2209 Madison Ave.		2320 Pleasant Blvd.		2003 Franklin St.	
Proximity to Subject		within half-mile		within half-mile		within half-mile		within half-mile		within half-mile	
Sales Price		$113,000		$119,000		$117,500		$127,500		$125,000	
Data Source	owner	sales agent		sales agent		sales agent		sales agent		sales agent	
VALUE ADJUSTMENTS	DESCRIPTION	DESCRIPTION	+(-)$ Adjustment	DESCRIPTION	+(-)$ Adjustment	DESCRIPTION	+(-)$ Adjustment	DESCRIPTION	+(-)$ Adjustment	DESCRIPTION	+(-)$ Adjustment
Sales or Financing Concessions	n/a	none	$	none	$	none	$	none	$	none	$
Date of Sale/Time	n/a	6 wks. ago	$	1 yr. ago	+10,700 (ROUNDED) $	2 mos. ago	$	5 wks. ago	$	5 wks. ago	$
Location	quiet st.	heavy traf.	+9,000	quiet st.		quiet st.		quiet st.		quiet st.	
Site/View	50 × 200 gd.	50 × 200 gd.		50 × 200 gd.		50 × 200 gd.		50 × 200 gd.		50 × 200 gd.	
Design and Appeal	ranch/good	ranch/good		ranch/good		ranch/good		ranch/good		ranch/good	
Quality of Construction	good	good		good		gd./alum sd.	+6,000	good		good	
Age	6 yrs.	8 yrs.		7 yrs.		8 yrs.		6 yrs.		7 yrs.	
Condition	good	good		good		good		good		good	
Above Grade Room Count	Total 7 / Bdrms 3 / Baths 2½	Total 7 / Bdrms 3 / (Baths) 2	+3,000	Total 7 / Bdrms 3 / (Baths) 2	+3,000	Total 7 / Bdrms 3 / (Baths) 2	+3,000	Total 8 / (Bdrms) 4 / (Baths) 2	-5,000 / +3,000	Total 7 / Bdrms 3 / Baths 2½	
Gross Living Area	1,300 Sq. Ft.	1,275 Sq. Ft.		1,350 Sq. Ft.		1,300 Sq. Ft.		1,400 Sq. Ft.		1,300 Sq. Ft.	
Basement & Finished Rooms Below Grade	full basement	full basement		full basement		full basement		full basement		full basement	
Functional Utility	adequate	adequate		adequate		adequate		adequate		adequate	
Heating/Cooling	central h/a	central h/a		central h/a		central h/a		central h/a		central h/a	
Garage/Carport	2-car att.	2-car att.		2-car att.		2-car att.		2-car att.		2-car att.	
Other Ext. Improvements	none	none		none		none		none		none	
Special Energy Efficient Items	none	none		none		none		none		none	
Fireplace(s)	none	none		none		none		none		none	
Other Int. Improvements	none	none		none		none		none		none	
Add'l Adj.		☒+ □- $ 12,000		☒+ □- $ 13,700		☒+ □- $ 9,000		□+ ☒- $ 2,000		□+ □- $ -0-	
Adjusted Value	$	$ 125,000		$ 132,700		$ 126,500		$ 125,500		$ 125,000	

Achievement Examination 4

SALES PRICE ADJUSTMENT CHART

COMPARABLES

	1	2	3	4	5	6	7
SALES PRICE	$119,500	$123,000	$116,600	$122,500	$112,800	$116,300	$123,000
FINANCING	80% S/L	75% S/L	70% S/L	75% S/L	75% S/L	70% S/L	80% S/L
DATE OF SALE	current	current	1 yrs. ago	current	current	current	current
LOCATION	quiet resid.	quiet resid.	quiet resid.	quiet resid.	quiet resid.	quiet resid.	quiet resid.
SITE/VIEW	good	good	good	good	good	good	good
SIZE OF LOT	65' × 145'	65' × 145'	65' × 145'	65' × 145'	65' × 145'	65' × 145'	65' × 145'
DESIGN AND APPEAL	good	good	good	good	good	good	good
CONSTRUCTION	brick	brick	brick	brick	brick	brick	brick
AGE	7 yrs.	6 yrs.	6 yrs.	7½ yrs.	7 yrs.	7 yrs.	7 yrs.
CONDITION	good	good	good	fair to good	good	good	good
NO. OF RMS./BEDRMS./BATHS	7/3/2	7/3/2	7/3/2	7/3/2	7/3/2	7/3/2	7/3/2
SQ. FT. OF LIVING SPACE	1,600	1,600	1,600	1,575	1,575	1,575	1,590
OTHER SPACE (BASEMENT)	finished half-bsmt.	finished half-bsmt.	finished half-bsmt.	finished half-bsmt.	finished half-bsmt.	finished half-bsmt.	finished half-bsmt.
FUNCTIONAL UTILITY	adequate	adequate	adequate	adequate	adequate	adequate	adequate
HEATING/COOLING	central heat	central heat/air	central heat/air	central heat/air	central heat	central heat/air	central heat/air
GARAGE/CARPORT	2-car att.	2-car att.	2-car att.	2-car att.	none	none	2-car att.
OTHER EXT. IMPROVEMENTS	porch	porch	porch	porch	porch	porch	porch
SPECIAL ENERGY EFFICIENT ITEMS	none	none	none	none	none	none	none
FIREPLACE(S)	one/brick	one/brick	one/brick	one/brick	one/brick	one/brick	one/brick
OTHER INT. IMPROVEMENTS	none	none	none	none	none	none	none
TYPICAL HOUSE VALUE	$123,000	$123,000	$123,000	$123,000	$123,000	$123,000	$123,000
VARIABLE FEATURE	NO CENTRAL AIR	—	YR.-OLD SALE	CONDITION	NO CENTRAL AIR/NO GARAGE	NO GARAGE	—
ADJUSTMENT VALUE OF VARIABLE	$3,500	—	$6,400	$500	$10,200	$6,700	—

Achievement Examination 4 (cont.)

	SUBJECT	COMPARABLE NO. 1	+(-)$ Adjustment	COMPARABLE NO. 2	+(-)$ Adjustment	COMPARABLE NO. 3	+(-)$ Adjustment	COMPARABLE NO. 4	+(-)$ Adjustment	COMPARABLE NO. 5	+(-)$ Adjustment
Address											
Proximity to Subject											
Sales Price		$119,500		$123,000		$116,600		$122,500		$112,800	
Data Source											
VALUE ADJUSTMENTS	DESCRIPTION	DESCRIPTION		DESCRIPTION		DESCRIPTION		DESCRIPTION		DESCRIPTION	
Sales or Financing Concessions	n/a	NONE	$	NONE	$	NONE	$	NONE	$	NONE	$
Adjusted Value											
Date of Sale/Time		2 MOS. AGO		3 WKS. AGO		1 YR. AGO	+6,400	2 WKS. AGO		1 MO. AGO	
Adjusted Value						$123,000					
Location	quiet res.	QUIET RES.		QUIET RES.		QUIET RES.		QUIET RES.		QUIET RES.	
Site/View	good	65×145 GD.		65×145 GD.		65×145 GD.		65×145 GD.		65×145 GD.	
Design and Appeal	Split lvl/gd	SPLIT LVL/GD.		SPLIT LVL/GD.		SPLIT LVL/GD.		SPLIT LVL/GD.		SPLIT LVL/GD.	
Quality of Construction	gd./brick	GD./BRICK		GD./BRICK		GD./BRICK		GD./BRICK		GD./BRICK	
Age	7 yrs.	7 YRS.		6½ YRS.		6 YRS.		7½ YRS.		7 YRS.	
Condition	good	GOOD		GOOD		GOOD		FAIR TO GOOD	+500	GOOD	
Above Grade Room Count (Total / Bdrms / Baths)	7 / 3 / 2	7 / 3 / 2		7 / 3 / 2		7 / 3 / 2		7 / 3 / 2		7 / 3 / 2	
Gross Living Area	1,600 Sq. Ft.	1,600 Sq. Ft.		1,600 Sq. Ft.		1,600 Sq. Ft.		1,575 Sq. Ft.		1,575 Sq. Ft.	
Basement & Finished Rooms Below Grade	finished half-bsmt.	FINISHED HALF-BSMT.		FINISHED HALF-BSMT.		FINISHED HALF-BSMT.		FINISHED HALF-BSMT.		FINISHED HALF-BSMT.	
Functional Utility	adequate	ADEQUATE		ADEQUATE		ADEQUATE		ADEQUATE		ADEQUATE	
Heating/Cooling	central h/a	CENTRAL HEAT	+3,500	CENTRAL H/A		CENTRAL H/A		CENTRAL H/A		CENTRAL HEAT	+3,500
Garage/Carport	none	2-CAR ATT.	-6,700	2-CAR ATT.	-6,700	2-CAR ATT.	-6,700	2-CAR ATT.	-6,700	NONE	
Other Ext. Improvements	porch	PORCH		PORCH		PORCH		PORCH		PORCH	
Special Energy Efficient Items	none	NONE		NONE		NONE		NONE		NONE	
Fireplace(s)	one/brick	ONE/BRICK		ONE/BRICK		ONE/BRICK		ONE/BRICK		ONE/BRICK	
Other Int. Improvements	none	NONE		NONE		NONE		NONE		NONE	
Add'l Adj.		☐+ ☒- $ 3,200		☐+ ☒- $ 6,700		☐+ ☒- $ 6,700		☐+ ☒- $ 6,200		☒+ ☐- $ 3,500	
Adjusted Value		$ 116,300		$ 116,300		$ 116,300		$ 116,300		$ 116,300	

Achievement Examination 4 (cont.)

COMPARABLE SALES CHART

	SUBJECT	COMPARABLE NO. 6		COMPARABLE NO. 7					
		DESCRIPTION	+(-)$ Adjustment	DESCRIPTION	+(-)$ Adjustment	DESCRIPTION	+(-)$ Adjustment	DESCRIPTION	+(-)$ Adjustment
Address									
Proximity to Subject									
Sales Price		$ 116,300		$ 123,000		$		$	
Data Source									
VALUE ADJUSTMENTS	DESCRIPTION	DESCRIPTION	+(-)$ Adjustment	DESCRIPTION	+(-)$ Adjustment	DESCRIPTION	+(-)$ Adjustment	DESCRIPTION	+(-)$ Adjustment
Sales or Financing Concessions		NONE		NONE					
Adjusted Value		$		$		$		$	
Date of Sale/Time		5 WKS. AGO		3 WKS. AGO					
Adjusted Value		$		$		$		$	
Location		QUIET RES.		QUIET RES.					
Site/View		65 x 145 GD.		65 x 145 GD.					
Design and Appeal		SPLIT LVL/GD.		SPLIT LVL/GD.					
Quality of Construction		GD./BRICK		GD./BRICK					
Age		7 YRS.		7 YRS.					
Condition		GOOD		GOOD					
Above Grade Room Count (Total / Bdrms / Baths)		7 / 3 / 2		7 / 3 / 2					
Gross Living Area	Sq. Ft.	1,575 Sq. Ft.		1,590 Sq. Ft.		Sq. Ft.		Sq. Ft.	
Basement & Finished Rooms Below Grade		FINISHED HALF-BSMT.		FINISHED HALF-BSMT.					
Functional Utility		ADEQUATE		ADEQUATE					
Heating/Cooling		CENTRAL H/A		CENTRAL H/A					
Garage/Carport		NONE		2-CAR ATT.	- 6,700				
Other Ext. Improvements		PORCH		PORCH					
Special Energy Efficient Items		NONE		NONE					
Fireplace(s)		ONE/BRICK		ONE/BRICK					
Other Int. Improvements		NONE		NONE					
Add'l Adj.		□+ □- $		□+ □- $	6,700	□+ □- $		□+ □- $	
Adjusted Value		$ 116,300		$ 116,300		$		$	

Chapter 5

Exercise 5.1
1. to value vacant sites
2. to apply the cost approach to value
3. to levy special assessments for public improvements
4. for taxation purposes
5. to estimate building depreciation
6. to apply the building residual technique
7. may be required in condemnation appraising
8. to determine if the site is realizing its highest and best use

Exercise 5.2

	SALES PRICE	TIME	LOCATION	PHYSICAL FEATURES	NET ADJ. + OR −	ADJUSTED PRICE
Dollar basis	$20,000	+$2,400	+$2,000	−$3,000	+$1,400	$21,400
Percentage basis	$20,000	+12%	+10%	−15%	+7%	$21,400

Exercise 5.3
Land value is $147,000 ÷ 4, or $36,750.

Exercise 5.4
Total projected sales:

48 lots at $27,000 per lot	$1,296,000	
16 lots at $32,000 per lot	512,000	
8 lots at $36,000 per lot	288,000	$2,096,000
72		

Total projected development costs	934,000
Estimated value of raw land	$1,162,000
Raw land value per lot: $1,162,000 ÷ 72	$ 16,139

Present worth of lot sales:

First year: 48 lots at $16,139 per lot = $774,672
$774,672 discounted to present
worth at 12 percent for one year
(.893) $ 691,782

Second year: 16 lots at $16,139 per lot = $258,224
$258,224 discounted to present worth
at 12 percent for two years (.797)   205,805

Third year: 8 lots at $16,139 per lot = $129,112
$129,112 discounted to present worth
at 12 percent for three years (.712)   91,928

Amount subdivider should pay for raw land $ 989,515

Achievement Examination 5

1. The earth's surface, and everything under it or on it, is considered *land*. When the land is improved by the addition of utilities (water, gas, electricity) or other services (such as sewers), it becomes a *site* and may be considered suitable for building purposes.

2. a. In applying the cost approach, site value must be distinguished from the cost of improvements, as indicated by the following formula:

$$\frac{\text{Cost of}}{\text{Improvements New}} - \frac{\text{Depreciation on}}{\text{Improvements}} + \text{Site Value} = \frac{\text{Estimated}}{\text{Property Value}}$$

   b. Assessments for public improvements, such as streets, water lines and sewers, often are based on their estimated effect on site values.

3. sales comparison method
   allocation or abstraction method
   subdivision development method
   land residual method
   ground rent capitalization

   The sales comparison approach is preferred whenever sales of similar vacant sites are available. The underlying presumption is that recent sales of comparable sites competitive with the subject site are the most reliable guide to the probable current market behavior and reactions of informed buyers.

Chapter 6

Exercise 6.1
The Bottom Photograph

It is an old house that cannot be economically produced today.

Exercise 6.2
$$\frac{537.8}{158.2} \times \$39,000 = \$132,580$$

Exercise 6.3
Area of comparable building: $45' \times 50' = 2,250$ sq. ft.
$\$184,500 \div 2,250 = \$82$ (cost per square foot)

Area of building under appraisal:

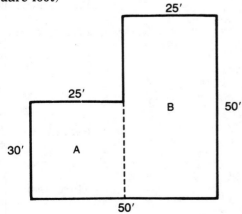

A = 30′ × 25′ =   750 sq. ft.
B = 25′ × 50′ = 1,250 sq. ft.
      Total area = 2,000 sq. ft.

Cost estimate: 2,000 sq. ft. × $82 = $164,000

Exercise 6.4
Unit-in-place costs:
  Foundation:
    Perimeter, 750 ft. @ $37.30 $ 27,975

  Floor
    31,250 sq. ft. @ $3.10   96,875

  Roof
    31,250 sq. ft. @ $3.60 ($2.40 + $.65 + $.55)   112,500

Interior construction
  Painting and partitions   4,500

Front exterior wall
  125′ × 15′ equals 1,875 sq. ft. minus
  144 sq. ft. for windows minus
  120 sq. ft. for door equals 1,611 sq. ft. @ $9.50   = $15,305
Windows 144 sq. ft. @ $15.30   =   2,203
Door   =   1,300   18,808

Rear exterior wall
  1,875 sq. ft. – 120 sq. ft. = 1,755 sq. ft. @ $9.50 = $16,673
Door   =   1,300   17,973

Side exterior walls
  500′ × 15′ equals 7,500 sq. ft. minus 20% for
    windows equals 6,000 sq. ft. @ $7.10   = $42,600
Windows 1,500 sq. ft. @ $14.20   = 21,300   63,900

Steel framing
  Area supported by frame,
    100′ × 225′ = 22,500 sq. ft. @ $4.50   101,250

Electric
  31,250 sq. ft. @ $3.25   101,563

Heating
  31,250 sq. ft. @ $2.75   85,938

Plumbing
  31,250 sq. ft. @ $1.60 $ 50,000

        Total Reproduction Cost $681,282
$681,282 ÷ 31,250 sq. ft. = about $21.80 per sq. ft.

Exercise 6.5
Economic age-life method:

$$\frac{100\%}{25} = 4\% \text{ depreciation rate}   4\% \times \$450,000 = \$18,000$$

$18,000 × 7 = $126,000 total accrued depreciation.

Exercise 6.6
1. External obsolescence—incurable
2. Physical deterioration—long-lived incurable
3. Physical deterioration—short-lived incurable
4. External obsolescence—incurable
5. Physical deterioration—curable
6. Physical deterioration—short-lived incurable
7. Functional obsolescence—incurable
8. Functional obsolescence—incurable
9. Functional obsolescence—incurable
10. Functional obsolescence—curable

Exercise 6.7
$1,100 − $980 = $120 loss in rent

$120 × 125 monthly rent multiplier = $15,000 loss in property value

Exercise 6.8
$156,000 − $142,000 = $14,000 loss in property value

Exercise 6.9

	Reproduction Cost	Observed Depreciation	Amount of Depreciation
heating system	$12,800	60%	$ 7,680
plumbing	15,200	30	4,560
electric and power	23,000	40	9,200
floors	18,200	45	8,190
roof	16,500	55	9,075
Total	$85,700		$38,705

Reproduction cost: 125′ × 160′ = 20,000 sq. ft.

20,000 × $55 = $1,100,000

Depreciation itemized above   −85,700

Balance of building depreciation $1,014,300 × .20   202,860

Total depreciation $241,565

Applying the formula for the cost approach:

$1,100,000 − $241,565 + $180,000 = $1,038,435 property value

Achievement Examination 6
1. Total factory area: 100′ × 150′ = 15,000 sq. ft.
2. Total office area: 50′ × 50′ = 2,500 sq. ft.
3. Total building area: 15,000 sq. ft. + 2,500 sq. ft. = 17,500 sq. ft.
4. Building perimeter:
   100′ + 150′ + 50′ + 50′ + 50′ + 50′ + 200′ = 650 linear ft.
5. Total parking area: 90′ × 200′ = 18,000 sq. ft. = 2,000 sq. yd.
6. Area covered by common brick:
   100′ + 150′ + 50′ + 150′ = 450′ × 14′   = 6,300 sq. ft.
   Plus area above office roof 50′ × 4′   =   200
   Plus area along office walls
                  50′ + 50′ = 100′ × 10′ = 1,000   7,500 sq. ft.
   Less—   Door area   12′ × 12′ =   144 sq. ft.
                           5(3′ × 7′) =   105
                 Window area 10(6′ × 12′) =   720   −969
               Total area covered by common brick   6,531 sq. ft.

7. Area covered by face brick:
   50' × 10'   =   500 sq. ft.
   Less—   Door area 3' × 7' =   21 sq. ft.
                                            Window area 6' × 12' = 72   −93
                        Total area covered by face brick   407 sq. ft.

8. Interior wall area for office:
   Private office 32' × 2 sides = 64' × 8'   = 512 sq. ft.
   Private office 34' × 2 sides = 68' × 8'   = 544
   Storage room 24' × 2 sides = 48' × 8'   = 384
   Washrooms 46' × 2 sides = 92' × 8'   = 736   2,176 sq. ft.
   Less door area 6(3' × 7') × 2 sides   −252
                        Total interior wall area for office   1,924 sq. ft.

9. Perimeter of office:
   50' + 50' + 50' + 50' = 200' × 8'   1,600 sq. ft.
   Less—   Door area 3(3' × 7') = 63 sq. ft.
                                Window area 6' × 12' = 72   −135
                        Total perimeter of office   1,465 sq. ft

10. 50' × 14'   = 700 sq. ft.
    Less one door 3' × 7'   −21
                                         Total   679 sq. ft.

11. Steel frame: 75' × 125' = 9,375 sq. ft.

12. Total land area: 210' × 230' = 48,300 sq. ft.

13. Land value:
    Of the four sales listed, the price of only the smallest parcel, C, appears
    to be out of line. The remaining sales are priced from $2.20 to $2.25
    per square foot, a rather narrow range.

    Because no additional information is given, and parcel D is closest to
    the subject lot in size, $2.25 per square foot seems appropriate in esti-
    mating the land value.

    Land value = 48,300 sq. ft. × $2.25 = $108,675

14. Foundation: 650 linear feet, 12" concrete @ $30.70 = $19,955

15. Exterior walls:
    Common brick, 12" block 6,531 sq. ft. @ $10.20 $66,616
    Jumbo face brick veneer 407 sq. ft. @ $3.80   1,547
                        Total for exterior walls $68,163

16. Roof construction:
    sheathing $ .65
    1⅞" fiberglass insulation   1.10
    4-ply tar and gravel covering   2.40
       Total   4.15
    17,500 sq. ft. of building area @ $4.15 = $72,625

17. Framing: 9,375 sq. ft. @ $4.50 = $42,188

18. Floor construction:
    17,500 sq. ft. 6" reinforced concrete @ $3.10 = $54,250

19. Windows: 11(6' × 12') = 792 sq. ft. @ $20.10 = $15,919

20. Exterior doors:
    6(3' × 7') metal @ $355   = $2,130
    12' × 12' rolling steel @ $1,425   =   1,425
                        Total for exterior doors $3,555

21. Interior construction:
    Wall area for office (drywall on wood studs),
    | 1,924 sq. ft. @ $3.15 | = | $6,061 |

    Concrete block dividing wall 679 sq. ft. @ $4.40 = 2,988

    Perimeter of office,
    | 1,465 sq. ft. @ $.25 (painting) | = | 366 |
    | | Total for walls | $9,415 |

    Doors: 7 (3′ × 7′) @ $275 = $1,925

    Floor covering: 2,500 sq. ft. vinyl tile in office @ $1.90 = $4.750

    Ceiling (office): 2,500 sq. ft. mineral fiber acoustic tile @ $1.65 = $4,125

22. Electric: 17,500 sq. ft. @ $3.10 = $54,250

23. Plumbing: 17,500 sq. ft. @ $2.75 = $48,125

24. Heating and air-conditioning: 17,500 sq. ft. @ $5.75 = $100,625

25. Miscellaneous:
    Parking area: 2,000 sq. yd. @ $7.20 = $14,400

26. Reproduction Costs:
    Exterior construction

Foundation	$19,955
Floor construction	54,250
Exterior walls	68,163
Framing	42,188
Roof construction	72,625
Windows	15,919
Exterior doors	3,555

    Interior construction

Walls	9,415
Floor covering	4,750
Ceiling	4,125
Interior doors	1,925
Electrical	54,250
Plumbing	48,125
Heating and air-conditioning	100,625

    Miscellaneous

Parking	14,400
Total reproduction cost	$514,270

27. Depreciation
    Observed depreciation, deterioration—short-lived incurable

brickwork $68,163 × 40%	$ 27,265
roof (asphalt and gravel) $42,000 × 60%	25,200
exterior doors $3,555 × 75%	2,666
floor (vinyl tile) $4,750 × 55%	2,613
acoustic tile ceiling $4,125 × 45%	1,856
electrical $54,250 × 35%	18,988
plumbing $48,125 × 30%	14,438
heating and air-conditioning $100,625 × 30%	30,188
asphalt paving $14,400 × 40%	5,760
Deterioration—short-lived incurable	$128,974

Total reproduction cost	$514,270	
Full cost of short-lived incurable items	−339,993	
Balance of building	$174,277	
Deterioration—long-lived incurable	× .25	43,569
Total physical deterioration		$172,543

Incurable functional obsolescence

Net value after physical deterioration: $514,270 − 172,543 = $341,727

Incurable functional obsolescence: $341,727 × 5% = $17,086

28. Cost valuation

Reproduction cost		$514,270
Depreciation:		
Deterioration—curable	-0-	
—short-lived incurable	$128,974	
—long-lived incurable	43,569	
Functional obsolescence—curable	-0-	
—incurable	17,086	
External obsolescence	-0-	
Total accrued depreciation		−189,629
Building value estimate		324,641
Land value estimate		108,675
Total property value indicated by cost approach		$433,316

Chapter 7

Exercise 7.1
Scheduled rent:
$900 per room per year or $900 × 5 rooms = $4,500 per year per unit
$4,500 per year per unit × 6 units = $27,000 per year

Market rent:

Because property 2 is an apartment building containing apartments with three bedrooms, it has been dropped as a comparable sale.

Property 1: $1,260 × 5 rooms = $6,300 per year per unit
$6,300 per year per unit × 6 units = $37,800 per year

Property 3: $1,176 × 5 rooms = $5,880 per year per unit
$5,880 per year per unit × 6 units = $35,280 per year

If the comparable properties reflect typical rents in the area, then rental income ranges from $35,280 per year to $37,800 per year, or from $1,176 per room per year to $1,260 per room per year. The subject property should be expected to rent for about $1,220 per room per year, or $36,600 annually.

Exercise 7.2
Apartment rental income	$32,000
Income from washers and dryers	900
Rent on parking space	1,000
Potential gross income	$33,900

Exercise 7.3

Sale No.	Adjustment	GIM
1	+	8.9
2	−	10.9
3	−	17.0
4	+	10.7
5	−	5.3

Sales 3 and 5 appear out of line. The range for the subject, then, is between 8.9 and 10.9, and weighted toward the high side by the indicated adjustments.

Our estimate:
GIM = 10.8
Value of subject property = $18,000 × 10.8 = $194,400

Exercise 7.4

Apartment rental income	$32,000
Income from washers and dryers	900
Rent on parking space	1,000
Potential gross income	$33,900

Six units provide 312 possible weeks of rent
(6 × 52 = 312).
Six weeks of vacancy means a 2% vacancy loss
(6 ÷ 312 = .019).

Vacancy and collection losses	
(2% + 3% = 5%) × $33,900	1,695
Effective gross income	$32,205

Exercise 7.5

Potential gross income		$210,000
Allowance for vacancy and collection losses		9,900
Effective gross income		$200,100
Variable expenses:		
Salaries—janitor	$9,200	
Employee benefits	600	
Management	6,000	
Gas (+25%)	15,500	
Water	3,800	
Electricity	8,700	
Janitorial supplies	700	
Redecorating	2,000	
Legal and accounting fees	2,400	
Fixed expenses:		
Taxes (+20%)	7,200	
Reserves for replacement	2,500	
Total operating expenses		58,600
Net operating income		$141,500

Exercise 7.6

Property	Capitalization rate (rounded)
A	10.9
B	11.7
C	11.8
D	11.4
E	21.3

The capitalization rate of property E appears out of line with the rest of the comparables and should be discarded.

Based on the four remaining comparables, the value of the subject property is in a range from about $144,100 ($17,000 ÷ .118) to about $156,000 ($17,000 ÷ .109).

Exercise 7.7

Sales price	$435,000
Site value	−125,000
Building value	$310,000
Recapture rate = 100% ÷ 25 years =	.04
NOI available for building recapture	$12,400
Total NOI	$57,000
NOI for building recapture	−12,400
NOI available for site	$44,600

$$\text{Discount rate} = \frac{\$44,600}{\$435,000} = .1025 = 10\tfrac{1}{4}\%$$

Exercise 7.8

First mortgage (65% × 10%)	=	6.5%
Second mortgage (20% × 13%)	=	2.6
Equity (15% × 14%)	=	2.1
Total discount rate		11.2%
Recapture rate = 100% ÷ 25 years	=	4.0%
Total capitalization rate		15.2%

Exercise 7.9

Estimated land value		$100,000
Net operating income	$50,000	
Discount on land value ($100,000 × 10½%)	−10,500	
Residual income to building	39,500	
Cap rate for building		
Discount rate	10.5%	
Recapture rate (100% ÷ 40)	2.5	
Building value (rounded) $39,500 ÷ .13	13.0%	303,800
Total property value		$403,800

Exercise 7.10

Estimated building value			$300,000
Net operating income		$53,000	
Cap rate for building			
Discount rate:	60% × 10¼% =	6.15%	
	40% × 12% =	4.8	
		10.95%	
Recapture rate (100% ÷ 50)		2.0	
Total		12.95%	
Discount and recapture on building			
value ($300,000 × .1295)		38,850	
Residual income to land		$14,150	
Land value (rounded) $14,100 ÷ .1095			$129,200
Total property value			$429,200

Exercise 7.11

Average cap rate = .1257

Subject: $\dfrac{I}{R} = V$ $\dfrac{\$16,000}{.1257} = \$127,300$ (rounded)

Achievement Examination 7

1. c
2. a
3. b
4. a
5. b
6. d
7. b, f, h, m, n, q, v
8. Discount rate
   Recapture rate
9. Discount rate:

65% × 11% =	7.15%
35% × 12% =	4.2 %
Total	11.35%

Recapture rate: 100% ÷ 25 yrs. = 4%

a. Building residual technique:

Estimated land value		$50,000
Net operating income	$40,000	
Discount on land value ($50,000 × .1135)		−5,675
Residual income to building		$34,325
Cap rate for building		
Discount rate	11.35%	
Recapture rate	4.00	
	15.35%	
Building value (rounded) ($34,325 ÷ .1535)		223,600
Total property value		$273,600

b. Land residual technique:

Estimated building value		$223,600
Net operating income	$40,000	
Cap rate for building		
Discount rate	11.35%	
Recapture rate	4.00	
	15.35%	
Discount and recapture on building value ($223,600 × .1535)		−34,323
Residual income to land		$5,677
Land value (rounded) $5,677 ÷ .1135		50,000
Total property value		$273,600

10. a. Reconstruction of operating statement:

Potential gross income		
(4 stores × $10,200 per yr.)		$ 40,800
Allowance for vacancy and collection		
losses (4%)		−1,632
Effective gross income		$39,168
Variable expenses:		
Repairs and maintenance		
(12% of effective gross income)	$4,700	
Legal and accounting fees	550	
Miscellaneous expense	816	
Fixed expenses:		
Insurance ($3,000 ÷ 3 yrs.)	1,000	
Real estate taxes	4,000	
Reserves for replacement:		
Roof ($2,000 ÷ 20 yrs.)	100	
Furnaces ($950 × 4 ÷ 10 yrs.)	380	
Total operating expenses		11,546
Net operating income		$ 27,622

b. Capitalization rate estimate:

Discount rate		
First mortgage (75% × 11%)	8.25%	
Equity (25% × 13%)	3.25	
Total discount rate		11.5%
Recapture rate (100% ÷ 40 yrs. remaining		
economic life)		2.5
Total capitalization rate		14.0%

c. Estimate of total property value:

Building residual technique		
Estimated land value		$55,000
Net operating income	$27,622	
Discount on land value ($55,000 × 11.5%)	6,325	
Residual income to building	$21,297	
Cap rate for building		
Discount rate	11.5%	
Recapture rate	2.5	
	14.0%	
Building value rounded ($21,297 ÷ .14)		152,121
Total property value		$207,121

Achievement Examination 8

Property Description & Analysis **UNIFORM RESIDENTIAL APPRAISAL REPORT** File No. _____

SUBJECT

Property Address 4807 CATALPA ROAD		Census Tract	LENDER DISCRETIONARY USE
City WOODVIEW County COOK State IL Zip Code 60000			Sale Price $ _____
Legal Description ATTACHED			Date _____
Owner/Occupant		Map Reference	Mortgage Amount $ _____
Sale Price $ _____ Date of Sale _____		PROPERTY RIGHTS APPRAISED	Mortgage Type _____
Loan charges/concessions to be paid by seller $ _____		[X] Fee Simple	Discount Points and Other Concessions
R.E. Taxes $ 2,277.32 Tax Year _____ HOA $/Mo. _____		[ ] Leasehold	Paid by Seller $ _____
Lender/Client		[ ] Condominium (HUD/VA)	
		[ ] De Minimis PUD	Source _____

NEIGHBORHOOD

LOCATION				NEIGHBORHOOD ANALYSIS	Good	Avg.	Fair	Poor
	[ ] Urban	[X] Suburban	[ ] Rural	Employment Stability	[X]			
BUILT UP	[X] Over 75%	[ ] 25-75%	[ ] Under 25%	Convenience to Employment	[X]			
GROWTH RATE	[ ] Rapid	[X] Stable	[ ] Slow	Convenience to Shopping	[X]			
PROPERTY VALUES	[X] Increasing	[ ] Stable	[ ] Declining	Convenience to Schools	[X]			
DEMAND/SUPPLY	[X] Shortage	[ ] In Balance	[ ] Over Supply	Adequacy of Public Transportation	[X]			
MARKETING TIME	[X] Under 3 Mos.	[ ] 3-6 Mos.	[ ] Over 6 Mos.	Recreation Facilities	[X]			

PRESENT LAND USE	%	LAND USE CHANGE	PREDOMINANT	SINGLE FAMILY HOUSING				
			OCCUPANCY	PRICE $ (000)	AGE (yrs)	Adequacy of Utilities	[X]	
Single Family	100%	Not Likely [X]				Property Compatibility	[X]	
2-4 Family	___	Likely [ ]	Owner [X]			Protection from Detrimental Cond.	[X]	
Multi-family	___	In process [ ]	Tenant [ ]	90 Low 7		Police & Fire Protection	[X]	
Commercial	___	To: _____	Vacant (0-5%) [ ]	120 High 7		General Appearance of Properties	[X]	
Industrial	___		Vacant (over 5%) [ ]	110 Predominant 7		Appeal to Market	[X]	
Vacant	___							

Note: Race or the racial composition of the neighborhood are not considered reliable appraisal factors.
COMMENTS: _____

SITE

Dimensions 65' x 130'		Topography	LEVEL
Site Area 8,450 sq. ft.	Corner Lot	Size	65' x 130'
Zoning Classification R-2, SINGLE FAMILY RES.	Zoning Compliance YES	Shape	RECTANGULAR
HIGHEST & BEST USE: Present Use YES	Other Use	Drainage	VERY GOOD

UTILITIES	Public	Other	SITE IMPROVEMENTS	Type	Public	Private		
							View	NO
Electricity	[X]		Street	ASPHALT	[X]		Landscaping	AVERAGE
Gas	[X]		Curb/Gutter	CONCRETE	[X]		Driveway	ASPHALT
Water	[X]		Sidewalk	CONCRETE	[X]		Apparent Easements	NONE
Sanitary Sewer	[X]		Street Lights		[X]		FEMA Flood Hazard	Yes* ___ No [X]
Storm Sewer	[X]		Alley				FEMA* Map/Zone	

COMMENTS (Apparent adverse easements, encroachments, special assessments, slide areas, etc.): UNDERGROUND ELECTRIC AND TELEPHONE
LINES; NO EASEMENTS OR ENCROACHMENTS

IMPROVEMENTS

GENERAL DESCRIPTION		EXTERIOR DESCRIPTION		FOUNDATION		BASEMENT		INSULATION	
Units	1	Foundation	CONCRETE	Slab		Area Sq. Ft.		Roof	[ ]
Stories	1	Exterior Walls	BRICK VENEER	Crawl Space	CON. WALLS	% Finished		Ceiling	[X]
Type (Det./Att.)	DETACHED	Roof Surface	ASPH. SHINGLE	Basement		Ceiling		Walls	[X]
Design (Style)	RANCH	Gutters & Dwnspts.	GALV/PAINT	Sump Pump		Walls		Floor	[ ]
Existing	YES	Window Type	DOUBLE HUNG	Dampness		Floor		None	[ ]
Proposed		Storm Sash	COMBINATION/	Settlement		Outside Entry		Adequacy	[ ]
Under Construction		Screens	ALUMINUM	Infestation				Energy Efficient Items:	
Age (Yrs.)	7	Manufactured House							
Effective Age (Yrs.)									

ROOM LIST

ROOMS	Foyer	Living	Dining	Kitchen	Den	Family Rm.	Rec. Rm.	Bedrooms	# Baths	Laundry	Other	Area Sq. Ft.
Basement												
Level 1		x	x	x		x		3	2		6 CLOS-	1,950
Level 2											ETS	

Finished area **above** grade contains: 7 Rooms; 3 Bedroom(s); 2 Bath(s); 1,950 Square Feet of Gross Living Area

INTERIOR

SURFACES	Materials/Condition	HEATING		KITCHEN EQUIP.		ATTIC		IMPROVEMENT ANALYSIS	Good	Avg.	Fair	Poor
Floors	VINYL/CARPET – OAK	Type	AIR	Refrigerator	[X]	None		Quality of Construction	[X]			
Walls	DRYWALL;PAINT/PAPER	Fuel	GAS	Range/Oven	[X]	Stairs		Condition of Improvements	[X]			
Trim/Finish	AVERAGE – PINE	Condition	VERY GD	Disposal	[X]	Drop Stair	[X]	Room Sizes/Layout		[X]		
Bath Floor	CERAMIC	Adequacy	GOOD	Dishwasher	[X]	Scuttle		Closets and Storage	[X]			
Bath Wainscot	CERAMIC	COOLING		Fan/Hood	[X]	Floor		Energy Efficiency	[X]			
Doors		Central	x	Compactor		Heated		Plumbing-Adequacy & Condition	[X]			
		Other		Washer/Dryer		Finished		Electrical-Adequacy & Condition	[X]			
		Condition	GOOD	Microwave				Kitchen Cabinets-Adequacy & Cond.	[X]			
Fireplace(s) 1 MASONRY, FAM RM		Adequacy	GOOD	Intercom				Compatibility to Neighborhood	[X]			

AUTOS

CAR STORAGE:	Garage	[X]	Attached		Adequate	[X]	House Entry		Appeal & Marketability	[X]			
No. Cars 2	Carport	[ ]	Detached	[X]	Inadequate		Outside Entry	[X]	Estimated Remaining Economic Life	43-48		Yrs.	
Condition	None	[ ]	Built-In		Electric Door		Basement Entry		Estimated Remaining Physical Life			Yrs.	

Additional features: 6" INSULATION ABOVE CEILING AND BEHIND DRYWALL; SIX-FOOT REDWOOD
FENCE AROUND REAR YARD

COMMENTS

Depreciation (Physical, functional and external inadequacies, repairs needed, modernization, etc.): NORMAL WEAR & TEAR ONLY

General market conditions and prevalence and impact in subject/market area regarding loan discounts, interest buydowns and concessions:
Strong housing market reflecting healthy local economy.
Conventional financing readily available with interest rates at 10-3/4 percent to 11-1/4 per-
cent.

UNIFORM RESIDENTIAL APPRAISAL REPORT   File No. _____

Valuation Section

Purpose of Appraisal is to estimate Market Value as defined in the Certification & Statement of Limiting Conditions.

COST APPROACH

BUILDING SKETCH (SHOW GROSS LIVING AREA ABOVE GRADE)
If for Freddie Mac or Fannie Mae show only square foot calculations and cost approach comments in this space

ESTIMATED REPRODUCTION COST - NEW - OF IMPROVEMENTS:

Dwelling	1,950	Sq. Ft. @ $	65	= $ 126,750
		Sq. Ft. @ $		=
Extras				=
				=
Special Energy Efficient Items	Ex. Insul.			= 600
Porches, Patios, etc.				=
Garage/Carport	500	Sq. Ft. @ $ 20		= 10,000
Total Estimated Cost New				= $ 137,350

	Physical	Functional	External	
Less Depreciation	13,735	-0-	-0-	= $ 13,735
Depreciated Value of Improvements				= $ 123,615
Site Imp. "as is" (driveway, landscaping, etc.)				= $ 5,400
ESTIMATED SITE VALUE				= $ 35,000

(If leasehold, show only leasehold value.)

INDICATED VALUE BY COST APPROACH .... = $ 164,015

(Not Required by Freddie Mac and Fannie Mae)
Does property conform to applicable HUD/VA property standards? ☐ Yes ☐ No
If No, explain: _____

Construction Warranty ☐ Yes ☐ No
Name of Warranty Program _____
Warranty Coverage Expires _____

SALES COMPARISON ANALYSIS

The undersigned has recited three recent sales of properties most similar and proximate to subject and has considered these in the market analysis. The description includes a dollar adjustment, reflecting market reaction to those items of significant variation between the subject and comparable properties. If a significant item in the comparable property is superior to, or more favorable than, the subject property, a minus (–) adjustment is made, thus reducing the indicated value of subject; if a significant item in the comparable is inferior to, or less favorable than, the subject property, a plus (+) adjustment is made, thus increasing the indicated value of the subject.

ITEM	SUBJECT	COMPARABLE NO. 1		COMPARABLE NO. 2		COMPARABLE NO. 3	
Address	4807 CATALPA	4310 W. GLADYS		3840 W. MONROE		316 IOWA	
Proximity to Subject							
Sales Price	$	$ 158,000		$159,500		$ 167,250	
Price/Gross Liv. Area	$	$		$		$	
Data Source							
VALUE ADJUSTMENTS	DESCRIPTION	DESCRIPTION	+ (–)$ Adjustment	DESCRIPTION	+ (–)$ Adjustment	DESCRIPTION	+ (–)$ Adjustment
Sales or Financing Concessions		NONE		NONE		NONE	
Date of Sale/Time		6 WKS. AGO		3 WKS. AGO		6 WKS. AGO	
Location	QUIET RES.	QUIET RES.		QUIET RES.		QUIET RES	
Site/View	65' x 130'GD	65'x 130'GD		65'x130'GD		65'x130'GD	
Design and Appeal	RANCH/GOOD	RANCH/GOOD		RANCH/GOOD		RANCH/GOOD	
Quality of Construction	GOOD	GOOD		GOOD		GOOD	
Age	7 YEARS	7 YEARS		7 YEARS		7 YEARS	
Condition	GOOD	GOOD		GOOD		GOOD	
Above Grade Room Count	Total 7 Bdrms 3 Baths 2	Total 7 Bdrms 3 Baths 2		Total 7 Bdrms 3 Baths 2		Total 7 Bdrms 3 Baths 2	
Gross Living Area	1,950 Sq. Ft.	1,975 Sq. Ft.		1,950 Sq. Ft.		1,940 Sq. Ft.	
Basement & Finished Rooms Below Grade	CRAWLSPACE	CRAWLSPACE		CRAWLSPACE		FINISHED BASEMENT	(5,000)
Functional Utility	ADEQUATE	ADEQUATE		ADEQUATE		ADEQUATE	
Heating/Cooling	CENTRAL H/A	CENTRAL H/A		CENTRAL H/A		CENTRAL H/A	
Garage/Carport	2-CAR DET.	2-CAR DET.		2-CAR DET.		2-CAR DET.	
Porches, Patio, Pools, etc.	NONE	NONE		NONE		NONE	
Special Energy Efficient Items	EXTRA INSULATION	YES		YES		YES	
Fireplace(s)	1 MASONRY	NONE	2,000	1 MASONRY		1 MASONRY	
Other (e.g. kitchen equip., remodeling)	NONE	NONE		NONE		NONE	
Net Adj. (total)		x + ☐ – $ 2,000		☐ + ☐ – $ -0-		☐ + x – $ 5,000	
Indicated Value of Subject		$ 160,000		$ 159,500		$ 162,250	

Comments on Sales Comparison: _____

INDICATED VALUE BY SALES COMPARISON APPROACH .... $ 160,000

INDICATED VALUE BY INCOME APPROACH (If Applicable) Estimated Market Rent $ 1,075 /Mo. x Gross Rent Multiplier 147 = $ 158,025

This appraisal is made ☐ "as is" ☐ subject to the repairs, alterations, inspections or conditions listed below ☐ completion per plans and specifications.

Comments and Conditions of Appraisal: _____

RECONCILIATION

Final Reconciliation: INCOME APPROACH VALUE LOW SINCE RENTS USUALLY COVER MORTGAGE LOAN AMOUNT ONLY: WHILE REPRODUCTION COST IS HIGHER, PREVAILING MARKET PRICES ARE BEST INDICATOR OF VALUE.

This appraisal is based upon the above requirements, the certification, contingent and limiting conditions, and Market Value definition that are stated in
☐ FmHA, HUD &/or VA instructions.
☐ Freddie Mac Form 439 (Rev. 7/86)/Fannie Mae Form 1004B (Rev. 7/86) filed with client _____ 19 ____ ☐ attached.

I (WE) ESTIMATE THE MARKET VALUE, AS DEFINED, OF THE SUBJECT PROPERTY AS OF _____ 19 ____ to be $ 160,000

I (We) certify: that to the best of my (our) knowledge and belief the facts and data used herein are true and correct; that I (we) personally inspected the subject property, both inside and out, and have made an exterior inspection of all comparable sales cited in this report; and that I (we) have no undisclosed interest, present or prospective therein.

Appraiser(s) SIGNATURE _____   Review Appraiser SIGNATURE _____ ☐ Did ☐ Did Not
NAME _____   (if applicable) NAME _____   Inspect Property

Freddie Mac Form 70 10/86   Fannie Mae Form 1004 10/86

Appendix B

Exercise B.1
1. 3 square feet or 432 square inches
2. 1.875 square feet or 270 square inches
3. 42 square feet or 6,048 square inches
4. 144 square inches
5. 10.5 square feet
6. 75 feet × 125 feet = 9,375 square feet

Exercise B.2
A = ½(BH) = ½(50′ × 85′) = ½(4,250 sq. ft.) = 2,125 sq. ft.

Exercise B.3
a. Area of A = 25′ × 19′ = 475 sq. ft.
   Area of B = 13′ × 8′ = 104 sq. ft.
   Area of C = 9′ × 7′ = 63 sq. ft.
   Total area = 642 sq. ft.

b. Area of rectangle:
      A = L × W = 18′ × 7′ = 126 sq. ft.
   Area of triangle:
      A = ½(BH) = ½(22′ − 18′) × 7′ = ½(4′ × 7′) = ½(28 sq. ft.) = 14 sq. ft.
   Total area = 126 sq. ft. + 14 sq. ft. = 140 sq. ft.

c. Area of A = ½(20′ − 12′) × 8′ = 32 sq. ft.
   Area of B = 18′ × 20′ = 360 sq. ft.
   Area of C = ½(8′ × 18′) = 72 sq. ft.
   Area of D = ½(14′ × 20′) = 140 sq. ft.
   Area of E = ½ (20′ − 8′) × 20′ = 120 sq. ft.
   Area of F = 8′ × 20′ = 160 sq. ft.
   Total area = (32 + 360 + 72 + 140 + 120 + 160) sq. ft. = 884 sq. ft.

Exercise B.4
<u>AREA</u>

A	= 5′ × 16′	= 80 sq. ft.
B	= 3′ × (20′ + 16′) = 3′ × 36′	= 108
C	= 12′ × 20′	= 240
D	= 10′ × (40′ − 22′) = 10′ × 18′	= 180
E	= (50′ − 25′) × 22′ = 25′ × 22′	= 550
F	= (50′ − 10′) × (74′ − 22′) = 40′ × 52′	= <u>2,080</u>
		TOTAL = 3,238 sq. ft.

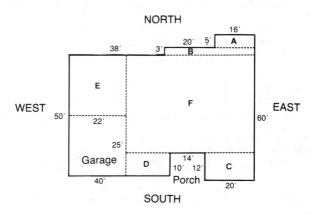

Exercise B.5

1. $8' \times 7' = 56$ sq. ft. $= 8,064$ sq. in. $= 6$ sq. yds. (rounded)

    $9' \times 3' \times 2' = 54$ cu. ft. $= 93,312$ cu. in. $= 2$ cu. yd.

2. A. $B = (33' + 55') - 83' = 5'$ $\frac{1}{2}(5' \times 16') = 40$ sq. ft.

    B. $83' \times 16' = 1,328$ sq. ft.

    C. $B = 132' - 110' = 22'$ $H = (16' + 82' + 28' + 28') - 110' = 44'$

    $\frac{1}{2}(22' \times 44') = 484$ sq. ft.

    D. $82' \times 33' = 2,706$ sq. ft.

    E. $55' \times (82' + 28') = 55' \times 110' = 6,050$ sq. ft.

    F. $132' \times 110' = 14,520$ sq. ft.

    Total area = 40 sq. ft. + 1,328 sq. ft. + 484 sq. ft. + 2,706 sq. ft. +

    6,050 sq. ft. + 14,520 sq. ft. = 25,128 sq. ft.

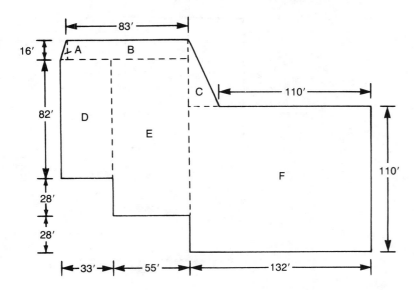

3. $80' \times 35' \times 10' = 28,000$ cu. ft. $\div 27 = 1,037.037$ cu. yd.

    $\frac{1}{2}(80' \times 35' \times 6') = 8,400$ cu. ft. $\div 27 = 311.111$ cu. yd.

    $1,037.037$ cu. yd. + 311.111 cu. yd. = $1,348.148$ cu. yd.

    $1,348.148$ cu. yd. $\times \$45 = \$60,666.66$

Achievement Examination B

1.

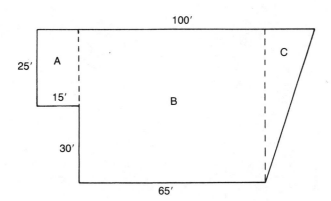

A = $25' \times 15' = 375$ sq. ft.

B = $65' \times (30' + 25') = 65' \times 55' = 3,575$ sq. ft.

$C = \frac{1}{2}(BH)$ $B = 100' - (15' + 65') = 20'$ $H = 30' + 25' = 55'$
    $\frac{1}{2}(20' \times 55') = 550$ sq. ft.
  Total area = 375 sq. ft. + 3,575 sq. ft. + 550 sq. ft. = 4,500 sq. ft.

2. $35' \times 20' \times 14' = 9,800$ cu. ft.
    $\frac{1}{2}(35' \times 20' \times 6') = 2,100$ cu. ft.
    9,800 cu. ft. + 2,100 cu. ft. = 11,900 cu. ft.
    $11,900 \times \$2.75 = \$32,725$

3. $40.83' \times 60.67' = 2,477$ sq. ft. (rounded)
    $80.5' \times 25.25' = 2,033$ sq. ft. (rounded)
    Total area = 4,510 sq. ft. (rounded)

4.

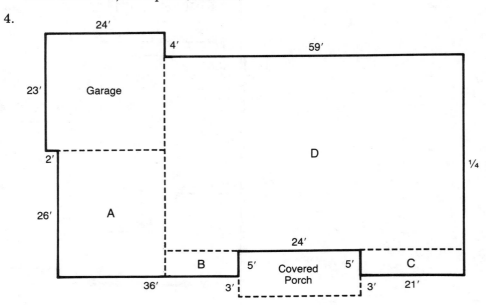

<u>AREA</u>

A	= $26' \times (24' - 2') = 26' \times 22'$	=	572 sq. ft.
B	= $36' - (24' - 2') = 36' - 22' = 14' \times 5'$	=	70
C	= $21' \times 5'$	=	105
D	= $59' \times (45' - 5') = 59' \times 40'$	=	2,360
		TOTAL =	3,107 sq. ft.

Appendix D

Exercise D.1

Estimated land value		$ 75,000
Total net operating income	$ 26,400	
Discount on land value ($75,000 × 11%)	8,250	
Residual income to building	$18,150	
Building value (using annuity factor of 8.694 × $18,150)		157,796
Total property value		$232,796

Exercise D.2

Total operating net income	$ 30,000
Annuity factor (25 years at 12 percent)	× 7.843
Present worth of net operating income	$235,290
Reversion factor (25 years at 12 percent = .059)	
Present worth of reversion ($150,000 × .059)	8,850
Total value of property	$244,140

Exercise D.3

1. Annuity
2. Straight-line

Achievement Examination D

1. Both residual techniques would produce essentially the same value.
2. a
3. b
4. Highest—annuity; lowest—straight-line
5. a
6. The value indications are different in cases "a" and "b" because of different assumptions in types of income streams and methods of recapturing capital.

a. Building residual—straight-line method

Estimated land value		$100,000
Net operating income	$50,000	
Return on land value ($100,000 × .15)	−$15,000	
Residual income to building	$35,000	
Cap rate for building		
Discount rate	15%	
Recapture rate	+ 4	
	19%	
Building value ($35,000 ÷ .19) (rounded)		184,211
Total property value		$284,211

b. Property residual—annuity method

Total net operating income	$50,000
Annuity factor (25 years at 15 percent)	× 6.464
Present worth of net operating income	$323,200
Present worth of reversion—$100,000 × .030	3,000
(25 years at 15 percent)	
Total value of property	$326,200

or

Building residual—annuity method

Estimated land value		$100,000
Residual income to building	$35,000	
Annuity factor (25 yrs. @ 15 percent)	× 6.464	
Value of building		226,240
Total value of property		$326,240

Appendix E

Exercise E.1
A leasehold estate of value is created when scheduled rent under the lease is less than the fair market rental, or economic rent.

Exercise E.2
$419,100
$393,200

Achievement Examination E
Leased fee interest:

Net operating income	$36,000
Annuity factor (30 yrs. @ 11 percent)	× 8.694
Present worth of net income	$312,984
Present worth of reversion ($150,000 × 0.44 reversion factor)	6,600
Value of the leased fee interest	$319,584

Leasehold interest:

Market rent	$ 45,000
Scheduled rent	36,000
Excess rent	$ 9,000
Present worth of excess rent discounted at 14%	× 7.003
Value of leasehold interest	$ 63,027

Total value of leased fee and leasehold interests = $319,584 + $63,027 = $382,611, rounded to $382,600.

Index

354

(Based upon the Uniform Standards of Professional Appraisal Practice as promulgated by the Appraisal Standard Board of The Appraisal Foundation)

Table of Contents

Section I – Introduction
Preamble

It is essential that a professional appraiser arrive at and communicate his or her analyses, opinions, and advice in a manner that will be meaningful to the client and will not be misleading in the marketplace. These Uniform Standard of Professional Appraisal Practice reflect the current standard of the appraisal profession.

The importance of the role of the appraiser places ethical obligations on those who serve in this capacity. These standards include explanatory comments and begin with an Ethics Provision setting forth the requirements for integrity, objectivity, independent judgement, and ethical conduct. In addition, these standards include a Competency Provision which places an immediate responsibility on the appraiser prior to acceptance of an assignment. The standards contain binding requirements, as well as specific guidelines. Definitions applicable to these standard are also included.

These standards deal with the procedures to be followed in performing an appraisal or review and the manner in which an appraisal or review is communicated. Standards 1 and 2 relate to the development and communication of a real property appraisal. Standard 3 establishes guidelines for reviewing an appraisal and reporting on that review.

These standards are for appraisers and the users of appraisal services. To maintain the highest level of professional practice, appraisers must observe these standards. The users of appraisal services should demand work performed in conformance with these standards.

Comment: Explanatory comments are an integral part of the Uniform Standard and should be viewed as extensions of the provisions, definitions, and standard rules. Comments provide interpretation from the Appraisal Standards Board concerning the background or application of certain provisions, definitions, or standards rules. There are no comments for provisions, definitions, and standards rules that are axiomatic or have not yet required further explanation; however, additional comments will be developed and others supplemented or revised as the need arises.
Ethics Provision

Because of the fiduciary responsibilities inherent in professional appraisal practice, the appraiser must observe the highest standards of professional ethics. This Ethics Provision is divided into four sections: conduct, management, confidentiality, and record keeping.

Comment: This provision emphasizes the personal obligations and responsibilities of the individual appraiser. However, it should also be emphasized that groups and organizations engaged in appraisal practice share the same ethical obligations.

Conduct. An appraiser must perform ethically and competently in accordance with these standards and not engage in conduct that is unlawful, unethical, or improper. An appraiser who could reasonably be perceived as a disinterested third party in rendering an unbiased appraisal, review, or consulting service must perform assignments with impartiality, objectivity, and independence and without accommodation of personal interests.

Comment: An appraiser is required to avoid any incident that could be considered misleading or fraudulent. In particular, it is unethical for an appraiser to use or communicate a misleading or fraudulent report or to knowingly permit an employee or other person to communicate a misleading or fraudulent report.

The development of an appraisal, review, or consulting service based upon a hypothetical condition is unethical unless:

(1) The use of the hypothesis is clearly disclosed;

(2) The assumption of the hypothetical condition is clearly required for legal purposes, for purposes of reasonable analysis, or for purposes of comparison and

would not be misleading; and

(3) The report clearly describes the rationale for this assumption, the nature of the hypothetical condition, and its effect on the result of the appraisal, review, or consulting service.

An individual appraiser employed by a group or organization conducts itself in a manner that does not conform to these standards should take steps that are appropriate under the circumstances to ensure compliance with the standards.

Management. The acceptance of compensation that is contingent upon the reporting of a predetermined value or a direction in value that favors the cause of the attainment of a stipulated result, or the occurrence of a subsequent event is unethical.

The payment of undisclosed fees, commissions, or things of value in connection with the procurement of appraisal, review, or consulting assignments is unethical

Comment: Disclosure of fees, commissions, or things of value connected to the procurement of an assignment should appear in the certification of a written record and in any transmittal letter in which conclusions are stated. In groups or organizations engaged in appraisal practice, intracompany payments to employees for business development are not considered to be unethical. Competency, rather than financial incentives, should be the primary basis for awarding an assignment.

Advertising for or soliciting appraisal assignments in a manner which is false, misleading or exaggerated is unethical.

Comment: In groups or organizations engaged on appraisal practice, decisions concerning finder or referral fees, contingent compensation, and advertising may not be the responsibility of an individual appraiser, but for a particular assignment it is the responsibility of the individual appraiser to ascertain that there has been no breach of ethics, that the appraisal is prepared in accordance with these standards, and that the report can be properly certified as required by Standards Rules 2-3 or 3-2.

The restriction on contingent compensation in the first paragraph of this section does not apply to consulting assignments where the appraiser is not acting in a disinterested manner and would not reasonably be perceived as performing a service that requires impartiality. This permitted contingent compensation must be properly disclosed in the report.

Comment: The preparer of the written report of an assignment where the appraiser is not acting in a disinterested manner must certify that the compensation is contingent and must explain the basis for the contingency in the report, certification, executive summary and in any transmittal letter in which conclusions are stated.

Confidentiality. An appraiser must protect the confidential nature of the appraiser-client relationship.

Comment: A appraiser must not disclose confidential factual data obtained from a client or the result of an assignment prepared for a client to anyone other than: (1) The client and persons specifically authorized by the client; (2) such third parties as may be authorized by due process of law; and (3) a duly authorized professional peer review committee. As a corollary, it is unethical for a member of a duly authorized professional peer review committee to disclose confidential information or factual data presented to the committee.

Record Keeping. An appraiser must prepare written records of appraisal, review and consulting assignments-including oral testimony and reports-and retain such records for a period of at least five (5) years after preparation or at least two (2) years after final disposition of any judicial proceeding in which testimony was given, whichever period expires last.

Comment. Written records of assignments include true copies of written reports, written summaries of oral testimony and reports (or a transcript of testimony) all data and statements required by these standards, and other information as may be required to support the findings and conclusions of the appraiser. The term written records also includes information stored on electronic, magnetic, or other media. Such records must be made available by the appraiser when required by due process of law or by duly authorized professional peer review committee.

Competency Provision

Prior to accepting an assignment or entering into an agreement to perform any assignment, an appraiser must properly identify the problem to be addressed and have the knowledge and experience to complete the assignment competently; or alternatively:

1. Disclose the lack of knowledge and/or experience to the client before accepting the assignment; and

2. Take all steps necessary or appropri-ate to complete the assignment competently; and

3. Describe the lack of knowledge and/or experience and the steps taken to complete the assignment competently in the report.

Comment: The background and experience of appraisers varies widely and a lack of knowledge or experience can lead to inaccurate or inappropriate appraisal practice. The competency provision requires the appraiser to perform a specific appraisal service competently. If an appraiser is offered an opportunity to perform an appraisal service but lacks the necessary knowledge or experience to complete it competently, the appraiser must disclose his or her lack of knowledge or experience to the client before accepting the assignment and then take the necessary or appropriate steps to complete the appraisal service competently. This may be accomplished in various ways including, but not limited to, personal study by the appraiser; association with an appraiser believed to have the necessary knowledge or experience; or retention of others who possess the required knowledge or experience.

Although this provision requires an appraiser to identify the problem and disclose any deficiency in competence prior to accepting an assignment, facts or conditions uncovered during the course of an assignment could cause an appraiser to discover that he or she lacks the required knowledge or experience to complete the assignment competently. At the point of such discovery, the appraiser is obligated to notify the client and comply with items 2 and 3 of the provision.

The concept of competency also extends to appraisers who are requested or required to travel to geographic area wherein they have no recent appraisal experience. An appraiser preparing an appraisal in an unfamiliar location must spend sufficient time to understand the nuances of the local market and the supply and demand factors relating to the specific property type and the location involved. Such understanding will not be imparted solely from a consideration of specific data such as demographics, costs, sales and rentals. The necessary understanding of the local market conditions provides the bridge between a sale and a comparable sale or a rental and a comparable rental. If an appraiser is not in a position to spend the necessary amount of time in a market area to obtain this understanding, affiliation with a qualified local appraiser may be the appropriate response to ensure the development of a competent appraisal.

Jurisdictional Exception

If any part of these standards is contrary to the law or public policy of any jurisdiction, only that part shall be void and of no force or effect in that jurisdiction.

Supplemental Standards

These Uniform Standards provide the common basis for all appraisal practice. Supplemental standard applicable to appraisals prepared to specific purposes or property types may be issued by public agencies and certain client groups, e.g., regulatory agencies, eminent domain authorities, asset managers, and financial institutions. Appraiser and clients ascertain whether any supplemental standards in addition to these Uniform Standard apply to the assignment being considered.

Definitions

For the purpose of these standards, the following definitions apply:

Appraisal: (noun) The act or process of estimating value; an estimate of value. (adjective) of or pertaining to appraising and related functions, e.g. appraisal practice, appraisal services.

Appraisal practice: The work or services performed by Appraisers, defined by three terms in these standards: appraisal, review, and consulting.

Comment: These three terms are intentionally generic, and are not mutually exclusive. For example, an estimate of value may be required as a part of a review or consulting service. The use of other nomenclature by an appraiser (e.g. analyses, counseling, evaluation, study, submission, valuation) does not exempt an appraiser from adherence to these standards.

Cash Flow Analysis: A study of the anticipated movement of cash into or out of an investment.

Client: Any party for whom an appraiser performs a service.

Consulting: The act or process of providing information, analyses of real estate data, and recommendations or conclusions on diversified problems in real estate, other than estimating value.

Feasibility Analysis: A study of the cost benefit relationship of an economic endeavor.

Investment Analysis: A study that reflects the relationship between acquisition price and anticipated future benefits of a real estate investment.

Market Analysis: A study of real estate market conditions for a specific type of property.

Market Value: Market value is the major focus of most real property appraisal assignments. Both economic and legal definitions of market value have been developed and refined.

A current economic definition agreed upon by federal financial institutions in the United States of America is:

The most probable price which a property should bring in a competitive and open market under all conditions requisite to a fair sale, the buyer and the seller each acting prudently and knowledgeably, and assuming the price is not affected by undue stimulus. Implicit in this definition is the consummation of a sale as of a specified date and the passing of title from buyer to seller under conditions whereby:

1. Buyer and seller are typically motivated;

2. Both parties are well informed or well advised, and acting in what they consider their best interests;

3. A reasonable time is allowed for exposure in the open market;

4. Payment is made in the terms of cash in United States dollars or in terms of financial arrangements comparable thereto; and

5. The price represents the normal consideration for the property sold unaffected by special or creative financing or sales concessions granted by anyone associated with the sale.

Substitution of another currency for *United States dollars* in the fourth condition is appropriate in countries or in reports addressed to clients from other countries.

Persons performing appraisal services that may be subject to litigation are cautioned to seek the exact legal definition of market value in the jurisdiction in which the services are being performed.

Mass Appraisal: The process of valuing a universe of properties as of a given date utilizing standard methodology, employing common data, and allowing for statistical testing.

Mass Appraisal Model: A mathematical expression of how supply and demand factors interact in a market.

Personal Property: Identifiable portable and tangible objects which are considered by the public as being "personal," e.g.

furnishings, artwork, antiques, gems and jewelry, collectibles, machinery and equipment; all property that is not classified as real estate.

Real Estate: An identifiable parcel or tract of land, including improvements, if any.

Real Property: The interests, benefits, and rights inherent in the ownership of real estate.

Comment: In some jurisdictions, the terms "real estate" and "real property" have the same legal meaning. The separate definitions recognize the traditional distinction between the two in appraisal theory.

Report: Any communication, written or oral, of an appraisal, review or analysis; the document that is transmitted to the client upon completion of an assignment.

Comment: Most reports are written and most clients mandate written reports. Oral report guidelines (See Standards Rule 2-4) and restrictions (See Ethics Provision: Record Keeping) are included to cover court testimony and other oral communications of an appraisal, review, or consulting service.

Review: The act or process of critically studying a report prepared by another.

Section II–Real Property Appraisals

Standard 1

In developing a real property appraisal, an appraiser must be aware of, understand, and correctly employ those recognized methods and techniques that are necessary to produce a credible appraisal.

Comment: Standard 1 is directed toward the substantive aspects of developing a competent appraisal. The requirements set forth in Standard Rule 1-1, the appraisal guidelines set forth in Standards Rules 1-2, 1-3, 1-4, and the requirements set forth in Standards Rule 1-5 mirror the appraisal process in the order of topics addressed and can be used by appraisers and the users of appraisal services as a convenient checklist.

Standards Rule 1-1. In developing a real property appraisal, an appraiser must:

(a) Be aware of, understand, and correctly employ those recognized methods and techniques that are necessary to produce a credible appraisal;

Comment: Departure from this binding requirement is not permitted. This rule recognizes that the principle of change continues to affect the manner in which appraisers perform appraisal services.

Changes and developments in the real estate field have a substantial impact on the appraisal profession. Important changes in the cost and manner of constructing and marketing commercial, industrial, and residential real estate and changes in legal framework in which real estate property rights and interests are created, conveyed, and mortgaged have resulted in corresponding changes in appraisal theory and practice. Social change has also had an effect on appraisal theory and practice. To keep abreast of these changes and developments, the appraisal profession is constantly reviewing and revising appraisal methods and techniques and devising new methods and techniques to meet new circumstances. For this reason it is not sufficient for appraisers to simply maintain the skills and the knowledge they possess when they become appraisers. Each appraiser must continuously improve his or her skills to remain proficient in real property appraisal.

(b) Not commit a substantial error of omission or commission that significantly affects an appraisal;

Comment: Departure from this binding requirement is not permitted. In performing appraisal services an appraiser must be certain that the gathering of factual information is conducted in a manner that is sufficiently diligent to ensure that the data would have a material or significant effect on the resulting opinions or conclusions are considered. Further an appraiser must use sufficient care in analyzing such data to avoid errors that would significantly affect his or her opinions or conclusions.

(c) Not render appraisal services in a careless or negligent manner, such as a series of errors that, considered individually, may not significantly affect the results of an appraisal, but which, when considered in the aggregate, would be misleading.

Comment: Departure from this binding requirement is not permitted. Perfection is impossible to attain and competence does not require perfection. However, an appraiser must not render appraisal services in a careless of negligent manner. This rule requires an appraiser to use due diligence and due care. The fact that the carelessness and the negligence of an appraiser has not caused an error that significantly affects his or her opinions or conclusions and thereby seriously harms a client or a third party does not excuse such carelessness or negligence.

Standards Rule 1-2. In developing a real property appraisal, an appraiser must observe the following specific appraisal guidelines:

(a) Adequately define the real estate, identify the real property interest, consider the purpose and intended use of the appraisal, consider the extent of the data collection process, identify any special limiting conditions, and identify the effective date of the appraisal;

(b) Define the value being considered; if the value to be estimated is market value, the appraiser must clearly indicate whether the estimate is the most probable price:

(i) In terms of cash; or

(ii) In terms of financial arrangements equivalent to cash; or

(iii) In such other terms as may be precisely defined; if an estimate of value is based on submarket financing or financing with unusual conditions or incentives, the terms of such financing must be clearly set forth, their contributions to or negative influence on value must be described and estimated, and the market data supporting the valuation must be described and explained;

Comment: For certain types of appraisal assignments in which a legal definition of market value has been established and takes precedence, the Jurisdictional Exception may apply to this guideline.

If the concept of reasonable exposure in the open market is involved, the appraiser should be specific as to the estimate of marketing time linked to the value estimate.

(c) Consider easements, restrictions, encumbrances, leases, reservations, covenants, contracts, declarations, special assessments, ordinances, or other items of a similar nature;

(d) Consider whether an appraised fractional interest, physical segment, or partial holding contributes pro rata to the value of the whole;

Comment: This guideline does not require an appraiser to value the whole when the subject of the appraisal is a fractional interest, a physical segment, or a partial holding. However, if the value of the whole is not considered, the appraisal must clearly reflect that the value of the property being appraised cannot be used to estimate the value of the whole by mathematical extension.

(e) Identify and consider the effect on value of any personal property, trade fixtures or intangible items that are not real property but are considered in the appraisal.

Comment: This guideline requires the appraiser to recognize the inclusion of items that are not real property in an overall value estimate. Additional expertise in personal property or business appraisal may be required to allocate the overall value to its various components. Separate valuation of such items is required when they are significant to overall value.

Standards Rule 1-3. In developing a real property appraisal, an appraiser must observe the following specific appraisal guidelines:

(a) Consider the effect on use and value of the following factors: existing land use regulations, reasonably probable modifications of such land use regulations, economic demand, the physical adaptability of the real estate, neighborhood trends, and the highest and best use of the real estate;

Comment: This guideline sets forth a list of factors that affect use and value. In considering neighborhood trends, an appraiser must avoid stereotyped or biased assumptions relating to race, age, color, religion, gender, or national origin or an assumption that racial, ethnic, or religious homogeneity is necessary to maximize value in a neighborhood. Further, an appraiser must avoid making an unsupported assumption or premise about neighborhood decline, effective age, and remaining life. In considering highest and best use, an appraiser should develop the concept to the extent that is required for a proper solution of the appraisal problem being considered.

(b) Recognize that land is appraised as though vacant and available for development to its highest and best use and that the appraisal of improvements is based on their actual contribution to the site.

Comment: This guideline may be modified to reflect that, in various legal and practical situations, a site may have a contributory value that differs from the value as if vacant.

Standards Rule 1-4. In developing a real property appraisal, an appraiser must observe the following specific guidelines, when applicable:

(a) Value the site by an appropriate appraisal method or technique;

(b) Collect, verify, analyze, and reconcile: (i) Such comparable cost data as are available to estimate the cost new of the improvements (if any); (ii) Such comparable data as are available to estimate the difference between cost new and the present worth of the improvements (accrued depreciation); (iii) Such comparable sales data, adequately identified and described, as are available to indicate a value conclusion;

(iv) Such comparable rental data as are available to estimate the market rental of the property being appraised;

(v) Such comparable operating expense data as are available to estimate the operating expenses of the property being appraised;

(vi) Such comparable data as are available to estimate rates of capitalization and/or rates of discount.

Comment: This rule covers the three approaches to value. See Standards Rule 2-2 (j) for corresponding reporting requirements.

(c) Base projections of future rent and expenses on reasonably clear and appropriate evidence;

Comment: Although the value of the whole may be equal to the sum of the separate estates or parts, it also may be greater than or less than the sum of the separate estates or parts. Therefore, the value of the whole must be tested by reference to appropriate market data and supported by an appropriate analysis of such data.

A similar procedure must be followed when the value of the whole has been established and the appraiser seeks to estimate the value of a part. The value of any such part must be tested by reference to appropriate market data and supported by appropriate analysis of such data.

(f) Consider and analyze the effect on value, if any, of anticipated public or private improvements, located on or off the site, to the extent that market actions reflect such anticipated improvements as of the effective appraisal date;

Comment: In condemnation evaluation assignments in certain jurisdictions, the Jurisdictional Exception may apply to this guideline.

(g) Identify and consider the appropriate procedures and market information required to perform the appraisal, including all physical, functional, and external market factors as they may effect the appraisal;

Comment: The appraisal may require a complete market analysis.

(h) Appraise proposed improvements only after examining and having available for future examination:

(i) plans, specifications, or other documentation sufficient to identify the scope and character of the proposed improvements;

(ii) evidence indicating the probable time of completion of the proposed improvements; and

(iii) Reasonably clear and appropriate

evidence supporting development costs, anticipated earnings, occupancy projections, and the anticipated competition at the time of completion.

Comment: The evidence required to be examined and maintained under this guideline may include such items as contractor's estimates relating to cost and the time required to complete construction. Market and feasibility studies; operating cost data; and the history of recently completed similar developments. The appraisal may require a complete feasibility analysis.

(i) All pertinent data in items (a) through (h) above shall be used in the development of an appraisal.

Comment: See Standards Rule 2-2 (k) for corresponding reporting requirements.

Standards Rule 1-5. In developing a real property appraisal, an appraiser must:

(a) Consider and analyze any current Agreement of Sale, option, or listing of the property being appraised, if such information is available to the appraiser in the normal course of business;

(b) Consider and analyze any prior sales of the property being appraised that occurred in the following time periods:

(i) One year for one-to-four-family residential property; and

(ii) Three years for all other property types;

Comment: The intent of this requirement is to encourage the research and analysis of prior sales of the subject; the time frames cited are minimums.

(c) Consider and reconcile the quality and quantity of data available and analyzed within the approaches used and the applicability or suitability of the approaches used.

Comment: Departure from this binding requirement is not permitted. See Standards Rule 2-2 (k) Comment for corresponding reporting requirements.

Standard 2

In reporting the results of a real property appraisal an appraiser must communicate each analysis, opinion, and conclusion in a manner that is not misleading.

Comment: Standard 2 governs the form and content of the report that communicates the results of an appraisal to clients and third parties.

Standards Rule 2-1. Each written or oral real property appraisal report must:

(a) Clearly and accurately set forth the appraisal in a manner that will not be misleading;

Comment: Departure from this binding requirement is not permitted. Since most reports are used and relied upon by third parties, communications considered adequate by the appraiser's client may not be sufficient. An appraiser must take extreme care to make certain that his or her reports will not be misleading in the marketplace or to the public.

(b) Contain sufficient information to enable the person(s) who receive or rely on the report to understand it properly;

Comment: Departure from this binding requirement is not permitted. A failure to observe this rule could cause a client or other users of this report to make a serious error even though each analysis, opinion, and conclusion in the report is clearly and accurately stated. To avoid this problem and the dangers it presents to clients and other users of reports, this rule requires an appraiser to include in each report sufficient information to enable the reader to understand it properly. All reports, both written and oral, must clearly and accurately present the analyses, opinions, and conclusions of the appraiser in sufficient depth and detail to address adequately the significance of the particular appraisal problem.

(c) Clearly and accurately disclose any extraordinary assumption or limiting condition that directly affects the appraisal and indicate its impact on value.

Comment: Departure from this binding requirement is not permitted. Examples of extraordinary assumptions or conditions might include items such as the execution of a pending lease agreement, atypical financing, or completion of onsite or offsite improvements. In a written report the disclosure would be requires in conjunction with statements of each opinion conclusion that is affected.

Standards Rule 2-2. Each written real property appraisal report must:

(a) identify and describe the real estate being appraised;

(b) identify the real property interest being appraised;

Comment on (a) and (b): These two requirements are essential elements in any report. Identifying the real estate can be accomplished by any combination of a legal description, address, map reference, copy of a survey or map, property sketch and/or photographs. A property sketch and photographs also provide some description of the real estate in addition to written comments about the physical attributes of the real estate. Identifying the real property rights being appraised requires a direct statement substantiated as needed by copies or summaries of legal descriptions or other documents setting forth any encumbrances.

(c) State the purpose of the appraisal;

(d) Define the value to be estimated;

(e) Set forth the active date of the appraisal and the date of the report;

Comment on (c), (d), and (e): These three requirements call for clear disclosure to the reader of a report the "what, why, and when" surrounding the appraisal. The purpose of the appraisal is used generically to include both the task involved and rationale for the appraisal. Defining the value to be estimated requires both an appropriately referenced definition and any comments needed to clearly indicate to the reader how the definition is being applied [See Standards Rule 1-2 (b)]. The effective date for the appraisal establishes the context for the value estimate, while the date of the report indicates whether the perspective of the appraiser on the market conditions was prospective, current, or retrospective. Reiteration of the date of the report and the effective date of the appraisal at various stages of the report in tandem is important for the clear understanding of the reader whenever market conditions on the date of the report are different from the market conditions on the effective date of the appraisal.

(f) Describe the extent of the processes of collecting, confirming, and reporting data;

Comment: It is suggested that assumptions and limiting conditions be grouped together in an identified section of the report.

(h) Set forth the information considered, the appraisal procedures followed, and the reasoning that supports the analyses, opinions, and conclusions;

Comment: This requirement calls for the appraiser to summarize the data considered and the procedures that were followed. Each item must be addressed in the depth and detail required by its significance to the appraisal. The appraiser must be certain that sufficient information is provided so that the client, the users of the report, and the public will understand it and will not be misled or confused. The substantive content of the report, not its size, determines its compliance with this guideline.

(i) Set forth the appraiser's opinion of the highest and best use of the real estate, when such an opinion is necessary and appropriate;

Comment: This requirement calls for written report to contain a statement of the appraiser's opinion as to the highest and best use of the real estate, unless an opinion as to highest and best use is unnecessary, e.g., insurance valuation or value in use appraisals. If an opinion as to highest and best use is required; the reasoning in support of the opinion must also be included.

(j) Explain and support the exclusion of any of the usual valuation approaches;

(k) set forth any additional information that may be appropriate to show compliance with, or clearly identify and explain permitted departures from, the requirements of Standard 1;

Comment: This requirement calls for a written appraisal report or other written communication concerning the results of an appraisal to contain sufficient information to indicate that the appraiser complied with requirements of Standard 1, including the requirements governing any permitted departure from the appraisal guidelines. The amount of detail required will vary with the significance of the information to the appraisal.

Information considered and analyzed in compliance with Standards Rule 1-5 is significant information that deserves comment in any report. If such information is unattainable, comment on the efforts undertaken by the appraiser to obtain the information required.

(l) include a signed certification in accordance with Standards Rule 2-3.

Comment: Departure from binding requirements (a) through (l) above is not permitted.

Standards Rule 2-3. Each written real property appraisal report must contain a certification that is similar in content to the following form:

I certify that, to the best of my knowledge and belief:

- The statements of fact contained in this report are true and correct.

- The reported analyses, opinions, and conclusions are limited only by the supporting assumptions and limiting conditions, and are my personal, unbiased professional analyses, opinions, and conclusions.

- I have no (or the specified) present or prospective interest in the property that is the subject of this report, and I have no (or the specified) personal interest or bias with respect to the parties involved.

- My compensation is not contingent upon the reporting of a predetermined value or direction in that value that favors the cause of the client, the amount of the value estimate, the attainment of a stipulated result, or the occurrence of a subsequent event.

- My analyses, opinions, and conclusions were developed, and this report has been prepared, in conformity with the Uniform Standards of Professional Appraisal Practice.

- I have (or have not) made a personal inspection of the property that is the subject of this report. (If more than one person signs the report, this certification must clearly specify which individuals did and which individuals did not make a personal inspection of the appraised property.)

- No one provided significant professional assistance to the person signing this report. (If there are exceptions, the name of each individual providing significant professional assistance must be stated.)

Comment: Departure from this binding requirement is not permitted.

Standards Rule 2-4. To the extent that it is both possible and appropriate, each oral real property appraisal report (including expert testimony) must address the substantive matters set forth in Standards Rule 2-2.

Comment: In addition to complying with the requirements of Standards Rule 2-1, an appraiser making an oral report must use his or her best efforts to address each of the substantive matters in Standards Rule 2-2.

Testimony of an appraiser concerning his or her analyses, opinions, or conclusions is an oral report in which the appraiser must comply with the requirements of this Standards Rule.

See *Record Keeping* under the ETHICS PROVISION for corresponding requirements.

Standards Rule 2-5. An appraiser who signs a real property appraisal report prepared by another, even under the label of "review appraiser," must accept full responsibility for the contents of the report.

Comment: Departure from this binding requirement is not permitted. This requirement is directed to the employer or supervisor signing the report of an employee or subcontractor. The employer or the supervisor is as responsible as the individual preparing the appraisal for the content and the conclusions of the appraisal and the report. Using a conditional label next to the signature of the employer or supervisor or signing a form report on the line over the words "review appraiser" does not exempt that individual from adherence to these standards.

This requirement does not address the responsibilities of the review appraiser, the subject of Standard 3.

Section III–Review Appraisals

Standard 3

In reviewing an appraisal and reporting the results of that review, an appraiser must form an opinion as to the adequacy and appropriateness of the report being reviewed and must clearly disclose the nature of the review process taken.

Comment: The function of reviewing an appraisal requires the preparation of a separate report or a file memorandum by the appraiser performing the review setting forth results of the review process. Review appraisers go beyond checking for a level of completeness and consistency in the report under review by providing comment on the content and conclusions of the report. They may or may not have first-hand knowledge of the subject property or of data in the report. The COMPETENCY PROVISION applies to the appraiser performing the review as well as the appraiser who prepared the report under review.

Reviewing is a distinctly different function from that addressed Standards Rule 2-5. To avoid confusion in the marketplace between these two functions, review appraisers should not sign the report under responsibility of a cosigner.

Review appraisers must take appropriate steps to indicate to third parties the precise extent of the review process. A separate report or letter is one method. Another appropriate method is a form or checklist prepared and signed by the appraiser conducting the review and attached to the report under review. It is also possible that stamped impression on the appraisal report under review, signed or initialed by the reviewing appraiser, may be an appropriate method for separating the review function from the actual signing of the report. To be effective, however, the stamp must briefly indicate the extent of the review process and refer to a file memorandum that clearly outlines the review process conducted.

The review appraiser must exercise extreme care in clearly distinguishing between the review process and the appraisal or consulting process. Original work by the review appraiser may be governed by STANDARD 1 rather than this standard. A misleading or fraudulent review and/or report violates the ETHICS PROVISION.

Standards Rule 3-1. In interviewing an appraisal, an appraiser must:

(a) Identify the report under review, the real estate and real property interest being appraised, the effective date of the opinion in the report under review, and the date of the review;

(b) Identify the extent of the review process to be conducted;

(c) Form an opinion as to the completeness of the report under review in light of the requirements in these standards;

Comment: The review should be conducted in the context of market conditions as of the effective date of the opinion in the report being reviewed.

(d) Form an opinion as to the apparent adequacy and relevance of the data and the propriety of any adjustments to the data:

(e) Form an opinion as to the appropriateness of the appraisal methods and techniques used and develop the reasons for any disagreement;

(f) Form an opinion as to whether the analyses, opinions, and conclusions in the report under review are appropriate and reasonable, and develop the reasons for any disagreement.

Comment: Departure from binding requirements (a) through (f) above is not permitted. An opinion of a different estimate of value from that in the report under review may be expressed, provided the review appraiser:

1. Satisfies the requirements of STANDARD 1;

2. Identifies and sets forth any additional data relied upon and the reasoning and basis for the different estimate of value; and

3. Clearly identifies and discloses all assumptions and limitations connected with the different estimate of value to avoid confusion in the marketplace.

Standards Rule 3-2. In reporting the results of an appraisal review, an appraiser must: (a) Disclose the nature, extent, and detail of the review process undertaken;

(b) Disclose the information that must be considered in Standards Rule 3-1(a) and ((b);

(c) Set forth the opinions, reasons, and conclusions required in Standards Rule 3-1 (c), (d), (e) and (f);

(d) Include all known pertinent information;

(e) Include a signed certification similar in content to the following:

I certify that, to the best of my knowledge and belief:

-The facts and data reported by the review appraiser and used in the review process are true and correct.

-The analyses, opinions, and conclusions in this review report are limited only by the assumptions and limiting conditions stated in this review report, and are my personal, unbiased professional analyses, opinions and conclusions.

-I have no (or the specified) present or prospective interest in the property that is the subject of this report and I have no (or the specified) personal interest or bias with respect to the parties involved.

-My compensation is not contingent on an action or event resulting from the analyses, opinions, or conclusions in, or the use of this review report.

-My analyses, opinions, and conclusions were developed and this review report was prepared in conformity with the Uniform Standards of Professional Appraisal Practice.

-I did not (did) personally inspect the subject property of the report under review.

-No one provided significant professional assistance to the person signing this review report. (If there are exceptions, the name of each individual providing significant professional assistance must be stated.)

Comment: Departure from binding requirements (a) through (e) above is not permitted.